PARTY IN POWER

Published under the auspices of
The Center for Japanese and Korean Studies
University of California, Berkeley

THE CENTER FOR JAPANESE AND KOREAN STUDIES of the University of California is a unit of the Institute of International Studies. It is the unifying organization for faculty members and students interested in Japan and Korea, bringing together scholars from many disciplines. The Center's major aims are the development and support of research and language study. As part of this program the Center sponsors a publication series of books concerned with Japan and Korea. Manuscripts are considered from all campuses of the University of California as well as from any other individuals and institutions doing research in these areas.

PUBLICATIONS OF THE CENTER FOR JAPANESE AND KOREAN STUDIES

Chong-Sik Lee
The Politics of Korean Nationalism. 1963.

Sadako N. Ogata
Defiance in Manchuria: The Making of Japanese Foreign Policy, 1931–1932. 1964.

R. P. Dore
Education in Tokugawa Japan. 1964.

James T. Araki
The Ballad-Drama of Medieval Japan. 1964.

Masakazu Iwata
Ōkubo Toshimichi: The Bismarck of Japan. 1964.

Frank O. Miller
Minobe Tatsukichi: Interpreter of Constitutionalism in Japan. 1965.

Michael Cooper, S.J.
They Came to Japan: An Anthology of European Reports on Japan, 1543–1640. 1965.

George Devos and Hiroshi Wagatsuma
Japan's Invisible Race. 1966.

Postwar Economic Growth in Japan. 1966,
Edited by Ryutaro Komiya
Translated from the Japanese by Robert S. Ozaki

Robert A. Scalapino
The Japanese Communist Movement, 1920–1966. 1967.

Soon Sung Cho
Korea in World Politics, 1940–1950. 1967.

C. I. Eugene Kim and Han-Kyo Kim
Korea and the Politics of Imperialism, 1876–1910. 1967.

Kozo Yamamura
Economic Policy in Postwar Japan: Growth versus Economic Democracy. 1967.

Japanese Poetic Diaries
Selected and translated, with an Introduction, by Earl Miner. 1969.

PARTY IN POWER

The Japanese Liberal-Democrats and Policy-making

HARUHIRO FUKUI

UNIVERSITY OF CALIFORNIA PRESS

BERKELEY AND LOS ANGELES · 1970

University of California Press
Berkeley and Los Angeles, California
© Haruhiro Fukui 1970

SBN 520 01646 7
Library of Congress Catalog Card Number 78-84046
Manufactured in Australia

Preface

The doctoral thesis out of which the present book grew was originally prepared during the period 1964-7 in the Department of International Relations of the Australian National University Research School of Pacific Studies. Throughout this period I enjoyed the generous assistance of many individuals and organisations, both in Canberra and in Japan. I am indebted especially to Professor J. D. B. Miller, then head, and to Mr D. C. S. Sissons, then a Fellow, of that department. Professor Miller was responsible for the general administrative arrangements for my stay and work in the Australian National University, and facilitated the completion of the thesis in innumerable ways. As my thesis superviser, Mr Sissons helped me directly throughout the three years of research and writing I spent in the Australian capital. Not only with the general planning and execution of the research program but also with the presentation of the arguments and evidence in the original thesis, Mr Sissons offered me most valuable advice and innumerable suggestions. I also owe a great deal to Dr J. A. A. Stockwin for his generous assistance, particularly in improving the style of my writing. In fact, the problem of language proved to be one of the most difficult I had to solve in writing the thesis and in this connection Dr Stockwin's assistance was indispensable. But for the unfailing help and encouragement so generously given to me by these two competent scholars, this book would never have been written in anything close to its present form.

My sincere appreciation is due to Professor Colin Hughes of the University of Queensland, Professor Ronald P. Dore of the London School of Economics and Political Science, and Professor Nobutaka Ike of Stanford University. All three supplied me with many valuable and detailed criticisms and suggestions for the book's improvement. I am most grateful for the personal courtesy as well as the expert advice they so liberally gave me.

I must also express my gratitude to the Australian National University for having made it possible for me to undertake and complete the research by offering me not only a generous scholarship grant but also a most congenial environment in which to work. Both the Oriental Section of the

University Library and the National Library of Australia greatly facilitated my work by letting me freely use their valuable collections and also in many cases by purchasing new materials specifically for the sake of my research.

In Japan so many people contributed either information, useful insight and advice, or both, to the preparation of the book, especially during my three months fieldwork in Tokyo from December 1965 to March 1966, that it is difficult to acknowledge them individually. I should like, however, to mention the special co-operation and courtesy I received from the Committee on Public Relations and the Committee on National Organisations of the Liberal-Democratic Party, the Kokumin kyōkai, the Kokumin seiji ken-kyūkai, and the political affairs sections of the principal national dailies. It is also appropriate that I should express my appreciation of the help given by the Liberal-Democratic Party members of the National Diet, their secretaries, and the officials of various factions, who not only responded willingly to my request for interviews but often helped me attend and observe party functions and meetings, including the 17th Party Conference of January 1966.

Finally, I would like to thank Mrs Ruth M. Schneider and members of her staff in the Department of Political Science of the University of California at Santa Barbara who kindly typed the final manuscript with their usual efficiency and care.

H.F.

Contents

Tables

Abbreviations

CG	Consultative Group
CHINCOM	China Committee
COCOM	Co-ordinating Committee
GSS	*Gikaiseido shichijūnen shi*
HC	House of Councillors
HR	House of Representatives
JCP	Japan Communist Party
JSP	Japan Socialist Party
KSK	*Kokumin seiji kenkyūkai*
LDP	Liberal-Democratic Party
MHC	Member of the House of Councillors
MHR	Member of the House of Representatives
PARC	Policy Affairs Research Council

Introduction

Numerous articles and books have been already written on various aspects of party politics in postwar Japan, including treatments of the conservative parties. Few detailed studies, however, of the actual process of policy-making in the Liberal-Democratic Party have yet been undertaken despite the growing awareness of the urgent need for a better understanding of the government and politics in contemporary Japan, of which this is an important aspect.

The reasons for the scarcity of such studies are both numerous and understandable. The lack of reliable and readily available information concerning the organisational and behavioural details involved is one of the more obvious obstacles. The size and complexity of the party's organisation and activities make it difficult to draw neat and clear-cut generalisations about the processes involved. As far as Japanese academics are concerned, there may also have been a reluctance to take positive interest in the conservative party on the grounds that conservative politicians are somehow not really worth studying because of their 'reactionary' and, perhaps, secretive inclinations.

In spite of such real or imagined obstacles, several considerations lead one today to make some initial attempts, albeit tentative and inconclusive, at a description and interpretation of the party's structure and behaviour in terms rather more specific and inclusive than those offered so far. One reason for doing this concerns the enhanced status and role of the parties, especially the ministerial party, in the postwar system of Japanese government. Another is the development in recent years of a comparative approach to the study of politics with emphasis on parties and interest groups. A third is the actual availability of empirical information about the selected aspects of the party's organisation and behaviour and the feasibility of making some meaningful, if tentative, generalisations about their nature on the basis of this information.

The first of these considerations has been implicit in virtually all discussions, whether academic or otherwise, of the parties and, indeed, politics in general in contemporary Japan. Even in the days of the prewar Imperial Constitution, parties no doubt played an important, often crucial, role in

1

determining the course of the government's actions and the fate of the nation. This was especially true in the years between Hara Takashi's appointment as Prime Minister in 1918 and the 15 May Incident of 1932. Under the new constitution the status of the parties has been vastly enhanced and their role in governmental decision-making has become central. Now that the National Diet is 'the highest organ of the state power', the parties have put themselves in control of the nerve-centre of the nation's public decision-making, for it is they, and they alone, that may legitimately dominate and speak in the name of that highest organ. It is true today, as it was in prewar times, that the national bureaucracy with its tight control of the administrative machinery of the state decisively influences the process of governmental decision-making. In its competition with the parties the bureaucracy is the winner more often than not. It is equally true, however, that few decisions can be made by the bureaucracy or any other groups which clearly contravene or ignore the wishes and interests of the parties. In practice, moreover, the relationship between a ministerial party and the bureaucracy usually takes the form of collaboration rather than competition. Under the present parliamentary cabinet system, in theory more than half and in practice virtually all of the ministers who make up a cabinet and head the ministries are drawn from the membership of the ministerial party. As a result, they are morally responsible to the party as much as they are legally responsible to the bureaucracy. Such collaboration at the summit is supplemented and reinforced at the base by the institutionalised custom of constant day-to-day contact and consultation between party members and senior public servants. This takes place at various levels of party and government decision-making, notably in the Diet standing committees and the policy-making organs of the party, especially the Policy Affairs Research Council.

It is therefore meaningless, even impossible, to discuss contemporary Japanese politics without explicitly or implicitly referring to the role of the parties, especially the ministerial party. Furthermore, the emphasis on the role of the parties in governmental decision-making has become increasingly evident as time passes and is likely to continue to do so. This is the first of the considerations which call for fuller examination of the Liberal-Democratic Party as a prerequisite to a better understanding of contemporary Japanese government and politics as a whole.

The second consideration relates to the encouraging developments in the postwar years in the social sciences in general and political science in particular—developments which have resulted from the growing interest in cross-cultural comparative analyses of various social structures and functions, including parties. These developments have involved efforts to expand the area of both theoretical and empirical investigation beyond the traditionally accepted geographical limits of the Western world. As is well known, the research efforts inspired by such an interest have already produced a series of highly significant works and many more of a comparable or even higher quality are bound to follow in the years ahead.[1]

A sound development of investigation with a cross-cultural and comparative emphasis naturally depends on the presence not only of raw data but also of some analytical models or working hypotheses built on a firm empirical basis relating to each area involved. From this point of view, it is regrettable that both description and analysis of the major Japanese parties should have remained, with rare exceptions, so incomplete and unsystematic that it is difficult to make even a few meaningful generalisations about their actual behaviour. The problem involved here is not that many of the assumptions held about the nature of contemporary Japanese parties are necessarily wrong or unfounded. It is that many of these assumptions are based on such limited evidence and presented in a manner so unsystematic and conjectural that one cannot be certain how relevant or how important they are to the actual process of party or government decision-making. What is needed is, therefore, an effort to re-examine and explicitly spell out such assumptions on the basis of as much reliable empirical information as is available.

The scarcity of reliable and readily accessible information concerning the organisation and behaviour of the contemporary Japanese parties has no doubt been a very real obstacle to any attempts to make a scientific investigation of them. It should be pointed out, however, that all the parties, including the Liberal-Democratic Party, have taken steps in recent years to increase the number and diversify the contents of their official publications which are, as a rule, available to the general public. In September 1965, for example, the Liberal-Democratic Party alone was regularly publishing five periodicals—the *Jimintōhō* (quarterly), *Jiyūminshu* (three times a month), *Soshiki Jōhō* (three times a month), *Seichō Shūhō* (weekly), and *Seisaku Geppō* (monthly)—without counting the large number of various occasional publications. It is also well known that officials of the parties have shown, at least privately if not officially, considerable willingness to respond to requests for personal interviews from outsiders, especially large newspapers and magazines, and to furnish information concerning certain specific issues and their personal views on them.

There are some important limitations to the use of information thus made available to a researcher in the form of party publications and interviews with party officials. One of these limitations is that most party publications deal almost exclusively with doctrinal or policy matters for purposes of dissemination or propaganda and seldom with the process of party decision-

[1]For a selective list of works with comparative focus, see the 'General Bibliography' in the Appendix to Robert E. Ward and Roy C. Macridis (eds.), *Modern Political Systems: Asia* (Englewood Cliffs, N.J.: Prentice-Hall, 1963), pp. 457-8. See also the 'Studies in Political Development' series published by the Princeton University Press on behalf of the Committee on Comparative Politics of the Social Science Research Council for more recent achievements in this field.

making or organisational problems. Nor is it easy to obtain specific and detailed information regarding such problems through personal interviews. As a rule, party officials are extremely cautious and timid about discussing with an outsider questions which inevitably involve references to the more unpleasant and undignified aspects of party activity, such as the delicate matters of intra-party factionalism, inter-personal rivalries, financial arrangements, and so forth.

Notwithstanding such limitations and numerous other difficulties that spring to mind, one may well question whether all possible approaches have yet been tried in order to collect enough relevant empirical information to enable one to study at least some of the important aspects of party organisation and decision-making. The impression that sufficient has not been done in this respect is reinforced by the realisation that much information may also be found in the many biographies written by or for party politicians, which have traditionally been an important part of publishing and book-reading in modern Japan. A judicious use of information collected through the above-mentioned sources—party publications, interviews with party officials, and biographies—should make possible a reasonably detailed and accurate description and analysis of contemporary Japanese parties.

The present study of the Liberal-Democratic Party was undertaken with the foregoing considerations in mind. Its primary purpose is to describe and analyse with as much specificity and accuracy as possible the actual behaviour of that party in various decision-making situations. The focus of its attention centres on the processes involved in the formulation of policies over issues of a more or less controversial character, as interpreted in terms of the organisational framework and the interaction of persons and of groups, rather than of doctrinal or ideological factors. This is not because the latter are deemed to be less important or less worth examining, but simply because it is felt that the former set of factors has so far been most inadequately treated.

Underlying this view is the assumption that in contemporary Japanese politics the organisational and group environment influences public decision-making as importantly as do elements of an ideological and doctrinal nature. In choosing to focus the discussion of the particular political party in contemporary Japan on the organisational, rather than ideological, aspects the writer had been inspired to a very important extent by a number of theoretical insights and suggestions found in the existing literature on the parties of the Western nations. Particularly relevant in this respect have been the three great classics in the field of the empirical theory of political parties, namely the works of M. Y. Ostrogorski, Robert Michels, and Maurice Duverger. Combined with the useful suggestions made more recently by Avery Leiserson,[2] many of their ideas, especially those which relate to the critical

[2]M. Y. Ostrogorski, *Democracy and the Organization of Political Parties* (New York: Macmillan, 1902), 2 vols.; Robert Michels, *Political Parties* (Glencoe: Free Press,

functions and characteristics of group and organisation in political behaviour, have guided the writer's efforts throughout the entire period of the research.

The book which has resulted from research premised on the above considerations consists of three fairly distinct parts: a historical introduction; then a section dealing with four selected factors in policy-making in the Liberal-Democratic Party; the third part consists of three case studies. On the assumption that different individuals and groups are likely to play leading roles in the process of party policy-making when these involve different kinds of issue, two basically domestic issues and one foreign policy issue were chosen. One of the domestic issues (that of compensating former landlords) is pre-eminently practical and socio-economic in its implications, whereas the other (the issue of constitutional revision) is primarily political and ideological. The issue of the policy towards China chosen to represent foreign policy issues, is both highly ideological and practical and presents a most complex pattern of interactions between the factors.

The three case studies are used to illustrate the relative significance and roles of the four selected factors in the context of dynamic party policy-making processes. Their selection, however, cannot be justified on a strictly logical and categorical basis alone, for it was made without careful comparison with other issues falling in the same categories, as would have been required to justify a claim for true representativeness in each case. In fact, the choice was dictated in part by the relative ease with which relevant empirical information was collected in the limited space of time available. For this reason, the possibility is not denied that in any of the three fields a more representative case might be found, or that any possible bias might be reduced by increasing the number either of categories or of cases in each category to be examined. In any event, the present study should be considered not as a finished product in itself, but merely as a preliminary, exploratory step towards a fuller description and analysis of this particular party.

In order to make the best use of such insights as have been provided by the relatively small number of scholars and a somewhat larger number of journalists concerning the behaviour of the Liberal-Democratic Party, existing books and articles relevant to the study were consulted with some thoroughness. The three big national newspapers of contemporary Japan— the *Asahi*, the *Mainichi*, and the *Yomiuri*—were checked with care and the *Asahi* in particular was used as the standard source of reference for majoi historical events involved. The periodical and occasional publications of the party were examined with even greater care. Biographies relevant to the book as a whole or to its sections were read and considered as thoroughly as possible.

1949); Maurice Duverger, *Political Parties* (New York: Wiley, 1954); Avery Leiserson, *Parties and Politics: An Institutional and Behavioral Approach* (New York: Knopf, 1958).

During the period between December 1965 and March 1966 a series of personal interviews was conducted by the writer in Tokyo. Twenty-four members of the National Diet affiliated with the Liberal-Democratic Party and about ten secretaries to Diet members were thus interviewed. In addition, the secretaries-general or their equivalents of the Fujiyama faction (*Tōyūkai*), Fukuda faction (*Tōfūsasshin renmei*), Ishii faction (*Suiyōkai*), Kawashima faction (*Kōyūkurabu*), former Kōno faction (*Shunjūkai*), and Miki faction personally assisted the writer's information hunt by furnishing a substantial amount of factual information either orally or in the form of various mimeographed documents.[3] Similarly, about twenty journalists (including reporters affiliated with the political affairs sections of the largest newspapers) were interviewed and most contributed factual information as well as interpretations which were sought by the writer. Several non-parliamentarian officials and clerks of the party headquarters, including two leading officials of the Policy Affairs Research Council, also helped the writer both directly and indirectly. Several incumbent and former cabinet ministers were heard at the weekly meetings of the *Kokumin seiji kenkyūkai*. Interviews were held also with the officials of the *Kokumin kyōkai* (the fund-raising agency of the Liberal-Democratic Party), the *Kokusaku kenkyūkai* (a private research organisation allegedly having enormous influence on both the party and the successive cabinets), the *Nōchi dōmei* (the pressure group of former landlords), and so forth.

The specific contributions of individuals and groups who consented to direct attributions will be explicitly acknowledged in the relevant parts of the book. The contributions of those who expressed a desire to remain anonymous were accepted with equal gratitude and profitably used as part of the background information.

[3]Neither the former Ikeda faction (*Kōchikai*) nor the Satō faction (*Shūzankai*), which had been officially closed, nor the two rival groups which had issued from the former Ōno faction and were busy setting up their separate faction offices at the time responded to the writer's requests for personal interviews. On the other hand, the quasi-factional group, *Soshinkai*, was visited and its secretary-general interviewed.

**Part One
Historical Background**

1 Evolution of the Prewar Party Models

The organisational and behavioural characteristics of the Liberal-Democratic Party (hereafter referred to as the LDP throughout the book) are defined by and explicable in terms of its historical background in the same way as any other contemporary institutional structures. It is impossible, indeed, to understand or explain many of the most salient and interesting aspects of its behaviour without referring to the weight and role of tradition, custom, and habit, which stretch back into the first years of the Meiji era.

The following description of the LDP's historical background concentrates on the evolution of the basic organisational framework and characteristics of conservative party politics in modern Japan. This will be considered primarily with reference to the developments associated with the four particular factors chosen for intensive analysis in the subsequent chapters—party membership, organisation, intra-party groups, and connections with extra-party groups.

The purpose of the two chapters contained in this part is not to trace in great detail the development of parties and party politics in modern Japan for its own sake, but merely to examine the evolution of the factors considered responsible for the LDP's organisational and behavioural characteristics as they are found today.

Original Forms and Structures

The first embryonic forms of party emerged in post-Restoration Japan during the first phase of the movement for freedom and popular rights in the mid-1870s. At first these groups, known frequently as *seisha* (political company) rather than *seitō* (party), were formed mainly by discontented members of the *shi* class (originally the warrior class) and relatively well-to-do owner-farmers who had traditionally dominated village politics under the Tokugawa system of government.[1] These primordial groups sprang up throughout the

---

[1]The word *seitō* (party) derived probably from *seiron tōha* used by Katō Hiroyuki in his translation of J. K. Bluntschli's *Allgemeine Staatrecht*, which was published in 1872 under the title of *Kokuhō hanron*. See Osatake Takeshi, *Nihon kenseishi taikō,*

country and probably numbered nearly two hundred in the middle of the 1880s.

Most of these early *seisha* groups were formed at the village or county level. Their organisation was very simple and membership small. In Fukushima Prefecture, for example, the earliest and best known of such groups was the *Sekiyōsha*, formed in 1875 in Ishikawa village with Kōno Hironaka as president and 207 members. Similarly, the *Hokushinsha*, formed in 1877 and located in Odaka village, had a president, a secretary, a treasurer, and a total of 170 members. The *Sanshisha*, formed in the same year, had a president, a secretary-general, two secretaries, a clerk, a treasurer, and 79 members.

It was not until after 1880 that the many small *seisha* groups scattered all over the country began gradually to be brought together to form larger units of organisation operating at the prefectural, regional, and eventually national levels. This process of amalgamation and consolidation corresponded roughly to the growth of the movement to establish a popularly elected national assembly which reached its climax in October 1881 when an imperial rescript promised the convocation of such an assembly in 1890. Many of these groups formed originally in the 1880s were subsequently incorporated into a few national party organisations, notably the Liberal Party (*Jiyūtō*) and the Constitutional Progressive Party (*Rikken kaishintō*). The process of transsition was no doubt extremely complex and variable from place to place and from group to group, but its organisational implications may be illustrated by the example of the *Aikokusha*.

The *Aikokusha* (Patriotic Company), originally formed in Osaka in February 1875, quickly lapsed into inaction, but was revived in September 1878 and was renamed the *Kokkai kisei dōmei* (the League for the Establishment of a National Assembly) in March 1880. According to its original constitution, it was essentially a federation of *seisha* groups and each of its prefectural affiliates was to send three permanent representatives to its headquarters in Tokyo and a few delegates, including its president, twice a year to meet at a national conference. The first conference was attended by only about forty representatives from half a dozen prefectures. However, the second conference held in March 1889 fared much better and was attended by some eighty representatives from twenty-one local *seisha* groups in eighteen prefectures. When its two leaders, Kataoka Kenkichi and Kōno Hironaka, presented to the Cabinet in April 1880 a petition on its behalf for the establishment of a national assembly, they claimed to represent some 87,000 members in twenty-four prefectures. The conference held in November of the same year was attended by sixty-four delegates said to represent some 130,000 people in twenty-two prefectures.

Vol. II (Nihonhyōronsha, 1939), pp. 438-9. The concept of political party was definitely foreign in origin and the founders of the early *seisha* groups often referred to European precedents for guidance.

It is impossible to determine exactly what percentage of these 87,000 or 130,000 people was actually affiliated with the local *seisha* groups making up the Aikokusha. There is no doubt, however, that it was significantly larger than its predecessors in so far as its membership is concerned. This developmental process involved, moreover, an important change in the general class basis of the membership as well as its geographical distribution.

Whereas the participants of its 1878 Conference all belonged to the *shi* class and came almost exclusively from western Japan (especially the Shikoku and Kyūshū regions) at least thirty-four of the sixty-four delegates attending the November 1880 Conference were from the commoner class (*heimin*) and many came from the eastern prefectures.

As the Aikokusha's organisational scope and membership grew to include increasingly heterogeneous geographical elements, geographically-based factionalism emerged within it and began to influence its behaviour. The effects of this kind of intra-group conflict became very pronounced in the Liberal Party which was formed in October 1881.

Four different groups initially participated in the efforts to build the Liberal Party. Subsequently, however, sharp divisions of opinion developed between them and two dropped out. As a result, two groups—the *Risshisha* of Tosa and the *Kokuryūkai* of Tokyo—were the sole organised groups comprising the party when it came into being.

According to its constitution, the Liberal Party consisted of a headquarters in Tokyo and local branches established at the prefectural level. A president, a vice-president, several standing committee members, and five secretaries were selected each for a term of one year. Interestingly, no official party posts of treasurer or accountant were provided, and instead the secretaries were charged with the task of looking after party finance. It is worth noting that throughout the subsequent period of Japanese party politics the most important function of the secretary-general of a conservative party has been to raise funds for the party. Each local branch of the Liberal Party was to send no more than five delegates to the annual party conference. Funds needed by the local branches had to be raised by themselves, whereas those for the headquarters were to be collected from the branches.

Most of the above-mentioned party posts were initially filled by Itagaki and his followers from the Tosa region associated with the Risshisha. This domination of the party organisation by a particular geographical group continued officially until April 1883, when the party conference nominated new officials, a majority of whom came from branches other than that in Tosa. It should be noted, however, that the move on the part of the 1883 party conference and the resulting composition of the Liberal Party's leadership group did not appreciably lessen, much less end, the factional power struggle but merely drove it underground. This type of factionalism was reactivated later in the Constitutional Liberal Party (*Rikken jiyūtō*).

Despite the apparently national character of the Liberal Party, its membership was very small in the beginning, in fact even smaller than those claimed by some of the local *seisha* groups which had preceded it, not to speak of the Aikokusha. When it was formed in October 1881 it had 101 members and by May 1884 this figure had increased to about 2,350. It should be noted, however, that its membership was based in principle on individual affiliation in contrast to the Aikokusha (renamed *Kokkai kisei dōmei*) which had been a loosely bound federation of autonomous local *seisha* groups.

The Constitutional Progressive Party, formed in March 1882 by Ōkuma Shigenobu and his associates, differed from the Liberal Party both organisationally and in reference to membership composition. In contrast to the extensive geographical basis on which the Liberal Party was built, the Constitutional Progressive Party consisted exclusively of groups of public servants, journalists, and businessmen who were personally acquainted with Ōkuma and most of whom lived in Tokyo. When it was formed, roughly four different groups joined it: a group of public servants, such as Maejima Hisoka, Kitabatake Harufusa, and Mutaguchi Gengaku who had been associated with Kōno Togama; those graduates of Keiō Gijuku (subsequently Keiō University) who had formed the *Tōyō giseikai* (Eastern Political Association), such as Fujita Mokichi, Inukai Tsuyoki, Ozaki Yukio, and Minoura Katsundo; members of the *Ōtokai* (Seagull Society), made up of the graduates of the Imperial University (subsequently Tokyo University), such as Takada Sanae, Okayama Kanekichi, Yamada Ichirō, and Amano Tameyuki; and those who had formed the *Ōmeisha* (Singing Birds' Society) under Numa Morikazu, such as Shimada Saburō, Ōkoa Ikuzō, Koezuka Ryū, and Tsunoda Shimpei. The Progressive Party's relatively high degree of intellectual sophistication and moderate progressivism gave the party a distinctive air of urbanity and cosmopolitanism in contrast to the rural, even parochial, outlook which characterised the Liberal Party.

The Rules of the Constitutional Progressive Party adopted at its inaugural meeting of 16 April 1882 provided for an extremely simple leadership structure consisting of only two kinds of office—party president and secretaries. These offices were filled respectively by Ōkuma and his closest associates, Ōno, Mutaguchi, and Haruki Yoshiaki. The Party Constitution which replaced the Rules in February 1885 abolished the post of president and substituted for it a 7-man administrative committee elected by party members at large by a simple majority vote. In September 1889 a Local Affairs Committee was established and each prefectural branch was bound to send at least one of its members to participate in it at the party headquarters.

Originally members of the Constitutional Progressive Party paid membership fees on an annual basis, but an amendment of the Constitution in 1889 abolished such fees and made the headquarters dependent entirely on voluntary contributions for its income. To the best of the writer's knowledge, however, it is not certain how and from what sources such contributions came.

The membership of the Constitutional Progressive Party was initially just as small in number as that of the Liberal Party and thereafter did not grow as quickly as the latter's. It seems to have started off at slightly over 100 in April 1882, grown to about 1,700 by the spring of 1884, and then dropped to about 1,500 by 1889. Characteristically, a very high percentage of these members came originally from Tokyo. Of the 116 members officially reported to the government in June 1882, 60 came from Tokyo, followed by 8 from Nagasaki (which was Ōkuma's birthplace), and 7 from Nīgata. This geographical distribution, however, did not last very long as the party grew gradually from a Tokyo-based intellectuals' debating society into a national party. By 1889 Tokyo's contribution dropped to a mere 2·7 per cent, while outside the Kantō region, Hyōgo and Osaka in Kinki, Ehime in Shikoku, Toyama in Hokuriku, and Miyagi in Tōhoku, contributed fairly substantial numbers.

The number of prefectural assembly members belonging to the two parties in June 1883 were respectively 163 for the Constitutional Progressive Party and 46 for the Liberal Party. Judging from the figures available for the end of 1882 and the spring of 1884 for the former and May 1884 for the latter, their total memberships at the time may be assumed to have been about 1,500 and 2,000 respectively. This suggests that, compared with the situation in the Liberal Party, the percentage of prefectural assembly members in the membership of the Constitutional Progressive Party was significantly higher, accounting for about 10 per cent in the middle of 1883 as compared with 2 or 3 per cent in the Liberal Party.

The formation in September 1890 of the Constitutional Liberal Party marked a turning point in the history of Japanese parties and party politics. Up to this point, the parties and their antecedent prototypes had necessarily operated outside any parliamentary organ of the state. From this time onwards, however, their principal forum became the Imperial Diet, which was established in 1890. The impact of the institutional change brought about by this event was bound to cause the existing parties some difficult problems of adjustment which they had to solve if they were to survive and establish a status and role of their own under the new circumstances. The task before them was as much one of utilising, reshaping, or abandoning the old structures and practices inherited from the pre-parliamentary days as of creating and developing new structures and practices.

The Constitutional Liberal Party was governed not by a single president but by a 70-member standing committee. In addition, five secretaries and a 6-member Policy Affairs Research Committee were elected. On 2 September 1890, prior to the election of these party officials, a parliamentary group called a *Yayoi kurabu* was formed by those members who had been elected to the House of Representatives in the first Diet election in Japanese history. For the purposes of investigation in matters of policy this parliamentary group was divided into six departments, roughly, though not exactly, corresponding to the ministerial divisions in the national public service.

The organisational innovations introduced by the Constitutional Liberal Party represented two new and important developments in the theory and practice of party politics in Japan. One was the realisation that a party should undertake its own independent and organised research into policy matters. When in the middle of 1892 the party officially established a policy research bureau at its headquarters with a chairman, two secretaries, and ten members, it had made a significant advance in this respect. The other was the tendency for the parliamentary component of the party to assert and gradually acquire a role and organisation of its own, separate from and, to a certain degree, independent of the national party organisation.

The relative importance and power of the parliamentary and the extra-parliamentary components of the party during the first Diet session may be inferred from the fact that in the Constitutional Liberal Party thirty-nine of the sixty-five initial standing committee members, three of the five secretaries, and all of the twenty-eight policy affairs research committee members were non-parliamentarian. In other words, a majority of the party officials were not members of the Diet. In theory, if not in practice, this supremacy of the extra-parliamentary elements was done away with by an amendment to the Party Constitution in October 1891 which was inspired by the belief that 'a party under a parliamentary system of government should be constituted with members of parliament as its core'.[2] Other amendments made on the same occasion included also the replacement of the collegiate form of top party leadership, represented by the standing committee and the board of secretaries established under it by a single president. At the same time, the word 'Constitutional' was dropped from the party's name.

Another important and burdensome heritage from the previous period which called for attention and effective action by the Constitutional Liberal Party was the prevalence of geographical factionalism. The party was formed through the merger of four distinctive regional groups, representing respectively the Tōhoku, the Kantō, the Kyūshū, and the Shikoku regional factions. It was inevitable that relationships between these groups should have been marked by strains and conflicts even after they were formally brought together and united in a single party organisation. Of the four factions the Tōhoku group was drastically weakened after its founder and leader, Kōno Hironaka, withdrew from the party in February 1897, while the Tosa (Shikoku) faction remained the single most powerful group throughout this period.[3]

[2]Ōkubo Toshiaki (ed.), *Kindaishi shiryō* (Yoshikawa Kōbunkan, 1965), p. 275.

[3]Masumi Junnosuke, 'Nihon seitōshi ni okeru chihōseiji no shomondai' (III), *Kokka-gakkai Zasshi*, LXXIV, 5 and 6 (April 1961), pp. 54-6, 59, and 65. For the circumstances of Kōno's withdrawal from the Liberal Party, see Kōno Banshū den hensankai (ed.), *Kōno Banshū den*, Vol. I (Kōno Banshū den kankōkai, 1923), pp. 448-57.

Remarkable as it may seem, considering the situation in the Liberal Party, this type of factionalism was almost totally absent from the Constitutional Progressive Party. For one thing, the party had been founded by Tokyo-based groups of intellectuals rather than by the geographical groups which had constituted the Liberal Party. Despite the subsequent rapid increase of members from prefectures other than Tokyo, Ōkuma and other original founders retained their control over the relatively centralised power in the party until December 1884. In that year, however, these men withdrew from the party and the effective leadership which had so far bound the party members tightly together collapsed. Factionalism which grew under these circumstances was based, however, not on geographical factors but mainly on the differences in occupational backgrounds and connections, as was the case with the groups of former journalists, lawyers, school teachers, or prefectural assembly members.

In 1896 the Constitutional Progressive Party led other anti-Liberal Party groups to merge their organisations, and formed a new Progressive Party (*Shimpotō*). The Progressive Party was also governed by a collegiate body called an executive council made up of five members, assisted by a 30-member standing committee, while Ōkuma remain the *de facto* president.

It was characteristic of the membership composition of these two parties' parliamentary groups that nearly three-quarters were former local politicians and that entrepreneurs and public servants were the next largest categories (see Appendix I). Since the entrepreneurs were often local politicians at the same time, one may say that an overwhelming majority of their members were in fact one-time local politicians. This was one of the most important reasons for the prevalence of geographical factionalism in the Liberal Party.

In June 1898 the Liberal and the Progressive parties were united to form the *Kenseitō* (Constitutional Government Party). The leadership structure of this party was characteristically a combination of the Liberal Party and the Progressive Party models. On the one hand, it dispensed with the office of president and substituted for it an executive council made up of two former Liberals and two Progressives. On the other hand, a 5-man board of secretaries was instituted on the Liberal Party model. It was only a week after the formation of this short-lived united party that the first 'party Cabinet' in Japanese history, headed by Ōkuma, came into being. Only two months after the unification, however, the former Liberals and Progressives were at loggerheads over the distribution of Cabinet posts. By early November of the same year they had again formed separate parties, that of the Liberals continuing to call itself the Kenseitō while that of the Progressives was named the *Kenseihontō* (True Constitutional Government Party). Both inherited almost intact the platform and the constitution of the old Kenseitō and therefore continued to be governed by an executive council.

From this time onwards, a quasi-two-party system built around two competitive parties of conservative persuasion became an established pattern of Japanese party politics. This was the case until the middle of 1940 when all existing parties were dissolved and absorbed by the *Taiseiyokusankai* (Imperial Rule Assistance Association). After World War II the same pattern was revived but significantly modified by the appearance of a powerful socialist party.

The Seiyūkai as a Prewar Party Model

Following the split of the Kenseitō in October 1898, the possibility of having the most eminent statesman of the time, Itō Hirobumi, lead the liberal wing of the defunct party began to be seriously considered among its leaders. In September 1900 this seemingly fantastic plan became a reality and the *Rikken seiyūkai* (Constitutional Association of Political Friends, hereafter referred to as the *Seiyūkai*) was established under Itō's leadership. As Kōtoku Shūsui commented in his famous contribution to the *Yorozuchōhō* on the eve of the party's official inauguration, one of the two major parties which had publicly claimed to represent the 'people's' will and interests against the bureaucracy dominated by the Sat-Chō clique thus submitted itself to the most illustrious member of this same clique.[4] The formation of the Seiyūkai was accomplished completely on Itō's terms and, in fact, took the form of donation of the party to Itō by the party's leaders.

That the bureaucratic elements claimed equality, if not necessarily superiority, of status and power *vis-à-vis* party politicians was symbolically demonstrated by the composition of the founding committee appointed by Itō on 25 August 1900. Five of its twelve members, including the chairman, were leading public servants. In 1913 seven top-ranking public servants became officially affiliated with the party to make its relationship with the top stratum of the bureaucracy even more pronounced.

In subsequent years the percentage of high-ranking public officials in the total membership of the Seiyūkai's parliamentary party was never higher than about 10 per cent. However, their contribution to the membership of the top party leadership group showed a significant increase. At the time it was formed in 1900 their share was a mere 3 per cent, but by 1920 it had risen to 16 per cent. In other words, their share in the top leadership group was about twice as high as the percentage of high-ranking public servants in the parliamentary party of the Seiyūkai as a whole, which was about 8 per cent at the time.

Another aspect worth special mention concerns Itō's deliberate attempt to base the new party on the support not only of the bureaucracy but also the business community, by inducing prominent businessmen to join or at least to be sympathetically interested in it. For example, Itō personally invited Shibusawa Eiichi, one of the most outstanding businessmen of his time, to be

---

[4]See the quotation from the *Yorozuchōhō* in Ōkubo, op. cit., p. 317.

officially a member of the party, although the latter declined to go beyond promising assistance from outside. Or again, Inoue Kaoru, acting on Itō's behalf, asked the businessmen associated with the Mitsui shūkaijo to participate. On the occasion of the party's inaugural ceremony, representative businessmen were specially invited together with independent members of the House of Representatives, local politicians and administrators, well-known lawyers, and so forth.

Apart from the importance of businessmen among the Seiyūkai-affiliated members of the House of Representatives (hereafter referred to as MHRs), it should be noted that lawyers too were numerically significant, accounting for over 15 per cent. The percentage of local politicians steadily declined from over three-quarters of the total number in 1902 to less than a half in the 1930s (see Appendix I).

Organisationally, if not behaviourally, the Seiyūkai was a well-developed party from the beginning. According to its constitution and the rules relating to the branches, it consisted of a headquarters in Tokyo and local branches set up at the prefectural level. The headquarters was governed by a president, an executive council, a secretary-general, and secretaries. An annual party conference was convened in Tokyo by the president and was attended by MHRs affiliated with the party and delegates from the local branches. The president might also convene, when special need arose, an MHRs' meeting during a Diet session.

Absent from the original Seiyūkai constitution were provisions relating to the organisation and officers of the parliamentary party (excepting the MHRs' meeting), and—even more important—policy research organs both at the headquarters and in the parliamentary group. It was, however, not long before additional organisational devices were introduced to fill such gaps. In January 1901 practical needs compelled President Itō to appoint five executive officers of the parliamentary party who in turn nominated nine secretaries of the parliamentary party. From this time onwards it became a rule for a variable number of such officers and secretaries to be appointed for each Diet session separately from the executive council members and secretaries at the headquarters. The amendments of the constitution in April 1927 provided explicitly for their election by the MHRs' meeting.

A policy research organ was first set up in the Seiyūkai in June 1901 in accordance with the rules of the policy research bureau. The bureau thus established consisted of five departments, each headed by a chairman and two directors and staffed by five research officers. These departments dealt respectively with public administration, finance, economy, foreign affairs, and education.

At the same time, the party conference of 3 December 1901 formally resolved to maintain the policy research departments of the parliamentary party which had been inherited from the Kenseitō. According to the Rules

Relating to the Policy Research Department Assignments adopted in December 1903, each MHR affiliated with the party might become a member of more than one department at a time, but he might vote in only one of them. This practice has been preserved in the present-day LDP. The dual structure of the policy research organs, represented on the one hand by the bureau and its successors at the headquarters (functioning mainly during the periods between Diet sessions) and, on the other, by the research departments of the parliamentary party (operating only during Diet sessions), continued until January 1911. In the years between 1903 and 1910 a series of Special Investigation Committees were set up to deal with specific and topical issues. In the meantime, by 1909 it had become customary for the Policy Affairs Research Council (hereafter referred to as the PARC) of the headquarters to establish within itself several divisions dealing with particular problems. By April 1913 ten divisions had been set up, each headed by a division chief.

Thus during the first decade of the century the policy-making activities in the Seiyūkai became well organised and systematic, as indicated by the development of the PARC described above. So far as the organisational framework of such activities is concerned, it was almost exactly the same as that found in today's LDP. It was not until March 1929, however, that a decision of the PARC came to be regarded as the party's official decision, and at the same time it became obligatory for all party officials to participate in the work of this particular organ. It was after this important decision that the PARC began to attempt to draw up broad political and economic policy programs, such as the twelve-point economic program of 1930, the ten-point Party Platform of December 1931, the 'Five-Year Industrial Development Plan' of February 1932, and so forth.

Apart from the parliamentary organisation and the policy research machinery of the party, several other important changes were made in the Seiyūkai's organisational structure in the first thirty years of its life. One of these changes concerned the composition of the executive council. In May 1903 a 30-member consultative council was set up to take over a large part of the small executive council's functions. According to the rules relating to this new organ, adopted by the party conference of December 1903, it was to consist of thirty members, twenty of whom were to be elected by and from the party-affiliated MHRs while the remaining ten were to be appointed by the president. What was significant about this new arrangement was the peculiar manner in which its members were nominated. Ten of them, in practice including the council chairman, were appointed by the president, this obviously being a device designed to enhance the latter's power and authority. On the other hand, the remaining twenty were selected from among the MHRs *on a regional basis*. For the purpose of their election eight regional groups were officially formed and the twenty available posts were distributed among these groups according to the number of party-affiliated

MHRs returned from each region in the preceding House of Representatives election. On the basis of this principle the initial plan of distribution was as follows: Kyūshū–4, Tōkai–3, Kinki–3, Chūgoku–3, Kantō–2, Tōhoku–2, Hokushin–2, and Shikoku–1.

Although the actual plans of distribution have naturally changed subsequently,[5] the division of the country into eight regions has remained almost intact into the postwar period and has been inherited by the LDP.

In January 1915 an election committee and in May of the same year a party affairs committee were set up at the Seiyūkai headquarters. Like its contemporary counterpart in the LDP the former consisted of the party's top leaders, all of the ten members having a status at least equal to that of the executive council member. The party affairs committee was a remote antecedent of today's LDP National Organisation Committee. It was originally set up as an *ad hoc* organ, but after April 1916 it became permanent and greatly expanded its activities.

The revision of the Seiyūkai constitution approved by the Extraordinary Party Conference of 15 April 1927 for the first time specified the method of electing the party president. According to Article 2 of the revised constitution, a president was to be elected by the party conference for a term of seven years.[6] The method which has come to be referred to as *kōsen* (election by the party at large) was thus for the first time formally introduced (at least in theory) as one of the important principles of party politics in Japan. In practice, however, a vote was never taken for the election of a Seiyūkai president but, instead, a nomination submitted by a senior member at the party conference on behalf of the party's decision-making organs was invariably approved unanimously.

The precedent for nomination by recommendation rather than by ballot was set, in fact, the day that the revised constitution was adopted. Following its adoption, a senior member of the standing council, Nakahashi Tokugorō, proposed 'to dispense with the troublesome formality of vote-counting and to nominate Tanaka Giichi (incumbent president) unanimously for re-election'. The proposal was carried 'unanimously'. Following Tanaka's sudden death in 1929, the advisers of the party and Cabinet members agreed first among themselves to choose Inukai Tsuyoki, and that decision was subsequently referred to and approved by both the executive council and the standing council before it was submitted to the Extraordinary Party Confer-

[5]An amendment of the rules made in May 1915 increased the total number of the council's members to 45, 25 to be elected from among the party-affiliated MHRs on the basis of regional representation, 10 from the House of Peers, and 10 to be appointed by the president. See Kobayashi Yūzo (ed.), *Rikken seiyūkai shi* (Rikken seiyūkai shuppankyoku, 1925), Vol. IV, pp. 166-7.

[6]The original constitution of September 1900 had said nothing about the method of choosing a party president and the matter had so far been left entirely to convention. For the text of the revised Seiyūkai Constitution of 1927, see Kikuchi Gorō, *Rikken seiyūkai shi* (Rikken seiyūkai shi hensanbu, 1933), Vol. VI (*Tanaka sōsai jidai*), pp. 269-71.

ence of 12 October 1929. At the Conference an adviser, Motoda Hajime, moved to dispense with the vote and to leave the nomination to the former president, Takahashi Korekiyo, who duly recommended Inukai. The recommendation was 'unanimously' approved.[7]

This evasion of the elective method in the selection of party president was bound to make the party conference essentially a formality. In this respect, the model of a party conference built by the Seiyūkai was also followed faithfully by its postwar successors, until in April 1956 the LDP for the first time implemented both the spirit and letter of the historic article of the revised Seiyūkai constitution by making Hatoyama Ichirō president through a genuine election. It is nevertheless significant that the basic idea was officially accepted by the Seiyūkai as early as 1927.

Combined with the effects of the unusually long term of office, its extensive powers relative to the personnel administration of the party invested the office of party president in theory with authority and prestige unmatched in the party. In practice, however, his power was not quite as great as the provisions of the party constitution made it sound, for it was restricted not only by the particular personality of the man who happened to occupy the post but also, as we shall see later, by the countervailing, centrifugal influence of intra-party factionalism.[8]

As the parties' role in the prewar system of government became increasingly important after the Russo-Japanese War and especially after the formation of the first Saionji Cabinet in 1906, the centre of power and activity in the Seiyūkai shifted gradually from the extra-parliamentary to the parliamentary organs. This tendency was clearly shown in the first twenty years of that party's existence by the fact that, whereas in 1900 nine of its forty-six top leaders (19·5 per cent) were non-parliamentarian, by 1921 the comparable percentage had decreased to 2·7 per cent (2 out of 72). In fact, during the period of 'party politics' after the Russo-Japanese War, the extra-parliamentary elements ceased to be represented to any significant degree on any of the formal organs of the party's headquarters.

This did not mean, however, that these extra-parliamentary elements ceased to play a role in the party's decision-making process or, indeed, in the politics of the nation at large. On the contrary, their activities became in many respects more organised and regularised during this period than previously. In December 1903 an Extra-Parliamentary Union of the Seiyūkai

[7]Ibid., p. 271; Vol. VII, pp. 1-7.

[8]The office of president in the Seiyūkai reached the apex of power and prestige under Hara Takashi during the period between June 1914 and November 1921. About the extent of Hara's authority as felt by other members of the party, see, for example, Wakatsuki Reijirō, *Kofūan kaikoroku – Meiji taishō shōwa seikai hishi* (Yomiuri shimbunsha, 1950), pp. 137-8. In this connection, it may be noted in passing that the word *jingasa* (backbencher), suggestive of the stratification between 'leaders' and the led in the party, came to be used widely by 1912. See Miyake Setsurei, 'Seitō no jingasa to shiteno anshinritsumei', *Nihon oyobi Nihonjin*, 585 (1 November 1912), p. 8.

was officially established. From this point onwards the organisation acted as an effective pressure group to work on the parliamentary party, government agencies, and extra-party groups. The campaign it sponsored and directed in late 1909 for the reduction of tax rates was a good example of the union's pressure group activity. Apart from such pressure group activities, the union also sent canvassing teams of speakers recruited from party members to various districts of the country and sponsored numerous political rallies and meetings. Like the party itself the union made it a rule to hold an annual conference in Tokyo to elect its officers and adopt manifestoes.

It is difficult to assess with a reasonable degree of accuracy the influence the union exerted on the behaviour of the Seiyūkai and the nation's politics in general. There is no doubt, however, that it represented the original pre-parliamentary party tradition which was inevitably overshadowed by the development of the parliamentary party and yet refused to pass away completely under the changed circumstances. In fact, the tradition has managed to survive the vicissitudes of the subsequent wartime and postwar years and is still visibly alive in the LDP.

One of the most important functions of the Extra-Parliamentary Union was to use its members for the purpose of disturbing and obstructing the election campaigns of candidates from rival parties, and indeed a characteristic of this period was that elections, whether to the Imperial Diet or prefectural assemblies, became matters of the greatest concern to the parties. In 1915 not only was the Election Committee, an organ specialising in electoral affairs, established in the Seiyūkai but also two important principles concerning the endorsement of candidates by the party were worked out. One was that priority should be given to an incumbent member at the expense of someone who had never been an MHR, or had been an MHR and been defeated. The other was that the headquarters should have a veto power over the local branches in the selection of party-endorsed candidates.[9] Both these principles have been fastidiously observed by the postwar parties and remain today the most respected of the prewar traditions in the practice of the LDP.

The second of these principles relating to electoral politics indicated the general pattern of the relationship between the headquarters and local branches, which was just as grossly one-sided in the Seiyūkai as in the LDP. The reasons for the inequality which characterised this relationship were found largely in the character of the branches. Generally speaking, a branch formed and operating at the prefectural level was a group made up almost exclusively of a handful of MHRs who had been returned from the prefecture and a somewhat larger number of prefectural assembly members. In many

[9]See Points 2 and 9, Point 1, and Points 3 and 6, respectively of the instructions sent by the headquarters to branches before the House of Representatives elections of March 1904, March 1915, and May 1920, in Kobayashi, op. cit., Vol. II, pp. 71-3; Vol. IV, pp. 104-5 and 635-7.

C

cases one would find, for example, the post of branch president occupied by
an MHR and the posts of branch secretaries by prefectural assembly members. Within a branch so composed it was, as a rule, the MHRs who held
the position of superiority and these men were naturally under the control
of the headquarters and its leaders.

The growth in importance of House of Representatives elections led the
party leaders to make deliberate efforts to broaden and consolidate voter
support for the party by winning the support and co-operation of local men
of influence. The most important of these were local politicians and administrators, especially prefectural assembly members. Under these circumstances
a sharply increasing percentage of prefectural assembly members were led
to join the major national parties, notably the Seiyūkai and the Kenseikai
(renamed *Minseitō* in 1927). Of those, for example, returned to the prefectural assemblies in the local elections of 1907, 1911, 1919, 1923, and 1935,
between 43 and 68 per cent were officially affiliated with the former and
between 17 and 41 per cent with the latter, as the table below shows: [10]

	1907	1911	1919	1923	1935	Average
	%	%	%	%	%	%
Seiyūkai	47·2	47·8	54·5	67·7	43·1	52·0
Kenseikai	16·8	22·9	29·5	24·9	40·6	26·9
Total	64·0	70·7	84·0	92·6	83·7	78·9

The figures eloquently testify to the extent to which local politics and politicians had become part of national party politics and organisation during
this period.

At the height of prewar party influence in politics, which roughly corresponded to the time of Hara Takashi's leadership of the Seiyūkai, the regional
groups in the party were considered the basic units of opinion and interest
aggregation and were regularly utilised as such by the party leaders. Whenever a controversial issue arose, the party leaders would have party-affiliated
MHRs attend the meeting of the regional groups (referred to as the 'village
meeting'—*mura no kai*) to which they belonged and unify their views in
such a manner as to conform to and strengthen the positions preferred by
the leaders. Each one of these regional groups was led by a particularly
influential member—such as Hoshi Tōru and Hara Takashi of the Kantō
group, Sugita Teiichi of the Hokushin group, Matsuda Masahisa of the
Kyūshū group, and so forth. The authority and prestige of these individuals
was such that they would sway the backbenchers' views one way or another
with relative ease. Exactly as in the case of postwar faction leaders, especially
of the LDP, their influence depended to a considerable extent on the practice
of distributing important party offices according to their advice on the basis

[10]The percentage figures were derived from the following sources: Kobayashi,
op. cit., Vol. II, pp. 408-11; Vol. III, pp. 443-9; Vol. IV, pp. 572-4; Kikuchi, op. cit.,
Vol. V, pp. 228-9; *Tokyo Asahi Shimbun*, 17 October 1935.

of regional representation and balance. A backbencher would need their help and recommendation for his promotions in the party.

In contrast to the opinion-aggregating function which the regional groups evidently performed, the other conspicuous role attributed to them was divisive and at times even disintegrative. For example, in the mid-1900s a conflict developed between Hara and his group on the one hand and Matsuda and his supporters on the other. This conflict sprang from the traditional hostilities between the Kantō and the Kyūshū groups as much as from the antagonisms between the bureaucratic elements dominant in the former and the old party politicians associated with the latter. This divisive influence of regional groups remained very pronounced until it was overshadowed by a newer form of intra-party factionalism based on factors other than geography.

The point of transition from the old to the newer form of factionalism in the Seiyūkai may be found in the conflict in early 1922 between groups favouring a Cabinet reshuffle and those opposed to it. This took the form of a conflict between a dominant faction led by the party president and Prime Minister, Takahashi, and a faction led by two dissident members of the Cabinet, Nakahashi and Motoda. It was thus clearly a harbinger of the postwar type of factionalism, particularly that of the LDP.

As factionalism grew increasingly more prevalent and vicious, the prestige and authority of the party president naturally suffered and became less and less readily accepted by the faction leaders, whose influence was steadily rising. The following conditions no doubt accelerated such a process. After the formation of the Hara Cabinet in 1918 the central role of the parties in the system of government became accepted much more widely than previously in the name of the 'norm of constitutional government'. As a result, the position of a party president became a main, though never quite exclusive, route to premiership. It was not, however, the simple fact of being the leader of the largest opposition party that determined ultimately who should succeed a resigning Prime Minister. What mattered were particular personal relationships maintained by the competing party politicians with the upper stratum of the extra-parliamentary, often extra-constitutional, power structure represented by the semi-institutionalised *genrō* (council of elder statesmen), the Privy Council, and the House of Peers. These two interrelated conditions led many faction leaders to aspire to the post of president and, for the purpose of attaining it, to engage in factional manoeuvres against one another. Should the incumbent president be found unable to obtain the imperial appointment to the premiership for any reason, his competitors within the party would criticise him as unfit. Factionalism naturally thrived on this kind of rivalry and mutual suspicion between influential members.

Following President Tanaka's death in 1929, the struggle over the problem of succession was fought between Suzuki Kisaburō and Tokonami Takejirō. The danger of another major split of the party posed by this conflict was barely averted by the intervention of Inukai Tsuyoki, but after the latter's assassination in May 1932 it was resumed with renewed intensity. Assisted by two younger but extremely shrewd 'brains', Mori Kaku and Hatoyama Ichirō, Suzuki emerged victor from the struggle. Partly, however, because of illness and partly because of mounting dissatisfaction with his ineffectual leadership he was compelled to resign in February 1937. Following his resignation, it was found to be impossible to choose a single successor without running the risk of a major split once again. Consequently, a collegiate form of leadership was substituted for the post. This device, called a 'Presidential Proxy Committee', involved four party leaders—Hatoyama Ichirō, Maeda Yonezō, Nakajima Chikuhei, and Shimada Toshio—and was designed to contain, at least temporarily, the intra-party factional strife symbolised by the relationship between these four individuals. For precisely the same reasons and purposes, the device was revived eighteen years later by the LDP in November 1955.

By the end of May 1938, however, pressure for reversion to the simple presidential system became so great that it was evidently impossible to continue under the committee system much longer. On the other hand, both Hatoyama and Nakajima were determined to bid for the post of president as soon as it was reinstated, and neither was likely to give up the fight. This conflict led in April 1939 to the final break up of the Seiyūkai into the two separate parties, one led by Hatoyama's deputy, Kuhara, and the other by Nakajima.[11] By the time all existing parties were absorbed by the Taiseiyoku-sankai on the eve of World War II one of the two major prewar parties was thus irrevocably divided and factionalism had become its most conspicuous attribute.

Furthermore, factionalism had completely shifted by this time from a geographical to a personal and monetary basis. Nakajima and Kuhara were both 'businessmen-politicians' and represented the newly rising *zaibatsu* interests. On the other hand, Hatoyama was Suzuki's brother-in-law and Mori's father had been an intimate friend of Hatoyama's father. These facts suggest that monetary considerations and personal (or familial) ties were factors of basic importance in the growth of the new form of factionalism.

The relationship between the Mitsui House and the Meiji oligarchy is legendary, dating back to the first years of Meiji when Mitsui Takafuku and Minoura Rizaemon were semi-official financiers of the Imperial Court and the Meiji government. It was, however, following the Russo-Japanese War that the relationship between the *zaibatsu* concerns and the parties became more or less formalised and accepted almost as a matter of course. The sudden

---

[11]There were a dozen of the Seiyūkai members who refused to associate themselves with either group and, consequently, there emerged three separate groups—the Nakajima group with 98 members at the end of 1939, the Kuhara group with 70, and the third group led by Kanemitsu Tsuneo with 12 affiliates. See *Gikaiseido shichijūnen shi* (*GSS*): *Seitō haiha hen* (1961), pp. 601-3.

and substantial increase in the number of voters following that war made an election a much more costly affair than previously and drove the parties to seek progressively more funds from the wealthy monopolies, and so to increase their dependence on them.

The revision of the Election Law in 1919, which lowered the minimum amount of direct state taxes to be paid by a qualified voter from ten to three yen, tripled the number of voters, while the introduction of universal manhood suffrage in 1925 further quadrupled it from three to well over twelve million. The resultant increase in the number of voters and the diversification of their socio-economic backgrounds inevitably resulted in a sharp rise in the cost of campaigning.

Although the relationship between Mitsui and the Seiyūkai could not be inferred so easily from the composition of its leadership group as in the case of Mitsubishi and the Minseitō, it was nevertheless clear that some of its prominent leaders—Yamamoto Jōtarō, Yamamoto Teijirō, and Mori Kaku —were well-known 'Mitsui-men' and acted as such.[12] Although it is impossible to make an accurate estimation of the amount of money that flowed from the Mitsui-affiliated firms to the Seiyūkai, it was probably in the order of a few million yen per election, as suggested by Iwai Ryōtarō.[13] In any event, it was indicative of the approximate value of the resources which Mitsui seems to have been in a position to throw into the party that between 1932 and 1934 it gave away an annual average of ¥3·9 million in various donations, not counting those of less than ¥50,000 each.

Between World War I and the 15 May Incident of 1932 Mitsui's role as the provider of the Seiyūkai's electioneering funds was predominant. This made it possible for fairly centralised control to be maintained over party funds by the party president and secretary-general at the expense of their potential competitors who might have wished to cultivate independent sources of revenue of their own to compete with the dominant group in the party. As is well known, however, Mitsui gradually and deliberately withdrew from active participation in party politics after the 'change of policy' in the wake of the 15 May Incident.

It was under such circumstances that the role of the 'newly rising' concerns, represented by Kuhara Fusanosuke's Nihon Sangyō (Nissan) and Mori Nobuteru's Mori Kōgyō, rapidly became predominant. The diversification of the sources of financial contributions brought about by the rise of

---

[12]Shinobu Seizaburō, *Taishō seijishi*, Vol. IV (Kawade shobō, 1952), p. 1335. As Shinobu points out, however, it is important to bear in mind that neither the Seiyūkai nor the Minseitō depended exclusively on Mitsui and Mitsubishi for donations. Behind the former were also the Yasuda, the Sumitomo, the Furukawa, the Kuhara, the Fujita, the Nakahashi, the Wakaba, and the Katakura concerns, while the latter was tied also to the Yamaguchi and the Nezu families, the Japan Electric Power and the Tōhō Electric Power companies, and so forth. See also Takahashi Kamekichi, *Nihon shihonshugi hattatsushi*, rev. ed. (Nihonhyōronsha, 1929), pp. 328-9.
[13]In *Mitsui Mitsubishi monogatari* (Chikurashobō, 1934), p. 224.

these new concerns rendered increasingly difficult the maintenance of centralised control of funds flowing into the party from external sources. Such a situation in turn encouraged the growth of plural factions in the party, each tied to one or more of these sources. Apart from the emotional and interpersonal factors mentioned already, these new developments among the nation's business circles had a considerable effect on the state of the intraparty factionalism. Thus a situation closely akin to what has become so typical of the LDP had already emerged by the end of the 1930s.

The Minseitō as an Alternative Model

While the Liberal Party wing of the Kenseitō formed the Seiyūkai following the split of 1898, the Progressive Party wing continued to exist as the *Kenseihontō* (renamed the *Rikken kokumintō* in March 1910). Its membership of fewer than one hundred split in February 1913, when half the members joined the newly formed *Rikken dōshikai*, leaving the other half to continue to call themselves the *Kokumintō* (National Party). It was not until the House of Representatives election of March 1915 that the Rikken dōshikai half of the former Progressives managed to defeat the Seiyūkai 153 to 108 and proved their competitive position. In October 1916 the Rikken dōshikai formed the *Kenseikai* together with two minor parties, the *Chūseikai* and the *Kōyū kurabu*.

The membership composition of the parliamentary party of the Kenseikai and its successor was similar to that of the Seiyūkai. By far the largest occupational category was that of local politicians, who continued well into the 1930s to account for over a half of the total number (see Appendix I). The rate of decline of this particular category was not as conspicuous in the Kenseikai and the Minseitō as in the Seiyūkai. Before the Russo-Japanese War the percentage of public servants had been very high, but subsequently it decreased sharply, especially in the 1920s. As in the Seiyūkai, businessmen and lawyers were numerically most important next to local politicians.

The organisation of the Kenseikai was also almost identical with that of the Seiyūkai. All organs found in the latter were either expressly provided for in the Kenseikai constitution of 1916 or subsequently created as need arose. There were, however, a few notable differences between the two parties in the actual working of these organs.

One difference related to the role played by the policy research organ in the party decision-making process and the status accorded to it. While it was not until the late 1920s that the Seiyūkai began to recognise the great importance of its PARC, the Kenseikai placed a much greater emphasis on the activities of its own PARC from the beginning. It was only two weeks after the party was formed in 1916 that a decision was made to the effect that any bill which party-affiliated MHRs might wish to introduce or have introduced by the party in the Diet must be submitted to the PARC in advance for consideration and approval. Here was clearly present the concept of a formal party decision and a regularised process of decision-making.

In August 1917 the Kenseikai's PARC was dealing with eighteen specific issues, ranging from the revision of the Election Law to the economic relations with Russia. Each of these concrete issues was examined in the first instance by one of the divisions set up in the organ and then reported back to the plenary meeting of the PARC with concrete recommendations for further action. By October 1918 it became customary for the plenary meetings of the PARC to be attended by all leading officials of the party, including the secretary-general and secretaries, advisers, and members of the executive council. In terms, therefore, of both the form and substance of policy research activities, the Kenseikai after about 1920 resembled the LDP of the mid-1960s even more closely than did its Seiyūkai counterpart on the eve of World War II.

Another noteworthy aspect concerned the role of the *kambukai*, which was roughly equivalent to the present *yakuinkai* (leaders' meeting) in the LDP. The practice for the principal party officials to meet on a fairly regular basis was started in the middle of 1917. Who should participate in these consultations was never rigidly fixed. Regular attendance was, however, gradually limited to the senior members of the executive council, the secretary-general and secretaries, and advisers, occasionally supplemented by the president and the PARC chairman. In contrast to the 'Three Leaders' Meetings' and the 'Seven Leaders' Meetings' of the LDP, the number of officials present at the *kambukai* meetings of the Kenseikai remained greater than ten as a rule, and was often closer to twenty.

In the Seiyūkai's leadership composition high-ranking public servants were accorded high priority. In comparison, the relative weight given to former local politicians in the Kenseikai's organs was of quite impressive proportions. The comparative percentages of the five principal occupational categories in the composition of the two parties' leadership groups in three years in the Taishō era were as follows:[14]

		Local politicians	Public servants	Business-men	Lawyers	Journalists
		%	%	%	%	%
1919	Seiyūkai	31·5	15·7	15·7	21·0	5·2
	Kenseikai	46·6	10·0	6·6	–	26·6
1922	Seiyūkai	13·0	13·0	13·0	21·7	26·0
	Kenseikai	54·5	6·0	9·0	6·0	15·1
1925	Seiyūkai	21·7	8·6	21·7	17·3	13·0
	Kenseikai	43·1	7·8	–	9·8	23·5

[14]The 'top leadership groups' refers here to: members of the executive council, secretary-general and secretaries, and the executive officers and the secretaries of the parliamentary party. The percentages were derived from Kobayashi, op. cit., Vol. IV, pp. 521-2 and 558-9; Kikuchi, op. cit., Vol. V, pp. 27, 102, 392-3, and 453-4; Yoko-yama Katsutarō and Higuchi Hideo, *Kenseikaishi* (Kenseikaishi hensanjo, 1926), pp. 151-2, 356, 363-71, 708-9, and 712-14; GSS: *Shūgiingiin meikan* (1962), *passim*.

As the statistical evidence clearly demonstrates, local politicians were by far the predominant group in the leadership positions of the party in these years, while the percentage of journalists was also quite substantial. On the other hand, businessmen, lawyers, and public servants were relatively few.

The preponderance of local politicians in the leadership composition of the Kenseikai had a considerable effect upon the relationship between the party's headquarters in Tokyo and local branches. In the case of the Seiyūkai the relationship was evidently one-sided, as we have already seen. In contrast, that obtaining between the Kenseikai's headquarters and branches seems to have been much more equal and deliberately so. A branch was allowed to have its own screening committee to decide, with the *ex post facto* consent of the headquarters, which particular candidates to endorse in a Diet election, although the principle of giving priority to an incumbent member was generally observed. In February 1924, for example, the Tokyo branch elected a 23-member screening committee which chose eight candidates for the Tokyo election district to run in the next House of Representatives election.

The relatively large scope of initiative and freedom of action which the Kenseikai allowed its branches to enjoy was justified by and further encouraged regularised and effective party activities at the grass-roots level as well as growth of membership. By early 1925 it had succeeded in creating branches in at least twenty-seven of the forty-six prefectures and in having regional meetings of branch members held at least once a year in all nine regions of the country. The fact that Secretary Yamaji Jōichi publicly announced at the party conference of December 1919 that it had a current membership of 262,260 was symbolic of its interest in the size of its grass-roots membership. Apparently prompted (directly or indirectly) by the policy of the party's leaders in this respect, a few dozen or a few hundred farmers and shopkeepers from a particular village or town would become members of the party *en bloc*.

Combined with the singularly high status accorded to the PARC and the functions of the *kambukai* in the general framework of the party's decision-making machinery, the great concern for grass-roots support and numerical strength made the Kenseikai look, if anything, more modern than the Seiyūkai. It was more typically a mass, or mass-oriented, party and as such resembled the LDP of the mid-1960s more closely.

After the Kenseikai was reorganised and became the *Rikken minseitō* (hereafter referred to as the *Minseitō*) in June 1927 the distinctive air of modernity both in its general organisational policy and ideological outlook was preserved and even emphasised. The role of the PARC grew in importance and prestige, its work becoming more systematic and sophisticated, and its broad orientation showing a distinct preference for welfare policies.

In terms of organisational programs the party attempted to establish branches at the township and village, as well as the prefectural, level and to encourage young people in particular to join it. What was more interesting from the point of view of our contemporary concern was that in the middle of 1936 it published a plan to increase the number of dues-paying members to 450,000 as the initial target, and to divide the one-yen per head membership fee between the headquarters and the local branch concerned on a fifty-fifty basis. This plan could well have come from the LDP in the 1960s. In terms of public relations activities of a more general type, the party sponsored a series of 'political education lectures' which were periodically held at the nation's principal urban centres and were attended each time by hundreds of prefectural assembly members and other kinds of local politician. For example, the 'lecture meeting', which was third in the series and held in Osaka in November 1935, was attended by about 250 local politicians. The Minseitō headquarters sent on this occasion a team of top party leaders as speakers. This was again almost exactly what the LDP would be doing thirty years later.

The relationship between the Kenseikai (and the Minseitō) and Mitsubishi was similar to that between the Seiyūkai and Mitsui. In the early days Ōkubo Toshimichi and Ōkuma Shigenobu had been to Mitsubishi what Itō Hirobumi and Inoue Kaoru had been to Mitsui. Subsequently, however, the Minseitō-Mitsubishi relationship became more direct and personal, as indicated by the fact that the Kenseikai's first president, Katō Takaaki, had not only been a leading official of a Mitsubishi concern but was married to the first daughter of the founder of the *zaibatsu*, Iwasaki Yatarō. In addition to Katō, another top leader of the party, Sengoku Mitsugu, was also a prominent 'Mitsubishi-man', while the Minseitō president Hamaguchi Yūkō's trusted confidant, Shidehara Kijūrō, was married to Iwasaki's second daughter.

Although it is again impossible to estimate the size of monetary contributions made by Mitsubishi to the Kenseikai or the Minseitō, it seems clear that the latter depended very considerably on them, especially at the time of elections. Such a situation continued until the 'change of policy' which Mitsubishi underwent in the footsteps of Mitsui and which was officially acknowledged in the 'Principles of Mitsubishi Spirit' (*Mitsubishiseishin kōryō*) in March 1934.

As we have seen above, the prewar Japanese conservative parties developed from small local *seisha* groups made initially of *shi* class citizens. Following the establishment of the Imperial Diet in 1890, parliamentary party organisations began to play a predominant role, and the bulk of their members were recruited from local politicians and entrepreneurs. In the first few years of the existence of parliamentary parties public officials also contributed a significant percentage of their members, but before long lawyers became numerically more important. In the meantime, the percentage of local politicians gradually but steadily decreased from the initial 72 per cent to less than 50 per cent in the middle of the 1920s. Even in the late 1930s, however, local politicians were the largest single category in both major parties, followed by businessmen, lawyers, and jonrnalists.

Conscious efforts to recruit local politicians into the party organisation as the core of its grass-roots membership began to be made by the Seiyūkai before 1907 and to receive very serious attention in the Kenseikai after 1920. The latter showed genuine interest in building the party organisation as a mass organisation and in 1936 even introduced the idea of collecting membership fees from all members.

Despite these developments, however, there was an evident tendency in the Seiyūkai from the outset to treat high-ranking public servants as a special group. This tendency was reflected very clearly in the disproportionately high percentage of them found in the party's leadership group. Seeds of 'bureaucratisation' of the conservative parties were sown, in fact, when the Seiyūkai was formed under Itō Hirobumi's leadership in 1900.

In terms of organisation, virtually all basic structural characteristics of the postwar conservative parties had emerged before World War II. Before 1900 the 'Three Leaders' offices—a secretary-general, the chairmen of an executive council and a PARC—had all become permanent attributes of the basic organisation of a conservative party. By 1911 the PARC of the Seiyūkai had come to consist of specialised divisions and in 1928 was officially empowered to make decisions on behalf of the party as a whole.

The principle of having a party president elected by the Party Conference at large (known as the *kōsen*) was introduced in the Seiyūkai in the late 1920s and the peculiar system of collegiate leadership called a 'Presidential Proxy Committee' was experimented with in the late 1930s. Almost as soon as it was formed in 1916, the Kenseikai introduced the semi-official highest decision-making organ, the *kambukai*, which was identical with the *yakuinkai* of the LDP. An election committee and a party affairs committee had been set up as the Seiyūkai's official organs in 1915.

The subordination of local branches to the party headquarters was a feature of the Seiyūkai, especially in relation to the endorsement of candidates in elections. In contrast, the Kenseikai deliberately encouraged the exercise of much more initiative and freedom of action by its branches, especially after 1920.

Intra-party factions emerged in the Constitutional Liberal Party primarily on a geographical basis and, as such, subsequently provided a principle to be applied in the filling of key party organs. Its transformation into the more contemporary form of factionalism—based primarily on factors other than geographical—became evident in the Seiyūkai around 1922, and the split of the party in 1939 occurred basically because of the effects of this new kind of factionalism.

Relationships between one or the other of the major conservative parties and a *zaibatsu* concern were well known from the earliest days of Japanese party politics. They assumed increasing importance after the Russo-Japanese War and reached a peak following World War I during the era of 'Taishō Democracy'. This state of affairs lasted until the early 1930s, when Mitsui and then Mitsubishi underwent a 'change of policy' and put an end to their active intervention in party politics.

These were the most important heritages from prewar party politics which on the eve of World War II were there to be picked up or abandoned. In the next chapter we shall see how they survived the big changes in the nation's international and domestic conditions in the following fifteen years and were transmitted to the LDP in 1955.

2 Transmission of the Prewar Heritage to Postwar Parties

Wartime Interregnum

The 'New Party' and 'New System' movement of the late 1930s, which eventually led to the creation of the *Taiseiyokusankai* (Imperial Rule Assistance Association) in October 1940, provoked contrasting responses from the *Seiyūkai* and the *Minseitō*. When in early 1938 the National Mobilisation Bill (*kokkasōdōin hōan*) was introduced into the Imperial Diet by the first Konoe Cabinet, the PARC of the Minseitō decided to oppose it, while a majority in the Seiyūkai wanted not only an affirmative vote on the bill but prompt dissolution of the party itself to facilitate the creation of a new party headed by Konoe. There were individuals in the former, such as Nagai Ryū- tarō, who publicly advocated the New Party and New System plans, but they were a minority among the Diet members affiliated with that party, whereas those who opposed these plans in the Seiyūkai, such as Hatoyama Ichirō, were just as hopelessly outnumbered in that party by those who subscribed to the pro-military blueprint of a one-party system.[1] For this reason, the 'Kazami Plan' drafted towards the end of May 1940 with a view to establish- ing a new political system, called for the creation of a new party without the participation of the majority in the Minseitō and the minority in the Seiyūkai.

Following Konoe's announcement on 24 June 1940 to the effect that he was prepared to lead the movement for a new system, the three Seiyūkai groups swiftly proceeded to disband themselves. In the Minseitō, however, President Machida Chūji rejected the demand for the party's prompt disso- lution submitted to him by Nagai and his followers and forced them to secede on 25 July. It was not until 15 August that it was finally compelled to bow to the mounting pressures outside the party for its dissolution and association with the Taiseiyokusankai. Thus even before it was officially formed this 'united national' organisation faced opposition in the form of resistance from the Minseitō leaders.

[1] *GSS: Kenseishi gaikan*, pp. 416-17. The 'New Party' and 'New System' movement was not a unidirectional and homogeneous movement but an agglomeration of at least five interrelated yet separately conceived movements. Yabe Sadaji, *Konoe Fumimaro*, Vol. I (Kōbundō, 1952), pp. 565-73.

The Taiseiyokusankai, which finally emerged in October 1940, was initially governed by President Konoe and Secretary-General Arima Yoriyasu and consisted of a headquarters and local branches. The headquarters was made up of advisers and standing advisers, an executive council, and a standing executive council, and under these offices five bureaux, a Central Co-operation Council, and a secretariat staffed with counsellors. Under this initial arrangement the Imperial Diet was brought under the supervision of the Diet Bureau and robbed of its independent deliberative functions.

In the course of the 76th Diet session (December 1940-March 1941), however, members bitterly criticised the organisation on account of its all-inclusive, monopolistic character. The reorganisation undertaken as a result of such pressure in April 1941 reduced the number both of its organs and its functions and left it to continue with only three bureaux and a central training school. As a result, the Diet Bureau was abolished.[2] This reorganisation not only put an end to the political activities of the Taiseiyokusankai but led to the withdrawal of most members of the Diet from it.

In May 1942, however, a new body, the *Yokusan seijikai* (Imperial Rule Assistance Political Association), was established as an all-inclusive national party and on this occasion only eight members of the Diet remained outside it as independents. The revived one-party system continued until March 1945, when two separate minor groups, the *Gokoku dōshikai* and the *Yokusōgiin dōshikai*, were formed by those who had withdrawn from that organisation. At the same time, the Yokusan seijikai was renamed the *Dainihon seijikai* (Great Japan Political Association). The Gokoku dōshikai was disbanded on 15 August and its members rejoined the Dainihon seijikai, while the latter and the Yokusōgiin dōshikai remained alive until early September 1945.

Like the Taiseiyokusankai, the Yokusan seijikai and the Dainihon seijikai were national political organisations with a membership recruited from a wide range of occupational groups other than members of the Diet, notably the military services, the bureaucracy, business circles, and mass communications. MHRs formed only one of the more important categories and did not enjoy a position of superiority to any significant degree. Structurally, however, these

[2]The three bureaux kept operative were those of General Affairs, Organisation, and East Asian Affairs. The reorganisation followed the mass resignation of all who had initially been officials of the organisation, except President Konoe. Their resignations resulted from the conflict between the radical right in control of its key positions and supported by the *tōseiha* faction in the army and an alliance of the *kōdōha* faction in the army, the bureaucracy, and big business. The opposition to the continued rule by the former came from the latter three groups—the *kōdōha* objected to the foreign dogma of Nazism espoused by the former, the bureaucracy feared that the powerful national organisation might attempt eventually to replace it as the executive arm of the state, and the big business circles were apprehensive about the possibility that it might unduly interfere with their free profit-making activities. Under the combined pressure brought to bear on them by these three groups, Arima and other original leaders of the organisation were forced to resign. See Aritake Shūji, *Maeda Yonezō den* (Maeda Yonezō denki kankōkai, 1961), pp. 441-3.

organisations obviously inherited prewar party models and, in fact, the degree to which they were accepted by them became more, rather than less, evident as time passed.

In the original organisational framework of the Taiseiyokusankai as it was founded in October 1940 there were two kinds of party organ (apart from the post of president) directly inherited from the prewar parties—namely the executive council and the advisers. The Diet Bureau itself had no independent organs comparable with those of a party. It consisted of seven divisions, three dealing with affairs relating to the House of Peers and four with those relating to the House of Representatives. The secretary-general of the Taiseiyokusankai was not the conventional *kanjichō* but a *jimusōchō*, while the policy research organs were absent until the reorganisation of April 1941. The Yokusan seijikai inherited intact the structure of the reorganised Taiseiyokusankai. It underwent, however, a drastic reorganisation in May 1943, as a result of which an MHRs' meeting was set up as a permanent organ and both the executive council and the PARC were greatly strengthened. Moreover, the bureaux were replaced by the familiar divisions when four of them were established to deal respectively with matters relating to the House of Representatives, planning, the nation's general conditions, and information and propaganda. Furthermore, as the office of the advisers was preserved, the only major difference which still remained between either of the prewar parties and the Yokusan seijikai in terms of organisation structure was the appellation given to the post of secretary-general. When it was reorganised into the Dainihon seijikai in March 1945, even that difference disappeared and the familiar appellation of *kanjichō* was revived.

The reappearance in these wartime organisations of the more or less established models of party leadership structure proceeded parallel to the process whereby members of the Diet reasserted, and to a certain extent regained, their role as one of the central forces in the policy-making process of the state. This process was started as soon as the organic tie between the Taiseiyokusankai and the Diet was severed by the reorganisation of April 1941. As a result of that reorganisation the Diet Bureau was abolished and the Taiseiyokusankai became a purely administrative agency of the state under the direct and exclusive control of the Minister of Home Affairs. After the Yokusan seijikai was formed as its political arm in May 1942 MHRs became bolder than before in their bid to recover initiative and independence. Although the influence of the bureaucrats in the Yokusan seijikai was no doubt very substantial, members of the Diet also played a leading part in its activities.

Moreover, once the balance of power in the organisation had been tipped in the party politicians' favour, its existence actually provided them with a convenient shelter behind which to preserve the prewar ideological and organisational heritage and traditions of party politics and to pass them on to the postwar parties when they were formed following the end of the war.

Despite the apparent wartime interruption in the development of parties and party politics, the organisation and probably also behaviour of the prewar parties was thus kept alive and ready to be made use of in the postwar years.

Resurrection under the Occupation

If it is surprising that the prewar traditions of party politics were preserved without major modifications during World War II, it is even more remarkable that they should have survived the prolonged period of the Allied Occupation following the end of the war. The key to an understanding and explanation of this remarkable fact lies in the timing of the formation of the first postwar parties and the peculiar legal status of a party in the Japanese system of government.

As soon as the war came to an end in August 1945, several groups of prewar party politicians began to prepare for the formation of new parties, and by the middle of November two major conservative parties—the *Jiyūtō* (Liberal Party) and the *Shimpotō* (Progressive Party)—had come into being side by side with some thirty other groups all calling themselves 'parties'.[3]

A few days before the war officially came to an end Hatoyama Ichirō and his associates began to make serious preparations for the formation of a postwar party. Hatoyama discussed the problem with Ashida Hitoshi on 11 August when the latter visited him at Karuizawa. On 15 August, still unaware of the decision made by the Supreme Council on the Conduct of the War to accept the Potsdam Proclamation, his close associates gathered at the office of Kōjunsha in Tokyo to exchange their views on forming a new party and decided to bring Hatoyama to Tokyo from his Karuizawa hideout. Following Hatoyama's return to Tokyo on 22 August, a 15-member founding committee was set up, a platform was drafted, and on 9 November the inaugural meeting was held.

The Liberal Party which thus came into being was first and foremost Hatoyama's party in the sense that it could not have been formed without his personal leadership and presence. It was also essentially a successor to the Kuhara faction of the Seiyūkai, as suggested by the factional breakdown of the MHRs initially affiliated with it. Of the forty-six MHRs who comprised the original Liberal Party in November 1945, eighteen had been elected for the first time in the wartime election of 1942, while twenty-eight had been elected in an earlier election. Of this latter number only seven had been members of the Minseitō, two of the Tōhōkai, and nineteen of the Seiyūkai. All but two of this last number had belonged to the Kuhara faction after the

---

[3]By the middle of November 1945 at least 33 'parties' had been formed, including the two mentioned above and the Socialist and the Communist parties. By the time the first postwar House of Representatives election was held in April the following year the number had gone up to 363, although only 13 of them operated at the national level and the rest were confined in organisation and activities to a single prefecture or an even smaller unit of administration. *Asahi*, 17 November 1945 and 9 April 1946.

split of 1939, while one of the remaining two had been associated with the Nakajima and the other with the Kanemitsu factions.

In organisation, the Liberal Party was almost identical with both major prewar parties. It had a president, advisers, an executive council, a secretary-general, and a PARC. Its original leadership composition had a rather novel aspect in that two of the four advisers and six of the sixteen members of the executive council were non-parliamentarian intellectuals, public servants, and a businessman. As the overall organisational structure subsequently became increasingly more complex, however, this factor disappeared rather quickly. Moreover, the old method of distributing the membership of the executive council among seven or eight geographical regions according to the number of MHRs returned from each (the method which had been formalised in the Seiyūkai's Consultative Council in 1903) was revived in May 1946.

Before the spring of 1946, when Hatoyama and other party founders were removed from their party posts by the Purge, the prewar organisational model of a conservative party had been fully and effectively re-established. Had the Purge come six months earlier, it might have caused a genuine break in the evolution of Japanese parties and party politics. In reality, however, it came too late to prevent the resurrection of the prewar traditions which had been preserved, rather than destroyed, by the wartime pseudo-party organisations.

Precisely the same conditions existed for the Progressive Party. While the preparations for the formation of the Liberal Party proceeded under Hatoyama's personal and unitary leadership, the initial efforts to form the Progressive Party came from three separate groups. Those who had formed an internal opposition in the Dainihon seijikai—including Matsumura Kenzō, Ōta Masataka, and Ogaswara Sankurō—first set out to build a party to compete with Hatoyama's. This group established a Postwar Political and Economic Research Association as the basis of its party building efforts. Those who had been in control of the principal posts in the Dainihon seijikai, including Ōasa Tadao, Uchida Nobuya, and Miyoshi Hideyuki, constituted the second group interested in forming a new party separate from the Liberal Party. The third group consisted of relatively young men, such as Inukai Takeru, Baba Motoharu, and Noda Takeo, who set up a Research Association for the Construction of a New Japan. By early November these three groups had reached agreement among themselves to unite and establish a single party.

On 24 November 1945, when its parliamentary party was officially formed, 273 MHRs were affiliated with the Progressive Party. Of them 163 had been elected in the twentieth election of April 1937 or earlier and of these 163 89 had been associated with the Minseitō, 39 with the Nakajima faction of the Seiyūkai, and 7 with its Kuhara faction. In contrast to the Liberal Party, which was an alliance of the Kuhara faction of the Seiyūkai and those elected during the war, the Progressive Party was an alliance of the Minseitō, the

Nakajima faction of the Seiyūkai, and those elected in the wartime election.

The original organisational structure of the Progressive Party was similar to those of the prewar parties and of the postwar Liberal Party. Following in the footsteps of the latter, in December 1946 it officially adopted the old formula of forming the executive council on the basis of regional representation and the prewar principle of having its president elected at the party conference.

Another important factor which contributed to the wholesale transmission of the prewar heritage to the postwar parties was the vague and indefinable legal status of the parties in the system of government. Most of the drastic changes in the nation's social and political institutions accomplished under the Occupation took the form of revisions of specific existing laws or the enactment of new ones. Thus the principal Occupation-sponsored reforms were tied to a series of legislation, such as the new constitution (1946); the Diet Law, the Court of Justice Law, the National Public Servants Law, the Local Self-Government Law, the Police Law, the Education Basic Law, the Labour Standard Law, and the Anti-Monopoly Law (1947); the National Administrative Organisation Law, the Criminal Procedure Law, and the Public Enterprise Labour Relations Law (1948); the Labour Union Law (1949); the Public Office Election Law, and the Criminal Case Compensation Law (1950).

In contrast with these reforms successfully undertaken, it was impossible to 'reform' the parties either structurally or behaviourally because a firm, tangible legal basis was lacking for them. Ever since the days of the humble *seisha* groups, the parties had evolved pre-eminently as *de facto* institutions and, consequently, neither their organisation structures, their status in the system of government, nor their basic functions had ever been explicitly defined in legal terms. This made it possible for the groups of prewar politicians to model the original postwar parties on forms with which they were familiar without as much American interference as in the other areas. It also encouraged those who took over from them to maintain the same forms intact.

This is not to suggest, however, that interest in legislating about the parties was totally lacking in the years immediately following the end of the war. In fact, as soon as the preparations for the revision of the Election Law were started towards the end of 1946, the drafting of a political party law began to be seriously contemplated, particularly by a group of Home Ministry officials who were planning at the time to experiment with an electoral system based on proportional representation. Although their initial attempt was soon given up in the face of opposition from most of the parties, the chaos created around the time of the 1946 House of Representatives election by the emergence of hundreds of purely nominal 'parties' led the Diet to deal with the problem during the first Diet session under the new constitution.

D

The Special Committee on the Political Party Bill and the Election Law, established in the House of Representatives in August 1947, examined such specific questions as the definition, organisation, and financing of a party and its role in the electoral process. A drafting sub-committee which this committee set up actually prepared a draft of a Political Party Bill and this was supported by the four largest parties—the Liberals, the Democrats (Progressives), the Socialists, and the National Co-operative Party (*Kokumin kyōdōtō*).[4]

The opposition of the smaller parties, however, notably the Peasant Party (*Nōmintō*) and the Japan Communist Party, rendered the efforts of the sub-committee abortive. The bill was shelved and, in its place, a National Election Administration Committee Bill was passed. In the second Diet a sub-committee established to draft a bill relating to the parties as well as regulation of corrupt electoral practices ended up by drafting a Political Fund Regulation Bill.

The failure of these efforts was due partly to the fact that the organisational structures and practices which had been inherited from the prewar parties were not particularly undemocratic or authoritarian. Also the belief was widely shared that parties should be left to themselves to develop freely without the interference of legal restrictions. For these reasons, it was felt that the restrictions contemplated by the draft bill were unnecessary, if not positively harmful.

Under the circumstances described above the first postwar conservative parties started their lives as the direct descendants of the prewar parties. The Purge, however, caused a change of far-reaching importance in their membership characteristics and in the patterns of inter-personal and intergroup relationships both within and between them. Its more immediate and short-range effect was to make it possible for the postwar politicians, represented by Yoshida Shigeru and his close coterie, temporarily to enjoy almost uncontested hegemony in conservative politics of the Occupation period, and to build the basis for more sustained influence in the politics of the post-Occupation period.

The magnitude of the blow dealt to the two major conservative parties by the Purge was clearly indicated by the fact that of the 270 MHRs affiliated with the Progressive Party on 19 December 1945, 250 were purged and of the 45 who belonged to the Liberal Party 20 were likewise affected.[5] As these

---

[4]For the contents of the draft bill, see Tsuji Kiyoaki (ed.), *Shiryō: Sengo nijūnenshi: 1 Seiji* (Nihonhyōronsha, 1966), pp. 327-31.

[5]Yoshimura Tadashi, 'Sengo ni okeru wagakuni no hoshutō', *Shakaikagaku Tōkyū*, I, 1 (January 1956), p. 3. For the official pronouncements of SCAP relating to the purge program, see Government Section, Supreme Commander for the Allied Powers, *Political Re-orientation of Japan, September 1945 to September 1948*, 2 vols. (Washington, D.C.: Government Printing Office, 1949). For discussions of the program and its effects, see Hans H. Baerwald, *The Purge of Japanese Leaders under the Occupation*, University of California Publications in Political Science, Vol. VIII (Berkeley and Los Angeles: University of California Press, 1959); Hans H. Baerwald, Tsurumi

comparative figures suggest, the effect of the Purge on the Progressive Party was far more crippling than on the Liberal Party. Even with the Liberal Party, however, the effect was serious enough to cause an almost complete change in the composition of the party's leadership group.

In the Progressive Party, President Machida Chūji and other officials were forced to resign *en masse* in February 1946 and were replaced by the party's remaining Diet members, supplemented by some who had never been or were not currently members of the Diet. The change in the prewar-postwar ratio of the Progressive Party leadership became more evident after the twenty-second House of Representatives election of April 1946. By February 1947 only three of the ten elected members of the executive council had been Diet members before the war, while both the chairman and all four vice-chairmen of the PARC were postwar MHRs. By early 1947 the party had thus come under the sway of postwar politicians.

The developments in the Liberal Party were of essentially the same nature. What the Purge would mean to it was dramatically brought home in early May 1946, when President Hatoyama was removed from the highest party post at the moment the party had won the first postwar House of Representatives election. To fill the post thus suddenly vacated by Hatoyama, attempts were made first to induce Kojima Kazuo and then Matsudaira Tsuneo to succeed him as the party's president. Having failed in these initial attempts, however, its leaders turned to Yoshida Shigeru and finally persuaded him to accept the offer of the post on the condition that Hatoyama would be responsible for financing party activity and, at the same time, would refrain from interfering with Yoshida's choice of Cabinet ministers. It was also understood that Hatoyama would take over as soon as he was free to do so and that Yoshida would be free to resign any time he wanted to do so. In any event, Yoshida was thus brought to head the Liberal Party and eventually to build his own independent and powerful following among the postwar conservative politicians to compete with Hatoyama's group when they returned to active political life several years later.

This change in the prewar-postwar ratio of the Liberal Party leaders was not as complete as was the case with the Progressive Party, but it was nevertheless significant. In the party's executive council, for example, the ratio of 11 to 4 in favour of prewar Diet members in May 1946 had shifted to 7 to 9 by June 1947. By March 1948, when the party was joined by a group of defectors from the Democratic Party (the Progressive Party was renamed the Democratic Party on 31 March 1947) and formed the Democrat-Liberal Party (*Minshujiyūtō*), the prewar and wartime politicians had decreased so much in number that they amounted to less than a quarter of the newly

---

Shunsuke, and Matsuura Sōzō, 'Tsuihō wa nihon no seiji wo dou kaeta ka', *Shisō no Kagaku*, 53 (August 1966), pp. 2-12; Matsuura Sōzō, 'Sempantsuihō kara reddo pāji made', ibid., pp. 13-22.

elected and appointed members of its executive council. Except in the more or less nominal posts of advisers and counsellors, prewar or wartime politicians never became again a numerically significant group in the composition of the party's official organs.

The wholesale replacement of prewar by postwar Diet members in the Liberal and the Democratic (Progressive) parties posed a serious problem of personnel administration to their leaders. The problem arose basically from the shortage of experienced professional politicians and administrators to guide party activities in the Diet and in the nation at large.

The seriousness of this problem was magnified by the drastic decline in the April 1946 elections of those MHRs who had bureaucratic backgrounds (see Appendix I). What made the situation even worse was the fact that those few former public servants who managed to get elected on this occasion had been mostly local, as opposed to national, government officials and tended to differ little from local politicians both in general outlook and in terms of administrative and legislative skills. Whether by design or by chance, however, this gap was filled at the election of January 1949 by the influx of large numbers of high-ranking public servants who have subsequently formed the nucleus of the postwar elements in both parties. Compared with the pre-war percentages of public servants among Seiyūkai and Minseitō MHRs (invariably less than 10 per cent), and also with the average of the two conservative parties at the April 1947 elections (7·8 per cent), it is remarkable that 17·4 per cent of the Liberals and 12·8 per cent of the Democrats successfully returned in the 1949 election were former high-ranking public servants. Moreover, these percentages continued to increase in the subsequent elections until they stabilised at about 25 per cent after 1960.

In the Liberal Party they apparently formed a temporary factional group among themselves under President Yoshida to counterbalance the power of the older prewar politicians. Although the strongly individualistic tendencies and the effects of inter-ministerial rivalries among them prevented a solidly united group from growing, they became rapidly and firmly entrenched in the party's hierarchy and came to constitute the core of the dominant faction supporting Yoshida against his critics, especially those led by Hatoyama.

On the other hand, the steady decline before the war in the percentage of local politicians in the Seiyūkai and, to a somewhat more limited extent, in the Minseitō, continued into the postwar period. Except for the first postwar election in April 1946 their contribution to the membership of the two parties' parliamentary contingents decreased until it became stabilised at about 25 per cent after 1955.

The fact that only one of the opposing Seiyūkai factions—the Kuhara faction—joined the Liberal Party and that most of the prewar politicians were purged meant that it was relatively free from intra-party factionalism. Such intra-party groups as the *Nihachikai* and the *Tōkakai* appearing during this period in the Liberal Party were very loosely organised, almost haphazard, groupings of those who happened to be elected in the same elections, and there is no evidence to show that they acted in ways similar to the factions of the later period.

The apparent ideological homogeneity and emotional unity thus generated among its members made it possible for the Liberal Party to identify itself almost completely with the Occupation administration and all that it represented, particularly the series of reforms, including the writing of the new constitution. To that extent, the Liberal Party under Yoshida's uncontested 'one-man' rule in the first five years of its existence represented a break away from the prewar political system and its ideological and emotional foundations.

In sharp contrast, the Progressive Party was internally divided from the outset and underwent a series of violent conflicts ultimately leading to a major split in March 1949. As early as the spring of 1947 rival factions, the *Taiyōkai* and the *Shinshinkai*, came into being. The former was positively interested in uniting with the Liberal Party, while the latter was opposed to such a scheme and insisted on building a middle-of-the-road party to promote the idea of 'modified capitalism' against the traditional conservatism embodied by the Liberals.

Two interrelated aspects of the factional strife in the Progressive Party during this period deserve special attention. One is that it was based at least partially on genuine differences of ideological assumptions and policy preferences between the two groups. To generalise, the 'collaborationist' group, represented by the Taiyōkai, was ideologically and emotionally committed to the constitutional and political order created under the Occupation, which represented a maximal departure from the prewar traditions. To that extent, this group identified itself with Yoshida's Liberal Party. On the other hand, the 'oppositionist' group, represented by the Shinshinkai, was dissatisfied with the constitutional *status quo* for one reason or another. Paradoxically, this latter group embodied the opposite tendencies of traditionalism on the one hand and, on the other, fairly radical progressivism akin to that held at the time by the right-wing Socialist groups. This is seen in the group's inaugural proclamation, where such terms as 'patriotism' and 'progressive capitalism' were juxtaposed. In fact, the first point of the 'collaborationist' platform pledged loyalty to the new constitution of Japan and the democratic system built on its basis, while the inaugural proclamation issued by the 'oppositionists' advocated solidarity and co-operation between different social classes and called, at the same time, for 'progressive capitalism' and 'patriotism'.

The other aspect of factionalism in the Progressive Party was that one of the rival groups persistently sought union with the Liberal Party. The possibility of unifying the two parties was first suggested officially barely a month after the first postwar election of April 1946, when Saitō Takao and Inukai Takeru, both members of the party's executive council, expressed views in favour of such a plan. In about a week a positive response from the Liberal Party officially conveyed by its secretary-general, Kōno Ichirō, led to the formation of a Joint Committee on Policy Agreement to deal with a series of concrete issues, such as the revision of the Meiji Constitution, the food shortage, inflation, and so forth. In the meantime, about sixty members from both parties proceeded to form a body specifically designed to promote their merger. By February of the next year President Shidehara was in a position to propose officially to Yoshida immediate unification. Although the latter's negative response on that occasion retarded the pace and changed the direction of the movement in the subsequent months, the unification efforts were continued throughout 1947 and 1948, until the purpose was partially achieved in 1950 when nearly thirty 'collaborationist' Democrats joined the Liberal Party.

As far as the 'collaborationist' Democrats are concerned, the desirability of uniting with the Liberals to oppose the Socialists and the Communists was self-evident from the beginning. The only problem to be solved was to decide which party and which group in either party should control the key positions in the proposed unified party. The difficulty in reaching agreement on this point, coupled with ideological reservations of the 'oppositionist' groups in the Democratic Party, prevented a genuine unification from taking place before the situation became complicated by the return to political life of those politicians who had been caught up in the Purge.

During wartime it had been plainly impossible to conduct normal party and electoral activities and, consequently, it was unnecessary for the pseudo-party organisations to make large financial outlays. Under the circumstances it was no doubt possible to finance the greater part of their activities by the contributions from their own members. The income from this normal source may have been supplemented to some extent by donations from the military, as one commentator has suggested.[6] After the war came to an end in August 1945, however, the situation changed drastically. On the one hand, the reappearance of a competitive multi-party system made it at least as costly as before the war to run a party and, especially, to win an election. In the January 1949 elections, for example, each candidate endorsed by the Democrat-Liberal Party is believed to have spent at least ¥800,000 and an average of ¥2.5 million. Most of those who ran for the first time are said to have spent upwards of ¥5 million and, in some cases, as much as ¥10 million. On the other hand, conditions brought about by the series of Occupation-sponsored reforms, especially the dissolution of the zaibatsu, made it impossible for the parties to depend on conventional connections to raise funds.

[6]Togawa Isamu, *Seijishikin: Seikai no chikasuidō wo saguru* (Uchida rōkakuho, 1961), pp. 102-7.

Pressed by the great and increasing needs for funds and unable to continue to rely on connections with such prewar *zaibatsu* concerns as the Mitsui and the Mitsubishi, the postwar conservative parties began to search for new sources of revenue. As a result of their efforts they no doubt succeeded in establishing links with a number of individual entrepreneurs and enterprises. However, the pattern of relationships between the conservative parties and extra-party groups which thus emerged during this pre-independence period was basically transitional and unstable. Often they were based on purely personal ties and involved obscure individuals, rather than established firms or business associations.

For example, an important part of the funds which went into the building of the Liberal Party by Hatoyama and his associates in 1945 is said to have been supplied by a well-known nationalist ideologue, Kodama Yoshio. After Hatoyama was purged and began to suffer from serious financial hardships, it was Hagiwara Kichitarō of the Hokkaidō Coal Mining and Steamship Company who helped him out and made it possible for his large faction to begin to operate as soon as the Purge was lifted. The individual who acted as the intermediary between Hatoyama and Kodama, Tsuji Karoku, was accused of having received ¥2·5 million from a broker dealing in surplus uniforms from the wartime Japanese army, as well as ¥6·5 million from Kodama, and of having passed it on to the Liberal Party. The series of criminal cases involving illegal contributions to the parties by individuals and groups of company directors which occurred during this period testify to the peculiarly personal and secretive character of the relationships which obtained between particular party politicians and their financial patrons.

In theory, under the system of government established by the new constitution the parties were to play a leading part in the public decision-making of the state. In reality, however, their status was inferior and subordinate to the authority of the Supreme Commander for the Allied Powers, General MacArthur, and his General Headquarters. Moreover, in the Japanese sphere of politics and public administration (which was as a whole subordinate to SCAP), it was not the parties but the bureaucracy which played a predominant role as the official interpreter and executor of SCAP's orders. Such restrictions tended to discourage various interest groups (which numbered over 15,000 in 1950) from seeking special relationships with a particular party, even a party in power. Under the circumstances it was much more sensible for a person or group desiring to have a specific action taken by a government agency or official to approach and bring pressure to bear either directly on that agency or official, or petition SCAP.

The same circumstances which prevented the parties from playing a leading role in the nation's public decision-making processes also kept to a minimum the overt pressure group activities of the large employer organisations which had come into being by the middle of 1948. Apart from the *Nihon shōkō*

kaigisho (the Japanese Chamber of Commerce and Industry, hereafter referred to as the *Nisshō*), which had originally been established in 1878 as the
Shōhō kaigisho, and the *Nihon kōgyō kurabu* (the Japanese Industrialists'
Club), which had existed since 1917, three important national organisations
of employers were established during the Occupation period. The *Keizaidantai rengōkai* (the Federation of Economic Organisations, hereafter referred
to as the *Keidanren*) was officially formed in August 1946 as successor to
the Nihon keizai renmeikai, the *Keizaidōyūkai* (the Committee for Economic
Development, hereafter referred to as the *Dōyūkai*) in April of the same year,
and the *Nihon keieishadantai renmei* (the Japan Federation of Employers'
Associations, hereafter referred to as the *Nikkeiren*) in April 1948. However,
whatever monetary contributions were made during this period by these
business groups to a party came almost invariably from individual firms or,
more frequently, a particular director or directors of a firm. It was not until
party politics was freed from the legal and psychological restrictions of the
Occupation period that the large business organisations began to play a
decisive role as the *de facto* representatives of the nation's business interests
and principal providers of political funds for the conservative parties.

Independence and After

Following the conclusion of the San Francisco Peace Treaty in 1951, conditions significantly different from those which had existed during the Occupation period emerged in the general temper of conservative party politics. One
of the most important of such new conditions in terms of its effects on subsequent developments arose from the mass reinstatement of the prewar and
wartime leaders who had been temporarily barred from public office by the
Purge program.

Between October 1950 and April 1952 the 210,282 prewar and wartime
leaders who had been involved in the Purge were freed from restrictions.
Many of them naturally attempted to re-enter the arena of active party
politics by running in the House of Representatives election of October 1952.
As a result, this particular election was characterised above all by bitter competition between the depurged prewar politicians and bureaucrats and the
incumbent postwar politicians.

Significantly, the election itself resulted from an unexpected dissolution of
the House by Prime Minister Yoshida, who obviously hoped to deny adequate
time for electoral preparations to the depurged politicians not only in the
opposition parties but also in his own party, which demanded his replacement
by Hatoyama as head of the party and the government. Only two days before
the election the two most outspoken depurged opponents of Yoshida—Kōno
Ichirō and Ishibashi Tanzan—were expelled from the Liberal Party on
account of anti-party activities. Thereafter, the anti-Yoshida group led by
Hatoyama, Kōno, and Ishibashi campaigned independently.

The result of the election, however, confirmed the suspected strength of the depurged candidates and revealed Yoshida's waning popularity. The Liberal Party lost forty-five seats to the opposition parties. On the other hand, the victory of the depurged candidates was spectacular. Of the 329 of them who ran in this election 139 were successfully returned. Seventy-nine of these belonged to the Liberal Party and thirty-two to the Progressive Party (*Kaishintō*),[7] accounting respectively for 33 and 37 per cent of the new members of their parliamentary parties.[8]

Before the election of 1952 there had been three distinctive factional groups in the Liberal Party—the Yoshida faction with about 140 Diet members, the Hatoyama faction with 120 members, and a loosely-knit group of about 25 non-aligned members. The Yoshida faction had been divided roughly into seven sub-units within itself, led respectively by Yoshida himself, Hirokawa Kōzen, Masuda Kaneshichi, Inukai Takeru, Satō Eisaku, Ikeda Hayato, and Hori Shigeru. The Hatoyama faction had been similarly subdivided into nine units—the Ōno, Ishibashi, Uehara, Kuhara, Matsuno, Hayashi, Masutani, Hoshijima, and *Dōshi kurabu* groups. The 1952 election drastically reduced the numerical strength of both the Yoshida and the Hatoyama factions respectively to 105 and 69, while increasing that of the non-aligned group to 66. It was, however, not until the House of Representatives election of April 1953 that a distinctive pattern of intra-party factionalism began to emerge.

As soon as Ogata Taketora entered the scene by winning a seat in the House of Representatives in the October 1952 election, Hirokawa's relationship with Yoshida and his other confidants, such as Satō, Ikeda, and Hori, began to show considerable strains. After he was defeated in February 1953 by Satō in their competitive bid for the post of party secretary-general, he was led to dissociate himself definitely from the Yoshida faction and proceeded to create a separate faction of his own. When Hatoyama and his followers separated from the party in March of the same year and set up the separatist Liberal Party, Hirokawa joined them. Prior to this formal separation from the Liberal Party he had in fact made his break with Yoshida complete and irrevocable by deliberately choosing to absent himself and members of his faction from the crucial vote in the House of Representatives on the motion of censure against the latter introduced by the Socialists, thus helping its passage.

In the Hatoyama faction, on the other hand, in the last weeks of 1952 Ōno began gradually to dissociate himself from the more militant anti-Yoshida elements among its members. By the spring of 1953 he had drifted away from

---

[7]The Democratic Party merged with the National Co-operative Party to form a National Democratic Party (*Kokumin minshutō*) in April 1950, which was renamed the Japan Progressive Party (*Nihon kaishintō*) in February 1952.

[8]Of the remaining 28, 12 belonged to the Right Socialist Party, 3 to the Left Socialist Party, one each to the Co-operative Party and the newly formed *Saiken renmei*, and 11 were independents. *Asahi*, 3 October 1952; *Mainichi nenkan: 1954*, p. 149.

the faction to the extent of refusing to join the separatist Liberal Party when it was formed.

After a majority in the Hatoyama and the Hirokawa factions was reunited with the Liberal Party towards the end of November 1953 the factional divisions in that party naturally underwent a substantial change. Compared with the conditions which had prevailed about a year before, the Hirokawa group had shifted from the Yoshida to the Hatoyama camp, while the latter had been reduced to a much simpler composition by losing four of its sub-units. The Hayashi, the Masutani, and the Matsuno groups had shifted to the Yoshida faction by this time, while the Ōno group had become independent. At the end of 1953 there were therefore roughly ten factional aggregations in the Liberal Party—three pro-Yoshida but separate groups led respectively by Satō, Ikeda, and Masuda; the 'bureaucrats' represented by Kawarada Kakichi, Asaka Tadao, and others; the newly formed Ogata and Kishi factions; a group of former *Seiyūkai* members led by Maeda Yonezō; the former Dōshi kurabu; the Ōno faction; and the Hatoyama faction.

When in November 1954 the Japan Democratic Party came into being through the merger of the Progressive Party, the remaining group of the separatist Liberal Party (now calling itself the Japan Liberal Party), and defectors from the Liberal Party, both the Hatoyama and the Kishi factions joined it. As a result, the pattern of factional divisions in the Liberal Party was somewhat simplified.

Factionalism in the Progressive Party during this period was not as complex as that in the Liberal Party. Basically, there were only four distinct factional groups in this party in 1953 and 1954—the Radicals, the Conservatives, the Neutrals, and the Independents. The Radicals consisted of two fairly large factions represented respectively by Miki Takeo and Kitamura Tokutarō, while the Conservatives were a small minority of only half a dozen members led by Ōasa Tadao. The Neutrals contained two groups, one called the 'Collaborationists' for their advocacy of collaboration and eventual unification with the Liberals, and the other called the 'Bureaucrats'. Apart from these four distinct groups, there was a fifth built around Matsumura Kenzō which was closely associated with the Miki faction. In addition, three individuals—Tsurumi Yūsuke of the House of Councillors and Matsuura Shūtarō and Oyama Kuranosuke of the House of Representatives—formed a link between the Miki and the Kitamura factions in the Radicals' camp.

The factions in the two conservative parties described above responded differently to the movement for unification which led to the formation of the LDP in November 1955. Such differences in turn influenced the interfactional balance and relationships in both parties and moulded the dominant characteristics of factionalism subsequently found in the LDP.

In the spring of 1953 Miki Bukichi publicly stated that he was determined to work towards a conservative merger. This call, coming from one of the most influential conservative party politicians, began to be taken seriously early the next year both by the leaders and rank and file of the three rival conservative parties in existence at the time. At their meeting of 30 March 1954 members of the Hatoyama faction agreed to work towards the same goal, while in April the executive council of the Liberal Party officially approved the plan. Paradoxically, however, no sooner had the efforts towards unification been placed on a non-partisan basis than the same old question, on whose terms and under whose direction the unification should be achieved, began to bedevil all such efforts. In both the Liberal and the Progressive parties, those who were in control of key party positions began to try either to realise the unification plan on their own terms or else to forestall it.

In the Liberal Party Yoshida and his confidants became increasingly critical and suspicious of the more ardent proponents of the merger plan associated with the three factions led by Ogata, Kishi, and Ishibashi. In order to present themselves as advocates of the unification plan, for which pressures were steadily mounting among the rank and file, and at the same time obstructing it in the most acceptable manner possible under the circumstances, they began to insist on a particular formula for unification. According to this, both the Liberal and the Progressive parties would first be disbanded, an entirely new party formed, and its president chosen by ballot. In view of the relative numerical strength of the two parties at the time, it was obvious that such a procedure would inevitably lead to Yoshida's re-election as president.

Similarly, the Central Executive Committee of the Progressive Party resolved to reject the unification plan unless the Yoshida Cabinet would resign first. This position reflected the views held by men like Matsumura Kenzō, Miki Takeo, and Kawasaki Hideji who had always been and were to remain consistently anti-Yoshida and anti-Liberal. On the other hand, the group led by Ashida Hitoshi and those associated with the Dōyūkai wanted unification at almost any price.[9]

The unification efforts following the initial moves of April and May 1954 centred around the Council to Promote the Establishment of a New Party which came into being towards the end of May as a joint forum of volunteers from the two parties. This non-partisan group was from the beginning openly opposed to Yoshida's continued rule. In the view of this group the new party was to have 'new leadership, new policies and new organisation'.[10] By the time it was reorganised and renamed the Preparatory Committee for the Establishment of a New Party in September it became to all intents and purposes a citadel of depurged prewar and wartime politicians designed to organise opposition not only to Yoshida as a person but also to many of the

[9]The *Dōyūkai* was formed as an intra-party group on 2 February 1954 and its five-point program included the unification and consolidation of the conservative parties as well as the revision of the constitution of Japan. See *Asahi*, 3 February and 30 April 1954.
[10]Ibid., 31 May 1954.

changes which had been accomplished under his administration during the period of the Allied Occupation. In terms of its composition, for example, not only its president, Kanemitsu Tsuneo, and secretary-general, Kishi Nobusuke, but all except two of the fifteen members of its executive council elected in July 1954 were prewar men. On 20 October 1954 it set up a five-member directorate consisting exclusively of anti-Yoshida prewar men— Hatoyama, Kanemitsu, Kishi, Ishibashi, and Ashida. This made it impossible for the Yoshida faction to participate in it and, as a result, the Japan Democratic Party which issued from it comprised the Progressive Party, the Japan Liberal Party (separatist), and only a part of the main Liberal Party.

The creation of the Democratic Party made it possible for Hatoyama to take over when Yoshida finally resigned in December 1954. The minority position of the Hatoyama Cabinet, however, made it imperative to continue the efforts towards a total merger with the Liberal Party. On the other hand, a minority in the Democratic Party led by Matsumura and Miki Takeo did not give up their opposition to the proposed merger. As late as September 1955 the Radicals were insisting on making the merger conditional on agreement between the two parties to have Hatoyama, instead of Yoshida, nominated as head of the new party. This position was subsequently confirmed by five Cabinet ministers representing the anti-Yoshida elements in the party, namely Matsumura, Ōasa, Miki, Ishibashi, and Kōno. When the merger was finally accomplished in November, it was despite the persistent opposition of this group whose presence was destined to remain a disruptive factor in the LDP in the years to follow.

In the Liberal Party it was the Yoshida faction which continued to resist the attempt to unite the two parties. When it became evident that the process leading to unification could neither be reversed nor halted for long, its members began to insist strongly on the strict implementation of the *kōsen* principle (election of the president by the party conference) in choosing the new president. As late as a week before the inaugural meeting of the LDP they kept insisting on postponing the ultimate merger until that principle was explicitly accepted by the Democrats and Yoshida's re-election ensured.

If Matsumura and his faction represented an extreme position of prewar elements, characterised by a certain dissatisfaction with the *status quo* in reference both to domestic constitutional arrangements and to the emphasis in foreign policy, the Yoshida faction and its descendants represented the other extreme, characterised by firmer commitment to the 'democratic' system established under the Occupation and unreserved co-operation with the United States. These two positions could be held together in the LDP only because of a delicate balance maintained by the other factional groups which represented, to a greater or lesser degree, moderating and unifying influences.

The differences in the degree and nature of personal involvement in the complex process leading to the merger of 1955 had far-reaching effects on the subsequent development of intra-party factionalism in the LDP. As already suggested, it was inevitable that the Yoshida and the Matsumura factions should remain ideologically and emotionally opposed to each other. It was just as natural for this antagonistic relationship to be carried on between their respective successors, the Miki-Matsumura faction and the Satō and Ikeda factions which issued from the Yoshida faction. Ōno's personal involvement in the merger movement after the middle of May 1955 contributed to the consolidation of his faction but also led to his estrangement from Yoshida and his close followers.

Similarly, it was mainly because of the decision of Ogata and Ishii Mitsujirō to support Ōno in his behind-the-scenes activities designed to help the merger plan that a factional unit separate and independent from Yoshida's crystallised under the leadership of these two men. Again, it was no doubt in the course of, and in a large measure thanks to, these developments that Kōno Ichirō established himself as the number three man in the hierarchy of the Hatoyama faction, ranking next to Hatoyama and Miki Bukichi. Thus he put himself in a position to take over the faction's reins as soon as the two older men passed away. Nor is it likely that the Kishi faction would have registered the phenomenal growth rate it showed in the subsequent few years leading to Kishi's attainment of the LDP presidency in 1957, had it not been for the impressive leadership and political tact that he demonstrated as the Democratic Party's secretary-general in assisting Miki in his campaign for the merger. Fujiyama Aiichirō's entry into politics in July 1957 as Minister of Foreign Affairs in the Kishi Cabinet and the emergence of the Fujiyama faction resulted as much from his personal involvement in the merger movement as from his long-standing personal friendship with Kishi.

The conditions of factionalism in the two parties on the eve of the merger in 1955 were thus essentially of a recent origin. It was in the course of a few short years between the conclusion of the San Francisco Peace Treaty in 1951 and the middle of 1955 that the basic pattern of inter-factional relationships which one would find in the LDP in the subsequent years emerged. In this evolutionary process the unification issue had a very significant catalytic, if not germinal, effect.

However, the obvious aspects of novelty notwithstanding, it would be impossible to dissociate these post-independence developments completely from the traditions and *mores* of prewar party politics. The decisive role played by men like Hatoyama, Miki Bukichi, Ōno, Matsumura, and others in itself testifies to the importance of the prewar elements in the process involved. Furthermore, as we have seen above, many of the factional units and relationships between them which could be identified in the LDP on its formation in 1955 directly resulted from the effects of the return to politics in 1951-2 of the prewar politicians, especially Hatoyama and his Seiyūkai associates. Even the divisive tendencies which began to appear during this period among Yoshida's followers, such as Satō, Ikeda, and Hori, and which eventually led to the emergence of separate factions, were either caused or considerably accelerated by the appearance of Hatoyama and his group as the first serious contenders for power against Yoshida. In this sense the elementary pattern of factionalism in the LDP evolved directly out of the clashes between the groups of the prewar and postwar politicians represented by these two men.

The unification movement brought about significant changes not only in the conditions of intra-party factionalism but also in the role of business enterprises and their organisations *vis-à-vis* the conservative parties. Of basic importance in this respect is the fact that the four separate national organisations of the nation's largest employers—Keidanren, Nikkeiren, Nisshō, and Dōyūkai—began to wield a decisive influence both on the internal and external relations of the conservative party. Apart from this general consideration, there are a few particular aspects of the manner in which the business community came to involve itself in the process of party politics which deserve special mention.

One of these aspects was the composition of the group formed among leading businessmen which subsequently guided the employers' organisations in their approach and strategy towards the parties. Just as the prewar politicians and bureaucrats played a predominant part in the movement for conservative unification, so a group of businessmen who had been personally connected with the *Banchōkai* of the mid-1920s initially led the campaign for the same goal among employers. These men included Nagano Mamoru, Kobayashi Ataru, and Shōriki Matsutarō. Although it is hard to prove that the motivations of the prewar politicians and the businessmen who now worked together towards a conservative merger were identical, many of them seem to have acted on the assumption that they were. Beyond their obvious shared interest in political stability under conservative dominance, they seem to have shared also the desire to 'rectify' the 'excesses' of the Occupation-sponsored reforms, especially those relating to the deconcentration of economic power (the Anti-Monopoly Law). Unlike most advocates of revisionism in the parties, however, the business leaders showed primary interest in the practical and material, rather than the ideological and emotional, aspects of the problem. This can be illustrated by their approaches to the revision of the Anti-Monopoly Law and the resumption of military production.

The Anti-Monopoly Law had been enacted by the Diet in March 1947 and promulgated on 14 April of the same year. Under the strong pressure of business groups it was revised first in May 1949 and, for a second time, in August 1953. The Anti-Monopoly Law Committee set up in the Keidanren played a leading role in the revisionist campaign. The unofficial advisory committee set up in 1951 called the *Seirei shimon iinkai* functioned as the main channel of communication between the government and business circles on the question of the revisions of various laws passed under the Occupation, including the Anti-Monopoly Law. It was a prominent businessman, Hara Yasusaburō, who presided over this committee. On the other hand, the preparations for the resumption of military production were officially started by the Keidanren in August 1952, when a Defence Production Committee was set up in its Economic Co-operation Forum together with two other committees. Following the conclusion of the Mutual Security Agreement between Japan and the United States in March and the passage of the Self-Defence Force and the Defence Agency Organisation Laws in June 1954, this committee persuaded the government to approve production of jet aircraft and guardships. In the meantime, a Guided Missile (GM) Section was established within the same committee in September 1953 and subsequently developed into an independent committee by November of the same year and then into a GM Council by June 1957. Both these developments involved a very substantial change in the basic ideological premises of the whole political and social system erected under the Occupation. Nevertheless, the business groups engaged in these revisionist campaigns steered almost completely clear of ideological arguments and concentrated on the practical aspects.

Another interesting aspect was the tremendous increase in the function and prestige of large employer associations and their national federations as the formal representatives of the nation's business interests and providers of political funds. The collectivist tendencies, similar to those represented by the *zaibatsu* concerns in prewar days, became increasingly evident in the postindependence period. During the Occupation period it was mainly individual entrepreneurs who were responsible for the bulk of financial contributions to the parties. In the following period, however, various employer organisations were formed on an industrial basis and subsequently their national federations began to play a predominant part. In the case of the Liberal Party, for example, only about 20 per cent of the ¥27·7 million reported to the National Election Administration Committee as the total amount of the donations received by it during the 1951 fiscal year had come from such groups and the remaining 80 per cent had come from individual enterprises. By February 1955, however, more than half of the large donations (half a million yen or more) came from industrial associations and national organisations.

Individual enterprises and entrepreneurs still remained an important and indispensable source of contributions to the conservative parties, especially to factions within them. However, the role of the industrial associations and their national federations was steadily growing, and this tendency made the relationship between the parties and the business community much more stable than previously. In a sense the business organisations, represented by the four national organisations, were merely a substitute for the prewar *zaibatsu* concerns, but with an important difference. Because of the large numbers of enterprises directly represented by these organisations and therefore directly involved in the financial upkeep of the conservative parties, the relationship between the parties and the business circles gradually acquired an air of inclusiveness and totality, a quality which had been lacking in the prewar party-*zaibatsu* relationships.

In the fifteen turbulent years of Japanese history from 1940 to 1955 no basic changes were made in the traditional framework of conservative party organisation inherited from the prewar parties. Not only in their appellations but even in their basic functions virtually all of the characteristic party organs identified in the Seiyūkai and the Minseitō in the 1930s survived the war and the Allied Occupation with remarkably little change. The timing of the formation of the first postwar parties in relation to the initiation of the Purge program and the lack of any firm legal basis or definition of a party contributed more than other factors to the degree of continuity observed in this respect.

Regarding membership composition, intra-party factionalism, and relationships with business groups, there were some significant new developments in these years. The increase in the number of former high-ranking public servants among conservative Diet members and the corresponding decrease in the number of former local politicians was one of these developments. The conflicts between depurged prewar politicians and postwar Diet members not only gave rise to the forms of factional strife basic to the postwar parties but also lent to it peculiarly ideological implications. Both the factional units involved and the patterns of their interactions were strongly influenced by the unification movement which led to the 1955 merger. As a result, factionalism in the conservative parties in 1955 was far more complex both structurally and ideologically than its prewar counterpart.

The temporary disappearance of the *zaibatsu* concerns, especially Mitsui and Mitsubishi which had financially supported the two prewar parties, naturally brought about a very great change in the general characteristics of relation between conservative parties and business enterprises.

Following the dissolution of the *zaibatsu* concerns, the parties were compelled to look to a number of smaller enterprises and individual businessmen for funds. This state of affairs no doubt contributed to the growth of multiple parties and factional groups within each of them. After about 1950, however, large employers' organisations, such as Keidanren, began to exert a strong unifying influence both within and on behalf of the nation's business community. The oligopolistic tendencies promoted the unification of the channels of political contribution by business enterprises and a situation somewhat analogous to that which had existed in the prewar days of *zaibatsu* ascendancy emerged. There was, however, a basic difference. Whereas the *zaibatsu* concerns with all their wealth and influence had represented only a small part of the total number of enterprises in the country, the postwar business organisations like Keidanren and the three other national organisations represented a much larger percentage of the nation's business firms. It became impossible under these postwar conditions to associate either major conservative party with a particular enterprise or system of enterprises.

Despite all the new developments mentioned above, it is important to note that their seeds had in many cases been sown before the war. High-ranking public servants were consciously recruited by the Seiyūkai leaders from the very beginning. Their failure to gain the formal affiliation of a substantial number of high-ranking public servants did not result from any lack of awareness or interest in the value of their unique qualifications as party leaders. It resulted simply from the fact that a high-ranking public servant did not have to join a party under the prewar system in order to become a Cabinet minister, a member of the House of Peers, a prefectural governor, and so forth.

Factions based on inter-personal relationships, monetary considerations, ideological differences, and so on had appeared in the early 1920s. Furthermore, the multiplication of *zaibatsu* groups, represented by the rise of the 'new zaibatsu' in the 1930s, had diversified to some extent the sources of revenue available to a party and groups within it and, as a result, had also diversified the factional units. It is hard to distinguish the Yoshida-Hatoyama rivalry from the Kuhara-Nakajima conflict, since both were basically interpersonal power struggles within a single party, compounded by temperamental and ideological differences. The factional strife which went on in the Liberal and the Democratic parties on the eve of the 1955 merger was basically the same as its antecedent of the late 1930s.

When established in November 1955, the LDP had an enormous amount of tradition and experience behind it which it could fall back on or which might hold it back. This was so in terms of membership composition, organisation structure, factionalism, and relationships with extra-party groups, all of which had evolved over many decades. No part of this heritage was immutable or indispensable. It had, however, grown out of a long, continuous evolutionary process. As such it constituted an important part of the historical background without reference to which it would be impossible to understand or explain much of the LDP's behaviour.

E

Part Two
Factors underlying LDP
Policy-making

3 Membership

At the 17th Party Conference held on 22 January 1966 the LDP secretary-general, Tanaka Kakuei, proudly announced that during the past year a gain of 200,000 new members had been achieved and that consequently the current membership stood at 1,950,000. Due to the definitional problems involved, however, it is not quite as easy as it may appear at first sight to accept this officially announced membership figure at face value nor, indeed, even to talk about the size of LDP membership at all with any degree of certainty. In fact, estimates varying as widely as from 50,000 to 5,900,000 have been given on different occasions by the party itself and by others, nor are there any assurances that these two extremes really delimit the range of the error to be taken into account. If one is to discuss the LDP policy-making process in terms of its membership characteristics, it is therefore essential to define and specify the particular level or levels of its membership structure which are to be considered.

As far as the formal procedures and requirements laid down in the party constitution are concerned, any person may become an LDP member, provided that he is recommended by two or more party members, fills in an application form to be returned either to the headquarters, a prefectural federation, or a branch, and then undertakes to pay the membership fee of ¥200 per year (or an amount to be specified if he happens to be a member of the Diet or of a local assembly or a head of an autonomous local government body). It is nevertheless the difficulty of enforcing such simple procedural requirements and collecting such a nominal membership fee which has caused so much confusion in the counting of the party members. Even the relatively modest estimate of 150,000 members frequently cited is believed to be grossly inflated by the inclusion of a sizeable number of those who fail to pay the annual membership fee.

There are three distinct categories of members, which may be figuratively represented by three concentric circles, the radius of the middle circle being approximately twenty times that of the inner circle and about one-two hundredth that of the outer circle.

Members of the Diet as Party Members

During the period from late 1955 to late 1965 at the centre of the party membership structure there were between 280 and 300 LDP MHRs and between 120 and 140 members of the House of Councillors (hereafter referred to as MHCs), or an average of 420 LDP Diet members in all. In accordance with the established tradition inherited from the Liberal and the Democratic parties, the LDP charges each of its Diet members a special monthly fee of ¥50,000 as a 'legislative expense fee' deducted directly from his salary. In addition there is a special membership fee of ¥10,000. Both in terms of regular and punctual payment of membership dues and official membership registration, Diet members are the most obvious and readily identifiable members of the party. This is hardly surprising since the party was born in November 1955 from the merger of the 185 Democrats and 115 Liberals in the Diet, and a predominant role is still played by the Diet members in the management of party affairs.

Apart from the fact of their membership in the 'highest organ of state power', the parliamentary group of LDP members is distinguished from the other two categories by their occupational background characteristics. Ever since 1955 slightly over 25 per cent of the LDP MHRs have been consistently identified as former local politicians (mainly members of prefectural assemblies), another 25 per cent as former high-ranking public servants, somewhat more than 20 per cent as former businessmen, about 10 per cent as former journalists, and the remaining 20 per cent as miscellaneous (see Appendix I).

This pattern, in fact, had already begun to appear in the general elections of October 1952, and has changed little over the past fourteen years. In the House of Councillors, the pattern has been radically different from, and far less stable than, that observed among the Lower House members (see Table I). Taking the percentages of LDP Upper House members (including Ryokufūkai) for mid-1956 and mid-1965, they were respectively as follows: local politicians 15 per cent and 20 per cent; public servants 43 per cent and 38 per cent; businessmen 20 per cent and 25 per cent; miscellaneous 25 per cent and 28 per cent. The percentage of journalists was negligible throughout the period. This means that former bureaucrats have been numerically the most important occupational category among the LDP-affiliated Diet members in the past ten years or so, contributing in 1965 about 27 per cent of the total (followed by local politicians with 22 per cent, businessmen with 18 per cent, and journalists with 7 per cent).

The significance of these figures in terms of the source of recruitment of LDP Diet members becomes clear when compared with the corresponding figures relative to the total workforce. Of the 41,128,000 persons who were twenty years old or over (potential voters) and at work in the middle of 1965, national and local public servants (exclusive of the military personnel of the Defence Agency and teachers and police attached to local self-governing bodies) accounted for about 855,000 and 307,000 respectively, or a total of 1,162,000, that is, less than 3 per cent. When it comes to high-ranking officials, that is those holding a position of section chief or above in the national government, however, there were less than 1,780, or about a 250th of one per cent of the total workforce over the age of twenty. In other words, more than a quarter of the LDP Diet members have been drawn from an occupational group which is infinitesimal in size in terms of the total workforce of the nation. No other group in the society apart from local politicians is so grossly over-represented by the LDP parliamentary party as the upper echelon of the national bureaucracy.

The occupational category next in numerical importance to the higher public servants is that of local politicians. Although the members of the prefectural assemblies constitute only slightly over 3 per cent of local politicians, they constitute the overwhelming majority of the LDP Diet members recruited from this particular source. It is not, however, the prefectural assembly members at large from whom candidates may be recruited to stand in a Diet election with LDP endorsement; for unlike most other kinds of local politicians a relatively high degree of partisanship, that is official affiliation with the particular national parties, is found among them. In 1965, for example, only about 4 per cent of them were independents, while nearly 94 per cent were affiliated with one of the five national parties. It is therefore the LDP group of prefectural assembly members (in which category fell some 1,725 or 66 per cent of their total number) that should be regarded as the potential source of recruitment for over 20 per cent of the LDP Diet members. The local politicians thus narrowly defined constitute about the same minuscule percentage of the total workforce, that is about a 250th of one per cent, and are just as grossly over-represented as the high-ranking bureaucrats.

Businessmen and industrialists holding managerial posts with private concerns, on the other hand, accounted for 0·8 and 1·2 per cent of the total workforce respectively in 1955 and 1960 and have in all probability represented at least 1 per cent in the more recent years. That would mean that the 18 per cent of the LDP Diet members provided by this group is disproportionately large and yet far less so than is the case with the high-ranking public servants or local politicians. The same may be said about the category of former journalists. Considering that the combined percentage of journalists (in a rather loose sense) and writers at large was about 0·1 both in 1955 and 1960 and that this figure is unlikely to have changed significantly in the last few years, the fact that they make up 7 per cent of the LDP parliamentary force is certainly again a case of over-representation, but much less so than with the other three categories, particularly the first two.

Compared with the general occupational divisions of the population at large in contemporary Japanese society, the composition of the LDP parliament group is very peculiar indeed. On the one hand, the top-ranking public

TABLE 1

Occupational background of conservative MHCs, 1947–65

	Shinsei kurabu		Minshutō		Ryokufū-kai		Jiyūtō		Kokumin minshutō		Kaishintō		Jiyūminshutō	
	No.	%	No.	%	No.	%	No.	%	No.	%	No.	%	No.	%
1947														
Local politicians	16	31·3	11	23·4	4	4·5								
Public servants	4	7·9	4	8·5	21	24·1								
Businessmen	25	41·1	22	46·8	24	27·5								
Lawyers	0	0·0	2	4·2	2	2·3								
Miscellaneous	11	21·5	12	25·5	41	47·1								
1950														
Local politicians					3	5·0	23	27·7	5	16·6				
Public servants					16	27·1	18	21·6	2	6·6				
Businessmen					14	23·7	38	45·8	11	36·6				
Lawyers					2	3·3	2	2·4	3	10·3				
Miscellaneous					27	45·6	12	14·4	12	40·0				
1953														
Local politicians					2	4·6	19	19·0			2	11·1		
Public servants					23	46·9	33	33·0			3	16·6		
Businessmen					9	18·3	31	31·0			3	16·6		
Lawyers					1	2·0	1	1·0			1	5·5		
Miscellaneous					17	34·6	22	22·0			10	55·5		
1956														
Local politicians					1	3·4							22	17·0
Public servants					15	51·7							53	41·0
Businessmen					5	17·2							27	20·9
Lawyers					1	3·4							6	4·6
Miscellaneous					9	31·0							30	23·2

TABLE 1 (*continued*)

	Shinsei kurabu		Minshutō		Ryokufū-kai		Jiyūtō		Kokumin minshutō		Kaishintō		Jiyūminshutō	
	No.	%	No.	%	No.	%	No.	%	No.	%	No.	%	No.	%
1959														
Local politicians					0	0·0							14	10·1
Public servants					5	45·4							61	44·2
Businessmen					3	27·2							28	20·2
Lawyers					0	0·0							8	5·7
Miscellaneous					4	36·3							35	25·3
1962														
Local politicians													18	12·6
Public servants													57	40·1
Businessmen													27	19·0
Lawyers													7	4·9
Miscellaneous													38	26·7
1965														
Local politicians													28	20·1
Public servants													53	38·1
Businessmen													24	17·2
Lawyers													5	3·6
Miscellaneous													39	28·0

Note: Those with two or more occupations are counted twice for the two principal categories. Consequently, the totals of the numbers given for the five categories are larger than the actual numbers of members.

Source: GSS: Kizokuin sangiin giin meikan (1961). For other sources, see Appendix I.

servants and prefectural assembly members, together accounting for about
125th of one per cent of the working population of the country, provide just
about a half of it, reinforced by businessmen and journalists who together
account for between 1 and 1·5 per cent of the workforce but a quarter of
the LDP Diet members. On the other hand, neither the primary producers
(principally those engaged in farming and forestry) who account for about
26 per cent of the gainfully engaged workforce, nor the employees in secondary and tertiary industries (who make up about 58 per cent) are represented
in its composition except marginally. Such a situation also contrasts very
sharply with that obtaining in the principal opposition party, the Japan
Socialist Party, of whose 144 MHRs and 73 MHCs in late 1965 less than 2
per cent were former high-ranking public servants, about 20 per cent were
former local politicians, and 52 per cent were unionists, as is shown in Table 2.

TABLE 2

Occupational backgrounds of Socialist members of the Diet

	MHRs		MHCs		Totals	
	No.	%	No.	%	No.	%
Local politicians	34	23·6	11	15·0	45	20·7
Public servants	3	2·0	1	1·3	4	1·8
Businessmen	10	6·9	1	1·3	11	5·0
Journalists	6	4·1	2	2·7	8	3·6
Unionists	63	43·7	50	68·4	113	52·0
Miscellaneous	28	19·4	8	10·9	36	16·5
Totals	144	100·0	73	100·0	217	100·0

Sources: Kokkai binran, 31st ed. (November 1965), pp. 99-150; *GSS: Shūgiingiin
meikan* (1962); and *GSS: Kizokuin sangiin giin meikan* (1960).

The educational backgrounds of LDP Diet members are no less remarkable
than their occupations, and in fact the two are interrelated. In the population
at large, not more than 5·2 per cent of those 15 years old or over have
received university or college education and about 22 per cent either liberal
arts or vocational education at the intermediary level, while 63 per cent
have only primary school education.[1] In contrast, 82 per cent of the LDP
Diet members have gone to college or university, less than 15 per cent have
left school at the intermediary level, and less than 4 per cent went no further
than primary school, as Table 3 demonstrates.

These figures are even more impressive when it is realised that more than
half the university and college graduates among them (about 44 per cent
of the total) are graduates of the former imperial universities, with an overwhelming majority coming from the University of Tokyo. Comparing them
once more with the Socialists, the percentages of LDP Diet members from

[1]The percentage figures are derived from the 1960 national census.

TABLE 3

Educational backgrounds of LDP members of the Diet

	MHRs		MHCs		Totals	
	No.	%	No.	%	No.	%
Tokyo University (A)	99	35·1	51	36·6	150	35·6
Other former imperial universities (B)	23	8·1	12	8·6	35	8·3
(A) and (B)	122	43·2	63	45·2	185	43·9
Other universities and colleges (C)	110	39·0	50	35·9	160	38·0
(A), (B), and (C)	232	82·2	113	81·1	345	81·9
Middle and vocational schools and teachers' colleges	36	12·7	24	17·2	60	14·2
Primary school	14	4·9	2	1·4	16	3·8
Totals	282	100·0	139	100·0	421	100·0

Sources: As for Table 2.

former imperial universities with degrees are about three times as large as those of the Socialists and those with an intermediary or lower level of educational experience about three times as small (Table 4).

TABLE 4

Educational backgrounds of Socialist members of the Diet

	MHRs		MHCs		Totals	
	No.	%	No.	%	No.	%
Tokyo University (A)	15	10·4	6	8·2	21	9·6
Other former imperial universities (B)	11	7·6	1	1·3	12	5·5
(A) and (B)	26	18·0	7	9·5	33	15·1
Other universities and colleges (C)	44	30·5	24	32·8	68	31·3
(A), (B), and (C)	70	48·5	31	42·3	101	46·4
Middle and vocational schools and teachers' colleges	59	40·9	32	43·8	91	41·9
Primary school	15	10·4	10	13·6	25	11·5
Totals	144	100·0	73	100·0	217	100·0

The occupational and educational background characteristics of the LDP parliamentary party membership as shown in these statistics make it very distinctive both as a group in the society at large and also among the parties. It can hardly be regarded as even remotely representative of the average voter in terms of the two basic sociological factors determining status and roles in a modern society. Externally, therefore, the LDP's relationship to the voter tends to resemble that obtaining between a teacher and pupils, or even that which operated in pre-modern Japan between the *shi* class on the one hand and the farmers, artisans, and merchants on the other.

In order, however, to relate this to the policy-making process, it is not sufficient to point out the unusual membership composition of the LDP parliamentary group. One must also understand the relationships between

TABLE 5

Classification of LDP Diet members by occupational and educational backgrounds, November 1965

	Public servants	Local politicians	Business-men	Journalists	Miscel-laneous	Totals
	%	%	%	%	%	%
Tokyo University (A)						
MHRs	89·4	8·8	12·9	22·8	26·9	34·2
MHCs	90·5	—	12·5	—	14·2	40·7
Total	89·9	6·5	12·5	21·6	23·0	36·2
Other imperial universities (B)						
MHRs	7·8	2·5	16·1	—	7·9	7·3
MHCs	5·6	—	16·6	—	10·7	7·4
Total	6·9	1·8	16·2	—	8·7	7·3
(A) and (B)						
MHRs	97·2	11·3	29·0	22·8	34·8	41·5
MHCs	96·1	—	29·1	—	24·9	48·1
Total	96·8	8·3	28·9	21·6	31·7	43·5
Other universities and colleges						
MHRs	1·3	48·1	46·7	74·2	49·2	39·6
MHCs	3·7	64·2	45·8	50·0	53·5	33·3
Total	2·3	52·3	46·5	72·9	50·5	37·7
(A), (B), and (C)						
MHRs	97·2	59·4	75·7	97·0	84·0	81·1
MHCs	99·8	64·2	74·9	50·0	78·4	81·4
Total	99·1	60·6	75·4	94·5	82·2	81·2
Middle schools, vocational schools, and teachers' colleges						
MHRs	1·3	25·3	19·3	2·0	14·2	13·6
MHCs	—	35·0	20·8	—	21·4	15·5
Total	0·8	28·0	19·7	2·7	16·4	14·2
Elementary schools						
MHRs	—	15·1	4·8	—	1·5	5·0
MHCs	—	—	4·1	50·0	—	1·4
Total	—	11·2	4·6	2·7	1·0	4·0

Sources: As for Table 2.

occupation and education and define the nature of their interactions both in power and functional terms.

If one relates the distribution of the four or five levels of educational experience mentioned above to the four numerically most important occupational groups among LDP Diet members, a very clear contrast appears between former high-ranking public servants and local politicians, with businessmen and journalists falling in between the two (see Table 5). While nearly 90 per cent of the bureaucrats are Tokyo University graduates and almost 100 per cent are graduates of some university or college, local politicians rate 6·5 per cent and 60·6 per cent respectively. Journalists and businessmen are somewhere in between. This indicates conclusively that it is the presence of the former high-ranking public servants that determines the remarkable educational background characteristics associated with the LDP parliamentary party. In other words, the extraordinarily high proportion of graduates of the former imperial universities, especially Tokyo University, which characterises the membership of the LDP parliamentary party merely reflects on the one hand the importance of the upper stratum of the national bureaucracy as a main source of recruitment for the ministerial party and, on the other hand, the well-known fact of the domination of the nation's officialdom by the graduates of those particular universities. Regarding this latter point, it should be sufficient to point out the following statistical facts. In the most recent year for which sufficient evidence is available, 1965, all of the permanent vice-ministers (the highest ranking career public servants) of the twelve ministries were without exception graduates of Tokyo University (see Table 6). In five ministries 90 per cent or more of those occupying the three highest grades, that is the chiefs of the bureaux, divisions, and sections, were graduates of the former imperial universities, a majority coming

TABLE 6

Distribution of higher public servants by universities attended, 1965

	Tokyo University	Other former imperial universities*	Other universities and colleges	Total
Vice-ministers	12	0	0	12
Bureau chiefs	72	11	6	89
Division chiefs	25	5	5	35
Section chiefs	244	112	103	459
Uncertain†				
Total	353	128	114	595

*Kyōto, Ōsaka, Kyūshū, Tōhoku, Hokkaidō.

†All but one bureau chief in the Ministry of Finance herein classified as uncertain were section chiefs; not counted in total.

Sources: Shokuinroku: 1966, Vol. I, passim; Nihon kankai jōhōsha, Nihon kankai meikan, 18th ed. (1966), passim.

from Tokyo University. In eight ministries the figure was 80 per cent or more. Furthermore, in the period between 1962 and 1966 inclusive something like 58 per cent of those who passed the higher diplomatic service examinations and 67 per cent of those who passed the general higher public service examinations were Tokyo University graduates. The corresponding figures for the graduates of the former imperial universities as a whole were 75 and 83 per cent respectively. This strongly suggests that the situation is not very likely to change drastically in the foreseeable future.

The dichotomy suggested above between the former high-ranking public servants and the former local politicians in terms of their educational backgrounds clearly affects the leadership group composition of the various party organs, especially of those which are directly involved in the formal policy-making process in the party. On the one hand, the bureaucrats, who have consistently formed about 30 per cent of LDP Diet members since 1955, have (as Table 7 shows) provided between one-third and one-half of the ministers in the successive Cabinets during that period. (The one exception is the third Hatoyama Cabinet, of whose eighteen members only three were of this particular category.)

TABLE 7

Percentages of former public servants and local politicians in LDP cabinets, 1955–65

Cabinets		Public servants No.	%	Local politicians No.	%
3rd Hatoyama	(Nov. 1955–)	3	16·6	1	5·5
Ishibashi	(Dec. 1956–)	6	33·3	3	16·6
1st Kishi	(Feb. 1957–)	12	34·2	6	17·1
2nd Kishi	(June 1958–)	6	33·3	2	11·1
1st Ikeda	(July 1960–)	6	33·3	0	0·0
2nd Ikeda	(Dec. 1960–)	23	46·0	5	10·0
3rd Ikeda	(Dec. 1963–)	17	50·0	5	14·7
1st Satō	(Nov. 1964–)	22	36·6	10	16·6
Total		104	41·4	32	12·7

Even when the Hatoyama Cabinet is included, an average of 41·4 per cent of the 251 ministers appointed during this period were former high-ranking officials. Regarding party offices, it should be first noted that not only have the three most recent presidents—Kishi, Ikeda, and Satō—all been typical bureaucrats but three of the seven secretaries-general between November 1955 and June 1965 were also leading bureaucrats.

Even more impressive when compared with the local politicians is the degree to which the former high-ranking public servants dominate the deliberative and decision-making organs of the PARC. While as many as five

TABLE 8

PARC officials with public service backgrounds and those who were formerly local politicians

	1955 No.	%	1957 No.	%	1959 No.	%	1961 No.	%	1963 No.	%	1965 No.	%	Total No.	%
Public servants														
PARC vice-chairmen	7	70·0	4	40·0	4	25·0	5	45·4	1	25·0	2	33·3	23	40·3
Members of PARC Deliberation Commission	13	86·6	14	56·0	13	52·0	—	—	10	40.0	10	76·9	60	58.2
Local politicians														
PARC vice-chairmen	—	—	—	—	3	18·7	1	9·0	—	—	1	16·6	5	8·7
Members of PARC Deliberation Commission	1	6·6	3	12·0	2	8·0	—	—	—	—	—	—	6	5.8

Sources: Seisaku Geppō, 118 (November 1965), pp. 156-8; *Asahi*, 22 November 1955, 23 July (evening) and 19 September (evening) 1957, 10 July 1959, and 6 August 1963; Jiyūminshutō, *Seimuchōsakai meibo: Shōwa 40-nen 11-gatsu 10-ka genzai*, mimeo., p. 1.

of the twelve PARC chairmen appointed between November 1955 and June 1965 were former public servants of the highest rank, over 40 per cent of its vice-chairmen and nearly 60 per cent of the Deliberation Commission members belonged to that category, as shown in Table 8.

Similarly, in November 1965 about a third of the chairmen of the PARC divisions and Special Investigation Committees were drawn from the public servant category.

	Divisions		Investigation Committees		Totals	
	No.	%	No.	%	No.	%
Public servants	5/15	33·3	15/45	33·3	20/60	33·3
Local politicians	3/15	20·0	7/45	15·5	10/60	16·6

As these tables clearly indicate, at least there is conclusive statistical evidence that, with the exception of the executive council, the former high-ranking public servants have been more or less over-represented in each of the executive and decision-making organs of the party.

On the other hand, the situation of the former local politician category has been radically different. While they have accounted for over 20 per cent of the total LDP parliamentary party membership in the past ten years and their percentage ratio to the public servants has been somewhat better than 2 to 3, their share of Cabinet and party posts has been very small. In the case of Cabinet ministers, for example, the average number of former local politicians between November 1955 and December 1966 was only about 13 per cent. This is less than one-third of the public servants' share in Cabinet posts and only slightly over a half of their own percentage share of the party's total Diet membership. Of the five presidents and the seven secretaries-general between 1955 and 1966, only one belonged to the local politician category. The degree of under-representation has been almost as startling regarding the positions on the PARC, particularly in the case of its vice-chairmen and the Deliberation Commission members. From the viewpoint of the party policy-making process, it is highly significant that the local politicians should have been consistently and strikingly under-represented in those crucial policy-initiating and formulating areas where the former public servants have been just as consistently over-represented.

It is probably quite wrong to assume that retired high-ranking public servants have regarded party politics as the most attractive arena of activity; for a much higher percentage has no doubt entered private business concerns or public corporations than the parties. Nevertheless, there is no doubt that it has become one of the main outlets for a significant proportion of the top-ranking bureaucrats who often reach the highest public service posts of vice-minister or bureau chief in their late forties or early fifties and then are compelled by the unwritten yet well-observed rule to retire in order to give way to the younger aspirants on the long waiting list. Once elected, they are almost invariably associated with the nuclear group of party decision-makers thanks to their training and experience which are particularly relevant to the legis-lative functions and responsibilities of a ministerial party under the present parliamentary cabinet system. In this limited sense it is probably correct to say that the former public servants have come to dominate the LDP.

To characterise the ideological and behavioural tendencies associated with any specific occupational background categories in sweeping terms is extremely dangerous and a degree of internal heterogeneity and disagreement should be taken for granted. It seems nevertheless useful to emphasise the fairly obvious advantages of a former public servant as a legislator and a party member in comparison with those who belong to the other occupational categories, in terms of the degree of familiarity with and access to the sources of authoritative information, personal acquaintance with active public ser-vants, experience in the fine technicalities of administration in a specialised field, and so forth. As a general proposition, many of the professional attri-butes of a high-ranking public servant acquired through his particular educa-tional and occupational experience may with good reason be considered as contributing to his role and performance in the party policy-making process.

Considering the nature of his educational and occupational experience, a former local politician may be very different from a former public servant. Because of his intimate relationships with local interests and groups (whose support was no doubt essential to his entry and survival, first in local politics and then in his election to the National Diet) he can be expected to speak and act as boldly as anybody else in the party and the Diet where special local interests are at stake.[2] When, however, it comes to the task of formu-lating national policies and drafting legislative bills, he can hardly be expected to match an experienced bureaucrat in performance, for the simple reason that both the information and facilities essential for effective execution of such a task are monopolised by the national bureaucracy and, as a rule, only the 'ins' or those who have been 'ins' have access to them.

[2]The almost single-minded preoccupations with the advancement of local interests on the part of a former local politician were typified by the incident caused in the autumn of 1966 by the alleged abuse of power by the then Minister of Transportation, Arafune Seijūrō, to make a National Railway express train make regular stops at a station located in his own constituency. As a result of this incident, aggravated by the additional charges of his attempt to induce a group of transportation operators to join an association of his electoral supporters and his having taken a couple of textile manu-facturers with him on his official trip to South Korea, he was eventually forced to resign on 11 October 1966. He kept insisting until the end, however, that there was nothing improper or immoral about what he had done 'for his people'. Arafune had served as a member of the Saitama Prefectural Assembly before he was elected to the Diet. The mentality of another former local politician turned Cabinet member, Director-General Kambayashiyama Eikichi of the Defence Agency, who caused a similar public uproar about the same time by visiting his constituency accompanied by top-ranking officials of the Agency, including the three chiefs of staff, was closely related. Kambaya-shiyama had been a member of the Kagoshima Prefectural Assembly. For the factual information concerning these incidents see *Asahi*, 12, 14, 17, 27 October 1966; *Maini-chi*, 13 October 1966. For a pertinent comment, see 'Senkyoku mo kokka no ichibubun' ('Konshū no shakai kansatsu), *Asahi Jānaru*, VIII, 46 (6 November 1966), pp. 87-8.

F

To the extent that educational and occupational background and experience may be expected to affect the characteristic pattern and effectiveness of a person's performance as a national law-maker and party member, the other three categories, businessmen, journalists, and 'miscellaneous', may be expected to fall somewhere between the above-mentioned two. It seems impossible to generalise more specifically about their roles and performance in the party policy-making process. It should therefore suffice to point out the generally intermediate and essentially indefinite positions they occupy in the dichotomy suggested above. If one considers national versus local interests, for example, they may well be found to approach the public servant rather than the local politician. If on the other hand one considers public versus private interests it is possible to find them opposing the former and siding with the latter, or opposing both.

The behavioural differences, however, which result from the differences in occupational and educational experience and connections may be significantly neutralised by what may be called a process of 'professionalisation' which has long been under way. This process tends to reduce differences between the members of the same party and works towards standardisation.

Partly because of the well-established tradition of giving priority to sitting members when candidates are being selected for official party endorsement and partly also because of their own natural staying power, the same members have been re-elected many times over. In the general election of 1946 nearly 90 per cent of the candidates sponsored by the Progressive and the Liberal parties and about 75 per cent of those successfully returned were 'new faces'. By 1955, however, the corresponding percentages for the Democrats and the Liberals combined had become as low as 16 and 9 and has since remained much the same in subsequent elections (see Appendix II). In other words, about 85 per cent of LDP candidates and 90 per cent of those successfully returned have been either incumbent or former MHRs.

In the case of the MHCs (who have a six-year term of office) the ratios of new candidates to re-elected members have been naturally much higher (see Appendix III). Nevertheless, the tendency for incumbent members to be preferred to new candidates has been quite pronounced even here. In recent elections 'old faces' have provided a majority of both candidates and elected members. It should be noted that 'new faces' have been proportionally fewer in the LDP than in the other major parties, particularly the Socialists, although the same tendency is more or less common to all of them.

Looked at from a slightly different angle, this tendency is clearly shown by the fact that, in November 1965, over half the LDP-affiliated MHRs had been returned six times or more, which means they had been members for nearly fifteen years. Even in the House of Councillors about two-thirds of the 139 LDP members who took their seats after the election of July 1965 had been returned twice or more and one-third three times or more. In other words, two-thirds had been members for at least six and up to ten years, while one-third had been for at least twelve and up to fifteen years.

Under such circumstances it seems inevitable that the behavioural characteristics attributed initially to each occupational background category are progressively modified by the effects of mutual interaction. In this way the original sharp and obvious contrasts between those belonging to different categories tend to become blurred and virtually disappear as time passes. That this is not a superficial impression gained simply by an observer outside the party but is shared even by some of the most experienced party men may be seen in the following exchange between a reporter and Kawashima Shōjirō:

> SAKIYAMA: How is one to look at the relative strengths and prospects of the 'pure politicians' and the 'bureaucrats' in the LDP?
> KAWASHIMA: They have become completely mixed up by now. There are no longer any sharp divisions between them. . . For example, you may say that Mr Kōno is a pure politician, but his closest friend, Mr Shigemasa, is a bureaucrat. Mr Ōno is a party man, but Mr Funada (who is intimate with him) is no doubt a bureaucrat. Mr Kishi of our own faction is a bureaucrat, but, as you know well, both Mr Akagi and myself are of the pure politician category. . . .[3]

Without denying the different roles played by former public servants and former local politicians in party policy-making, we may say that a stereotyped style among LDP members has been gradually emerging out of the constant interaction of the various behavioural characteristics they have brought with them.

In view of the extremely intimate relationship of the ministerial party and the national bureaucracy, or rather the former's dependence upon the latter both for personnel recruitment and also in the making and execution of policy, the professionalisation process has necessarily tended to 'bureaucratise' the categories other than former public servants. The process of party 'modernisation', which amounts to the bureaucratic rationalisation of its structural framework, has been accompanied by a progressive permeation of the whole parliamentary party membership by bureaucratic influence.

We have seen already that what makes the LDP parliamentary party look so distinctively an élite group with a level of educational experience (and therefore, presumably, of intellectual sophistication) far higher than that of the average voter is the influx of former high-ranking public servants and their predominant position in the intra-party power relationship, especially in the area of party policy-making. The above-mentioned process of professionalisation cannot but further accentuate this élitist aspect of the party. If, nevertheless, the party has not completely lost its mass-party character (or at least pretensions), this is because of the presence of two other very different

[3]Kawashima Shōjirō, *Ikeda kaizōnaikaku no seikaku to sono zento* (Kokumin seiji kenkyūkai 'Getsuyōkai' ripōto, No. 50, hereafter to be referred to as 'KSK Report', 50), mimeo. (31 July 1961), p. 39.

species of party member. But for the presence of the latter, the LDP would have conceivably become a mere appendage of the bureaucracy.

Local Politicians as Party Members

Of the non-parliamentary members of the LDP, active local politicians who constitute the middle ring between Diet members and grass-root supporters stand out and are the most stable. Whether as a source of recruitment for the parliamentary group almost as important as the national bureaucracy, as the executive personnel of the party branches and prefectural federations, or as the link between the party and voters, they play an indispensable part in the survival and growth of the LDP as an effective political party.

The influence of national parties in local politics, especially at the prefectural level, had already become quite significant in the period following the Russo-Japanese War in the first decade of the century. By the end of the Meiji era a fairly large proportion of prefectural assembly members had begun to act according to instructions issued by the headquarters of the national parties, such as the Seiyūkai and Kenseihontō. Since World War II the prefectural assemblies have been more deeply and extensively influenced by the national parties. Before the parties united in 1955 about 70 per cent of their members were affiliated with one party or another, while by 1963 nearly 100 per cent of them were so affiliated, as independent members decreased steadily from about 33 per cent in 1955 to 15·7 per cent in 1959, and 2·7 per cent in 1963. Nevertheless, with the outstanding exceptions of these prefectural assembly members and the members of the Tokyo Special Ward Assemblies, local politicians have been remarkably free from regularised and effective control by the national parties. This is shown by the fact that as late as October 1965 about 40 per cent of prefectural governors, 80 per cent of city mayors, 95 per cent of town and village mayors, 60 per cent of city assembly members, and 90 per cent of town and village assembly members were still independents.

So far as the LDP is concerned, the tradition (dating back to the first decade of the century) of regarding prefectural assembly members as an integral part of the membership of a national party has been apparently accepted as a matter of course from the beginning. In the local elections of 1963, moreover, efforts were made for the first time to induce candidates for the other kinds of local assembly and for the executive positions to join the party officially. In fact, the LDP went so far as to start providing material and moral support through official endorsement, even to candidates running in town and village assembly elections, as well as to repudiate candidates in gubernatorial contests unless they agreed to join the party formally. After the elections of that year official invitations to join the party were sent to independent members of town and village assemblies throughout the nation in the name of the LDP secretary-general and the chairman of the National Organisation Committee. Even as a reaction to the similar efforts on the part of the opposition parties, this indicated a much more aggressive recruitment policy on the part of the traditionally complacent ministerial party.

Thanks to such efforts as well as to the natural tendency among local politicians to join the ministerial rather than an opposition party, nearly 8,500 local politicians, or just over 10 per cent of the total, had become formally affiliated with the LDP by late 1965. The breakdown of this figure was as follows: 26 out of the 46 prefectural governors, 1,725 of the 2,606 prefectural assembly members, 80 of the 558 city mayors, 3,424 of the 17,930 city assembly members, 143 of the 2,808 town and village mayors, 2,478 of the 57,023 town and village assembly members, and 622 of the 1,033 Tokyo Special Ward Assembly Members, i.e. a total of 8,498 of the 82,004 local politicians.

This means that at the prefectural level over 55 per cent of the governors and 65 per cent of assembly members belonged to the LDP, at the intermediate, city level just under 15 per cent of mayors and 20 per cent of assembly members were so affiliated, while at the lowest, town and village level only about 5 per cent or less of mayors and assembly members belonged to the party. If, however, independents are excluded and only those affiliated with one or other of the national parties are counted, another significant aspect of the situation emerges: a relatively high percentage of executive heads and a relatively low percentage of assembly members had chosen the LDP rather than an opposition party; 96, 78, and 91 per cent respectively of the governors, city mayors, and town and village mayors were so committed as opposed to 69, 50, and 54 per cent respectively of the prefectural, city, and town and village assembly members. In the very limited areas of local politics that have been successfully 'politicised', the LDP can be identified with the top stratum of local bureaucracy more intimately than with the local legislatures.

There is little doubt that the affiliation of local politicians proves to be an enormous asset in Diet and other kinds of election for, generally speaking, they are much closer to the average voter both physically and psychologically than the bureaucrats living in Tokyo and, for that reason, are in a better position to influence his voting decisions. Yet when it comes to the making of decisions on policy issues by the party as such there is no evidence to suggest that any significant contributions are ever made by them. In view of the virtually complete control of the headquarters by the Diet members and the domination of the policy-making organs and processes by the former public servants among them, this is hardly surprising. Their participation in the process is merely incidental and marginal and is largely limited to attendance at occasional policy seminars arranged by the headquarters. They attend these in their capacity of officers of local branches or prefectural federations and listen to, rather than actively debate with, lecturers who are also nominated by the headquarters. What is expected of them in relation to the party policy-making process is obviously not more than support and assistance in implementation, as opposed to the initiation and formulation, of policy.

Grass-roots Membership

Much more difficult to define and describe than the above two categories of LDP members are the multitudes constituting the peripheral ring of the party membership structure. It is with this group that confusion often occurs when one tries to make a numerical estimate or describe its socio-economic and ideological characteristics. Such elusiveness is indeed its most obvious and significant characteristic.

Whereas 1·9 million was officially quoted in the annual organisational program as the number of registered LDP members in January 1966, the bona fide members (those who pay the ¥200 per annum membership fee more or less regularly) seem to be about 50,000 or one-fortieth of the officially quoted number. The rest are almost purely nominal members, in the sense that they neither pay the membership fee from their own pockets nor are much interested even in the fact of their affiliation with the party. As a rule, in fact, a large proportion of these 'registered' members have been passively recruited from among the members of the eight hundred or so supporters' associations built around individual Diet members, at the latter's request. The essence of the relationship obtaining between a Diet member and his supporters-turned-party-members is realistically summed up by the following statement of an experienced LDP Diet member:

> When pressed by the Party Headquarters to help increase the number of members, each Diet member asks some of his personal supporters to join the Party for his sake. To be sure, they have no intention at all of paying the membership fee themselves. They are bound to say, 'Oh well, I don't mind joining, if you pay the money for me'. The Diet member does not want to help much in the drive to increase members for obvious reasons. If he persuades one thousand members of his supporters' association officially to join the Party, he will be forced to spend ¥200,000 for the payment of their membership fee; if the number to be recruited is 10,000, he will then have to foot a bill for ¥2 million! . . . The majority of the supporters willing to join do not even dream of paying to do so. To them money is something the Diet member should spend for them, not something they should be expected to spend for him.[4]

A shopkeeper who had lately been recruited into the party in the manner described above was surprised when told by a journalist that he was a party member and exclaimed, 'You say I am a member of the LDP? Well, I remember Mr X, the city assembly member, calling the other day to ask me to become a member, and I did sign the form he brought with him. However, I do not believe that I have ever paid anything . . . '. As an indicator of the maximal limit of the nominally registered members, the figure of 1·9 million is not entirely useless for certain purposes. It must be, however, taken with utmost caution and qualifications, as the above examples suggest.

Of the 50,000 more or less stable members who regularly pay the membership fee about 420 are Diet members and 8,600 are local politicians. This

[4]'Seitō wa kore de yoi no ka' (9), Yomiuri, 12 January 1966.

leaves only about 40,000 to be considered as belonging to the peripheral members in the sense of the words used here. Considering that there are about 2,600 branches of the party at the city, town, and village level throughout the country, each of which must have a dozen or so officials to maintain it for a prolonged period, it is clear that a majority of these 40,000 are actually party office-bearers at the local level. As such they are no doubt also the most active organisers and constitute the hard core of the LDP local organisation. A statement made some time ago by a resident organiser from Nīgata Prefecture, to the effect that it was easy to find from ten to twenty men at each branch always willing to take part in meetings and rallies organised by the prefectural federations, underwrites this conclusion, at least partially.

It is still a valid assumption that a relatively high proportion of those engaged in primary industries, especially agriculture, tends to prefer the conservative LDP to the radical opposition parties. A study made in 1961 revealed, for example, that 67·4 per cent of the farmers responding to a questionnaire said they had voted for the LDP in the House of Representatives election of the previous year, as compared with 62·1 per cent of self-employed merchants and entrepreneurs, 57·1 per cent of corporation managers, 38·2 per cent of manual labourers, 27·4 per cent of white collar employees, and 33·3 per cent of those following professions. In a more sophisticated study of the Japanese voting behaviour made at about the same time a similar conclusion was drawn in the form of an urban-rural dichotomy.[5] It is nevertheless important to emphasise the dangers of equating the grassroots voter support for the LDP, that is the scope of its potential membership, with the primary industry population. The distribution of LDP votes in the recent Diet elections reveals that the level of voter support for the party has been considerably higher than that of the population engaged in agriculture, forestry, and fisheries and that the two do not correlate very significantly.

On the one hand, the drastic change in the employment pattern of the nation over the past twelve years has made it impossible for the LDP to continue to depend as heavily and comfortably as previously on the electoral support of the farmers. It would have been a bad policy to do so, even if the agricultural population as such had remained unchanged in its traditional conservatism and antipathy towards the radical parties; for its size has drastically decreased both relatively and in absolute numbers—between 1955 and 1965 it fell from about 16 million, or nearly 40 per cent of the total workforce, to 11 million, or just about a quarter of the workforce. Equally significant, however, is the fact that a substantial proportion of the farming population, especially that part of it which is organised in agricultural unions and co-operatives, can no longer be expected to supply votes for the LDP as a

[5]Naikakukambō naikakuchōsashitsu, *Chūkansō no ishiki to sono haikei* (*Shakaifūchō chōsashiryō*, No. 6), mimeo. (Febrary 1962), pp. 55-6; also see Kyōgoku Jun'ichi and Nobutaka Ike, 'Sengo sōsenkyo ni okeru tōhyōkōdō: Jō', *Shisō*, 434 (August 1960), pp. 35-7.

matter of course. The alienation of farmers from the LDP in some of the most predominantly agricultural prefectures, such as Aomori, Iwate, Akita, and Shimane, has been clearly registered by the gap between the percentage shares of the agricultural population and LDP votes in the House of Councillors elections of 1959, 1962, and 1965.

The organisational efforts made by the LDP in the past ten years or so have been predicated on the well-founded assumption that the profound socio-economic change symbolised by the sharp decline of agricultural population and the increase of floating votes in rural constituencies is bound, if left alone, to have seriously adverse effects on the future electoral performance of the LDP. By the middle of 1963 such efforts had resulted in the establishment of some 2,600 local branches throughout the country and the appointment of 22,000 resident organisers. These branches have been the principal and most orthodox agencies through which to recruit new members at the grass-roots, though they are frequently supplemented by the supporters' associations. Both the organisational details and membership composition of the branches no doubt vary from place to place, but they share the common function of recruiting new members as well as electioneering for incumbent LDP Diet members or potential LDP candidates on a semi-permanent basis.

According to accounts given in 1960 by several resident organisers, by early 1960 branches were formed in all but a few towns and villages in Nīgata Prefecture, the majority of their members being farmers and merchants. Those already affiliated with a branch would call on their relations and acquaintances to persuade them to join. In Yamanashi a branch was set up in each town or village and its members were assigned each to a hamlet and its subdivisions, that is neighbourhood associations. In Asahikawa City in Hokkaidō a sub-branch was set up in each of its seven school districts, each consisting of about 1,000 members and further sub-divided into several street committees of about a hundred members each. Through the activities of these branches, the LDP allegedly succeeded in having about 10 per cent of voters 'register' as members in some prefectures.[6]

In defining the character of LDP membership at this level it is particularly important to point out the prevalence of indirect or group affiliation, as opposed to direct and individual membership. As typified by the instances of 12,000 postmasters, 5,000 hairdressers and barbers, and 4,500 manufacturers of oils and fats who collectively joined the party several years ago, a substantial proportion of the party's members is provided by the three hundred organisations officially listed as groups sympathetic to the LDP, or

---

[6]In Wakayama Prefecture, for example, some 34,000 had signed up by early 1960 and in Yamanashi 41,000 had done so. See Matsushita Keiichi, *Gendainihon no seijiteki kōsei* (Tokyo daigaku shuppankai, 1962), p. 149. The fact that even the official estimate of 1·9 million for the party's current membership is only 3·2 per cent of the 58·2 million voters proves, however, that these were rather special cases and that the percentage figures for more urbanised prefectures were much smaller.

by their sub-divisions.[7] At the local level youths' and women's associations have often been instrumental in inducing their members to become party members *en masse* and in a few cases the employees of particular manufacturing establishments have joined in hundreds. In fact it is difficult to find many instances of individuals joining the party strictly of their own accord and independently of any group.

The fact that the branches of the party have apparently been as active in urban as in rural areas in their efforts to recruit new members, and that many of the large groups who have joined the party *en bloc* comprise those engaged in secondary or tertiary, rather than primary, industries, suggests that the membership at this level is occupationally quite variegated. Farmers are only one of the major categories.

The recruitment of members by indirect affiliation and through total or partial absorption of an existing organisation necessarily renders the peripheral membership of the LDP singularly unstable, even ephemeral. As already pointed out, most have been induced to join the party at the request of a Diet member, a party branch official, or a resident organiser. Few are interested sufficiently in the party and its general policy program to pay the membership fee from their own pockets or to desire continued formal association with it over a prolonged period. Hence the repeated calls at annual party conferences for a more effective collection of membership fees and registration and re-registration of bona fide members. Since no more than, say, 20 per cent of sympathetic organisations can be expected to be interested in a wide range of LDP policies not directly relating to the allocation of public funds, it is reasonable to assume that many members drawn from this source tend soon to drop out, in fact as soon as their specific economic demands are satisfied.

Nor are those drawn from the supporters' associations more likely to make stable and permanent party members, for their relationships to the particular Diet members or would-be candidates are often too personal to be transferred to the impersonal entity called the party. In fact, there is an element of rivalry and even antagonism in the relations between a party branch and prefectural federation on the one hand and a supporters' association on the other, which is bound to make a person's sustained loyalty to the one incompatible with his loyalty to the other, especially at the time of an election.

Under the circumstances described above, it is extremely difficult to differentiate clearly a nominal and sporadic party member from one of the ten million who belong to the eight hundred or so supporters' associations or organisations sympathetic to the party.[8] It is probably more accurate to

[7]Regarding the role of these organisations, see the discussion in Chapter 6.

[8]According to one estimate, there were about 800 supporters' associations with an aggregate membership of 9·8 million in the middle of 1964 (*Asahi*, 14 August 1964). Regarding the membership of the 'sympathetic' organisations, however, it is impossible to make a realistic estimate, although a substantial part of it seems to overlap that of the supporters' associations.

say that many of the 1·9 million peripheral members have regular and permanent membership of some such organisation, but are only temporarily and incidentally members of the party. Except for the purely nominal act of registering as a party member they are hardly distinguishable from non-party members associated with the former.

The involvement of the peripheral members in the party policy-making process is even more incidental and marginal than that of the local politician members. As a rule, it is limited to participation in the occasional study seminars and meetings sponsored by a branch or a prefectural federation, and the receipt of a few party publications each month. Apart from the annual meetings of the prefectural federations, such meetings are usually held for the benefit of two particular categories of members, youths and women, to whose role in the local party activities has been attached a special importance in the official organisational programs of the party.[9]

Such seminars and meetings, however, have been primarily designed, not to provide an opportunity for the opinions of grass-roots members to be heard and reflected in the formulation of new party policies, but rather to educate them in the policies already decided by the headquarters and to solicit their co-operation in propagating those policies.

A registered member is entitled in theory to receive various party publications either free or at a nominal cost. In reality, however, the number of copies available for each publication has been much too small to reach anything like 1·9 million members. The largest of the periodicals currently published by the LDP, *Jiyūminshu*, had in January 1966 a circulation of 150,000, while *Seisaku Geppō* had about 10,000. The circulations of *Soshiki Jōhō* and *Hōsō Shirīzu* were merely a few thousand each. Despite the vast improvement of the system of distribution reported from several prefectures in recent years, the number of copies made available to each prefecture still seems far too small to reach the majority of ordinary members.

The fact that participation in locally organised seminars and meetings and subscription to party publications represent virtually the only regularised mode of contact and communication between the party and a peripheral member shows that the latter's contribution to official policy-making at the headquarters is extremely indirect and limited, if not entirely absent. Since the headquarters is under the virtual control of Diet members, it would be necessary for an ordinary member or members to affect the latter's thought and behaviour in order to influence the party policy-making process one way or another. The fact, however, that a Diet member does not depend primarily on the party organisation for his electoral success (which is his main concern) but rather on the supporters' association built specifically as his per-

---

[9]The 'policy for youth and women' was made Point 5 of the 'Objectives of the Party Activities' ratified by the 17th Party Conference of January 1966. See *Wagatō no kihonhōshin* (January 1966), pp. 64-86.

sonal electioneering machine, makes it difficult to bring effective pressure to bear on him through the agency of a formal party branch or prefectural federation. Pressure likely to affect his actions as a policy-maker may be much more effectively and directly applied through his supporters' association. This amounts to saying that it is much more sensible and logical for anybody interested in influencing the party's decisions to join a supporters' association or associations rather than the party. Hence the difficulties of drastically increasing the number of bona fide members and the resulting numerical discrepancy between the ten million associated with the supporters' associations on the one hand and the 1·9 million nominal and 50,000 dues-paying party members on the other hand.

The LDP was initially formed essentially as a conservative Diet members' group but has subsequently made heroic efforts to transform itself into a 'mass' party primarily with a view to avoiding the consequences of the drastic change in the employment pattern of the nation and its effects on the relative electoral performance of itself and the rival parties. By 1966 it seemed to have made impressive gains in its much publicised efforts to win new members. When carefully examined, however, the bulk of the 1·9 million or so members are purely nominal and the size of the effective membership still remains at about 50,000. Moreover, the policy-making power is narrowly concentrated in the hands of slightly more than 400 Diet members who constitute the inner ring of the party membership and monopolise all party offices at the headquarters. Both as an important source of future Diet members and as a link to connect the party with the voter some 8,500 local politicians surround this inner group. Then there are some 40,000 ordinary members, constituting an outer, or peripheral, ring and cultivating and feeding the voter support for the party at the unit level of public administration. The rest of the 1·9 million may be regarded as a reserve army of regular LDP voters and potential members, hardly distinguishable from the eleven million members of the supporters' associations or the comparable numbers associated with various organisations and groups defined as sympathetic to the party.

The distance between the inner ring, especially that part of it which consists of former high-ranking public servants, and the middle and outer rings may be measured in terms of occupational and educational background, as well as the completely one-sided distribution of decision-making power. Just as the two categories of former bureaucrats and local politicians have between them contributed a half of the LDP Diet members, farmers and white collar workers have accounted for a majority of local assembly members, followed by officials of trade associations or civic groups, retail or wholesale dealers, and so forth. Of those elected in the local elections of 1959, for example, farmers and company employees accounted respectively for 26 and 31 per cent of prefectural assembly members, 28 and 26 per cent of city assembly members, and 63 and 7 per cent of town and village assembly members. Retail and wholesale dealers contributed 4, 13, and 11 per cent respectively of these three categories of local assembly members.

If one may assume that the educational level of the LDP local assembly members is not higher than that of the Diet members recruited from among them, the proportion of university and college graduates among them cannot be higher than 60·6 per cent (as compared with 81·2 per cent of the Diet members), and that of those who finished only elementary school cannot be lower than 11·2 (as compared with 4·0 of the latter). One may likewise assume that the average educational level of the LDP members at the periphery is not significantly different from that of the population at large, and compare the overall figures of 5·2 per cent for university and college graduates and 63·0 per cent for those with no more than primary education with the two sets of corresponding figures given above. Even with a fairly large margin of possible error involved in applying the figures for the population at large to the local members of the LDP, the contrasts seem to be sufficiently sharp and obvious to make such comparisons meaningful. The distance between these figures is bound to perpetuate the present monopoly of party policy-making power by the headquarters and the parliamentary party, while the same factors will continue to ensure the generally superior position of the former public servants within the inner group, and will perpetuate the process of bureaucratisation.

4 Party Organisation

As an organisation, the LDP consists of a headquarters located in Tokyo and branches established at the level of basic administrative units (such as city, county, town, and village) and in various voluntary associations.[1] These two are the basic components of the party's formal structure, but in addition to them there has been created an auxiliary institution designed for the systematic training of party cadres and organisers, the Central Academy of Politics. In the present chapter an attempt will be made to describe in a frame of reference broadly concerned with policy-making the more prominent characteristics of the formal organisation and its individual components, with a view to defining their nature and role in party policy-making processes.

Party Headquarters

There are two particularly conspicuous aspects worth noting about the organisational framework of the LDP party headquarters. One is the apparently complete control of all official party organs and positions by members of the Diet. The other is the great multiplicity of party organs and the resulting fragmentation of the organisational structure.

The LDP Constitution requires only a few particular categories of the party positions to be filled exclusively by members of the Diet, such as those of the president, members of the audit board, most of the executive council, and the party discipline committee, the chairman of the election policy committee, and those in the organs for Diet activities. In practice, however, virtually every formal position has been constantly occupied by an incumbent Diet member. In August 1965, for example, none of the 314 principal party

[1]The constitution of the Liberal-Democratic Party, originally established on 15 November 1955 and most recently amended on 17 January 1964 (hereafter referred to as the LDP Constitution, 1955, 1964, etc.). The original text is available in *Kokkai nenkan: 1959* (Kokkai nenkan kankōkai), pp. 312-15, and the amended text in Jiyūminshutō, *Wagatō no kihonhōshin* (January 1964), pp. 96-120. An official English translation of the latter is available in Jiyūminshutō, *The Constitution of the Liberal Democratic Party: and Its Declaration, Basic Principles, Characteristics, Mission* (April 1964), pp. 9-35. The terms used in this book to refer to the party organs and officials are taken as a rule from this official translation.

officials, except for nine of the twenty advisers, was outside the Diet, and even these nine advisers had formerly been leading members of the Diet. Even where the eligibility of non-parliamentary members is specifically mentioned in the constitution (e.g. 'not more than three places on the Party Discipline Committee may be filled from outside the Diet') none has so far been actually appointed. For all practical purposes, therefore, the LDP headquarters may quite legitimately be said to be under the complete and exclusive control of the party's parliamentary contingent. The fact that a substantial proportion of its routine work is discharged by the non-parliamentary employees of the secretariat does not contradict such a generalisation so far as the centre of power and source of dominant influence in its activities is concerned.[2]

The second aspect of the structure of the headquarters which strikes an outsider as surprising is the degree of functional differentiation and the multiplication of organisational units. In mid-1966 there were about twenty of these at the headquarters. These may be classified for convenience roughly under four categories: the executive, the decision-making, the parliamentary, and other organs.

As defined in the constitution, the first of these categories comprises the offices of the president, vice-president, secretary-general, deputy secretaries-general, three bureaux, and four functional committees. On the face of it, this category does not sound particularly complex, involving, as it does, four types of organisation. A closer look reveals, however, that two of the functional committees embrace a fair number of sub-divisions. These are the Committee on Public Relations, which involves five bureaux, and the Committee on National Organisations which contains nine bureaux subdivided into seventeen departments (see Table 9).

Similarly, the decision-making organs are officially only three in number: the party conference, the Assembly of the Members of Both Houses of the Diet, and the executive council. For present purposes, however, the PARC must be included in this category, for it constitutes an essential part of the formal decision-making mechanism, as will be shown later. Whereas there is nothing complicated about the three first-mentioned organs, the PARC is the most complex multi-unit organ of the party. It consists of a Deliberation Commission, fifteen divisions and, as of November 1965, nearly fifty special investigation committees. Moreover, the divisions and the special committees together involve nearly one hundred sub-units specialising in particular fields of investigation or in specific policy issues.

The third and the fourth categories are fairly simple in composition. The former comprises merely the Assemblies of the Members of the two Houses and a few separate organs set up only in the House of Councillors, while the latter includes the committees on election policy and party discipline, the

[2]In December 1965 there were 225 non-parliamentary employees working at the LDP headquarters. See *Asahi nenkan: 1966*, p. 293.

audit board, and such miscellaneous organs as the advisers, the councillors, the resident organisers, and the *ad hoc* Organisation Research Council. Even here, however, there has been a tendency for the number of the *ad hoc* special organs to increase steadily, as suggested by the emergence in the last few years of the National Movement Headquarters, the Anti-Disaster Policy Head-quarters, the Public Relations Research Committee, etc.

It is against the background of these two very prominent characteristics of the general structure of the LDP headquarters that the individual organs and their functions may be meaningfully discussed in a policy-making frame of reference. Both are bound to limit and define the effective roles of such organs and thus give a special slant or flavour to the process of party policy-making.

The Policy Affairs Research Council

As mentioned above, the party conference, the Assembly of the Members of Both Houses of the Diet, and the executive council make up the formal system of policy-making in the party, while the PARC also plays an informal but indispensable part in it. Of these four particular organs, the first two are concerned primarily with rubber-stamping such general and abstract aims and principles of the party activity as are prepared and presented to them by the latter two organs and seldom, if ever, with specific policy matters or initiation of a concrete policy program. As a result, practically every important policy decision of the party is formally initiated and determined by the PARC or the executive council or by both together.

According to Article 40, Paragraph 2, of the LDP Constitution, it is necessary for any bills or policy plans to be examined and approved by the PARC in order to become official party policies. Once formally approved by that organ, they are passed on to the executive council for its final decision which can be overruled in theory (but never in practice) by either the party conference or the Assembly of the Members of Both Houses of the Diet. A bill which has passed the scrutiny of these two organs normally goes directly to the Diet Policy Committee and through it reaches the floor of the Diet, usually as a Cabinet-sponsored bill.

As mentioned earlier, the PARC, which plays a crucial role in the formal policy-making process of the LDP, is an extremely complex organ. Under the direction of a chairman and not more than five vice-chairmen, a deliberation commission and fifteen divisions operate as its permanent organisational components. In addition to them an indefinite number of 'Special Investigation Committees' are set up on an *ad hoc* basis to deal with specific policy issues that may arise from time to time. Ever since the first nine of such special committees were created within two weeks of the formation of the LDP in November 1955, their number has steadily increased until today it has reached nearly fifty, despite sporadic attempts made every few years to

TABLE 9

LDP HEADQUARTERS

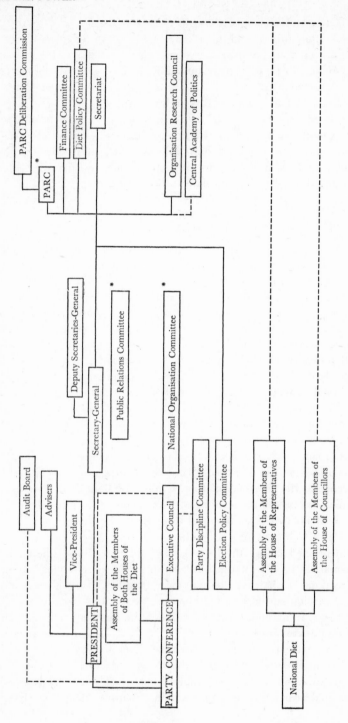

* See facing page.

PUBLIC RELATIONS COMMITTEE
— Education and Propaganda Bureau
  — Information Bureau — International Department
  — Publications Bureau
  — Party Organ Bureau
  — Cultural Affairs Bureau

PARC — PARC Deliberation Commission

(Divisions)
- Cabinet Affairs
- Local Administration
- National Defence
- Judicial Affairs
- Foreign Affairs
- Financial
- Educational Affairs
- Social Affairs
- Labour Affairs
- Agriculture & Forestry
- Fisheries
- Commerce & Industry
- Transportation
- Communications
- Construction

(Special Investigation Committees)
- Constitution
- Foreign Affairs
- Economic Affairs
- Education
- Election System
- Taxation System
- Basic Policy on Agriculture, Forestry & Fisheries
- Basic Policy on Medium & Small Enterprises
- Labour
- Social Security
- Road Administration
- Land Development
- Security
- Basic Problems in National Railway Administration
- Etc.

NATIONAL ORGANISATION COMMITTEE

(Bureaux)

— General Organisation
  (Departments)
  — General Affairs
  — Local Organisation
  — Civil Affairs

— Agriculture & Forestry Organisation
  — Agriculture & Forestry Organisation
  — Fishery Organisation

— Commerce & Industry
  — Medium & Small Enterprises Organisation
  — Commerce & Industry Organisation

— Labour
  — Industrial Labour
  — Government & Public Workers
  — Medium & Small Enterprise Workers

— Welfare
  — Public Health
  — Social Welfare
  — Social Security

— Youth
  — Youth
  — Student

— Women's
  — Women's Organisation
  — Women's Policy

— Public Speeches

— Education & Training

G

reduce it to a somewhat less unwieldy level by abolishing the relatively inactive ones. At the same time, the fifteen permanent divisions have also accelerated the tendency towards multiplication and fragmentation within the council by subdividing themselves into an increasing number of 'sub-committees' which today account for about thirty between them, or an average of two each.

According to the rules of the party, each Diet member affiliated with it must belong to at least one but not more than two PARC divisions at any one time. He may choose freely between the fifteen of the divisions, which correspond to the fifteen ministries of the national public services. The participation in the special investigation committees is entirely voluntary. Nor is there any limitation on the number of them one may belong to at the same time.[3]

Combined with the effects of monopolistic control of the formal organs of the headquarters by Diet members, the steady multiplication of these sub-units of the PARC has inevitably resulted in the ever wider and thinner spread of the limited number of the Diet members available to fill the increased number of party positions. In November 1965, for example, each of the 421 LDP-affiliated members of the Diet belonged concurrently to an average of 1·7 divisions and 6·1 special committees, that is nearly eight separate sub-units of the Council. In other words, every LDP Diet member was forced, in theory at any rate, to attend to at least eight different policy problems simultaneously, in addition to all the other kinds of party activity in which he might be called upon to participate as a member of the organs other than the PARC.

Increasing pressure exerted by interest groups, ministries and other government agencies has no doubt been responsible, at least partially, for the growth of this tendency. For every demand of an individual or group in the society to be satisfied by a public action of the government, it is necessary that it be translated either into a specific administrative measure explicitly authorised by a relevant existing law or into a legislative bill establishing a new law or amending an existing law. Under the present parliamentary cabinet system this means that it must be supported either by a section of the public service or by the ministerial party, for it is only the former which may authoritatively decide to satisfy such a demand within the limits of a relevant existing law, while it is the ministerial party alone that may have the specific demand introduced into and successfully passed by the Diet as a Cabinet-sponsored bill. Consequently, all kinds of demand for public decision are brought to these two possible sources of support by interest groups and even those which are initially taken to ministries are often referred to the party for additional support.

[3]Information on this particular aspect was provided by Mr Takakura Tadashi in an interview on 8 February 1966.

. Under such circumstances, the PARC and its subdivisions have inevitably become faithful mouthpieces of interest groups or particular ministries. Because of the enormous workload imposed on them and the hopelessly inadequate amount of time available to Diet members, it is patently impossible for them to formulate independent policy programs by themselves. The increasingly complex technicalities of policy-making in a modern and rapidly changing society only add to the difficulties facing PARC members in exercising their independent policy-making function.

Another factor which has no doubt contributed to the growth of very close relationships between each of the PARC subdivisions and particular ministries and sets of interest groups is the voluntary basis of the former's membership affiliation. According to the party constitution, only the chiefs and the deputy chiefs of the divisions have to be appointed by the chairman of the PARC (with the consent of the executive council), although in practice those of the special investigation committees are also appointed either by the executive council or the leaders' meeting. Other members of these sub-units are drawn on an entirely voluntary basis, the only restriction being that no member may join more than two divisions at any one time. This has resulted in each of them attracting only those members who are specially interested in a particular issue or category of issues because of pressures from their constituencies, interest groups, or sections of the public service. In this sense, it is most natural for each and every subdivision of the PARC to be closely and inseparably related to a particular ministry or ministries and sets of interest groups.

The record of the actual performance of the PARC, particularly its divisions, amply confirms the foregoing generalisations. To give only a few examples, in August 1957 the Transportation Division was no doubt echoing the demands of the nation's transportation industry and the Ministry of Transportation when it called for a ¥2,000 million government loan to Japan Air Lines, some ¥120,000 million investment in the improvement of the National Railways system, and the spending of ¥31,600 million for the improvement of the harbour facilities. Again, in August 1960 the Social Affairs Division finalised a new social insurance plan in accordance with the original plan presented by the Ministry of Welfare. The 'Road Improvement Plan' which the Construction Division decided to sponsor in September 1962 was merely the 1963 portion of the three-year plan previously prepared and announced by the Ministry of Construction. The list of similar examples could be enlarged almost indefinitely.

An important corollary of this dependence on the bureaucracy and preoccupation with economic or budgetary problems on the part of the PARC has been the exclusion from the deliberations of its subdivisions of issues of a more general political or ideological nature. Such a tendency has been in fact deplored by those party members who have been in a position to observe more closely and constantly than anybody else the manner in which the policy research organ actually functions. In May 1961, for example, a leading member of the newly established Party Organisation Research Council, Kuraishi Tadao, frankly admitted that the PARC was so busy considering budget drafts or bills to be introduced by the Cabinet that it was impossible for its members to pay much attention to more fundamental and general policy issues. Three years later the same criticisms were repeated by three former chairmen of the Council, Fukuda Takeo, Nakamura Umekichi, and Funada Naka. There is little evidence, moreover, that such criticisms have led so far to any effective steps to correct the situation. On the contrary, a progressive increase, rather than a decrease, of the elements thus criticised seems to be almost inevitable so long as Diet members continue to monopolise party positions, including those in the PARC, and the party is called on to deal with every conceivable demand of the ministries and other government bodies or interest groups.

According to the party constitution, decisions made by the divisions and the special investigation committees must be reviewed in the first instance by the PARC Deliberation Commission. Originally, the commission was to consist of the PARC chairman and vice-chairmen and, in addition, not more than twenty-five members specially appointed by the chairman. In November 1955 the commission was initially composed of twenty-six members, namely the chairman and ten vice-chairmen of the PARC and fifteen members specially appointed, twelve from the House of Representatives and three from the House of Councillors. However, the number of the last category of members quickly increased to twenty-five—the maximum permitted by the constitution—which made it virtually impossible for the group to deal effectively and promptly with the already enormous and steadily growing number of specific policy issues submitted to it by the PARC's working sub-units. Consequently, by early 1959 it became customary to have the meetings of the PARC vice-chairmen largely supersede it as a regular agency to review the decisions of the divisions and the special committees. This was in order to speed up the process and avoid the development of sharp divisions of opinion which would have inevitably arisen in the larger body. In the summer of 1961, however, a meeting of the PARC chairman and vice-chairmen decided to reduce the number of the specially appointed members to about fifteen. An amendment to the party constitution in January 1964 formally reduced it to 'not more than twenty', and today it consists of about a dozen members appointed in addition to the PARC chairman and half a dozen vice-chairmen.

Whereas, as already mentioned, the members of the divisions and the special investigation committees are recruited on a voluntary basis, both the vice-chairmen and the members of the deliberation commission are appointed formally by the PARC chairman with the consent of the executive council.

In practice they are appointed by the executive council either independently or jointly with the leaders' meeting. Just as the free choice open to the members regarding their affiliation with the divisions and special committees has inevitably turned them into faithful collaborators and agents of particular sections of the bureaucracy and of interest groups, the selection and appointment of the vice-chairmen and the members of the deliberation commission by a higher party organ has introduced elements of factionalism in their composition. In the case of vice-chairmen, for example, until the summer of 1963, it was a well-established practice to have each of the eight or so major factions represented by one vice-chairman, with an additional few drawn from the membership of the House of Councillors. In accordance with the interim report of the Party Organisation Research Council and under strong pressure from its chairman and leader of the party modernisation movement, Miki Takeo, in July 1963 the number of the PARC vice-chairmen was boldly reduced to four, and the considerations of inter-factional balance have been given up at least temporarily.

On the other hand, in the case of members of the deliberation commission, the reduction of their number to about twelve has evidently failed to affect the principle of inter-factional balance. In fact, just as the ten vice-chairmen once virtually replaced the unwieldy 36-man commission before the latter was reduced to a somewhat more manageable size in 1961, the fifteen commission members, particularly the twelve of them recruited from the House of Representatives, have now been substituted for the vice-chairmen as the inter-factional co-ordinators in the policy-making mechanism of the party.

The Executive Council

All policy recommendations initiated by a division or a special investigation committee of the PARC on behalf of particular sections of the bureaucracy or interest groups, and then approved by the PARC Deliberation Commission acting on behalf of the intra-party factions, finally reach the executive council to be made official party decisions. As pointed out earlier, the verdicts given by the executive council are officially final so far as the party is concerned, for the actual functions of the two higher organs of party decision-making, the Party Conference and the Assembly of the Members of Both Houses of the Diet, are entirely nominal. A draft bill approved by the executive council, for example, will be passed on directly to the Diet policy committee of the party. It will then be introduced into the Diet (normally as a Cabinet-sponsored bill) unless objections are raised by the bureaucracy (represented formally by the Cabinet but in fact by the meetings of the permanent vice-ministers).[4]

[4]The meetings of the Cabinet have traditionally been nominal for the simple reason that its members, i.e. the ministers, are too busy signing documents. Every draft bill is

The principles which govern the nomination of the executive council members are rather peculiar. There are three kinds of member involved: those elected from MHRs, those elected from MHCs, and those appointed by the party president. The original constitution of 1955 mentioned only the categories and did not specify the numbers, but the three strong men of Hatoyama's time, Miki Bukichi (then member of the Presidential Proxy Committee), Kishi Nobusuke (the secretary-general), and Kōno Ichirō (the Minister of Agriculture and Forestry), decided apparently arbitrarily on 17 November 1955 to have thirty elected from the MHRs and ten from the MHCs so that the former Liberals and the Democrats might each contribute twenty. By early 1957 the distinction between the elements formerly associated with the two parties became a much less significant factor and the present pattern of its composition began to appear. Under this new pattern ten of the forty members were appointed by the president, as required by the party constitution, twenty were elected from among the MHRs on a regional basis, and the remaining ten were elected from among the MHCs. Except for the contribution of the postwar institution, the House of Councillors, in place of the prewar House of Peers, this was of course an exact replica of the composition of the Seiyūkai's Consultative Council of December 1903. Although the number of its members was reduced to thirty in practice in July 1960 and officially in the form of a constitutional amendment in January of the following year, the basic principles underlying their nomination have not changed at all. Eight are appointed by the president, fifteen elected on a regional basis in proportion to the number of MHRs representing each of the nine regions, and seven are elected from the MHCs.

Superficially, the selection of at least half of the executive council members seems to be governed by the old principle of regional representation, or rather geographical factionalism, sharply different from both the voluntarism which operates in the case of the working sub-units of the PARC and the kind of factionalism which determines the composition of its deliberation commission. Such an impression, however, does not conform to reality, for regionalism in this instance is entirely nominal. It is true that the fifteen members are elected by and from the MHRs returned from the nine regions of Hokkaidō, Tōhoku, Kantō, Horuriku-shin'etsu, Tōkai, Kinki, Chūgoku, Shikoku, and Kyūshū, but it is equally true that they never act as regional representatives when voting on specific policy issues in the executive council. They neither consult with the other MHRs from the same regions before making a decision nor report to them the results of their actions taken in the council. From the point of view of effectiveness, the principle of regional

---

thoroughly examined, however, by the vice-minister's conferences before it is allowed to reach the floor of the Diet. The information relevant to this aspect was provided by Mr Miyazaki Yoshimasa, editorial writer of the *Yomiuri*, on 12 January 1966. See also Misawa Shigeo, 'Seisakukettei katei no gaikan', *Gendai nihon no seitō to kanryō* (*Nihon seijigakkai nempō 1967*) (Iwanami shoten, 1967), pp. 23-4.

representation is nothing but a dead carry-over from the past and does not affect the behaviour of this organ in any significant way.

Much more real in influencing the nomination of its members have been, in fact, the same pervasive elements of non-geographical factionalism and the pressure of interest groups, just as was the case with the subdivisions of the PARC. It has been and will be inconceivable for any of the factions to be left without at least one representative of its own participating in the executive council. For example, in August 1964 the Satō faction contributed six of its members, followed by the Ōno faction with five, the Ikeda, Miki, Kawashima, Kōno, and Ishii factions with three each, and the Fukuda and Fujiyama factions one each respectively. In June 1965 the distribution was as follows: the Satō and Ikeda factions and independents—4, the Ōno, Miki, Kōno, Fujiyama, and Ishii factions—3, and the Kawashima and Fukuda factions—1. In this respect the Executive Council may be said to function as something of an enlarged duplicate of the PARC Deliberation Commission.

At the same time, the executive council has been constantly subjected to the pressures of interest groups not only from outside but also from within. As the vice-president of the party, Kawashima Shōjirō, once deplored, at least some of its members habitually speak on behalf of a particular interest group or groups.[5] When a conflict of opinion develops between a PARC division or special committee (closely linked to an interest group or a ministry), and the deliberation commission (which tends to be under factional pressure but is relatively impervious to interest group pressures), the executive council is usually found to stand with the former and to overrule the latter's decision in favour of the interest group or the ministry concerned. It should be noted in this connection that any party member may speak before the executive council, though only its proper members have the right to vote, a situation which cannot but tempt many members harassed by lobbyists to take the matter directly to this body instead of leaving it to the discretion of the PARC Deliberation Commission.[6]

As previously pointed out, a decision made by the executive council is binding to every party member as an official decision of the party (at least in theory) and is usually passed on to the Diet policy committee to be introduced in the Diet as a bill. In practice, however, an official party decision thus made often gets shelved and kept from prompt legislative action in the Diet or administrative action by the Cabinet. A typical example is the case involving the proposed change in the status of the defence agency to ministry. It was in June 1963 that an official party decision was made by the executive

[5]See 'Seitō kindaika e no michi' (8), *Asahi*, 9 August 1964.
[6]The writer was furnished with useful information and insights on this aspect by Mr Nakajima Kiyonari of the Political Affairs Section of the *Asahi Shimbun* in an interview on 20 January 1966. It was pointed out, however, by a PARC research staff member, Mr Takakura Tadashi, that except in regard to matters relating to the preparation of a draft budget, the executive council seldom overrules a policy recommended by the PARC Deliberation Commission (interview on 8 February 1966).

council to have a bill amending the defence agency organisation and the Self-defence Forces laws in order to elevate the agency to the status of a regular ministry introduced in the next ordinary Diet session. Despite strong pressure applied by the Defence Division of the PARC and the defence agency itself, however, the Cabinet successfully postponed indefinitely the introduction of the bill into the Diet because of the fear that the fierce opposition from the Socialists and other opposition parties would endanger other important parts of its legislative program. The Cabinet persisted in this negative attitude even after a meeting of vice-ministers gave its final approval in March 1964 to the draft bill, as advised by the Cabinet Legislative Bureau, and the revised text was accepted by the LDP PARC and the defence agency. In the subsequent Diets, numbers 47 to 50, no action was taken by the Cabinet. The renewed efforts of the defence division during the 51st Diet of 1966 to have the bill promptly introduced have so far failed to change the Cabinet attitude.

This kind of situation arises mainly because of the peculiar role of the Cabinet as, on the one hand, the sponsor of an overwhelming majority of bills introduced in the Diet by the ministerial party and, on the other, as the formal representative of both the bureaucracy and the party. A related factor contributing to the lack of finality in the executive council decisions is the intervention of a quasi-official decision-making organ called the 'leaders' meeting'.

The Cabinet

According to the Diet Law and the rules of each House, a Diet member affiliated with the ministerial party has as much right to present a bill on his own initiative as does the Cabinet or a Diet member who belongs to an opposition party. Provided that he may secure the support of twenty or more members (fifty or more, if the bill relates to a budget) in the House of Representatives or ten or more (twenty or more, if the bill relates to a budget) in the House of Councillors, any member of the Diet may sponsor and present a bill on his own initiative. In fact, individual members of the ministerial party were responsible for half of the bills introduced by the Liberal Party during the last Diet session convened by the Yoshida Cabinet on 30 November 1954 and one-third or more of those introduced in the 8th (July 1950), 23rd (November-December 1955), and 25th (November-December 1956) sessions. There has, however, been a conspicuous and consistent tendency for Cabinet-sponsored bills to predominate among those introduced on behalf of the ministerial parties. Consequently a bill sponsored by an individual member has come to mean a bill originating in an opposition party. From the 40th (December 1961-May 1962) to the 50th (October 1965-December 1965) sessions, for example, 90 per cent of the bills introduced by the LDP (and 92 per cent of those which were successfully passed) were sponsored by

Cabinet. On the other hand, three-quarters of the member-sponsored bills introduced during the same period originated in the opposition parties. It has thus become an established rule (in practice, if not in theory) of the legislative process under the present parliamentary cabinet system for an important bill supported by the ministerial party to be officially endorsed and sponsored by the Cabinet, instead of individual members, especially if it must be passed against strong opposition from the other parties.

If the Cabinet officially represented only the ministerial party (from which all its members are drawn), it would be rather difficult for it to avoid prompt legislative or administrative action on decisions made by the executive council on behalf of the party. Constitutionally, however, the Cabinet is a formal institution entirely separate and independent from the party. The Cabinet represents the executive power, as opposed to the legislative power exercised by the Diet and therefore shared by the party. This independent constitutional status of the Cabinet makes it very possible for the 20-man body to refuse to act as dictated by the party if the prospective action is likely to lead to bitter opposition from the other parties and jeopardise the implementation of other priority measures in its policy program. A case in point was the proposed elevation of the defence agency's institutional status.

The Leaders' Meeting

The leaders' meeting is defined in the LDP Constitution merely as an *ad hoc* group consisting of the heads of various party organs and other members specially nominated by the president, the function of which is to ensure co-ordination and co-operation between them. Until the most recent revision of the LDP Constitution in January 1964 it had been an informal organ (like the Government-Party Liaison Meeting of late 1958 and its successor, the Senior Members' Meeting), and had consisted initially of six and subsequently seven particular party officials. Hence it was popularly called the 'Six Leaders' Meeting' or the 'Seven Leaders' Meeting'.[7]

Despite the *ad hoc* basis on which it had long operated, the leaders' meeting and its predecessors had frequently made very important decisions with no apparent delegation of power on the part of the executive council. It was the Six Leaders' Meeting, for example, that decided in September 1957 to

[7]The Six Leaders' Meeting consisted of the secretary-general, and the chairmen of the executive council, the PARC, and the committees on Diet policy, national organisation, and party discipline (see *Asahi*, 23 December 1958). The chairman of the newly-formed public relations committee was included in January 1959 to make it a Seven Leaders' Meeting and as such it continued until July 1960 when it was abolished by a decision of the executive council. In December of the same year, however, it was revived as a somewhat larger body with the vice-president, deputy secretaries-general, the secretary-general of the House of Councillors, LDP, etc., added to the above-mentioned seven and, finally, it was accorded a formal status of co-ordinating organ by the amendment of the constitution in January 1964. See ibid., 30 January 1959, 22 July, and 13 December 1960. For the memberships of the earlier Government-Party Liaison Meeting and the Senior Members' Meeting, see ibid., 18 July 1958 and 28 January 1959.

have the Anti-Prostitution Law enforced in its entirety after April 1958; in October 1957 it decided to have all future bills which might affect the budget presented exclusively under Cabinet sponsorship, instead of by individual members; in December 1957 it allowed four LDP Diet members to attend the Second Afro-Asian Peoples' Solidarity Conference in Cairo; in July 1958 it determined to reform administrative organisation; in October 1958 it agreed to prevent increases of private railway and bus fares. Similarly, it was the Seven Leaders' Meeting which decided in April 1959 to have the construction of additional underground railways started on two specified routes in 1960; again in September 1959 it allowed shipping concerns to suspend temporarily the payment of a significant portion of interest on loans extended by the Development Bank. The enlarged leaders' meeting continued to play such a decision-making role after it was made a formal party organ in January 1964, often causing confusion in and interference with the official party policy-making processes represented by the chain of the PARC sub-units, the deliberation commission and the executive council.

Serious conflicts can develop between the Cabinet and the executive council or, what is the same thing, between the dominant and dissident factions, as the constitutional status and role of the former described above suggest. It is, in fact, by the very possibility of such conflicts that the independent policy-making functions of the leaders' meeting are justified and encouraged, whatever elements of irregularity this may introduce to interfere with the formal party policy-making mechanism.

As previously mentioned, both the composition and policy decisions of the PARC and the executive council are determined largely by considerations of the inter-factional balance coupled with pressures from interest groups and the bureaucracy. To the extent that they reflect the inter-factional balance these decisions are products of compromise between the dominant faction or factions in control of the presidency and other key party positions, and the Cabinet and the dissident factions excluded from these posts. Such compromise frequently involves concessions on the part of the former group which it may find to be unacceptable for one reason or another. To the extent that they result from the pressures of particular interest groups and sections of the public service they may cause dissatisfaction among other interest groups and other sections of the bureaucracy which are adversely affected by the decisions concerned. This is invariably the case with practically every decision relating to budgetary appropriations.

The battles fought annually between the deflationist Ministry of Finance and every other ministry struggling to get as great a share of the budget as possible are well known. In certain cases almost as serious conflicts may develop between the ministries of the latter kind themselves, as happened over the proposed reduction of the enterprise tax between the Ministry of International Trade and Industry and the Autonomy Agency in 1957 and 1958.

Sometimes conflicts arise between an interest group and a ministry, as was the legendary case of the long-drawn battles fought between the Japan Medical Association and the Ministry of Welfare over the amounts of medical fees, or the less known fights between the National Federation of Agricultural Co-operative Unions and the Ministry of Agriculture and Forestry over the legislation of the Agriculture Basic Law. The examples of conflicts between interest groups are so many that they hardly deserve illustration. From the point of view of the dominant factions in control of the highest party positions, a decision of the executive council, of which only eight members are appointed by the president (while fifteen are nominated on a regional basis and seven elected from among MHCs), is not always acceptable and, for that reason, it is necessary to have a higher organ which is at the same time capable of overriding it and fully responsive to the interests of the dominant factions. In contrast to the composition of the executive council, the leaders' meeting, as it is customarily constituted, consists of up to eleven members of whom four are nominated by the president with the consent of the executive council and three are appointed by the secretary-general, who is in turn appointed by the president and is regarded as the latter's closest collaborator in the party. In other words, nearly two-thirds of its regular members are at least potentially pro-president and, therefore, any executive council decision filtered through its examination can be considered as at least innocuous, if not positively favourable to the interests of the dominant factions.

Whenever a conflict arises between two or more interest groups, an interest group and a ministry, or between two or more ministries, it is almost inevitably transferred to the party. This often takes the form of a conflict between the PARC divisions and special committees and will also involve the executive council which is, as already pointed out, as sensitive to the pressures of external groups as to those arising from intra-party factionalism. Under such circumstances whatever decision the executive council may make on an issue is bound to be controversial and to threaten party unity and the public image of the party. This makes it essential from the point of view of the dominant factions to have an independent organ higher in status than the executive council which can intervene to resolve disputes on the basis of concern for party unity and the maintenance of the *status quo*, thus assuring their own continued hegemony.

Party President

Underlying the foregoing discussion of the *raison d'être* and role of the leaders' meeting was the assumption that the president of the ministerial party, who is the highest party official, cannot be expected to play such a watch-dog role. As far as the constitutional powers of the party president are concerned, there seems in fact to be little need for the leaders' meeting to act on behalf of the top party leadership. The president is empowered to 'take the supreme responsibility' for the party and to 'represent and control' it, which should mean that he has the power to reject or override whatever executive council decisions he may regard, for his own reasons, as undesirable. Furthermore, there is nothing in theory to prevent him from initiating a particular policy and having it accepted according to his wishes either by the PARC or the executive council, whereby it will be declared an official party decision. In short, he has the constitutional power to become the most important, if not the only, actor in the party policy-making process. In reality, however, his powers are much more limited and conditional and there are good reasons for his finding it difficult to assert strong leadership and necessary to have a supplementary organ, such as the leaders' meeting, to make up for the limitations of his personal leadership.

It is unlikely, on the one hand, that a particular policy decision will be made by the executive council or that a decision already made will be acted upon against the president's strong objections, and a policy fully supported by him is likely to be made the official party line and carried out. It is after all the president who appoints the PARC chairman, who in turn appoints both its vice-chairmen and the members of the deliberation commission, and every official party decision must be first approved by these organs before it gets to the executive council. On the other hand, however, it appears that he does not in practice frequently exercise this power of veto nor does he positively identify himself with a particular policy in the face of opposition from a substantial section of the party or public opinion. There are at least two interrelated factors which inhibit him from aggressively asserting and exercising his full constitutional powers. One is the method of his election and the term of his office, and the other is the effects of intra-party factionalism.

According to the special rules governing the election of the LDP president, he must be elected by secret ballot at the party conference. Each Diet member affiliated with the party and one delegate from each prefectural federation of the party branches has one vote, but only members of the Diet are eligible to stand as candidates. If any of the candidates succeeds in winning a simple majority of valid votes cast in the first contest, he is automatically nominated president for a term of two years. If, on the other hand, no candidate succeeds in doing so, the two who win the highest scores of votes compete between them for a second time, and whoever wins a majority in the second trial is nominated.

The old principle of electing the party president by ballot at a party conference, which was adopted in the revised Seiyūkai Constitution of 1927, has now become not merely an abstract principle but the actual practice of the LDP. Up to the end of 1966 two or more candidates have contested the post at the party conferences of December 1956, January 1959, July 1960, and July 1964. Each of these occasions, however, has been characterised by intense inter-factional strife, allegedly accompanied by the spending of large amounts of money by each faction to buy uncommitted votes. The record of past performance suggests strongly that cut-throat competition between the factions is unavoidable, unless all but one of them can be persuaded to refrain from running a candidate in the contests, as happened at the party conferences of April 1956, March 1957, and July 1962. It also suggests that, given the pattern of membership distribution between the ten or so factions in recent years, it is essential for any one of them to secure the support of at least a few other factions in order to control a majority of votes. In the middle of 1966 a majority meant more than half of the 282 MHRs, 139 MHCs, and 46 delegates from the prefectural federations, in other words 234 votes. At the time each of the two largest factions led by Satō and Maeo had each forty-five adherents in the House of Representatives, followed by the Miki (31), Nakasone (30), and Fukuda (24) factions. In the House of Councillors the numerical strength of each faction following the election of July 1965 was Satō—52, Maeo—15, Kōno—14, Fujiyama—11, and Miki— 10. This would mean that in order to control a majority of votes at a presidential election even the largest Satō faction would need to gain the support of at least three major rival factions, or two of them reinforced by more than two-thirds of the prefectural federation delegates.

Because an incumbent president or a presidential aspirant obviously needs to depend upon the goodwill and co-operation of at least a few factions other than his own, he will inevitably avoid whatever course of action might threaten to estrange them. Furthermore, it is in the nature of factionalism that whether a particular faction will co-operate or continue to co-operate with another faction is not determined solely by genuine disagreement over specific policy issues but, more importantly and frequently, by tactical considerations of whether such co-operation will benefit it or not. Since most of the major factions have among their own leaders either the incumbent president or an aspirant for the presidential post, they are concerned most immediately with whether or not co-operation with or opposition to another faction will make it easier or harder for them to retain or capture the desired post.

The presidential position is made even more susceptible to the influences of factionalism because, according to the constitution, the term of his office is only two years. This is indeed twice as long as the term for other party offices but obviously too short to insure stable and aggressive leadership. Two years after Kishi Nobusuke had been forced to resign both the party presidency and premiership under the pressure of intra-party factionalism as well as opposition from the other parties and public opinion, he reminisced that a president spends his first year in office healing the wounds left by the bitter inter-factional competition at the last presidential election, and his

second year preparing for his re-election at the forthcoming party conference.[8]
Thus he is left with little time to think seriously about general policy problems, much less to cope with controversial issues at the risk of providing the
rival factions with an excuse, if not sound reason, to oppose his leadership
and obstruct his re-election. Under such circumstances it is inevitable that
an organ like the leaders' meeting should be called into being to fill the
vacuum of leadership and safeguard the interests of the dominant factions
in the policy-making process. Without such leadership it would be governed,
as we have seen, almost entirely by the logic of inter-factional balance and
interest group politics.

Local Organisation

As mentioned at the beginning of this chapter, the organisation of the LDP
consists not only of the headquarters but also of local branches. These
branches are established in counties, cities, wards of metropolitan and major
city areas, towns, villages, or any other unit areas or unit groups, and are
united into prefectural federations. In the organisational framework of the
headquarters they come under the jurisdiction of the General Organisation
Bureau of the National Organisation Committee.

Following the unification of the Liberals and the Democrats and the formation of the LDP, one of the most urgent tasks facing the new party was
promptly to expand and consolidate its national organisation. It was hoped,
rather too optimistically it seems from hindsight, that a rapid increase in the
membership through the establishment of branches at the city, county, town,
and village levels would automatically make it possible for it not only to cope
with the competition from the opposition parties in election campaigns but
also to rely on membership dues for a substantial part of its regular expenses.
With such a view the party headquarters proceeded to have prefectural
federations of party branches formed in eighteen prefectures by the end of
1955 and in practically all remaining prefectures by early 1956. Characteristically, the formation of the prefectural federations preceded that of unit
branches at the lower levels, in conformity with the traditional centrifugal
pattern of the flow of influence in the society.

By the middle of 1958 unit branches had been established in about 2,500
cities, towns, and villages (about 60 per cent of all these basic units of public
administration) and by early 1964 the actual number of such branches had
increased to nearly 3,000 or over 88 per cent of about 3,400 cities, towns,
and villages then in existence. At the prefectural level these come under the
forty-six prefectural federations, each of which has an organisational structure
closely resembling the headquarters, at least superficially. Practically every
federation has, for example, such standard organs as a president, secretaries,

[8]Kishi Nobusuke, *Jikyoku shokan: Naze tōkakai wo kaisan shita ka* (KSK Report,
116) (20 November 1962), p. 52.

an executive council, a policy affairs research council, committees on organisation, election policy, etc., divisions on public relations, cultural, youth and women's affairs, and advisers or councillors. In January 1960 the establishment of seven specific divisions in each prefectural federation, dealing with the organisational problems associated with different sectors of voters, became compulsory in accordance with the spirit of the organisational program adopted by the 7th Party Conference. In May 1961, the Committee on National Organisation decided to have a general secretary appointed by each federation as a full-time party official paid directly by the headquarters, as a further step towards standardisation of their organisational framework.

Despite the superficial impression conveyed by the foregoing description that LDP local branches are both ubiquitous and pervasive in their influence, as well as highly sophisticated organisationally, they have certain characteristics which considerably reduce their effectiveness in the party's organisational development and in its overall policy-making process. Such characteristics derive largely from their dependence upon the parliamentary party, the effects of factionalism and organisational dualism in the input-output feedback mechanism at the grass-roots, all of which are closely interrelated.

In terms of their leadership composition, it should first be noted that over 80 per cent of the presidents of the prefectural federations of party branches have nearly always been incumbent members of the National Diet and at least a quarter of the remaining 20 per cent have been former Diet members. Furthermore, an overwhelming majority of the rest of their officials are, as a rule, local politicians, mainly members of the prefectural assemblies. In one rather extreme case (Kanagawa Prefectural Federation in 1959), there were 82 officials, some of whom held two positions concurrently, of whom 10 were incumbent and 9 former Diet members (this included both the president and vice-president), 43 were members of the prefectural assemblies, 7 of city assemblies and 1 of a town assembly. In other words, 23 per cent were either incumbent or former Diet members, 52 per cent were prefectural assembly members, and 9 per cent were other local politicians. Thus a total of 84 per cent were professional politicians. This means that the prefectural federation is led by Diet members who are in turn assisted by party-affiliated local politicians, particularly prefectural assembly members.

The predominance of national and local politicians in the composition of the leadership groups in the prefectural federations naturally inclines them to be preoccupied with the one paramount concern of politicians—competition and victory in elections. This particular preoccupation is what, in fact, makes it inevitable for the factional divisions in the parliamentary party to permeate the behaviour of local branches. At the same time, it leads to the growth of organisational dualism at the base of the party structure and accounts for the peculiarly intimate and reciprocal relationships which emerge between Diet members and groups of local politicians. This is because

a Diet member needs to secure the co-operation of the influential residents
of his constituency in order to cultivate and maintain his bailiwick. He does so
in part by using the local politician's familiarity with the voters to his
advantage. Local politicians on the other hand are anxious to use the Diet
member's patronage and prestige to affect the results of local elections in
their favour. In order, however, to explain the aspects of factionalism and
dual organisational structure, it is necessary to refer also to the influence of
the present electoral system.

Under the present House of Representatives electoral system, each constituency returns three, four, or five MHRs, while the prefectural constituency
system for the House of Councillors returns a minimum of two and a maximum of eight MHCs from each constituency. It is inevitable under such a
system that a major party such as the LDP and the Japan Socialist Party
should run more than one candidate in each constituency in order to win a
majority of seats in the Diet. As it is logically impossible for a single prefectural federation to support and help, with complete impartiality, two or more
mutually competing candidates, it must necessarily work for a particular
candidate and against the rest. Furthermore, practically every LDP candidate
in recent years has run with the financial as well as moral support of a particular faction, a tendency which grows in proportion to the cost of electioneering. This means that a given prefectural federation cannot help being
identified with a particular candidate and also, through the support it gives
him, with a particular faction in the parliamentary party. This in turn makes
it necessary for those candidates who are excluded from its official support
to depend for funds and moral backing on a different faction, often opposed
to the prefectural federation, and to create an organisation separate from it.
The latter is the so-called supporters' association, which has generally proved
much more effective and reliable as a vote-getting device from the candidate's
point of view than the formal organ of the party.

The battles between two or more candidates begin as a rule over the question of who should be formally endorsed by the election policy committee of
the headquarters as an official LDP candidate entitled to the party's full
support and assistance. In practice the election committee (which is headed
by the president of the party in accordance with constitutional requirements
and consists by tradition of all faction leaders) instructs the prefectural
federations to submit to it by a specified date a list of candidates they would
recommend. It then proceeds to determine on the basis of such recommendations the final roll of party-endorsed candidates. The committee invariably
accords preference to incumbent members and limits the number of officially
endorsed candidates to not more than the total number of members to be
returned by each constituency. It usually proves impossible, however, for a
federation to present to the committee a unified list of recommended candidates which satisfies all the potential candidates and their factional supporters.

As a result, squabbles usually develop, first within the prefectural federations and then, through factional linkages, in the election policy committee at the headquarters.

In the election of 1958, for example, at least four federations had failed to present their recommendations as late as seven weeks after the due date, in each case because of factional divisions of opinion among their leaders. The Nagasaki and the Hiroshima prefectural federations managed to submit recommendations in time, but two separate lists were received from each of them, one authorised by a majority and the other by a minority group of their leaders. On the occasion of the November 1960 House of Representatives election Ōno Bamboku's influence and obstinacy were given as the reason for the endorsement of at least five candidates supported by his faction despite the fact that they had failed to win official recommendations from their prefectural federations. Kōno Ichirō was reported to have done the same for at least four unrecommended candidates. These examples could be multiplied many times.

Apart from their role in electioneering and factional conflict, the local branches and the prefectural federations engage in various activities in support of a policy program determined by the headquarters. For example, in relation to the Security Pact revision issue a Headquarters for the Revision of the Security Pact was established in each federation towards the end of 1959 and early 1960; in the spring of 1960 a series of regional meetings of prefectural federation general secretaries was held to strengthen their organisation and propaganda; finally, in June 1960, one of these meetings adopted a resolution calling for the earliest possible ratification of the revision. A more recent experience was in 1965, in connection with another controversial diplomatic issue, the ratification of the Japan-South Korea treaty. In September of that year organised campaigns by the prefectural federations supporting the government's efforts to have the treaty speedily ratified by the Diet began to be discussed in the *Soshiki Jōhō*. For example, a Kinki regional meeting of resident organisers heard reports about seminars sponsored by some other prefectural federations to inform local politicians of the issue and about relevant resolutions introduced into various local assemblies. On 1 October a big rally was held in Tokyo with about 3,000 participants representing some 600 organisations in order to launch an organisation specifically designed to promote ratification of the treaty. The role played by the prefectural federations in organising the local delegations to this rally was no doubt very substantial.

As a general proposition, however, the local branches and prefectural federations have played only a subordinate role in the party policy-making process and indeed have often been entirely passive. If the headquarters has frequently ignored or reversed the recommendations for candidates presented by the prefectural federations, it has seldom even invited them to contribute

H

their own original ideas or plans on policy matters. In this respect the flow of influence seems to have been almost entirely downward, from the headquarters to the prefectural federations and, where necessary, to the nearly 3,000 unit branches.

Such an impression is strengthened by a review of the 'Central Special Lectures' held in September 1960 for the education of prefectural assembly members, the conferences of the prefectural federation policy affairs research council chairmen, the training courses offered by the Central Academy of Politics, and meetings of various descriptions which have been organised at the local level in recent years. After examining the actual activities of the local branches and the prefectural federations, it is hard to escape the conclusion that their original contributions to the making of official party policy have been negligible. Decisions have been made by the headquarters and handed down to the prefectural federations for support, propagation, and implementation. Except to the extent that they may have been used by local interest groups as convenient linkages through which to funnel their particular demands into the channels of party policy-making, they seem to have been treated by the headquarters with little respect or attention.[9]

The Movement for the 'Modernisation' of Party Organisation

The organisation and behaviour of the LDP headquarters and branches have met increasing criticisms within the party itself in recent years. The experience of the anti-Security Treaty riots of 1960 and the narrowing electoral gap between the LDP and the opposition parties, rather than theoretical concern about the rationale or logic of the decision-making process, have probably been the most important reasons for the growth of a reformist movement, which has been associated since January 1961 with the newly formed Party Organisation Research Council. An overall reorganisation of the party structure seriously affecting the policy-making mechanism has been proposed and may some day be realised if it encounters more favourable circumstances than hitherto.

Behind the establishment of the Party Organisation Research Council in January 1961 was doubtless the fear that existing party organisation and behaviour was inadequate to meet changing needs, as shown by the increasing competitive power of the opposition parties. Such feelings have been subsequently expressed very clearly and forcefully by the leaders of the Council and of the modernisation movement it represents. Kuraishi Tadao, then chairman of the Council, bluntly stated in early 1962:

I say to anybody, whether in the party or outside, that the Liberal Democratic Party hardly deserves to be called a political party . . . We have been fortunate

[9]The demands of local interest groups may go directly to the ministries or the subdivisions of the LDP PARC, but also via local branches, prefectural federations, and the National Organisation Committee of the headquarters.

so far in that the Socialists have made mistakes from time to time to save us from what should have been a catastrophe. If they should learn to stand on their own feet again and begin seriously to think about organisational problems, then I have no illusion but that after a couple more elections we would lose to them even under the present election system . . . .[10]

Precisely the same view was expressed and developed by Ishida Hirohide, then chairman of one of the five sub-committees established in the Council, when he wrote a famous article in the *Chūōkōron* about a year later.[11] Summarising the problems confronting the LDP as those of intra-party factionalism, political funds, the election system, and party organisation, he warned that a projection of the trends observed in the electoral performance of the LDP and the opposition parties since 1952 would suggest that by 1970 the former would be overtaken by the latter in their respective shares of votes. In other words, the proportion of LDP voters would continue to run parallel to the decreasing percentage of the population engaged in primary industries, whereas the percentage voting for the opposition parties, particularly the Socialists, would increase in parallel to the rising proportion of those employed in secondary industries and of organised labour.

As soon as it was established the Party Organisation Research Council began to deal energetically with three broad problem areas, namely party finance, organisation, and public relations. By September 1962, when Miki Takeo was appointed chairman and gave it the appearance of evangelical dedication, it had suggested the creation of a finance committee, reorganisation of the executive council, establishment of a new policy research department to study developments in the opposition parties, appointment of resident organisers, and expansion of party publications. In November 1962, five sub-committees were established, in July 1963 an interim report of their findings was submitted to President Ikeda, and a final report was presented about three months later.

Of the five sub-committees the one on the party organisation dealt fully (and another on solidarity, partially) with the kind of organisational problems considered in the present chapter. According to the recommendations of the former, emphasis must be shifted from the parliamentary party to the national organisation, in other words from the headquarters to the local branches, the elements of leadership must be strengthened both at the national and the local levels, the practice of delegation and representation should be made more systematic, and both the geographical and occupational unit groups should be more effectively organised.

Apart from such general recommendations, a series of specific changes in particular party organs and their functions were also proposed, including some which would importantly affect the formal policy-making mechanism

[10]Kuraishi Tadao, *Jimintō tōfū sasshin ron* (KSK Report, 76) (12 February 1962), p. 3.
[11]Ishida Hirohide, 'Hoshuseitō no bijon', *Chūōkōron*, 903 (January 1963), pp. 83-97.

of the party. In relation to the headquarters, they involved the posts and functions of the presidency, the party conference, the executive council, and the PARC. Concerning local organisation, they implied a much tighter and more organic relationship between the local branches and the headquarters, and the adjustment of relations between formal branches and the supporters' associations.

The aims of the modernisation movement represented by the above-mentioned recommendations of the Party Organisation Research Council are very clear. They can be briefly summarised as attempts to transform the LDP into what is referred to in the party and journalist circles as an 'organised party', so that it might become capable of coping more effectively with the mounting competition of the opposition parties, especially the Socialists, both at elections and over particular issues, such as the Security Pact revision of 1960 and the ratification of the Japan-South Korea treaty in 1965. Modernisation in this sense has been assumed to involve expanded authority and power on the part of the formal party leadership, and also more complete and effective penetration of communities by the party organisation. However, both of these two broad areas have so far proved singularly resistant to modernisation and improvement. In the first of these areas not only have difficulties been encountered in exterminating the factions and other informal groups which have seriously interfered with the formal policy-making process, but also the formal organs themselves have taken a generally negative attitude. For example, in December 1964 Secretary-General Miki asked the Organisation Research Council to take steps to have all kinds of informal inter-party and intra-party groups in which LDP-affiliated Diet members participated disbanded without delay. This suggestion, however, was flatly turned down by that council itself. Similarly, the reform recommendations submitted by the latter relating to the method of election of the party president were killed by the executive council.

In the second area the continuation of the multi-member electoral district system and the predominant role of the supporters' associations have prevented the development of truly effective branch organisations at the community level, although renewed enthusiasm has been shown by the 'national movement' under the direction of the National Movement Headquarters established in January 1965.

The ultimate effects of the modernisation movement on the structure of the LDP, especially on its formal and informal policy-making process, are by no means easy to predict. Despite the fact that so far failures have been more prominent than successes, some of the basic changes proposed by the Party Organisation Research Council may yet be realised under the obvious and growing pressure of significant changes in the socio-economic environment of the society in which the party operates. The increasing competitiveness at national and local levels of the opposition parties, including the fast-growing Kōmeitō, will no doubt compel the LDP to make fairly drastic adjustments both in its electoral tactics and in its organisational structure. As the awareness of the new requirements (which are already clearly appreciated by Miki, Ishida, Kuraishi, and others) becomes more widely shared, certain basic changes will indeed prove unavoidable.

Without denying the probability of some important changes being enacted in the not too distant future, it is nevertheless important to consider them in relation to the structural and behavioural characteristics attributed above to the various party organs, as they are currently constituted. The most important of these may be summarised as follows:

Firstly, the development of party organisation, particularly of the cluster of policy-making organs represented by the PARC, has shown that it is much easier to multiply and fragment the operational and functional units involved than to rationalise and strengthen the existing ones. In fact, the over-expansion of these organs has obviously imposed excessively heavy strains on the available manpower which has been limited, as far as the responsible positions are concerned, to members of the Diet. No change aimed at modernising the policy-making and leadership structure of the party would prove really meaningful or helpful unless it involved effective control or reduction of the number of organs and possibly appointment of non-parliamentary members to party positions so far monopolised by Diet members. In view of the steadily increasing volume of demands for public decisions which come to the party, the ultimate solution may call for a basic re-definition of the role of the party in the system of government, negating the view that the ministerial party must not only be informed of, but actually review and pass judgment on, every single demand for public decision.

Secondly, the influence of the factions and other informal intra-party groups is detrimental to the assertion of effective leadership by the formal party organs and to their smooth functioning, particularly the policy-making chain represented by the PARC and executive council, and the party presidency. The efforts so far made to combat the growth of these informal groups have met little success. If the basic aim of the modernisation movement is to centralise the effective power of policy-making in the hands of the formal party organs, and if the factions, as is likely, should remain as resistant as in the past to a movement aimed at their liquidation, then they are bound to present the most formidable obstacle to that movement and may well ultimately defeat it.

Thirdly, the ineffectiveness and lack of authority of the formal party leadership in the intra-party decision-making process has been paralleled by its vulnerability and, at times, subservience to the influence of external groups, particularly the bureaucracy and interest groups. A similar pattern of relationship has obtained between formal party branches and prefectural federations on one hand and supporters' associations built around individual politicians on the other. The difficulty lies in balancing the need to secure material and spiritual support from a wide range of external groups (particularly for the purposes of elections), and the demand for the party's freedom of action and independence from pressures inevitably applied by such groups. This dilemma, which is certainly not peculiar to the LDP or the Japanese parties, is likely to remain unresolved and even aggravated for a long time to come and may prove, like factionalism, fatal to modernisation efforts.

5 The Intra-party Factions

In addition to, and often at variance with, the formal party organisation and its various components numerous informal groups have been formed by and among LDP Diet members ever since it was established in November 1955. Some of these groups have been interested in promoting the interests of particular external groups, usually in the form of facilitating special legislation and appropriation of public funds, and therefore may be regarded as intra-party interest groups. Typical of such groups have been, for example, those formed over the issues of ex-servicemen's pensions, the payment of reward to former landowners, and the medical insurance administration.[1] Some have been related to external groups only marginally and operated as independent and self-contained intra-party groups to promote particular causes or policies. These may be regarded as policy groups, typical of which have been the Soshinkai, the Asian Affairs Study Group, and the Afro-Asian Affairs Study Group.[2] Much rarer have been regionally-based groups, such as the Kantō MHRs' Association, which represent one of the oldest forms of intra-party grouping in the history of Japanese parties. In addition to these, there have been several groups formed around much more personal interests in sports, the arts, and so on, usually on a non-partisan basis.

Much more obvious, active, and durable than any of the above-mentioned kinds, however, have been the factions. So fundamental and pervasive has been their influence both within the LDP and in contemporary Japanese politics at large that it is essential to define and appreciate their role and functions both in terms of intra-party group dynamics and the party policy-making process. The other types of group may be considered meaningfully only in relation to the factions and the system they make up in the party.

[1]For much of the information on which this section is based the writer is indebted to many newspaper reporters covering the work of the LDP. He owes especially valuable factual information and helpful suggestions to Messrs Miyazaki Yoshimasa (*Yomiuri*), Nakajima Kiyonari (*Asahi*), Suzuki Yoshio (*Sankei*), Uchida Kenℶ (Kyodo News Agency), and Hirano Muneyoshi (NHK).
[2]For a discussion of these groups, see Chapters 8 and 9.

Factional Configuration, 1956-60

Following the unification of 1955 there were in the LDP three distinctive groupings which had originated in the former Liberal Party and four somewhat looser groupings issuing from the former Democrat Party. The Liberal groups were represented respectively by Yoshida Shigeru, Ogata Taketora, and Ōno Bamboku, whereas the Democrat groups were led by Kishi Nobusuke, Miki Bukichi, Hatoyama Ichirō, and other leaders of the former Progressive Party, such as Ōasa Tadao, Matsumura Kenzō, Miki Takeo, Kitamura Tokutarō, and Ashida Hitoshi. In addition, there were several 'non-aligned' groups, one of which consisted of former Liberals and all the others of former Democrats. Associated with these groups were about fifty former Liberals, twenty-five former Democrats, a few followers of Ishibashi Tanzan, and a few independents (factional), such as Ichimanda Hisato and Shōriki Matsutarō. Of these groups the four whose leaders formed the initial four-man presidential proxy committee in place of a president (Hatoyama, Miki Bukichi, Ōno, and Ogata), plus the Kishi group, whose leader held the next ranking post of secretary-general, constituted a 'dominant' coalition. On the other hand, the Yoshida group, the two conservative Progressives' groups led by Ōasa and Matsumura, the two radical Progressives' groups led by Miki Takeo and Kitamura, and the non-aligned Progressives' group represented by Ashida, formed a 'dissident' coalition to oppose the former. Most of these groups were already fully-fledged factions in the present sense of that word and met regularly on fixed dates of the month either singly or together with other factions.

Within about a year from the formation of the LDP, however, the original Ogata and Miki (Bukichi) factions had come respectively under the leadership of Ishii Mitsujirō and Kōno Ichirō upon the deaths of their founders. The latter also absorbed the Hatoyama and Kitamura factions, while both the Ōasa and Ashida groups joined the Kishi faction. The divisions of opinion both within and between the factions accompanying the party presidential election of December 1956, which was contested between Ishibashi, Kishi, and Ishii, led to the split of the Yoshida group into two separate factions represented respectively by Ikeda Hayato and Satō Eisaku, and also to the merger of the conservative Matsumura and the radical Miki Takeo groups of former Progressives.[3] During the three and a half years between the presidential election of December 1956 (which gave birth to the short-lived Ishibashi Cabinet), and that of July 1960 (which following the Security

[3]In the presidential contest Satō supported his own brother Kishi, while Ikeda aligned himself with the Ishibashi-Ishii coalition against Kishi. In the meantime, the majorities in the conservative Ōasa and the radical Kitamura factions of former Progressives voted for Kishi, leaving as a result the Matsumura and the Miki groups, who favoured Ishibashi, to form a coalition between them. Watanabe Tsuneo, *Habatsu: Nihon hoshutō no bunseki* (Kōbundō, 1964), pp. 46-7 and 88-9.

Treaty crisis replaced Kishi by Ikeda as party president), a fairly stable system of intra-party factionalism operated. The eight factions led respectively by Ikeda, Ishibashi, Ishii, Kishi, Kōno, Miki and Matsumura, Ōno, and Satō fought and co-operated with one another to form temporary and loose opposing alliances of changing memberships, one supporting the incumbent president (the 'dominant' factions) and the other opposing him (the 'dissident' factions).

TABLE 10

Factions in the LDP, 1955–67

	Dominant	Dissident	Neutral
Nov. 1955–Dec. 1956	Hatoyama* Ishibashi Kishi Miki, B. Ogata Ōno	Ashida Kitamura Miki, T. Ōasa Yoshida	
Dec. 1956–Feb. 1957	Ikeda Ishibashi* Ishii Miki, T.	Kishi Kōno Ōno Satō	
Feb. 1957–Jan. 1959	Kishi* Kōno Ōno Satō	Ikeda Ishii Miki	
Jan. 1959–July 1960	Ikeda Kishi* Ōno Satō	Ishii Kōno Miki	
July 1960–July 1962	Fujiyama Ikeda* Kishi Satō	Ishii Kōno Miki Ōno	
July 1962–Nov. 1964	Ikeda* Kawashima Kōno Miki Ōno	Fujiyama Fukuda Ishii Satō	
Nov. 1964–Jan. 1967	Fukuda Ikeda Ishii Kawashima Miki Satō*	Fujiyama Kōno Ōno	
Jan. 1967–	Fukuda Ishii Kawashima Miki Satō*	Fujiyama Matsumura Nakasone	Funada Maeo Mori Murakami

*Indicates the faction whose leader was party president.

Sources: 'Seitō wa kore de yoi no ka', Parts 5 and 6, *Yomiuri*, 6 and 7 January 1966.

Factional Configuration, 1960-7

The presidential election of July 1960 registered the opening of a new phase in the evolution of factionalism in the LDP. Within a period of about two years the large Kishi faction split into three separate factions, the Fujiyama faction, the *Tōfūsasshin renmei* (the Fukuda faction) and the *Kōyū kurabu* (the Kawashima faction).

The Fujiyama faction became a distinctive and independent entity when Fujiyama Aiichirō entered the presidential contest in July 1960, only to lose with 49 votes against Ikeda's 246 and Ishii's 196. In the meantime, the Committee on Party Modernisation, which was formed around the same time by about twenty volunteers, mainly from the Kishi faction, eventually became the *Jimintō tōfūsasshin konwakai* in May 1962 and was renamed the *Tōfūsasshin renmei* in August of the same year. On 31 October 1962 the Kishi faction was formally dissolved, and towards the end of November the 25 of its 49 members who refused to join the Tōfūsasshin renmei proceeded to form the Kōyū kurabu under the joint direction of Kawashima Shōjirō and Akagi Munenori.

The tendencies towards fragmentation of the existing factions, of which the emergence of these three groups out of the Kishi faction was symptomatic, quickly spread to the other factions and became especially acute, paradoxically, in the two factions which had prided themselves on firmer solidarity and tighter discipline than the others. More than a month before Ōno Bamboku's death in May 1964 journalists covering the LDP were predicting that not more than seven or eight of its members were certain to remain loyal to Ōno as long as he was alive and that several others were definitely shifting their allegiance to other factional leaders.[4] Following Ōno's death on 29 May, and especially after the Cabinet reshuffle of 17 July, the split of faction members into two opposing groups became evident. After an attempt to reunify its ranks through the intervention of an 8-man committee failed in early August the two groups emerged as *de facto* independent factions under their new leaders, Funada Naka and Murakami Isamu.[5]

Divisive tendencies developed just as rapidly in the Kōno faction long

[4]According to a group of journalists long associated with the LDP and its factions, as of April 1964 Tokuyasu Jitsuzō, Horikawa Kōhei, Nakamura Kōhachi, Nakagawa Ichirō, Watanabe Eiichi, Suhara Shōichi, and Harada Ken were certain to stay with Ōno, while Kuraishi Tadao, Murakami Isamu, Kanda Hiroshi, and Tanaka Masami were likely to identify themselves increasingly closely with Satō, and Mitzuta Mikio, Fukuda Hajime, Tamura Hajime, and Kamoda Sōichi might well move to the Fujiyama faction. For the factual information given in this and following notes concerning the divisions in the Ōno and the Kōno factions the writer is indebted to Mr Takeuchi Kei of *Kokumin seiji kenkyūkai*.

[5]The 8-man committee which was launched by the general meeting of the Ōno faction on 3 August consisted of two members each representing the Funada, the Murakami, and the neutral groups, and two more from the House of Councillors members. The meeting between Funada and Murakami on 6 August to discuss its four-point recommendations failed to produce reconciliation between them because of each man's refusal to recognise the other as the formal leader of the would-be reunified faction.

before its leader died in July 1965. As early as May 1964 three rival groups had emerged among its members, referred to by journalists respectively as the dominant group (Mori Kiyoshi, Shigemasa Seishi, and others), the dissident group (Yamaguchi Kikuichirō, Matsuda Takechiyo, and others), and the neutral group (Nakasone Yasuhiro, Sakurauchi Yoshio, and others). Following Kōno's death on 8 July 1965, the conflicts gradually became polarised between Shigemasa and Nakasone, and despite a temporary truce towards the end of August, resulting from mediation by the faction's financial patrons of the Sankinkai, the faction remained internally divided with a majority (about thirty) supporting Nakasone and a minority (about fourteen) rallying behind Shigemasa.[6] By early 1967 the two groups had become completely estranged from each other and formed separate factions under the leadership respectively of Nakasone and Mori Kiyoshi.

In the meantime, the Ishibashi faction ceased to function as an effective factional unit after the House of Representatives election of 1960 which greatly reduced its membership, and it virtually ceased to exist after Ishibashi himself was defeated in the next Lower House election of 1963. Towards the end of 1964 the six members of the Matsumura group in the Miki faction dissociated themselves from that faction allegedly because of their dissatisfaction with Miki's direct involvement in the nomination of Satō as Ikeda's successor in November of that year. Under Matsumura's leadership they thus began to operate as a small yet independent unit in the system of intra-party factionalism. Ikeda's sudden death in August 1965 made the prospects for the survival of his faction as a unified group uncertain for a while, but it managed, unlike the Ōno and the Kōno factions, to tide itself over the danger of split and to continue not only as a unified but also an effective and respected faction under Maeo Shigesaburō.

By early 1967 these structural changes and the deaths of some of the most influential leaders had altered quite considerably the general picture of factionalism in the LDP. In the summer of 1960 there were four factions headed by Kishi, Satō, Ikeda, and Ōno forming a dominant alliance, and three factions led by Kōno, Miki, and Ishii forming an alliance of dissidents. After the House of Representatives election of 29 January 1967 there were five dominant factions (Satō, Fukuda, Miki, Ishii, and Kawashima), four neutral

[6]On 26 August 1965 the representatives of the Sankinkai conferred with the five advisers and the eight secretaries of the faction after the 49th day memorial service given to the late Kōno at Hotel Okura in Tokyo. On that occasion the Sankinkai leaders, including Kawai Yoshinari of the Komatsu Manufacturing Co., Hagiwara Kichitarō of the Hokkaidō Coal Mining and Steamship Co., and Nagata Masaichi of the Daiei Motion Picture Co., strongly urged the faction representatives to put an end to the internal feud without delay. The latter accepted this advice and subsequently tried hard to hold the original faction together despite the continuing hostility and competition between the two groups. In Kōno's lifetime each of the twelve members of the Sankinkai used to contribute at least ¥10 million per annum or a total of ¥120 million to the faction's coffer, and the threat to stop this enormous contribution apparently sobered the two faction leaders and their followers.

factions (Maeo, Funada, Murakami, and Mori), and three dissident factions (Fujiyama, Nakasone, and Matsumura).

The Satō Faction

As of February 1967 the Satō faction is the largest of the twelve LDP factions with 49 MHRs and about 52 MHCs associated with it. As mentioned earlier, it was originally a twin brother of the Ikeda faction, both having issued from the former Yoshida faction at the first LDP presidential election in December 1956. Although until that date only about fifteen members of the Yoshida faction had been regarded as Satō's followers as against nearly twenty identified as Ikeda's, its membership steadily grew during Kishi's premiership (February 1957 to July 1960) under which Satō remained the number two man in the party and his faction was consistently in the dominant group. By September 1957 at least twenty MHRs were regularly present at the meetings of the two political associations run by the faction, the Shūzankai and the Mokuyōkai. The November 1960 House of Representatives election increased its membership in that House to forty-six and even after the Shūzankai was disbanded in January 1964 anything between seventy and eighty-five Diet members continued to meet at Satō's office. Shortly after this two groups of Diet members, the Seiji kōza and the Seikei kenkyūkai, began to receive financial donations from various business firms in the name of the faction.

Internally, the Satō faction had enjoyed a large measure of stability and harmony until about the end of 1964 and even as late as January 1965. Three of Satō's closest confidants, Tanaka Kakuei, Hori Shigeru, and Aichi Kiichi, formed a happy trio and shared the financial and political responsibilities between them. Apart from these three top leaders, Kuno Chūii, Setoyama Mitsuo, Tsukahara Toshio, Masuda Kaneshichi, and Matsuno Raizō formed a sub-leaders' group topping the faction's waiting list for ministerial and party appointment. The relationship, however, between two of the top leaders, Tanaka and Hori, and their respective supporters began to deteriorate in the months that followed, and after the Mokuyōkai's successor, the *Mokuyō kurabu*, was disbanded in September 1965 (as the Shūzankai had been twenty months before) the conflicts became very evident and intense. While Tanaka was apparently determined to succeed Satō as party president and Prime Minister with the support of the non-dominant factions (particularly the Ikeda faction), Hori was believed to distrust Tanaka's liberal inclinations and prefer Fukuda Takeo as Satō's eventual successor. By early 1967 the air of monolithic solidarity and stability seems to have virtually evaporated from the largest of the factions just as from most others.

The Fukuda Faction

The Fukuda faction, which had grown out of the Tōfūsasshin renmei, holds in the wake of the 1967 House of Representatives election twenty-seven MHRs and three MHCs and is firmly aligned with the Satō faction in a dominant coalition. As previously mentioned, the Tōfūsasshin renmei was originally founded in July 1960 as a party modernisation committee. According to its leader, Fukuda Takeo, the experience of the Security Treaty crisis in the summer of that year led him and his collaborators to organise the committee with a view to combating factionalism which, they believed, had rendered the LDP entirely impotent and unable to cope with the growing threat of international communism. Resolved ostensibly to put an end to factionalism, reform the electoral system, strengthen the formal party organs, enforce party discipline, and build a 'people's front' against 'Chinese and Soviet imperialism', they reorganised the committee into a *Tōfūsasshin konwakai* in May 1962, which was soon renamed the Tōfūsasshin renmei in early August of the same year.[7] During the summer of 1962 between 60 and 80 MHRs and MHCs were regularly present at its frequent meetings and by the spring of 1963 it claimed 103 members from the Lower House, 27 from the Upper House, and 7 former Diet members as its official members. At that stage it was governed by an 11-member presiding committee, a 19-member liaison conference for co-ordination between the factions, and a 39-member standing caretaker's committee.

It was characteristic of the Tōfūsasshin renmei and its immediate predecessors that they were a cross-factional group ostensibly dedicated to the task of purging the party of factionalism. In fact, all but the Kōno faction and the Kōyū kurabu (later the Kawashima faction) were represented by the Liaison Conference for Co-ordination between the Factions of which Fukuda was chairman. After the July 1963 reshuffle of the second Ikeda Cabinet, however, and especially after the House of Representatives elections in November of the same year, its leadership group led by Fukuda began to exhibit an undisguised hostility towards Ikeda and his faction. Henceforth the pretensions of this group to a supra-factional commitment to abolish all factions and to enhance the authority and prestige of the formal party leadership quickly faded out. Three days after the Cabinet reshuffle Fukuda declared at a press conference that he and his colleagues in the League had come to the conclusion that Ikeda was not in the least interested in the anti-faction campaign and that they would take the battle to the nation at large. In early August the twelve Kōyū kurabu members who had been so far associated with the group walked out on the grounds that it was being used

[7]The original committee had lapsed into inaction within a few months of its birth in 1960 and, therefore, its reorganisation in 1962 was rather nominal. In any event, a preparatory committee, alternatively referred to as a committee of sponsors, was formed in January 1962, and it was this organisation which became the basis for the Tōfūsasshin konwakai in May and Tōfūsasshin renmei in August. The information relating to the details of the successive events leading to the formation of this group was supplied to the writer by Mr Kawamura Yoshikuni, secretary-general of the Tō kindaika giin renmei, during an interview on 18 January 1966.

by the anti-Ikeda elements for their factional purposes. In the general election of November twenty candidates were elected with the endorsement and support of no other factions but the Tōfūsasshin renmei. And, finally, the faction's presiding committee decided to dissolve it in December 1963 ostensibly because the LDP Organisation Research Council chaired by Miki Takeo had submitted to Ikeda, the party president, a recommendation to make its own anti-faction campaign official party policy.

What emerged out of the Tōfūsasshin renmei and its campaign to put an end to the intra-party factionalism was therefore not a genuinely unified party freed from factionalism but just another faction led by Fukuda Takeo. While it is hard to deny that Fukuda and his associates were motivated partly by a genuine desire to strengthen the party so that it could compete more effectively with the opposition parties, it seems equally clear in retrospect that they were just as deeply interested in weakening the existing factions and their leaders (especially the Ikeda faction), and in building a new viable faction of their own. Ultimately the anti-faction campaign of this group represented Fukuda's bid for eventual hegemony at the expense of the senior aspirants for party presidency, such as Kōno and Kawashima, and the younger competitors, such as Tanaka and Nakasone. That its immediate aim was to replace Ikeda by Satō as party president and Prime Minister became even more evident when the Tō kindaika giin renmei was formed in July 1964 as a joint anti-Ikeda front by the six dissident factions under Fukuda's direction.[8] However, even after Satō was nominated party president in November, and thus became Prime Minister, this organisation continued to exist as a de facto new Fukuda faction built on a basis more extended than the existing Fukuda group. Through the campaign for a change in the electoral system (the institution of a single-member constituency system) in the winter of 1966 it succeeded in boosting its formal membership to about twenty-five. Another twenty-five or so who were currently and nominally affiliated with the Satō and other factions were said also to be under Fukuda's influence.

The Miki Faction

In February 1967 Miki Takeo led a large faction in the dominant camp with an estimated membership of thirty-five MHRs and fourteen MHCs.

During much of Hatoyama's reign following the conservative merger of November 1955, about twenty former Progressives had constituted the embryonic Miki faction and led the 'Radical' wing in opposition to the conservative or dominant wing represented by Shigemitsu Mamoru and Matsumura Kenzō. Expediency as well as accident led the Matsumura group to join the Miki faction a few months before the presidential election of

---

[8]The Tō kindaika giin renmei was originally formed as a Seikyokuisshin sōrengō hombu on 6 July and then renamed a week later. Participating in it were about 35 members of the Fukuda, Satō, Fujiyama, Ishii, Ōno, and Miki factions. See Asahi, 7 (morning and evening), 11 (evening), and 14 July 1964.

December 1956 and, as a result, the original Matsumura-Miki faction (subsequently called the Miki-Matsumura faction) emerged with an initial membership of twenty-six MHRs. This faction from the outset showed considerable interest in policy problems and policy research activities. In fact, by September 1957 the faction had come to be known officially as the *Seisaku kenkyūkai* (Policy Research Association) and in July 1958 four specialised research groups were formed on a permanent basis, dealing respectively with foreign policy, agricultural administration, social security, and economy. In the meantime, a 'summer school' held for a week every July at Karuizawa where the faction members would listen to lectures given by ten or so specialists on various subjects became an annual event after 1957. This example was subsequently followed by most other factions.[9]

Both temperamentally and ideologically, however, Miki and Matsumura differed from each other too widely to continue forever this marriage of convenience. While Matsumura consistently and relentlessly criticised and attacked Kishi over the controversial issue of the revision of the Police Duties Act in 1958, Miki was much more sympathetic towards the troubled Prime Minister and restrained his followers from mounting unreserved opposition to him. The precarious coalition survived the crisis of 1960 over the Security Pact controversy, but finally broke down in November 1964, when Matsumura and five of his followers left the faction in protest against Miki's support of Satō in the struggle for succession to the retiring President Ikeda. The secession of the Matsumura group left the Miki faction largely under the control of the pro-Satō group led by Hayakawa, who was reported to have threatened for a while to walk out with nearly twenty of the thirty remaining faction members but was dissuaded by the assurance that Miki would eventually nominate him his successor. Both the desertion of the Matsumura group and Hayakawa's bid for faction leadership no doubt had the effect of damaging Miki's stature as a faction leader and weakening his faction's bargaining power for a while, but the faction's relative success in the 1967 House of Representatives election ensured that it would remain one of the crucial groups in the future presidential contests, whether Miki himself stood for election or not.

The Kawashima Faction

The Kawashima faction with eighteen MHRs and four MHCs was another party to the dominant coalition. When Kishi announced his intention to dissolve his faction, the Tōkakai, at a press conference on 31 October 1962,[10]

[9]'Seisakuhabatsu ga taitō', *Mainichi*, 13 July 1958. The writer owes useful information on this particular aspect of the Miki faction's activities also to Mr Iwano, secretary to Mr Miki, through an interview on 17 January 1966.

[10]On that occasion Kishi himself justified his decision by his desire to stand above the narrow factional interests and views and to be able to pass judgment on various issues from the viewpoint of more general party or national interests. See Kishi Nobusuke, *Jikyoku shoken: Naze tōkakai wo kaisan shita ka* (KSK Report, 116)

about twenty-five of its members refused to join the Tōfūsasshin renmei, which had already been formed by Fukuda, and instead proceeded to form a separate faction under the joint leadership of Kawashima and Akagi Munenori. According to a leaflet entitled *Goaisatsu* (Greetings) distributed by the group in February 1963, there were twenty-seven MHRs and five former MHRs then affiliated with the Kōyū kurabu. In the House of Representatives election of the same year its membership was reduced to nineteen and in January 1964 it was officially dissolved as a political association as defined in the Political Funds Regulation Law. This did not mean, however, that the faction ceased to exist but merely that it became more of a Kawashima faction than the loose federation of the followers of Kawashima, Akagi, and Shīna that it had been. In fact, the faction resumed its regular meetings after the middle of that year and soon became one of the most unified and effective factions.

As of January 1966, a staff of five managed its factional activities, and three members were assigned to policy research; the faction meetings were held normally every other week and more frequently in the period from July to September when activities preparatory to the annual budget-making were in full swing. Each member paid a monthly membership fee of ¥10,000 to finance its activities and about fifty editions of the factional organ, *Seisaku Kenyū*, had been published by January 1966. Each edition consisted of nearly 700 copies circulated among businessmen who provided financial assistance, supporting groups, journalists and others, and a four-day 'summer school' was annually held at Hakone.

The Ishii Faction

A fifth factional unit which falls in this category is the Ishii faction with fifteen MHRs and eight MHCs regularly associated with it.[11] Ishii succeeded Ogata when the latter died in January 1956, but it was not until he personally fought the presidential election of December that year against Kishi and Ishibashi, allegedly spending from his own pocket nearly ¥100 million, that the faction began to be accepted as a viable entity both by its own members and others. During the following year and a half it existed as a very loosely knit group called the *Suiyō kurabu* with about thirty MHRs regularly attending its meetings. It was governed largely by a 5-man team made up of Nadao

(20 November 1962), pp. 11-12. A much more plausible reason was, however, the obvious difficulty he must have found in financially supporting the overgrown faction of some seventy members coupled with the growing rift between the pro-Ikeda group led by Kawashima and the pro-Satō group led by Fukuda. The writer owes much of the information on this and other aspects of the process leading to the formation of the *Kōyū kurabu* and the subsequent developments to Mr Kaneko Jun'ichirō, secretary to Kawashima and secretary-general of the Kōyū kurabu, through an interview held on 19 January 1966.

[11]For much of the information on which the following description of the Ishii faction is based the writer is indebted to Mr Sakata Michita, member of the House of Representatives (interview, 1 March 1966).

Hirokichi, Tsukada Jūichirō, Tanaka Isaji, Kanke Kiroku, and Baba Motoharu, but hostilities between a 'policy' or 'bureaucrat' group led by the first
two and an 'action' or 'politician' group led by the remaining three had made
it difficult for the faction to compete effectively under a unified command
against other factions. However, at a meeting held on 29 September 1958 the
faction was renamed the *Suiyōkai* and a decision was made to put an end to
the ineffectual 5-man leadership and to unify the command over the group
in the hands of Hayashiya Kamejirō, a senior faction member with a seat
in the House of Councillors, with a view to making it more competitive and
ensuring the success of Ishii's bid for presidency at the forthcoming contest.

After Ishii lost to Ikeda in the 1960 presidential election (196 to 246 in
the first ballot and 194 to 302 in the second), both the faction's membership
and influence quickly began to wane. Although in early 1966 about twenty
of its members still continued to attend its weekly breakfast sessions on Wed-
nesday mornings, it had apparently become a relatively ineffective group in
the intra-party power struggle, especially because some of its most influential
members had begun by that time to assert almost complete freedom of action.
In March 1966 its factional activities (apart from the weekly breakfast sessions) were limited to the annual 'summer school' held at Karuizawa, while
factional expenses were defrayed almost entirely by Ishii himself, although
each member paid a nominal membership fee of ¥2,000 a month.

The Maeo Faction

Of the four 'neutral' factions, numerically by far the most important is the
Maeo faction with forty-three MHRs and about nineteen MHCs attached
to it. Five months after it had separated from the Satō faction (with which
it had constituted the 50-man strong Heishinkai), Ikeda and about fifteen
of his followers formed the Kōchikai as a factional political association.
Throughout Kishi's period as Prime Minister the Ikeda faction remained
either definitely dissident or rather vaguely neutral, while the Kōchikai became known for its extensive and sophisticated policy research activities.
Especially after the middle of 1958 the group began to meet regularly at
weekly policy study sessions and its research department began to engage in
investigations of economic and foreign policy problems. The results of such
policy investigations undertaken in the name of the Kōchikai by a group of
specialists attached to the research department were circulated among its
own members and collaborators, particularly those in industry and the
bureaucracy, mainly in the form of a series of monographs and, to a more
limited extent, also through the faction's monthly organ, the *Shinro*.[12]

[12]The twenty-one titles of the Kōchikai's reference materials series published between
December 1959 and March 1962 included, for example, eight monographic studies of
contemporary Japanese economy, of which three dealt with agricultural problems, and
nine studies of foreign policy issues, six of which were devoted to a discussion of the
China problem. See the list of these publications in Kōchikai Chōsabu (ed.),

I

After Ikeda became Prime Minister in July 1960 the faction's membership considerably increased. In the November 1960 House of Representatives election forty-nine of the LDP-sponsored candidates who were successfully returned were identified with this faction and the corresponding figure at the November 1963 election was forty-seven. While the Kōchikai was officially disbanded less than a month after the 1963 election in accordance with the recommendations of the LDP Organisation Research Council, the factional activities continued with just as much vigour and publicity as before. Nor did Ikeda's resignation in October 1964 and death in August 1965 lead to the break-up of the faction, as was the case with both the Ōno and the Kōno factions. In fact, the New Year party held at Ikeda's residence on 19 January 1965 was reported to have been attended by as many as seventy-four LDP Diet members and founded the basis for the continued unity and prosperity of the faction under the leadership of Maeo Shigesaburō. It is true that a rift threatened to develop on Ikeda's death between a group of former bureaucrats from the Ministry of Finance (including Maeo, Ōhira, and Kurogane) and the rest of its members, and also that speculation was rife at the time that Ōhira was planning to build his own separate faction. Nevertheless, it maintained its unity without a single defection and quickly proceeded to form a new factional association, the *Shin zaisei kenkyūkai*, in place of the defunct Kōchikai. This new group has since been meeting regularly every Tuesday, just as the Kōchikai used to, and Maeo seems to be in firm control of the group with the evidently willing co-operation of Ōhira, Suzuki Zenkō, Niwa Kyōshirō, and others.

The Funada and Murakami Factions

Two of the neutral factions in existence in February 1967, the Funada and Murakami factions, originated in the former Ōno faction. Just before the LDP presidential election of December 1956, twenty-nine MHRs were said to be followers of Ōno and this number remained remarkably unchanged until his death in May 1964. The faction was formally named *Hakuseikai* following that presidential election and its office was opened at Kōjimachi, Tokyo, in March 1957, but was closed six months later. With a view to strengthening its factional solidarity in order to ensure Ōno's success in the presidential election of 1960 the Hakuseikai was revived as the *Bokuseikai*. This lasted until December 1963 as a political association in the sense defined in the Political Funds Regulation Law, and until well after Ōno's death as a *de facto* factional entity.

Ōno's death in May 1964 was followed by bitter power struggles between the senior faction members, which for about a month were contained under

---

Keizaiseichō: Sore wo suishin suru mono to sore ga motarasu mono (Shiryō 47-gō) (Kōchikai, March 1962). See also the articles in the *Shinro* attributed to the Chōsabu's authorship, e.g. 'Naigaikeizai no ugoki', in each issue.

the rule of an informal governing committee. By the end of June, however, the struggle had become clearly bipolarised with Funada and Murakami as the main contenders. After these two men failed to decide between themselves the question of succession to Ōno in October of the same year it became evident that the faction could not last very long. The final break came about ten months later, when, as mentioned previously, the efforts of an 8-man mediation committee failed to invent a leadership formula acceptable to both groups. By early 1966 the Funada faction had formed a factional association called the *Isshinkai* and the Murakami faction had followed suit by establishing the *Ichiyōkai*. In February 1967 the former had a membership of thirteen MHRs and five MHCs and the latter ten MHRs and two MHCs. The split has naturally rendered both groups far less effective in the game of intraparty factionalism than the firmly united Ōno faction used to be in its founder's lifetime.

The Mori and Nakasone Factions

The former Kōno faction, from which by February 1967 there had issued the 'neutral' Mori faction and the 'dissident' Nakasone faction, had during Kōno's lifetime been one of the largest and best organised. Made up largely of those who had been associated with the Hatoyama and the Hirokawa factions of the Liberal Party and the Kitamura faction of the Progressive Party, and long organised in an association called *Shunjūkai*, it was regarded, together with the former Ōno faction, as the mainstay of the 'politicians' groups. Its membership remained at about fifty, made up of thirty-five MHRs and fifteen MHCs until the November 1963 House of Representatives election when over forty-five of the candidates sponsored by the faction were successfully returned, thus boosting its total membership to nearly sixty-five. Under the pressure of the former radical Progressives, who had long been known for their unusually keen interest in policy problems, this faction too engaged in extensive and independent policy investigations of its own since relatively early days, especially in the fields of economic and foreign policy. In more recent years it had become customary for the Shunjūkai to publish for the benefit of its electoral and financial supporters a commentary on the annual government budget (*Kotoshi no yosan to watakushi-tachi no kurashi*) each year, in addition to reports on various lectures given by its members and invited guests.

As previously mentioned, Kōno's sudden death in July 1965 immediately caused the conflicts which had existed in the faction for some time seriously to threaten its factional unity and existence. A façade of unity was maintained by the nomination in July 1965 of Shigemasa (largely as a result of pressure from financial patrons in the Sankinkai) as the presiding secretary in July 1965 virtually to succeed Kōno as the faction's leader. However, the fact that he had won only slightly over a third of the votes cast at the election clearly indicated the precarious nature of his leadership and a continuation of divisive tendencies.[13] It was precisely because of the weakness of Shigemasa's leadership that a collegiate form of leadership was instituted by the nomination of a 9-man board while at the same time the Sankinkai brought direct pressure to bear on the members of the faction to maintain unity. Though its members continued to meet weekly at breakfast or lunch and even at 'policy study seminars' which were often held more than once a week, Shigemasa's apparent failure to establish a firm grip on the faction, especially over its junior members (those who had been returned not more than three times), aggravated by the dwindling faction funds, made its break-up only a matter of time. After the middle of 1966 it in fact ceased to exist as a united group and the split became open and formal by early 1967, when one of the groups led by Mori stayed with the neutral camp with twelve MHRs and the other group represented by Nakasone joined the dissident bloc with twenty-three MHRs attached to it.

The Fujiyama Faction

In addition to the Nakasone faction, the Fujiyama and the Matsumura factions remained dissident following the January 1967 election.

The Fujiyama faction claims sixteen MHRs and twelve MHCs as its bona fide members. It came into being as a viable factional unit in 1960, when Fujiyama ran for the first time in the presidential election against Ikeda and Ishii and lost in the first ballot.[14] Both his officially 'non-political' supporters' association, the Tōyūkai, and the 'political', fund-raising organisation, the *Kokusai seiji-keizai-bunka kenkyūkai* (subsequently the *Kokusai seikei chōsakai*), had been formed almost simultaneously with Fujiyama's entry into party politics in July 1957, when he was appointed Minister of Foreign Affairs in the first Kishi Cabinet. The faction had at least thirty-one affiliates among the LDP candidates successfully returned in the November 1960 House of Representatives election,[15] but the membership thereafter dwindled steadily as Fujiyama's personal wealth was dissipated, until it reached the low level indicated by the figures given already.

In January 1966, Fujiyama was still paying the faction bill almost entirely from his own pocket, although the Tōyūkai, a majority of whose members were businessmen and industrialists and whose monthly magazine, *Kokumin*

---

[13]Shigemasa's main adversary, Nakasone, did not officially run as a candidate for factional leadership on that occasion, and yet 13 votes were cast for him as against 17 for Shigemasa. Matsuda Takechiyo and Nakamura Umekichi also collected 6 and 2 votes each. The writer owes this piece of information to Mr Takeuchi of *Kokumin seiji kenkyūkai*.

[14]Fujiyama polled 49 to Ikeda's 246 and Ishii's 196 (*Asahi*, 14 July 1960 (evening)). The present discussion of the Fujiyama faction is based principally on the information supplied by Mr Ukai Takuo, secretary to Fujiyama, in an interview on 18 January 1966.

[15]Of the thirty-four candidates who were returned in that election and were claimed to be Fujiyama faction affiliates, two were claimed also by the Ōno and one by the Kishi factions. *Asahi*, 22 November 1960.

Saron, was sold for a nominal price (¥50 a copy), was apparently self-supporting.[16] The Diet members associated with the faction made it a rule to meet once a week when the Diet was in session either at breakfast or lunch, usually on Thursdays at the Hotel New Japan, and to hold a two-day study seminar once a year. They were meant for the Diet members, but about ten former or would-be Diet members also attended frequently. In addition the faction had since September 1960 co-operated in the organisation of semi-annual four-day study sessions for students (the *Fujiyama seiji daigakuin*), which had been sponsored and directed personally by Fujiyama with the help of the youth association called the *Yūai seinen dōshikai*.

The Matsumura Faction

The last and smallest, and yet in some ways the most interesting and militant, of the dissident factions in February 1967 was that of four members led by Matsumura Kenzō. When Matsumura with five others deserted the Miki faction in November 1964 in protest against Miki's support for Satō, he probably hoped not only to dissociate himself from the expressly pro-Satō majority in the Miki faction but also to create a preliminary group basis on which to build, if possible, a second conservative party more forward-looking than the present LDP. Matsumura has been known just as much for his consistent advocacy of such a second conservative party as for his passionate campaign for closer Japanese ties with the People's Republic of China.

As one of his closest associates once publicly stated, Matsumura's second conservative party was conceived primarily as a means of preventing the Socialists from replacing the LDP in the indefinite future either by themselves or in coalition with the other opposition parties, and was obviously modelled after the prewar Minseitō, the Seiyūkai's conservative competitor.[17] Notwithstanding the obviously backward-looking, even reactionary, implications of the plan, it is equally clear that he was deeply and sincerely concerned about the predominant influence of money and factionalism and the resulting subordination of policy considerations in the LDP decision-making

---

[16]Tōyūkai also charged, at least in principle, a ¥1,000 per month membership fee. Ukai (interview, 18 January 1966).

[17]For Furui Yoshimi's comments on Matsumura's two-conservative-party plan, see 'Nitchūkankei kaizen e no michi' ('Konohito to ichijikan'), *Ekonomisuto*, XLIV, 40 (11 October 1966), p. 45. In February 1962 Matsumura had said: 'I have no idea how long Mr Ikeda is going to stay in power, nor who will succeed him, Satō or Fujiyama. But will the people acquiesce in that sort of arrangement? Will you tolerate such a situation? I have no doubt that they will say, "This is not how it should be under a true two-party system. When you cannot continue, you must hand over the power to the Opposition party." That would of course mean a sort of revolution, for many in the Opposition party are extremely radical leftists. That is why I think it better for Fujiyama, for example, to separate himself from this party while Satō is in power and form another conservative party. Whichever of the two succeeds in winning public confidence should form a cabinet . . .' Matsumura Kenzō, *Nihon no zento wo ueru* (KSK Report, 78) (26 February 1962), p. 29.

process, a concern which was shared by many others in the party.[18] Despite the numerical insignificance of his following after the January 1967 House of Representatives election, the idea of a second conservative party has clearly been alive and some day may well be used as a weapon by the dissident factions and even the neutral factions to influence, if not blackmail, the dominant coalition over particular political issues or matters relating to the personnel administration of the party.

The Factions and LDP Members in the Upper House

The factional divisions of the LDP members of the Upper House did not become sufficiently clear to be identified and linked with those in the Lower House until about the time of the July 1960 LDP presidential election. There had existed three loose groupings formed in 1956 around the three candidates in the presidential election of that year: the *Seishin kurabu* (Kishi's supporters), the *Suiyōkai* (Ishii's supporters), and the *Washinkai* (Ishibashi's supporters). As Watanabe has pointed out, the reasons for such a state of affairs among the LDP MHCs have been, though diverse, fairly evident. Firstly, those who were elected from the national constituency depended, as a rule, much more on national interest groups such as the Medical Association or the ex-servicemen's associations than on the factions for financial and organisational aid; secondly, those elected from the prefectural constituencies found it sensible and profitable to campaign with the supra-factional, rather than factional, support of the MHRs returned from the area; thirdly, the long six-year term of office made it less urgent for a sitting MHC to 'cultivate' his constituency with as much care and spending as his Lower House counterpart; fourthly, the fact that every faction leader was an MHR dampened the MHCs' interest in and loyalty to a particular faction; fifthly, it had become an established custom for a candidate for a governmental or party post from the LDP membership in the House of Councillors to be recommended by the President of the House, and the President and Secretary-General of the Assembly of LDP MHCs instead of by a faction leader; and sixthly, it had also become an unwritten rule for three MHCs to be appointed Cabinet ministers

---

[18]For his impassioned condemnation of the influence of money and factionalism in the LDP and plea for greater interest in policy problems on the part of its leaders, see 'Seisaku koso ga seitō wo hagukumu: Seisaku hon'i de un'ei sareru hoshutō ni tsuite', *Waseda Kōron* (3 August 1962), pp. 88-92. Following the LDP presidential election of July 1960, Kōno and about twenty-five of the members of his faction decided to desert the LDP and form a separate conservative party, though the plan was soon given up, in part because of the objections raised by Ōno Bamboku. See *Asahi*, 11, 12, and 23 August 1960; Ōno Bamboku, *Ōno Bamboku kaisōroku: Girininjō ichidaiki* (Kōbundō, 1964), p. 109. Both Akagi Munenori of the then Kishi faction and Imamatsu Jirō, formerly of the same faction and currently independent, also expressed views at least mildly in favour of dividing up the LDP into two separate parties. See Akagi Munenori, *Kōyū kurabu no kessei ni tsuite* (27 November 1962), p. 26; Imamatsu Jirō, *Hoshutō no kindaika ipponka wa hatashite kanou ka* (KSK Report, 180) (25 February 1964), pp. 27-9.

at each Cabinet change. This made it sensible to have three, rather than eight or more, groups as the basis for such appointments.[19]

These conditions continued to discourage complete absorption of LDP-affiliated MHCs by the factions formed among Lower House members and to perpetuate the three rather loose and cross-factional groupings. By the middle of 1962, however, factional divisions modelled after and organically linked with those in the Lower House had emerged quite clearly among them and it became possible to count each faction's supporters with a measure of accuracy. In July 1962, for example, the factional distribution was roughly as follows: Satō—40, Ikeda—30, Kōno and Fujiyama—25 each, Ōno—18, Miki—13, Kishi—10, and Ishii—less than 10. By late 1967 it had changed to something like this: Satō—52, Maeo (former Ikeda)—11, Nakasone and Mori combined (former Kōno)—15, Fujiyama—9, Funada—6, Murakami—3, Miki—10, Ishii—10, independents and uncertain—20.

The three cross-factional groups still existed as the *Seishin kurabu* (the Satō and Kishi factions), the *Konwakai* (the Ishii, Ikeda, and Miki factions), and the *Mizuho kurabu* (the Ōno, Kōno, and Fujiyama factions). The individual factions, however, gradually extended their influence over the LDP members of the Upper House and were accepted increasingly as the basic units of intra-party politics by members of that House.

Types of Faction Leaders

As we have seen, one of the most obvious characteristics of the factions in the LDP is that each has been identified with and led by a particular politician. Consequently, except in a few recent cases, such as the Tōfūsasshin renmei and the Kōyū kurabu, every faction has been called by the leader's name. Furthermore, a faction has been passed on from one leader to another in the manner of common personal possession. Thus there seems to be little room to doubt that the factor of personality is involved and plays a significant role in the formation and growth of a faction in the party.

On the other hand, however, it seems to be equally evident that there are no special personality types or career patterns which qualify a party member to become a faction leader. In fact, any member with a seat in the House of Representatives who is able to help a group of his fellow party politicians perform the basic functions attributed to the faction may be regarded as a potential faction leader and these functions centrally relate, as we shall soon see, to the allocation of offices in the party and government and supply of political funds.

Of the twelve men leading their own factions in early 1967 four can be classified as former bureaucrats (Satō, Fukuda, Maeo, and Funada), three as former journalists (Kawashima, Ishii, and Matsumura), three as business-

[19]Watanabe, op. cit., pp. 191-2n.

men (Murakami, Mori, and Fujiyama), while the other two (Miki and Nakasone) belong to no particular category.

Like many of their fellow bureaucrats who have reached the highest positions in the national public services, the four ex-bureaucrats all come from relatively well-to-do families. Satō's father was a successful *sake* (rice wine) dealer, just like the late Ikeda's father, while Fukuda's grandfather, father, and elder brother had all served his native town of Kinko in Gumma Prefecture as mayor. Funada's father, too, was a large landlord in Tochigi Prefecture. In terms of family ties both Satō and Funada have some outstanding names among their close relations. Satō's two elder brothers are the late vice-admiral of the Imperial Navy, Satō Ichirō, and the former Prime Minister, Kishi Nobusuke, while his brothers-in-law, Tsunemitsu Shirō of Sanwa Bank and Hara Hidekuma of Daiichi Electric Industry are also well-known names among business circles. Similarly, Funada's two brothers are the active MHR, Fujieda Sensuke, and former MHR, Funada Kyōji, while his wife, Sumiko, is the fourth daughter of the former privy councillor, Motoda Hajime. Neither Fukuda nor Maeo, however, finds among his immediate relations any such outstanding names.

As is true with so many of the high-ranking bureaucrats, the four men were all graduates from the Law School of Tokyo Imperial University, but it was in the Ministry of Transportation (formerly Railway Administration Agency) that Satō made his successful career, in the Ministry of Finance that Fukuda and Maeo made theirs, and in the Ministry of Home Affairs that Funada had an almost equally outstanding record of promotions. Although their education and occupational backgrounds leave little room for doubt about their above-average intelligence and abilities, the ways in which these qualities have been demonstrated have given observers rather contrasting impressions.

Satō, who has been known as 'Eisaku the quick-eared', is believed to be ambitious and astute but rather self-conscious and shy, while Fukuda, who has been called an 'eel', is known for his stubbornness as well as tremendous manipulative ability. Funada may have been even better gifted with intellectual power, as his old nickname, 'the razor-blade', suggests, but because of his 'bureaucratic' personality he had seldom been counted as Ōno's successor in the latter's lifetime. Very different is the personality attributed to Maeo, who has been called a 'brown cow in the dark' for reasons the writer does not quite comprehend. Apart from his unusually inarticulate speech and slow-moving manners, he has been credited especially with those rare qualities among politicians, honesty and modesty.

Ideologically, Fukuda and Funada seem to be equally inflexible in their anti-communist commitments, while Satō is far more flexible or opportunistic and Maeo even more so.

None of the three former journalists who lead factions in the LDP today can point to names among their kin as illustrious as Satō or Funada, except that Ishii's wife is the eldest daughter of the prewar MHR, president of the Seiyūkai, and wealthy businessman, Kuhara Fusanosuke. None of them went to Tokyo Imperial University either, Kawashima having graduated from Senshū University, Ishii from Tokyo College of Commerce (present Hitotsubashi University), and Matsumura from Waseda University. Kawashima and Matsumura started their careers as newspaper reporters as soon as they had graduated, but Ishii had been an official in the Tokyo Metropolitan Police Office and then in the Office of the Government-General in Taiwan before he joined Asahi Newspaper Company's business section. The three share the common characteristic of old age, Matsumura being the oldest (born 1883) and the other two being not very much younger (born 1889 and 1890 respectively). Naturally their mannerisms tend to be rather old-fashioned and precisely for this reason they command certain special admiration and even reverence from their fellow party politicians.

Of the three Kawashima is probably regarded shrewdest as a politician, Ishii has been criticised for his indecisiveness, and Matsumura has been praised for purity of motivation and honesty.

The three businessmen have all extensive family ties in the entrepreneurial circles of the nation. Murakami's brother, brothers-in-law, and sons jointly run their family concern, Daiwa Construction Company, and several related interests. Mori, who is the fourth son of the founder of the enormous prewar industrial combination—the Mori concern—not only has a brother, Satoru, who is the president of Nihon Metallurgical Manufacturing Company and former MHR, but is also related through his many sisters to another LDP faction leader, Miki Takeo, an LDP MHR, Fukuda Tokuyasu, and above all to the president of Shōwa Electric Industry, Anzai Masao, who in turn is related through his son's marriage tie to the Shōdas, whose daughter has married the Crown Prince. In fact, the Mori-Anzai family connections represent the most illustrious and extensive kinship group in contemporary Japan, involving even the Satō (the Prime Minister), the Ōhashi (an LDP MHR), and the Iwasa (the president of Fuji Bank) families in addition to those mentioned already.

Fujiyama's family ties are almost as impressive. He was born the first son of one of the most successful businessmen in the Meiji period, Fujiyama Raita, who had served as the president of Tokyo Chamber of Commerce and Industry and a large number of corporations as well as being a member of the House of Peers. He married a daughter of the former Governor of the Bank of Japan and another outstanding businessman of the time, Yūki Toyotarō, and until his entry into politics in 1957 managed these corporations inherited from the father as the head of the family team which also involved his mother and two brothers.

Unlike the former bureaucrats and like the journalists none of these three former businessman faction leaders had attended Tokyo Imperial University. Murakami went to Waseda School of Engineering, Mori to Kyoto Imperial University's Department of Geology, and Fujiyama to Keiō University.

Both Murakami and Mori have reputations very similar to their respective predecessors, Ōno and Kōno. Neither of them has been known for particularly impressive intellectual performance, but Murakami is said to be broad-minded and tolerant, a quality so often associated with Ōno, while Mori has apparently been known best for his straightforward manners and energetic devotion to his work, characteristics which remind one of Kōno. Fujiyama has impressed many with his highly refined manners and strong interest in arts, especially painting. Both in terms of family background and personality he would be by far the most promising candidate for the title of 'the Playboy' in the LDP, but at the same time many question his qualifications as an effective party leader on account of his gullibility, a quality which does not seem to be an asset in that rather unique field of human activity called party politics.

As already indicated, Miki is married to a daughter of Mori Nobuteru, the founder of the prewar Mori concern and through this matrimonial tie related to that unusual kinship group involving the Imperial Court as well as some of the biggest politicians and businessmen in contemporary Japan and constituting in itself the postwar version of Japanese high society. In his youth Miki studied both at Meiji University in Tokyo and American University in Washington, D.C., U.S.A. Since his entry into politics in the mid-1930s he has been identified generally as a 'progressive' in the conservative party camp, but he has changed sides so frequently and with such apparent ease in the inter-party and inter-factional struggles that he has been also charged with opportunism and unreliability both by his fellow politicians and journalists.

In contrast, Nakasone does not have any significant kinship ties with the big family names, his father being a local timber merchant in Gumma Prefecture. He went to the Law School of Tokyo Imperial University and on graduation served briefly in the Ministry of Home Affairs as a minor official before he joined the Democratic Party in 1947. As the nickname, 'young army officers', given to him and his collaborators in the Democratic and Progressive parties suggests, he has been credited, just like his former associate Mori, with extraordinary stamina and forceful presentation of his political and ideological views.

Just as it seems to be futile to find some common criteria by which to judge the qualifications of a faction leader in terms of his family, educational, and occupational backgrounds, it seems to be equally difficult to regard seniority as a significant factor contributing to a man's eligibility for such a role. Of the twelve men reviewed above the youngest, Nakasone, was born in 1918, followed by Mori who was born in 1915. Since the average LDP-affiliated

MHR in 1965 was 53 years old, or born in 1912, both of them were younger than the average. Three others—Miki (born 1907), Fukuda (born 1905), and Maeo (born 1905)—were only slightly older than the average. Even if age may be said to have played a part in the case of the three venerable ex-journalists, it has obviously not been a decisive factor. Nor has the length of time one has served as an MHR been of any significant consequence in the making of a faction leader. Only four of the twelve men, that is Funada, Kawashima, Matsumura, and Miki, have been MHRs since the prewar days, while all the rest have been elected to that House after World War II, and Fujiyama in particular as late as 1958.

No less varied are the origins of the twelve factions. Only two of the leaders—Miki and Matsumura—have built their factional following more or less for themselves to begin with, whereas all the others have inherited theirs from their predecessors. Ishii and Maeo in particular succeeded to the factions built respectively by Ogata and Ikeda almost completely intact and without a fight. All the others except Fujiyama picked up part of the factional following left by the original leaders after some contest of power with their competitors within the factions (Satō v. Ikeda after Yoshida's resignation; Fukuda v. Kawashima and Akagi after the dissolution of the Kishi faction; Funada v. Murakami following Ōno's death; Mori v. Nakasone after Kōno's death). Fujiyama walked out of the Kishi faction with about thirty of the latter's affiliates in 1960. To inherit a faction is probably much easier than to build one anew, the determination of the successor depending in a large measure upon the elements of chance as well as the candidate's relationship with the previous leader.

As long as the factions are regarded, as we shall soon see, as the basic units of distributing party and government posts (and for that purpose a waiting-list of candidates for future appointments is prepared in each faction on the basis of members' relative lengths of affiliation as well as a few other forms of contribution to the factional interests), there naturally exists resistance to the dissolution of any one or more particular factions and shifts in affiliation. This situation favours continuation of a faction even after the death or retirement of its incumbent leader and consequently the practice of succession described above. Given, however, the intensely personal and emotive, as opposed to programmatic or issue-centred, character of the faction, there is little compelling reason why the average affiliate of a faction should be loyal to a new leader to whom he probably owes little either materially or psychologically. It is no doubt for this reason that splits have occurred in many of the original factions after the founding leaders ceased to exercise their effective control. For the same reason a faction which passes under a new leadership inevitably suffers from a period of instability and precariousness. The apparent absence of a fixed pattern or uniform type in the personality characteristics of the actual faction leaders and the resulting impression of haphazardness in the process of leader recruitment merely reflects this aspect of instability and fluidity in the situation.

Factions as Units for Distributing Posts

As described above, the faction has become the basic and apparently permanent unit of association within the LDP since the presidential election of December 1956. Each of the eight or more of these groups under successive LDP Cabinets has had its own headquarters and a fairly fixed and stable membership drawn exclusively from among LDP Diet members. In terms both of its daily activities and command of loyalty from its members each faction has been in many ways scarcely distinguishable from an independent party and obviously competed with the formal party organisation. Why such a system of factionalism should have come to flourish in the LDP and what specific functions it has performed must be carefully examined and explained as a prerequisite to a full understanding of the party policy-making mechanism.

The faction in the LDP evolved essentially as a device by means of which a member of the party in the Diet hoped to acquire either a government post, a party post, political funds, or all of these. In other words, a Diet member's desire for office and money was responsible for the growth of factionalism and all the benefits or evils associated with it. It is quite significant that the era of factionalism in the party was ushered in by the presidential election of 1956, on which occasion the three candidates, Kishi, Ishibashi, and Ishii, and their supporters are said to have spent at least ¥120 million, ¥90 million, and ¥60 million respectively in their vote-hunting efforts.[20] That event illustrated most dramatically how ambition for office, the magic power of money, and the game of factionalism could feed and flourish on one another.

According to the LDP Rules relating to the election of a party president, it is necessary for a presidential candidate to win a majority of votes cast by all LDP Diet members and the forty-six prefectural delegations in the first poll, or, failing that, to win either the first or the second place in the first poll and then a majority in the second poll. It is obvious that the surest way to succeed in such an electoral contest based on the principle of majority vote is to build in advance a sufficiently large and reliable group of one's own supporters and depend upon their bloc voting. Should one fail to build a single group embracing a majority of the qualified voters involved, however, it would become necessary to induce others outside the group (often including members of rival groups of a similar kind), to vote for one. As most LDP leaders themselves would readily admit, every one of the candidates who has run in a past competitive LDP presidential election has acted strictly in

[20]These figures are cited by the then *Asahi* reporter, Okada Tadao, while the *Yomiuri* reporter, Watanabe, gives ¥300 million, ¥150 million, and ¥80 million as the sums believed to have been spent by the three groups. See Okada Tadao, *Seiji no uchimaku* (Yūki shobō, 1963), p. 128; Watanabe, op. cit., p. 141.

accordance with this rule. As explained once by an advocate of the popular election of Prime Ministers, Nakasone Yasuhiro, each aspirant attempts to keep the votes represented by his own faction from slipping away to a competitor and at the same time to win to himself those controlled by other factions. Bribery either in money or promise of office has been liberally employed in this process.

Just as the few influential leaders, who hope to win a forthcoming presidential election in order to become president of the LDP and the nation's Prime Minister, have found in the faction a most effective and reliable weapon, so have the rank and file seen in it a sure guarantee for smooth promotions and the acquisition of political funds. According to LDP members themselves, they feel compelled to struggle for a high government or party post not so much by their personal pride or ambition as by the pressures applied by their constituencies. Even the self-assured Nakasone once confessed to great annoyance in this regard: 'many MHRs are terribly embarrassed when asked by their constituencies why they have not yet been appointed Cabinet ministers. They themselves don't care very much really, but it is hard to put up with this sort of pressure, especially if other members returned by the same constituency manage to get an appointment first.' About a month later Kuraishi spoke in a similar vein when he said that a Diet member who had been appointed a minister or parliamentary vice-minister had a far better chance of re-election and that to the majority of Diet members re-election is almost an end in itself.

Ever since Ishibashi resorted to the careful distribution of government and party offices in such a way as both to reward his supporters and collaborators in the previous presidential election and, at the same time, to maintain the extremely delicate inter-factional balance of power (represented by the narrow seven-vote margin he had won over Kishi in that election), factional and inter-factional considerations have become a basic factor in the LDP personnel administration. The Prime Minister (who is concurrently president of the party) assigns various government and party offices as a rule not to individual members as such but to the factions. To be more specific, the following offices are all more or less subject to assignments based on such factional or interfactional considerations, the relative importance attached to each office being roughly corresponding to the order in which they are mentioned on p. 130:[21]

[21]This list of the offices and their ranking in importance as perceived by LDP-affiliated Diet members was prepared on the basis of information furnished by several journalists as well as LDP politicians. Suggestions given by Mr Nakajima of the *Asahi shimbun* were especially employed as guidelines. It may be possible but probably not very helpful to rank the individual offices placed in each category, e.g. the twenty Cabinet ministerships lumped together in Category 2, because perceptions of their relative importance and preferences for them vary greatly from politician to politician and even between journalist observers.

1. Speaker of the House of Representatives, and President of the House of Councillors.
2. Deputy Speaker of the House of Representatives, Deputy President of the House of Councillors, and Cabinet ministers.
3. LDP Secretary-General, Chairman of the Executive Council and Chairman of the PARC.
4. LDP Chairmen of the Committees on Finance, National Organisation, Public Relations, and Diet Policy.
5. Chairmen of the Standing Committees in the House of Representatives, and those in the House of Councillors.
6. Chairmen of the *ad hoc* Special Committees in the two Houses.
7. Parliamentary vice-ministers.
8. Deputy secretaries-general, vice-chairmen of the executive council, and vice-chairmen of the PARC.
9. Chiefs of the PARC divisions and special investigation committees.

In order to facilitate the working of this rather peculiar system of appointments, a waiting list of candidates is carefully prepared in advance within each faction on the basis of the number of times they have been re-elected, the length of time they have been associated with the faction, and the monetary or other forms of contributions they have made to the faction or its leaders. For this reason it was relatively easy to predict in advance specific appointments to these positions in a reshuffle of a Cabinet or party leadership in the heyday of factionalism in the LDP. It was in the form of such waiting lists that, for example, the names of 'recommended' candidates for Cabinet posts were submitted to the Prime Minister by each faction in December 1960, July 1962, and July 1963. As the considerations of inter-factional balance came to be accepted as the criterion for appointments, it became unavoidable for practically every LDP Diet member interested in such appointments to associate himself with one faction or another on a semi-permanent basis.

A Source of Funds for Members

Just as important as the allocation of government and party posts and closely related to it as a cause of LDP factionalism have been the financial needs of most sitting and prospective Diet members. At the time of the 1958 House of Representatives election it was said that it took an LDP candidate at least ¥5 million to win a seat, of which ¥1 million was paid by the party but the remainder was for the candidate himself to raise. Obviously, many found it extremely hard to collect such a sum. It has become even harder in the subsequent years during which costs have increased several times. It is in fact not only the electioneering activities during the legally defined campaign periods but also the continuous and constant 'cultivation' of his constituency that an LDP Diet member must finance if he is to make sure of his re-election next time. Whenever a group of voters visits Tokyo from his electorate, he is expected to pay for their meals, their fares, their hotel accommodation and, not infrequently, to give them some pocket money. At the time of the annual summer Buddhist festival and at the end of the year, his local collaborators naturally expect him either to buy them drinks or to give them a few thousand yen for a present (or both) as a matter of traditional courtesy. And in a hundred other ways he is constantly under pressure to spend money.[22]

Under these circumstances the average LDP Diet member is compelled to turn to the few influential men who are able to exact large sums from various interest groups, corporations, individual businessmen, and industrialists. These privileged few are the faction leaders, either actual or potential. When asked whether he believed that he had been so successful in raising funds because the donors supported his particular policies or ideas, Kawashima Shōjirō once brusquely and characteristically said, 'I just go and get the money. Policy has nothing to do with it. I go and tell them that I need funds and just get them. Just as much as I need . . . It takes lots of money to make friends, you know.'[23]

To minimise the tax obligations of themselves and their donors the leaders have constituted their factions into 'political associations' within the meaning of the Political Funds Regulation Law. According to the relevant provisions of this particular law and related laws currently in force, a political party, association or any other form of group must satisfy certain legal requirements as a 'political association' in order lawfully to receive donations or expend money for purposes of political activity. These requirements include the following: the entity in question must (1) nominate an official representative and a treasurer and register with either an appropriate election administration commission or the Minister of Autonomy; (2) regularly report through its treasurer the donations and other income received and expenditures made (this must be done within ten days of 30 June and 31 December each year) to the election administration commission or the Minister of Autonomy; (3) regularly report within a prescribed period donations and incomes received and expenditures made for a particular election; and (4) refrain from receiving donations from persons or corporations in special contractual relationships with a public body, aliens or alien groups, and those either using pseudonyms or remaining anonymous. On the other hand, a party, association, or other form of group which satisfies these conditions may claim exemption from donation, corporation or income tax for the donations and incomes received by it. At the same time, a donor organisation or group may, if it is incorporated, include in its deductible debit statements the sum of its donations to political groups up to half of a total of 0·25 per cent of its gross capitalisation and 2·5 per cent of its gross income for the appropriate financial

[22]Okada, op. cit., pp. 125-6. In the mid-1960s the *minimum* monthly outlay for the average LDP Diet member was said to be about ¥1 million. 'Seijishikin wa dou nagareru', *Asahi*, 29 October 1966.
[23]Kawashima Shōjirō, *Ikeda kaizōnaikaku no seikaku to sono zento* (KSK Report, 50) (31 July 1961), pp. 23-4.

year. An unincorporated, partially profit-making organisation may count such donations as part of deductible losses up to 2·5 per cent of its total income for the appropriate financial year. When applied to one of the largest donors, the Yawata Iron Manufacturing Co., this means that in 1963 it could make tax-free political donations up to the value of some ¥207 million against its capitalisation of ¥90,500 million and an income of ¥6,200 million for that financial year. At election time each of the factional 'political associations' built at the receiving ends of such donor-beneficiary relationships has constituted an independent and self-contained quasi-party, providing its members with financial aid even more substantial than they have received from the party headquarters.

In the House of Representatives election of November 1960, for example, the Ikeda, Kishi, Ishii, and Miki factions in the name of their respective 'political associations'—the Kōchikai, the Tōkakai, the Hōankai, and the Shin seiji keizai kenkyūjo—officially expended a total of ¥341,000,000. At the same time, the Shūzankai of the Satō faction and the Daiichi kokusei kenkyūkai of the Kōno faction spent an estimated total of ¥318 million. In other words, the combined total of the expenditures made by six of the eight factions alone was nearly equal to the total of ¥666 million spent by the LDP Party Headquarters. Furthermore, practically all the money spent by the factions is believed to have gone directly to the individual candidates either as undisguised 'aid' or as allowances for 'organisation' and 'political research'. Thus on that occasion about forty supporters of Ishii and twenty-five followers of Miki officially received ¥2 million each, and the seventy-odd Ikeda faction candidates ¥1 million each, from their respective factions. This was compared with the ¥500,000 per head which the party headquarters managed to hand out uniformly to the 320 candidates.

The role of the factional political associations as fund-raising and distributing devices does not cease with the end of a legally defined election campaign period, for, as has already been pointed out, the financial needs of the average Diet member are constant and continuous. Thus in 1962, for example, the nine associations run by the eight factions (these include a second association run by the Kishi faction and called the *Shinyūkai*) spent between them a total of ¥1,286 million as compared with ¥1,607 million spent by the LDP. We have already seen how some significant changes in the general system of LDP factionalism had taken place by 1965 and the tendency towards fragmentation and multiplication of factional units was reflected in an increase to fifteen in the number of their political associations. Between them these fifteen fund-raising organisations (representing nine factions and one quasi-faction) collected in 1965 a total of ¥1,679 million, which was approximately half the ¥3,382 million collected by the LDP in that year. Here again it should be noted that the bulk of the money raised by the individual factions was probably distributed among their members, whereas a high percentage of that collected by the headquarters was consumed in the management of the party at large. Since the specific sums made available to a member by the party headquarters or a faction depend on various factors, such as his position and status in the party, the particular faction to which he belongs and his position therein, and the relative degree of his financial needs, it is difficult to make a significant generalisation about this. For example, Tanaka Kakuei, who was then LDP Secretary-General, received between 20 and 21 December 1965 as much as ¥63 million for 'Diet activities' and in addition ¥73 million for 'organisational activities'. In 1965, the per capita annual income of the factions varied from ¥1·8 million for the Fujiyama faction to ¥6·8 million for the Satō faction. In the House of Councillors election of 1962 Morita Tama of the Ikeda faction received ¥1 million from the headquarters and ¥3·5 million from a factional association called the *Tokyo Maeokai*, whereas Kijima Yoshio of the Fujiyama faction officially received ¥2 million from the party but nothing at all from the faction. Despite the fact that these figures are all based on reports made by the party, the factions, and the politicians concerned and thus cannot be trusted without qualification, there is little doubt that the situation has varied from faction to faction and individual to individual. Nevertheless, it seems reasonable to assume that in the mid-1960s most LDP Diet members receive, as a matter of routine, about half a million yen per year from the party and at least ¥1 million from the factions. When they run in an election they apparently get ¥2 million from the party and at least as much from the factions.

The Role of the Multi-member Constituency System

Another very important factor contributing to the growth and prevalence of factions in the LDP has no doubt been the multi-member electoral system under which each Lower House constituency returns three, four or five members. A party intent on winning a majority must accordingly enter two or more candidates in each constituency, a situation which inevitably leads to bitter competition not only between the parties but also between those candidates who are endorsed officially by the same party. Although the LDP may refuse to endorse more candidates in the same constituency than are likely to be returned, it is common for extremely bitter internecine competition to develop between two or more LDP candidates and for this to continue long after the election is over. Under such circumstances the competing candidates have to seek financial and other forms of support from rival factions and faction leaders during the election campaign and subsequently on their successful election associate themselves with the same antagonistic factions. In other words, expensive election campaigns force a candidate to seek financial support from a faction, while the competitive situation drives the two or more LDP candidates standing in the same constituency to seek such support from

K

opposing factions and subsequently continue to identify themselves with them.

In an assessment of the effects of the multi-member constituency system on LDP factionalism two factors are important: one is the inability of the party headquarters to supply each candidate officially endorsed by the party with sufficient campaign funds, and the other is that each prefectural federation of party branches has traditionally been dominated by a particular faction. As a result, the pattern of antagonisms between dominant and dissident groups of factions, which is such a familiar feature of LDP intra-party politics at the centre, is reproduced at the prefectural and constituency levels in the form of competition between those candidates who are supported by the prefectural federation and those who are not. Under these circumstances the formal party organisation itself becomes a tool of intra-party factionalism and a majority of the party's candidates are led to rely on their own electioneering machines (the supporters' associations) for votes and on the factions for funds. It is against this background that the replacement of the present multi-member district system by a single-member district system has been seriously discussed within the party in recent years as a possible cure for disruptive effects of factionalism.[24]

The Size of Factions

Each of the three principal factors that have been responsible for the growth of factionalism has defined both the size and functions of the factions as they have operated in the LDP. Ideally, a faction as a unit of competition would be most satisfactory if it controlled one person more than a half of the total party-affiliated MHRs. Such a faction would constitute in itself what is called in the theory of games a minimum winning coalition, ensuring a victory in the competition without spreading the benefits accruing from such a victory too widely and therefore too thinly. In practice, however, the limitations of available funds and effective co-ordination tend to reduce each factional unit to a much smaller size than the theory would suggest.

On the one hand, a faction with much fewer than twenty members has been considered to be rather too small to be effective in helping its leader bid successfully for the positions of party president and Prime Minister. Nor is such a numerically small faction likely to have a satisfactory share of the limited number of government and party posts and thus provide its members with the incentive to stay within it. A faction with much more than fifty members, on the other hand, will not only impose an unbearable financial burden on its leader but will also inevitably be faced with difficulties in adjusting the competing demands for priorities in the factional waiting list for appointments to the more desirable government and party posts. More-

[24]See Robert E. Ward, 'Recent Electoral Developments in Japan', *Asian Survey*, VI, 10 (October 1966), pp. 547-67; 'Seitō wa kore de yoi no ka' (14) and (15), *Asahi*, 23 and 26 January 1966.

over, in a very large faction it is likely that some of its members will compete in the same electorates and that divisive tendencies will thereby emerge. As already mentioned, the result of such electoral competition and antagonism is usually a split in factional affiliation. In a time of economic recession, when the flow of funds from sources outside the party tends naturally to dry up, the optimal size of a faction may be considered to be much smaller than fifty. Assuming that it costs a faction ¥5 million per head in a House of Representatives election (a modest estimate), a 50-man faction will need at least ¥250 million to fight a single election, on top of its regular expenses. It must be far from easy even for the most powerful faction leaders to raise that much money at short notice and every few years. It would seem, therefore, that, considering the fact that ten House of Representatives and seven House of Councillors elections have been held in the twenty-one postwar years (one election every fifteen months), a faction of fifty MHRs and fifty MHCs, which is approximately the size of the Satō faction both before and after the January 1967 election, has reached about the maximal numerical strength from an economic point of view. On the other hand, the smaller factions, such as those led by Murakami, Funada, Mori, and Matsumura in the wake of that election, should be rather unstable and in danger of either falling apart or being gobbled up by a larger faction.

Factions and Party Policy-making

The major functions of the faction should be fairly obvious from the foregoing discussion of the principal factors responsible for its development. In brief, it operates as the basic unit in the distribution of the important party and government posts, including the party presidency and the premiership, and looks after the financial needs of the rank and file Diet members. In terms of the party policy-making process, however, its role is somewhat more complex and harder to generalise about. In some important respects it has been dysfunctional, but in a few others it has been moderately functional.

On the negative side should be counted, first of all, the general effects of the considerations about inter-factional balance of power which have determined the appointment of members to the key party positions. As has been pointed out by an official committee as well as by individual members of the party itself, there is little doubt that inter-factional balance has sacrificed the principle of appointment on the basis of individual merit and thus reduced the possibilities of the most capable and best qualified members being appointed to the key party positions and participating in the crucial policy-making process. The factional waiting list does not take into consideration, except marginally, the factors of ability and achievement. This apparently means that the most influential formal party leaders are not necessarily the best qualified of its members for policy-making.

Far more critical, however, have been the effects of this principle of inter-factional balance upon the quality of leadership represented by the party president and the leaders' meeting. Under the circumstances they are not only not the best qualified but are seriously hampered in the exercise of the legitimate decision-making powers with which they are entrusted by the party constitution. Especially important in this connection is the fact that the official presidential term of office is only two years. Even more important are the effects of the familiar pattern of struggle between dominant and dissident alliances of factions, which logically results from the kind of factionalism under consideration operating generally in accordance with the principles of political coalitions. This type of intra-party, inter-factional struggle is bound to cripple party leadership when faced with an especially controversial issue or difficult situation. As was forcefully brought out by the conflicts which lasted almost continuously from about September 1958 to July 1960 under Kishi, this form of intra-party struggle may prove vicious enough to sap completely the energy of the formal party leadership and paralyse its functions.[25] Given the characteristically competitive instinct of the faction, a president who dares to deal with any controversial policy issue runs the risk of arousing all the destructive passions of his opponents in the dissident factions and even some of his fair-weather allies, and may well be found to be digging his own grave. As far as the role of the formal leadership group in the party policy-making process is concerned, therefore, factionalism doubtless exerts an inhibitive influence.

The Faction as a Unit of Intra-party Communication

On the positive side may be counted the role of the faction as a unit of intra-party communication and its generally decentralising, or rather polycentric, effects on the party policy-making process. While there seems no logical reason why a formal party organ, such as the Executive Council or the PARC, cannot be made the effective forum of policy deliberations and

[25]The conflicts became quite evident following the formation of the Foreign Policy Study Group in September 1958 by the dissident Ikeda, Ishii, Miki, and Ishibashi factions very obviously with a view to challenging the Kishi-Fujiyama line which aimed at an early revision of U.S.-Japan Security Treaty. A few months after the formation of that group, the dissident factions pounced on the clumsy handling by Kishi and his followers of the Police Duties Law Revision Bill and the extension of a Diet session in November as an excuse to intensify their internal opposition. A rather drastic realignment of forces occurred in June 1959, when Kōno moved to the dissident side because his wish to be appointed secretary-general was rejected, while Ikeda, now made Minister of International Trade and Industry in the new Cabinet, and Ishii, now nominated chairman of the executive council of the party, both joined the dominant coalition. As a result, when the controversy reverted to the issue of the Security Treaty in late 1959 and 1960, it was the three factions led by Kōno, Miki, and Ishibashi which engaged in various obstructionist tactics to interfere with the ratification of the Revision Bill, including a boycott of the final vote in the House of Representatives on 19 May 1960. It was as much due to the pressure of these internal opposition groups as to those of public opinion and external groups that Kishi was forced a month later to offer to resign. For a detailed account of the controversy over the Security Treaty, see George R. Packard, *Protest in Tokyo: The Security Treaty Crisis of 1960* (Princeton, N.J.: Princeton University Press, 1966).

frank exchange of views for all interested party members (which they are no doubt meant to be), it is true that, up to the present, such a purpose has been served more by the factions than by the formal party organs.[26] Whereas a meeting of four hundred members would no doubt make it rather difficult for each to express his views freely and for all to come to agreement on specific problems, a relatively small group of a few dozen members may find it much easier to satisfy such needs. The atmosphere of a faction headquarters, located often in a modern and clean office building or hotel, is much more informal and therefore more conducive to free and frank discussion than that of the party headquarters. Besides, the authority of a faction leader was such, at least in the heyday of LDP factionalism, that whoever objected to a view or course of action favoured by him could be quickly and effectively silenced and brought into line.[27] This means that the formal party leadership, represented by the president, needed to deal only with a dozen faction leaders, instead of four hundred members, when he wanted to have a decision made with the full support of the whole parliamentary party. He could rest assured of general support once he had succeeded in winning a promise of co-operation from them. For example, for the ratification of the ILO Convention 87, ten years after the Hatoyama Cabinet's decision to accomplish it in February 1955, Satō called upon the faction leaders individually and won their promise of co-operation in the first few months of 1965 and thus made it possible for it to be approved finally by the House of Councillors in May. Similarly, the ratification of the Japan-South Korea Treaty in November of the same year was made possible by the personal commitments of the two faction leaders, Ōno and Kōno, initially made while they were in the dominant coalition under Ikeda and honoured, after Ōno died, by Kōno, even though by this time he had shifted his position to the dissident side.[28]

All this does not deny in the least, however, that whatever integrative and co-ordinating functions are performed by the faction in the party decision-making processes depend in the final analysis upon the personal authority and influence of the leader, which in turn depend on his ability to raise sufficient funds and promote the chances of his factional followers' appointments to the desirable party and government posts.

The theory about the democratising influence of the faction, according to which its presence generally tends to prevent dictatorship by a particular individual or group, actually regards weak and ineffective leadership on the part of the president and other key party officials as a virtue. Whether such

[26] For views emphasising this positive aspect of LDP factionalism, see Watanabe, op. cit., p. 155; George O. Totten and Tamio Kawakami, 'The Functions of Factionalism in Japanese Politics', *Pacific Affairs*, XXXVIII, 2 (Summer, 1965), pp. 109-22.
[27] 'Kōno could make every one of the members of his faction turn either right or left as he wished with no trouble at all', according to Mr Fukushima of the Shunjūkai secretariat. (Interview, 20 January 1966.)
[28] The writer owes information concerning these two specific cases to Mr Miyazaki Yoshimasa of the *Yomiuri Shimbun*. (Interview, 12 January 1966.)

an influence should be considered positive or negative is, therefore, essentially a matter of degree and preference, as clearly demonstrated by the widely differing evaluations of Yoshida's 'one-man rule' which is often cited as an example of a situation likely to develop in the absence of plural factions in the LDP. It may be argued that the presence of factions makes it possible for a number of radically different and opposing views and policy preferences to coexist within the single party and thus justifies the transfer of public (governmental) power from one faction to another within the party. This argument springs from the long monopolisation of power by the LDP at the expense of the opposition parties. It means that the LDP, from a strictly partisan point of view, can pretend to be a self-contained party system in itself, embracing a dozen *de facto* parties within it and ensuring that power passes from one to another *democratically* through periodic presidential elections. In short, the presence and nature of the factions has made it possible for plural political views and attitudes to coexist at the informal level without destroying a semblance of party unity at the formal level of the party organisation.

Attempts to Disband the Factions

Whether or not factions are desirable from the point of view of intra-party democracy, the formal party leadership has seen them much more as the agents of dissident obstructionism and intransigence than as useful means of intra-party communication and co-ordination. Following the riotous presidential election of December 1956, the new President, Ishibashi, and his Secretary-General, Miki Takeo, immediately began to call for an end to factional strife. Governing in a period of unbridled factionalism, Kishi Nobusuke attempted in September 1957 not only to talk about but also to enforce the dissolution of the dozen or so factional groupings, although this failed to produce any tangible and lasting effects. Under Kishi's pressure Ōno's Hakuseikai and Miki's Sannōkai were nominally disbanded, Sunada Shigemasa's Senkenkai and Kōno's Shunjūkai as well as Kishi's own Kizankai withdrew their applications for official registration which had been lodged with the Autonomy Agency, while the Heishinkai of the former Yoshida faction and Satō's Mokuyōkai promised to follow suit. On the other hand, Ikeda's Kōchikai, Satō's Shūzankai, Ishibashi's Tanzankai, and Ishii's Suiyō kurabu all refused to comply with Kishi's order and continued just as before. Moreover, it soon became evident that the decisions of the ostensibly co-operative groups were in reality nothing but purely nominal. Following the submission of the Organisation Research Council's interim report in July 1963 (the 'Miki Report'), Ikeda proceeded in December to disband his own factional associations, the Iseikai and the Kōchikai, and thus compelled the others either to change their names or close down regular meeting places. For example, on this occasion Satō's Shūzankai was renamed *Tameike kurabu*, the management of the Miki faction's office passed nominally from Miki's to Matsuura Shūtarō's hands, and the Fukuda and Ishii factions ceased to meet officially and regularly. Finally, Satō invited all faction leaders to a well-known Akasaka restaurant in September 1966 to call on them to liquidate their factions without delay and announced his intention to do the same with his own Mokuyō kurabu, an intention which was eventually fulfilled but failed to induce the others to follow suit.[29]

Every one of these efforts by successive presidents and their allies in the dominant group have proved unsuccessful, as some of the most experienced LDP politicians had confidently predicted.[30] These failures seem to have been inevitable, for all the basic factors responsible for their growth still remained unchanged. The fact that the assurances given by Satō and Tanaka in 1966 that the party headquarters would officially look after members' financial needs (in fulfilment of the assurances some three hundred rank and file members received a uniform 'year's-end allowance') failed to shake their loyalty to the factions suggests that all three factors, and not just one, will have to be removed, if the factions are ever to be actually abolished.

The conventional faction as a form of grouping, however, is basically not very stable, for its unity and solidarity depend almost exclusively upon the loose network of bilateral ties binding each member to the leader in a highly personal relationship. As a rule, very little consideration is given to agreement on ideological or policy preferences between the leader and his followers, while the association between the rank and file members of a faction is often accidental and, at least in reference to the factional waiting list for posts, even overtly competitive. As a result, the weakening of the leader-follower ties (the extreme form of which is the leader's death) immediately threatens to cause open strife between the members which may eventually lead to the break-up of the faction.

The Decline of the Factions

While LDP presidents and other leaders of dominant factions have often preached self-righteously about the evils of factionalism and the need to dissolve the factions, this has failed to affect the general conditions of factionalism in the party. Nevertheless, several developments in its environment have conspired in recent years to produce some noteworthy changes, especially in the years following the Security Treaty crisis of 1960.

[29]'Seitō wa kore de yoi no ka' (5), *Yomiuri*, 6 January 1966. According to a journalist, Secretary-General Tanaka Kakuei, himself a member of the Satō faction, was not keen about the proposition and sabotaged its enforcement. As a result, the whole problem of factionalism and its effective cure was thrown back again to the Organisation Research Council (Nakajima Kiyonari, interview, 20 January 1966).
[30]Kawashima Shōjirō said in July 1961, 'The factions cannot be done away with. No, that is impossible as long as the presidential elections are held . . .' Kawashima, op. cit., p. 18. At a private meeting on 31 January 1966, Hori Shigeru assured his audience, including the present writer, that it was 'absolutely unthinkable for the factions to disappear within a year or so'.

Firstly, the various business and industrial groups supporting individual factions began to feel the strains of the vastly increased monetary contributions demanded of them, and therefore pressed for unification of the channels of donations. This was first attempted with the establishment of the Keizai saiken kondankai in January 1955 and then with its replacement by the Kokumin kyōkai in July 1961. Although the process has been both slow and tortuous, this situation has made it increasingly difficult for the faction leaders to raise sufficient funds.

Secondly, the slow but steady growth of the opposition parties, especially the JSP, and the relative decline in the effectiveness of the LDP as the dominant party (which was dramatically brought out in the Security Treaty crisis), emphasised the need for party-wide, instead of factional, solidarity and encouraged interest in ideological and policy problems, rather than merely personal and manipulative skills.

Thirdly, three of the most effective faction leaders, Ōno, Kōno, and Ikeda, died in quick succession in 1964 and 1965.

All these changes have combined to bring about a marked decline in the authority and prestige of the faction leaders and a general loosening of factional solidarity and discipline. It is significant in this connection that Satō arranged, following his nomination as party president in November 1964, to meet not only the leader but also other members of each faction in order to hear their suggestions concerning various policy issues. According to a newspaper report, practically every member of the Ishii faction was present at one of these consultations, while every one of the eighteen Kōno faction members present at another spoke. By early 1966, not only the Ōno and Kōno factions but almost every other faction was visibly suffering from internal divisions and antagonisms. On the other hand, interest in the ideological and policy implications of intra-party groupings began to grow at the expense of the traditional emphasis on the emotive and financial basis of the faction. Most immediately this shift of emphasis appeared in the guise of factional 'policy study sessions', which were not new but became much more frequent in the years following the Security Treaty crisis of 1960. Reinforced by the decline of factional unity, the emphasis on policy has led to the emergence of new cross-factional groupings based on policy or ideology, such as the two opposing groups interested in the China issue and the Soshinkai identified with the traditionalist and nationalist elements in the party. The fact that affiliation with such cross-factional groups has not entailed dissociation from the factions suggests coexistence (possibly involving an element of competition) between the two categories of intra-party grouping rather than supersession of the one by the other. Nevertheless, this new situation is bound in the long run to affect the basic characteristics of the system of factionalism in the LDP as it has existed in the past ten years or so.

As mentioned in Chapter 4, much of the routine decision-making and policy formulation takes place within the framework of the formal party organisation, represented by the PARC and its working sections and the executive council. Appointment to the key posts in such organs has traditionally been affected by the considerations of inter-factional balance. Indirectly but to a very important extent, therefore, the faction influenced their work and, in all probability, the content of their decisions wherever factional interests were involved.

More directly, the faction played a critical role whenever a controversial issue arose. Opinion would sharply divide over such an issue not only between the parties but frequently within the LDP itself, and the conflicts often proved insoluble if left to the formal decision-making organs. As a result the party leadership, interested in having a clear-cut decision made one way or the other in the name of the party and with at least a semblance of party-wide consensus to back it up, would resort to an informal and extra-constitutional decision-making mechanism, the council of faction leaders. Considering the basically competitive and expansionist nature and purposes of a faction, the leadership ran the risk of playing into the hands of its open opponents (the dissident factions) and its potential opponents (the allies in the dominant factional coalition) who would certainly make sure that no opportunity was missed to discredit the leadership and take over control of the party themselves. With good luck, however, the party president might persuade the faction leaders to co-operate with him in his efforts to create a semblance of consensus and thus to resolve the difficulties. In either case, the role of the faction in this kind of decision-making situation was direct and crucial.

Under the changed conditions reviewed above, however, the influence of the faction leader in the selection of party officials is likely to decline, although the election of a party president will probably continue much longer to be a game of inter-factional power politics. Consequently, the role of the faction in the formal party decision-making will probably become less important.

The growth of cross-factional groups primarily interested in specific policy issues will, moreover, deprive the factions of their utility as an informal decision-making mechanism over controversial issues and the role will shift to these cross-factional groups, if not to the formal party organs. Since opinion is bound to be divided over certain issues and a single group cannot conceivably represent two or more conflicting views at the same time, it is likely that more than one cross-factional group will grow over each specific issue and that these will fight each other. When the unchallenged authority of the faction leaders to impose their wills on their followers and generate consensus of a sort (either for their own or the party leaders' sake) is gone, it will no doubt become extremely difficult to reconcile the opposing views and groups with each other. Under such new conditions the façade of unity and harmony afforded by the emotional and irrational elements of factionalism will be replaced by much more harsh and direct, though no doubt rational, confrontation of ideological principles and political commitments.

The factions have grown in the LDP as a form of inter-personal relationship calculated to be mutually beneficial to the handful of influential members who aspire to the post of party president and the rank and file who desire lesser government or party posts and political funds. By entering into this special relationship, the leaders have secured a reliable bloc of votes in a presidential election as well as other, less tangible benefits, such as prestige and the sense of leadership. The rank and file, on the other hand, have benefited by securing opportunities for promotion in the intra-party hierarchy and very significant amounts of supplementary income to finance the electoral and other activities essential to their survival as members of the Diet. The effects of the multi-member constituency system have further encouraged tendencies towards factionalism by dividing party members among themselves. As long as these three basic factors remain, the factions are unlikely to die out, despite the repeated calls for their dissolution.

The most conspicuous of the influences of factionalism on the party policy-making process have been negative. By introducing elements unrelated to ability or achievement as determinants in intra-party allocation of manpower, it has no doubt worked against efficiency and rationality. More directly, it has interfered with the process of party policy-making by setting alliances of dominant factions against those of dissident factions on controversial issues. The essentially competitive and antagonistic relationships between the factions, especially between those identified with the dominant and those with the dissident positions, have made it inevitable for intense conflicts to develop over controversial issues. This in turn has weakened and often paralysed leadership on the part of formal party organs and officials represented by the party president and the leaders' meeting.

Less conspicuous has been the factions' positive role as the intermediate units of intra-party communication and co-ordination, intervening between the top party leadership group and the rank and file members. The replacement of the more than four hundred individual LDP-affiliated members of the Diet as the basic units of communication by a dozen or so groups, each led by a particularly influential member with a firm control over the actions of his followers, has facilitated the growth of some degree of consensus over certain issues. A faction leader who is potentially a competitor of the incumbent president has at times shown willingness to help the latter by bringing his followers into line, provided that the rewards given or promised in return have been sufficiently tempting.

From a strictly partisan point of view, the presence of the factions has benefited the LDP also by making it possible for the dozen or so quasi-parties to coexist within the single party organisation despite all the genuine or false divisions of opinion and conflicts. This has also made it possible for the LDP to remain continuously in power despite the many changes of Cabinets. Whenever an LDP Cabinet dominated by a particular coalition of factions fell, another LDP Cabinet dominated by a rival coalition of factions would take over. Thus a quasi-two-party or multi-party system has emerged and operated within the LDP itself, while the opposition parties have been effectively and perpetually kept out of power.

Whether positive or negative, and notwithstanding the repeated attempts to do away with them, the factions have played a decisive role in the process of party policy-making, particularly when the LDP has been faced with issues of a controversial nature. Neither the general pattern of their interaction nor their specific effects upon party policy-making will remain the same forever, as several important developments since about 1960 have indicated. Without fully taking into account the significance of the influence of factions, the process of policy-making in the LDP will be as impossible to explain as ever.

6 Connections with External Groups

In order to exist as a viable unit in the system of party politics the LDP naturally depends very considerably upon external organisations and groups for support in return for various services both general and particular which it is capable of performing.

Being essentially a parliamentary party with a weak grass-roots organisation, the party requires above all two specific forms of support—votes and funds. Neither of these is available in sufficient quantity within the existing party organisation itself, but both are so essential that too little of either would seriously damage its effectiveness and even threaten its survival. Hence the acquisition of votes and funds from outside sources, usually from organised groups of various kinds, becomes the *sine qua non* of its existence. In addition to such tangible support, the party also needs more general moral support of powerful external groups as a condition for the effective execution of its policies.

Any political party in a system similar to that in which the LDP operates needs funds not only to finance its own management and programs but also to attract votes. Up to a point funds represent votes in disguise and this is why money plays a crucial role in elections, which are basically contests for votes.

The linkages between the LDP and various external groups have developed broadly at two more or less distinctive levels—the level of the formal party organisation and that of individual party members. At the first level a few hundred enterprises used to make separate donations to conservative parties through party leaders, but this practice was replaced by a special organisation to co-ordinate these linkages and take care of the party's needs for funds and public relations in a more systematic manner. However, direct and personal connections between individual enterprises and other organisations on the one hand and the formal representatives of the party on the other continue to be an essential and important part of the intricate mechanism.

At the level of individual members consolidated and extensive ties have been maintained by the faction leaders with large numbers of external groups (mainly enterprises) for fund-raising purposes, ostensibly in the name of the factions rather than themselves. A large portion of the funds collected by them has been in fact expended on the upkeep of the factions and the welfare of their members, especially in relation to their electoral needs. The basic nature of this type of linkage remains predominantly personal and particular. Similar connections have also been established by less important or influential members principally for the purpose of raising funds for themselves. Their organisations are called 'supporters' associations' and have usually been crucial to the success or failure of the politicians concerned. Equally important as a linkage between the LDP and external groups at the level of individual members has been another kind of supporters' association, the primary function of which is to collect votes rather than funds. For the electoral success of individual LDP members and indirectly of the LDP itself, this type of organisation has apparently been indispensable.

Different again have been a host of groups involving particular party leaders (such as the president), on the one hand, and prominent industrialists, journalists, and public servants on the other. Their purposes and compositions have been various—some being plainly non-political—but most have either supplemented some of the types of linkage already mentioned or have provided moral, ideological, or technical support.

These groups usually claim rewards in the form of specific legislative or administrative actions by the party for support given at the official party level. When it comes, however, to relationships between individual members and their supporters' associations the reward claimed may be much more personal and private. In the case of the former kind of reward the legislative or administrative actions which the supporting groups expect the party to take on their behalf usually call for much more than goodwill and political commitment. They can be effectively taken only with the co-operation of and technical facilities provided by the national bureaucracy. Thus, connections between the party and the bureaucracy at both of the above-mentioned levels are a prerequisite for contacts between the party and private external groups.

Connections at the Level of Formal Party Organisation

Since 1955 the LDP has always depended heavily on the donations of various external groups for a very substantial proportion of its annual income.[1]

[1]Concerning the actual amounts of funds made available to the parties, especially the LDP, by various donor groups, widely varying estimates have been made. It has become almost a cliché that the 'actual' amounts are much larger than those officially reported to the appropriate authorities by the recipients of the donations. Very often it has been said that the former are at least twice as large. When it comes to specific evidence supporting these allegations, however, practically none that is sufficiently explicit, specific, and reliable has been offered. In the absence of firm evidence substantiating the rumours, I feel compelled to take the position, at least at the moment, that to make our discussion meaningful at all, we have to deal with the subject on the basis of the 'official' figures that are available. To multiply these figures by two, three, or four in an attempt to arrive at 'more realistic' figures may be a healthy exercise,

In the first ten years of its existence, however, relations between the LDP as the recipient and external groups as the donors of political funds tended to become less particular, personal, and unorganised and more general, impersonal, and regularised. This change was clearly reflected in the remarkable growth of two particular categories of external donor group and a corresponding decline of others.

As Table 11 shows, in 1957 nearly 30 per cent of the donations came from about twenty individual enterprises and less than 6 per cent from trade and professional associations. The *Keizai saiken kondankai* (Economic Reconstruction Forum), which was established in January 1955 by the business community as the official channel of its political contributions, accounted for about 60 per cent. By 1962 the situation had undergone a drastic change. Whereas, on one hand, the number of individual companies involved had increased six times to 121, their share of the total value of the contributions had dropped to about 10 per cent. On the other hand, the number of trade and professional associations had increased to thirty-eight and their percentage share of the contributions to 25 per cent. In the meantime, the Keizai saiken kondankai had been replaced by the *Kokumin kyōkai* (People's Association) which accounted for nearly 60 per cent of the donations, roughly equal to the share of the former five years before.

It was in the subsequent few years, however, that the most spectacular change occurred in the relative importance of the roles played by these different categories of donor group. The role of individual enterprises as a source of direct donations had dwindled to less than 2 per cent by 1965 and even that of the trade and professional associations had become quite inconspicuous. On the other hand, the Kokumin kyōkai had definitely established itself as the major supplier of funds for the party, handing out in a single year a total of ¥2,343 million, or 90 per cent of the total LDP income. Statistically, it is no exaggeration to conclude that this particular organisation is the financial patron and guarantor of the LDP in the late 1960s.

The Kokumin Kyōkai

In the six years following its formation the Keizai saiken kondankai provided the LDP with about ¥3,800 million on behalf of the nation's business community. In addition to ¥20 million regularly passed on to the party on a monthly basis, it paid the bill for the latter in every Diet election held during this period. To it belonged about 150 corporations as formal members. This organisation was abolished, however, in March 1961 as a result of mounting dissatisfaction with its performance among business leaders, especially those

---

but under the present circumstances does not seem to improve our knowledge of the situation very significantly. Hoping that at a later date we may be in a position to deal with the 'more realistic' figures supported by some evidence more conclusive than is available now, I will limit my attention in the present chapter to the information presented in the form of the officially reported figures.

TABLE 11

Sources of LDP income by categories of donations

'Unit: ¥1,000'

	1957	1960	1962	1965
Total income	226,945	1,890,285	1,558,677	3,382,465
Major donations (i.e. exceeding ¥100,000)	184,700	1,710,899	832,696	2,603,666
Major donations/Total income	81·3%	90·5%	53·4%	76·9%
Individual enterprises:				
Number of enterprises	21	42	121	20
Combined sum of donations	54,700 (29·6%)*	191,799 (11·2%)	86,895 (10·4%)	43,300 (1·6%)
Trade and professional associations:				
Number of associations	3	24	38	13
Combined sum of donations	10,000 (5·4%)	154,000 (9·0%)	208,401 (25·0%)	174,500 (6·7%)
Political associations (excl. Keizai saiken kondankai and Kokumin kyōkai)				
Number of associations	1	4	5	5
Combined sum of donations	11,000 (5·9%)	53,800 (3·1%)	41,000 (4·9%)	21,000 (0·8%)
Keizai saiken kondankai / Kokumin kyōkai	109,000 (59·0%)	1,309,300 (76·5%)	495,000 (59·4%)	2,343,866 (90·0%)
Individuals				
Number of individual donors	—	4	2	3
Combined sum of donations	—	2,000 (0·1%)	1,400 (0·1%)	21,000 (0·8%)

*Percentages of the major donations, not of the total income.

Sources: Kampō, No. 9286 (4 December 1957), pp. 36-9; No. 9414 (14 May 1958), pp. 256-9; 'Gōgai' No. 124 (24 December 1960), pp. 7-11; No. 10298 (19 April 1961), pp. 399-408; No. 10775 (15 November 1962), pp. 356-60; No. 10930 (27 May 1963), pp. 13-18; 'Gōgai' No. 44 (20 April 1966), pp. 3-20; 'Gōgai' No. 115 (22 September 1966), pp. 8-22.

associated with the Dōyūkai, who felt that the organisation had been a failure on several specific counts. They thought that the enormous amount of money which it had funnelled into the party had been obviously misused for factional and other unworthy purposes, that despite its efforts to unify the channels of political donations from business circles individual factions continued to ask firms for additional contributions, and that it had come to be regarded by the public as the symbol of a special relationship tying the party to big business.

Before the Keizai saiken kondankai was formally dissolved, President Kishi and Secretary-General Kawashima established in December 1959 a new organisation called *Jiyū kokumin rengō* (National Union for Freedom) with the collaboration of several business leaders, including Sugi Michisuke, Adachi Tadashi, Mizuno Shigeo, and Uemura Kōgorō. Its basic aim was to create a broad-based mass association to propagate LDP policies in opposition to various leftist popular organisations. The function of raising funds for the party was considered to be secondary and incidental. The amount of money it collected and passed to the LDP was never much over ¥5 million per month. When, however, the Keizai saiken kondankai was dissolved and it became necessary immediately to create a fund-raising group in its place, the Jiyū kokumin rengō was quickly reorganised into the Kokumin kyōkai, which aimed from the beginning to fulfil the dual purpose of building a basis for organised popular participation in LDP public relations and of raising funds.[2]

The Kokumin kyōkai officially came into being on 15 July 1961. According to its constitution (adopted one month earlier), it was to be governed by a president and a board of directors and each individual member could choose to pay a subscription of 100, 500, 1,000, or 10,000 yen and a corporate member 5,000, 10,000, 50,000, or 100,000 yen per month. By October 1964, 4,896 corporate members were paying a total of ¥49,225,920 per month in subscriptions, while 48,225 individual members supplemented this sum by ¥9,218,115. By the end of 1965, there were 6,152 corporate members paying a total of ¥64,770,814 per month and 58,689 individual members contributing another ¥12,138,286. In addition to income from regular subscription fees which amounted to about ¥850 million in 1965, the organisation managed to raise nearly ¥690 million in that year in special contributions and an additional ¥1,140 million from other sources, in other words a total of ¥2,678

---

[2]Maeo Shigesaburō, then LDP Secretary-General, once explained the ideological, organisational, and fund-raising functions of the organisation as follows: 'The formation of the Kokumin kyōkai is intended partly to build a sort of national front against the so-called popular front. Because of its position as the ministerial party, the LDP is forced to refrain from using extreme or inflammatory language in its official publications, but it is necessary to have propaganda materials printed and distributed with less restraint by a department of an organisation like the Kokumin kyōkai in order to counter more effectively the effects of the communist propaganda . . . If it proves capable of raising more than ¥50 million per month, that will be sufficient to enable the party to cultivate votes continuously between elections and, consequently, cut its expenses for a particular election . . .' Maeo Shigesaburō, *Tōsanyaku ni kiku: Hoshutō dappi no nayami* (KSK Report, 53) (28 August 1961), pp. 4-6.

million. Of this last amount, ¥2,343 million, or 87·5 per cent, was given to the LDP, as has already been mentioned.

It is quite evident from the statistical data cited above that by 1966 the Kokumin kyōkai had rapidly and effectively co-ordinated practically all groups and organisations willing to make financial donations to the LDP as such. Although it had not yet completely superseded the contributions made to individual factions and their leaders, it is highly significant that, as Table 12 shows, nearly 40 per cent of the 455 enterprises and associations

TABLE 12
Donor groups classified by the combined values
of their contributions and categories of their recipients, 1965

Recipients	¥10m. or over	¥5m. to ¥10m.	¥1m. to ¥5m.	Less than ¥1m.	Total
LDP (A)	8	4	8	7	27
	161·5	30·1	14·0	2·1	207·7
Kokumin kyōkai	13	7	29	130	179
(KK) (B)	398·1	47·2	54·5	34·2	534·0
(A) and (B)	21	11	37	137	206
	559·6	77·3	68·5	36·3	741·7
LDP (or KK) and one	14	15	21	2	52
or more factions	216·2	102·6	63·5	1·1	383·4
One faction (C)	1	3	45	90	139
	10·0	19·0	81·3	33·2	143·5
Two or more factions (D)	10	18	25	5	58
	255·3	115·3	67·7	2·8	441·1
(C) and (D)	11	21	70	95	197
	265·3	134·3	149·0	36·0	584·6
Total	46	47	128	234	455
	1,041·1	314·2	281·0	73·4	1,709·7

Note: The upper and the lower figures refer respectively to the number of donors and the combined values of their donations in ¥ million.

Sources: Kampō 'Gōgai' No. 44 (20 April 1966), pp. 2-40; 'Gōgai' No. 115 (22 September 1966), pp. 5-40.

which made donations to the LDP or its component parts in 1965 handed their money directly and exclusively to the Kokumin kyōkai. From any point of view, then, it should be admitted that one of the two basic functions the Kokumin kyōkai was built to fulfil has been discharged with remarkable success in a relatively short space of time.

It is somewhat harder to assess its achievements in providing a mass basis for the ideological and political programs of the party. However, notwithstanding the denials by its own officials of any intention to interfere with the policy-making process in the LDP,[3] it seems clear that efforts have not been spared over the political and ideological aspects of its task.

These activities have been carried out mainly through occasional lecture

[3]Mr Nojima Teiichiro, chief of the Public Relations Department of the Kokumin kyōkai, in an interview with the writer on 17 February 1966.

L

meetings in various localities and by periodical publications. In the first half of 1965, for example, a series of eleven lectures was held in ten prefectures, while the official organ of the organisation, *Kokumin kyōkai*, was supplemented by another periodical (also published every ten days), *Kokumin no Koe*. The basic themes of these activities have consistently been strong nationalism and virulent opposition to communism, together with support for government positions on controversial political and diplomatic issues. Side by side with its spirited verbal campaigns against opposition to the visit of a United States atomic-powered submarine in 1964 and against opposition to the signing of the Japan-South Korea treaties in 1965, it has also campaigned enthusiastically and extensively for restoring the custom of flying the national flag and singing the national anthem on national holidays, and reinstating the old National Foundation Day of 11 February. The anti-communist posture of the organisation is shown most dramatically by a small booklet called *Nihon ga moshi kyōsanka shitara* [If Japan became Communist], written by an ex-member of the Communist Party of the Soviet Union, Takaya Kakuzō, and published by the Kokumin kyōkai in June 1965. This simple-looking booklet, 700,000 copies of which were printed and distributed in the first seven months, tells its readers that a socialist government would inevitably be replaced by a communist régime and that all the horrors associated with this would visit Japan which would then be destroyed with utmost ruthlessness. Whether this is a gospel of political realism or paranoiac insanity, there is little doubt that it has been taken with absolute seriousness by the leaders of the organisation as well as by at least a segment of its readers.

Not only as the financial supporter but also as the propaganda arm of the LDP the Kokumin kyōkai had thus become a powerful influence by early 1966. Its militant, reactionary nationalism and crusading anti-communism cannot but exert enormous pressure on the party leadership and affect the party policy-making process. While its ideological pronouncements and actions in its major campaigns so far have followed, rather than led, party decisions, it is conceivable that the relationship between them could be reversed under certain circumstances and initiative pass from the party to the sponsoring organisation. Such an eventuality would no doubt benefit the more vehemently nationalist and anti-communist elements within the party, best represented by the Soshinkai and the 'Old Right' groups. It is significant in this respect that the Kokumin kyōkai is organisationally independent from the LDP, although it is ideologically and programmatically closely related to it. It is therefore not subject to the latter's formal decisions or discipline except in a moral sense. It may be relevant to point out in this connection that few of the Kokumin kyōkai officials were formally affiliated with the LDP as of February 1966 explicitly for the fear of losing their freedom of action.[4]

[4]Nojima (interview, 17 February 1966).

As will be seen later the scope of its lobbying or pressure group activities is clearly limited because of the conditions prevailing among the most important of its members, but there seems little doubt that its influence will be a crucial factor in any LDP decision over a controversial issue.

Individual Groups and Organisations

Most of the corporate members of the Kokumin kyōkai belong to the federations of business enterprises (which are in turn defined as the party's sympathetic organisations side by side with a number of professional, civic, and cultural groups). As such they get special treatment in the distribution of various party publications, invitations to party functions and meetings, and so on. While they refrain as a rule from making separate financial contributions to the party (and especially to particular factions), many of them apparently continue to act as independent pressure groups when it comes to putting their specific economic, budgetary, and other demands to the party. Individual Diet members are often chosen as the primary objects of their lobbying activities, but many also maintain direct and regular relations with the formal party organisation and its leadership.

Apart from the well-known and widely publicised activities of such powerful groups as the six local government organisations,[5] the *Chūshōkigyō seiji renmei* (Small and Medium Enterprise Political League), and the *Nihon ishikai* (Japan Medical Association), etc., numerous interest groups have maintained special relationships with the party mainly, though by no means exclusively, under the aegis of the LDP National Organisation Committee and the various sections of the PARC. Especially in the case of farmers' and small businessmen's groups liaison conferences have been established since 1960 to connect them with the appropriate departments and bureaux of the above-mentioned committee in accordance with a provision of the party constitution. Even outside the framework of such official agencies of communication party leaders have often been present at these organisations' meetings and functions. For example, the national meeting of the Federation of Small and Medium Enterprises (*Chūshōkigyō sōrengō*) held on 16 April 1962, which resolved to bring more pressure to bear on the government and the party to have the Small and Medium Enterprises Basic Bill enacted, was addressed personally by the LDP Secretary-General Maeo Shigesaburō, the PARC Chairman Tanaka Kakuei, the National Organisation Committee Chairman Ogawa Hanji, and others. Similarly, the rally of the Japanese League of Farmers' Organisations held in March 1963 was attended by

---

[5]The term refers to the associations of prefectural governors, the presidents of prefectural assemblies, city mayors, the presidents of city assemblies, town and village mayors, and the presidents of town and village assemblies. For a survey of these organisations and their lobbying activities, see Ari Bakuji, 'Chihōrokudantai: Chihōjichi wo meguru zenkoku soshiki' in Nihon seijigakkai (ed.), *Nihon no atsuryokudantai* (*Nempō seijigaku, 1960*) (Iwanami shoten, 1960), pp. 49-63.

President Ikeda, the National Organisation Committee Chairman Ogawa, the PARC Vice-Chairman Nohara Masakatsu, etc.

From the point of view of the external groups, these opportunities for formal and informal communication with the LDP are no doubt seen as occasions for putting over their demands. For the party, they enable party leaders to repay financial supporters with the promise of appropriate political action concerning their demands and to appeal for greater aid in money and votes. Although it is largely through the Kokumin kyōkai that funds flow into the party from the external groups, the amount of funds thus to be made available depends on the image of the party held by its individual members. This in turn reflects the nature of the relationships (usually direct and personal) between the party leaders and themselves. Thus the party leaders still have to maintain close personal relations not only with the officials of the Kokumin kyōkai but also with its individual members and their representatives. In other words, direct, emotive ties between particular party leaders and their financial and moral supporters outside the party, very similar to those which had existed between conservative party leaders and groups of prominent businessmen before the Keizai saiken kondankai was formed in 1955, still play an important role today, despite the growing influence of the Kokumin kyōkai. This situation is likely to be further perpetuated by the obvious fact that it is difficult for a single organisation to represent at once all the specific, diversified, and often mutually incompatible demands and interests of some 6,000 different groups involved.

In this connection the role and activities of the leaders of the nation's business community, represented by the four powerful national organisations of businessmen and industrialists—Keidanren, Nikkeiren, Nisshō, and Dōyū-kai—deserve special attention. As has already been pointed out, it was with the co-operation of several leading businessmen that both the Keizai saiken kondankai and the Kokumin kyōkai were originally established. The fact that the largest contributions received by the Kokumin kyōkai invariably come from the corporations and trade associations which dominate these organisations shows how important they are in its development and activities. In late 1966, for example, the five hundred or so corporations affiliated with Keidanren alone accounted for over 70 per cent of the Kokumin kyōkai's income, according to one estimate.[6] It is no doubt because of the well-known importance of the role played by these business organisations that in December 1963 the top LDP leaders, including President Ikeda, Secretary-General Maeo, and the Finance Committee Chairman Sudō, appealed personally to sixteen leading businessmen representing the four organisations for increased help and co-operation in strengthening the Kokumin kyōkai. Similarly, in October 1964 President Ikeda invited them to the Hotel Ōkura to beg for an

[6]See Suzuki Yukio, 'Seikyokufuan to zaikai', *Ekonomisuto*, XLIV, 46 (8 November 1966), p. 26.

additional donation of some ¥1,500 million through the Kokumin kyōkai so as to enable the party to meet the costs of the forthcoming House of Representatives elections. In December 1966 it was Secretary-General Fukuda who asked the officials of Keidanren for additional contributions.

Connections Maintained by Individual Faction Leaders

The LDP faction leaders continue to maintain political associations (as defined in the Political Funds Regulation Law) which are largely independent of the formal party organisation. These are their personal fund-raising machines, although they are ostensibly factional organisations. In 1965, for example, the political associations each officially collected between ¥54 million and ¥668 million, totalling ¥1,747 million among ten of them. As seen in the preceding chapter, it is remarkable that these enormous amounts of money were raised almost single-handedly by a dozen or so faction leaders on behalf of their factional followings. This provides one of the main reasons for the perpetuation of factionalism within the LDP.

As can be seen from Table 13, many faction leaders have formed more than one political association, obviously for the purpose of tax evasion. In sharp contrast to the rapid unification of the channels of contributions to the party (represented by the efforts of the Kokumin kyōkai), the bulk of donations to faction leaders come directly from individual corporations.[7] Nevertheless, a number of donor groups extending beyond the limits of single corporations have also emerged, with fairly fixed memberships. In Ikeda's lifetime, for example, the Kōchikai was organically linked with several groups of leading businessmen and industrialists, such as the Kayōkai, the Nikokukai, and the Suehirokai. All members of these groups were at the same time the leaders of the business community as such and there is little room for doubt that they helped to arrange financial contributions to the Kōchikai as well as to the LDP not only from their own enterprises but also from many others affiliated with any of the four national organisations of businessmen which they represented. Satō maintains even more extended relationships with over a dozen groups of businessmen. The Chōeikai, which is the largest and most representative of these groups, involved nearly sixty leading businessmen by early 1966, including some who had been formerly associated with Ikeda's groups. The others also play an important role, but especially the Misokakai, which involves the top leaders of business organisations and important trade associations, and the Itsukakai, which consists mainly of those businessmen who have been closely identified with Yoshida and his followers (sometimes

---

[7]Except the two groups associated with Satō and his faction, Fujiyama's Kokusai seikei chōsakai, and Tanaka Kakuei's Etsuzankai, between about 60 per cent (Miki) and over 80 per cent (Kōno) of the donations received by them in 1965 came directly from individual enterprises. That the Kokusai seikei chōsakai had been financed largely by Fujiyama himself was confirmed to the writer by his secretary, Mr Ukai Takuo, in an interview on 18 January 1966. The situation about Satō's and Tanaka's groups is not certain.

TABLE 13

Sources of factional incomes by categories of donors, 1965

(Unit: ¥1,000)

	A	B	B/A	C	D	E	F
Satō							
Seiji-kōza	464,203	19,500	4·2	1 / 2,000 (10·2%)	2 / 5,500 (28·2%)	2 / 12,000 (61·5%)	0 / 0
Seikei kenkyūkai	203,862	1,500	0·7	0 / 0 (–)	0 / 0 (–)	1 / 1,500 (100%)	0 / 0 (–)
Total	668,066	21,000	3·1	1 / 2,000 (9·5%)	2 / 5,500 (26·1%)	3 / 13,500 (64·2%)	0 / 0 (–)
Maeo							
Shin zaisei kenkyūkai	233,235	189,300	80·9	79 / 130,200 (68·7%)	8 / 29,100 (15·3%)	3 / 29,000 (15·3%)	1 / 1,000 (0·5%)
Fukuda							
Chiyoda keizai konwakai	55,617	0	0	0 / 0	0 / 0	0 / 0	0 / 0
Jikyoku keizaimondai konwakai	75,470	64,200	85·0	38 / 45,900 (71·4%)	3 / 5,300 (8·2%)	2 / 12,000 (18·6%)	1 / 1,000 (1·5%)
Shin seiji keizai kenkyūkai	35,000	35,000	100	21 / 17,000 (48·5%)	1 / 9,000 (25·7%)	2 / 9,000 (25·7%)	0 / 0
Total	166,087	99,200	59·7	59 / 62,900 (63·4%)	4 / 14,300 (14·4%)	4 / 21,000 (21·1%)	1 / 1,000 (1·0%)
Kōno							
Daiichi kokusei kenkyūkai	139,960	139,960	100	46 / 115,900 (82·8%)	4 / 11,500 (8·2%)	3 / 6,500 (4·6%)	3 / 6,060 (4·3%)

TABLE 13 (*continued*)

	A	B	B/A	C	D	E	F
Miki							
Seisaku kondankai	50,110	50,110	100	35 / 19,610 (29·1%)	1 / 2,000 (3·9%)	3 / 28,500 (56·8%)	0
Kindaika kenkyūkai	73,000*	73,000	100	52 / 52,100 (71·3%)	6 / 7,400 (10·1%)	4 / 13,500 (18·4%)	0 (—)
Total	123,110	123,110	100	87 / 71,710 (58·2%)	7 / 9,400 (7·6%)	7 / 42,000 (34·1%)	0 (—)
Ono							
Bokuseikai†	27,800	27,800	100	15 / 18,300 (65·8%)	2 / 2,500 (8·9%)	2 / 7,000 (25·1%)	0 (—)
Hompō seikei kenkyūkai†	54,800	2,380	4·3	3 / 2,380 (100%)	0 / 0 (—)	0 / 0 (—)	0 (—)
Isshinkai†	18,850‡	18,850	100	22 / 14,850 (78·7%)	2 / 1,500 (7·9%)	2 / 2,500‡ (13·2%)	0 (—)
Total	101,450	49,030	48·3	40 / 35,530 (72·4%)	4 / 4,000 (8·1%)	4 / 9,500 (19·3%)	0 (—)
Kawashima							
Kōshinkai	84,600	84,600	100	48 / 58,100 (68·6%)	3 / 7,500 (8·8%)	3 / 11,000 (13·0%)	2 / 8,000 (9·4%)
Ishii							
Hōankai	77,100	61,300	69·5	49 / 47,300 (77·1%)	2 / 3,000 (4·8%)	4 / 10,000 (16·3%)	1 / 1,000 (1·6%)
Fujiyama							
Kokusai seikei chōsakai	54,098	0	0	0 / 0 (—)	0 / 0 (—)	0 / 0 (—)	0 (—)

TABLE 13 (*continued*)

	A	B	B/A	C	D	E	F
Tanaka, K. Etsuzankai	99,605	0	0	0 0 (—) 409	0 0 (—) 34	0 0 (—) 31	0 0 (—) 8
Grand total	1,747,311	767,500	43·9	523,640 (68·2%)	84,300 (10·9%)	142,500 (18·5%)	17,060 (2·2%)

A = Total incomes.

B = Total value of donations received.

B/A = B as a percentage of A.

C = The top, middle and bottom figures refer respectively to the number of individual enterprises which made donations, the combined values of their donations, and the latter as a percentage of the total donations received by the faction.

D = Same as above from trade and professional associations.

E = Same as above from political associations.

F = Same as above from individuals.

*¥8,500,000 is given as the total income of this faction in *Kampō* 'Gōgai' No. 115 (22 September 1966), p. 6 and is cited in 'Seijishikin wa dou nagareru', *Asahi*, 29 October 1966. The writer's own calculation suggests, however, that the correct figure should be as given here.

†The Bokuseikai operated only during the first half of 1965 and was replaced in the latter half by the Hompō seikei kenkyūkai and the Isshinkai.

‡¥1,000,000 received by the Isshinkai from the Hompō seikei kenkyūkai is excluded from the figures given here.

Sources: As for Table 12.

called the 'strong men's group' or *jitsuryokuha*).[8] Kōno's Daiichi kokusei kenkyūkai was financially looked after largely by the Sankinkai, the twelve members of which used to contribute a minimum of ¥20 million per year each. This stable and reliable source of income was supplemented by several other sources, particularly the Tokyo shunjūkai, which also involved many leading businessmen and industrialists.

In this fashion several fairly distinctive clusters of businessmen and enterprises have emerged (admittedly with frequent overlapping of affiliations) in response to the financial demands of particular faction leaders. The latter are apparently so dependent for survival and success upon this kind of support that their political behaviour cannot but be seriously affected.

Despite, however, the seeming stability of these connections between the LDP faction leaders and groups of businessmen, it should be noted that their relative importance in comparison with connections at the level of the official party organisation has significantly declined over the past few years. Of the 455 donor groups which made financial contributions in 1965, 206 (45·2 per cent) contributed directly to the LDP itself or the Kokumin kyōkai, while 197 (43·2 per cent) contributed to a faction leader or leaders (see Table 12 above); 52 (11·4 per cent) split their contributions between the LDP or the Kokumin kyōkai on the one hand and one or more factions on the other. This means that a majority of the donor units had come by this time under the total or partial control of the Kokumin kyōkai and the party headquarters and were thus excluded from the reach of the faction leaders. Generally speaking, the largest donors (those who made a contribution of ¥10 million or more) preferred to give either to the Kokumin kyōkai and a faction or factions or to the Kokumin kyōkai alone. When they gave only to the factions, they characteristically split the bounty between two or more groups. In contrast, the small donors (those whose donations were worth less than ¥1 million) obviously found it difficult to split their modest contributions between two or more beneficiaries and gave them either to the Kokumin kyōkai alone or a single faction leader. Those in between tended to donate rather to a faction or factions than to the party or the Kokumin kyōkai, but there was a sharp division of behaviour between the relatively larger ones (with donations worth between ¥5 million and ¥10 million) and the relatively smaller ones (between ¥1 million and ¥5 million) when it came to deciding whether to favour a single faction leader or please two or more of them. Those of the former category have followed generally the example of the largest donors, while the latter type have acted like the smallest of donors.

[8]Kobayashi Ataru, Sakurada Takeshi, Nagano Shigeo, and Mizuno Shigeo represent this group of business leaders and have played a predominant role in the postwar relations between the conservative parties and the business community. For a brief review of their achievement and role, see Miyazaki Yoshimasa, 'Atsuryokudantai to shite no zaikai', *Kaigai Jijō* (Institute of World Affairs, Takushoku University), XIII, (2 February 1965), pp. 20-1; Yashiro Kenrō 'Seizaikai no jinmyaku wo saguru', *Ekonomisuto*, XLII, 15 (10 April 1964), pp. 63-6.

All this suggests above all that the growing influence of the Kokumin kyōkai seriously interferes with the fund-raising efforts of the individual faction leaders. This impression is corroborated by the fact that among the fund-raising groups associated with faction leaders about which systematic information is available in the selected years, only Satō's and Ikeda's groups managed to increase their total incomes between 1962 and 1965. Four others suffered varying degrees of loss, ranging from about ¥115 million in the case of Kōno's Daiichi kokusei kenkyūkai and ¥11 million in the case of Ishii's Hōankai. Even more significant, however, is the tendency on the part of the donors to avoid concentrating on a single particular faction leader as the object of their sustained financial support and instead to distribute favours among as many beneficiaries as possible. The comparative behaviour of the four categories of donor classified on the basis of the relative sizes of their contributions indicate that those who seem to concentrate on a particular faction do so not so much because of their preference for that faction leader but because they cannot afford to give enough to more than one. In other words, those who can afford to do so tend to oblige two or more leaders as well as the party leadership either directly or through the Kokumin kyōkai. Only one of the forty-six largest donors of 1965 acted contrary to this general tendency.[9]

The reasons for this tendency are not hard to seek. Factionalism in the LDP is basically concerned with the struggle for power, which involves rapid changes in the fortunes of individual factions and their leaders (and also leads to an enormous waste of energy and funds). It is therefore logical for an external group seeking the party's favours to spread its risk by contributing, not to one faction alone, but to many. In a period of rapid and unpredictable change in the factional situation, as in the years following the anti-Security Treaty crisis of 1960, this kind of caution and prudence has naturally become more pronounced.

The instability in relations between faction leaders and their financial supporters is shown in the relatively low level of consistency in the choice of beneficiaries by the donors, and is further accentuated by the strongly personal and emotive basis on which they depend. Whereas, for example, nearly 80 per cent of the groups which made donations to the Kokumin kyōkai or directly to the LDP in 1965 can be considered as stable and regular supporters, the same may be said of only about 53 per cent of those which contributed to a faction leader or leaders alone. Indeed, the percentage of regular supporters was as low as 44 per cent in the case of those who split their contributions between more than one faction leader. From this evidence it may be concluded that less than half of the one hundred or so groups (mainly smaller

[9]The *Zenkoku kouri shuhan seiji renmei* (National Political Association of Spirits Retailers) gave ¥10 million to the Satō faction alone in two instalments. See *Kampō* 'Gōgai', No. 44 (20 April 1966), p. 29; No. 115, p. 30.

corporations), which in 1965 gave money to faction leaders could be counted upon with confidence as a stable source of revenue by the latter. A change in the balance of power between the factions can result in a massive shift of allegiance on the part of a majority of the donors of this type.

Supporters' Associations

Like the fund-raising organisations maintained by the LDP faction leaders, most of the supporters' associations formed by LDP Diet members of lesser importance are registered with the Minister for Autonomy as 'political associations' in the sense of the term used in the Political Funds Regulation Law. They operate either through the offices of the Diet members at Nagata-chō or through separate offices maintained elsewhere. Although it is difficult to generalise about their financial effectiveness, it seems that in the mid-1960s most of them managed to raise a few million yen per year. A few apparently collect more than ¥10 million; fewer, less than ¥1 million. Since the regular expenses alone of an LDP Diet member reach ¥1 million per month and an election costs him at least ¥30 million, it is probably correct to assume that the income from this particular source is quite substantial but not sufficient to meet his rapidly increasing expenses. Moreover, only about eighty LDP Diet members have actually formed this type of supporters' association designed to help them financially.

The vote-collecting supporters' associations obviously account for the majority of the eight hundred or so supporters' associations which had come to exist by the middle of 1964. Every LDP Diet member has at least one of them to fall back upon as his personal vote-gathering machine at the time of an election. Referring to the value of his own association, Fukuda Takeo once said with unusual frankness: 'When we begin to prepare for an election, it is not the LDP that comes first to our minds as a possible source of help. No, we never think of the LDP at the time of elections. It is after all the *Fukudakai* to which I turn for help, and it must be the same with everybody else.'[10]

The weakness of the formal party organisation at the grass-roots, combined with the effects of the multi-member constituency system, has inevitably led every LDP Diet member and prospective candidate to organise a supporters' association to give him the practical help which the party cannot offer him. A vast network of these personalised and segmented organisations has become a central focus of attention and activities in LDP electoral strategy.

Whereas fund-collecting associations are almost invariably located in Tokyo, these primarily vote-gathering machines are necessarily based in local constituencies. In their membership they also differ rather sharply from each other, for the one consists mainly of businessmen and corporations and the

[10]Fukuda Takeo, *Habatsusenkyo no jishuku: Habatsuyūzei wo kinzeyo* (KSK Report, 160) (23 September 1963), p. 30.

other of influential local figures representing a variety of occupations and groups. However, they are both based essentially on personal ties between a particular politician and his electors, strongly tinged by the considerations of mutual interests and aid. Whereas the one operates by exchanging funds for legislative or administrative action, the other exchanges votes for a similar political output. With as much candour as Fukuda, and in a far more descriptive way, another LDP Diet member, Kuraishi Tadao, once explained his own supporters' association as follows:

> In my own constituency the small entrepreneurs and shopkeepers who are advisers to my association go to various small industrialists' and merchants' organisations to find out what they would want me to do for them. It is therefore much simpler for them to bring their problems and grievances to my office, than take them to, say, the Small Industry Finance Fund in Tokyo. We refer to the responsible offices in Tokyo on their behalf and such offices usually respond quite reasonably and promptly to our requests. Another example would be the question of taxes . . . This sort of service performed by my office makes them feel that they should be glad to pay 5 or 10 thousand yen per month in order to finance my political activities . . . This organisation, i.e. the *Hokushin jichi kenkyūkai*, as it is called, also sells pins to those who come to hear my speeches. These pins are produced at the cost of ¥20 each, but people pay at least 50 or 100 and not infrequently as much as 1,000 yen for them.[11]

The role played by small entrepreneurs and shopkeepers for Kuraishi's group can be played by leaders of any other politically significant local groups and organisations. They may be, for example, such semi-official groups as tax payment and saving unions, road safety and youth guidance councils, crime prevention, fire prevention, voluntary scavengers or community chest associations, such trade and professional groups as local chambers of commerce and industry, shopkeepers' associations, agricultural co-operative unions and local medical associations, or any of the various civic and functional groups such as the parents and teachers, youth, women's, aged people's and even war-bereaved families associations. Of Arafune Seijū-rō's supporters' association in Chichibu and its neighbouring areas in Saitama Prefecture it was said that virtually all officials of the local textile manufacturers' unions, farmers' co-operatives, forest owners' associations, parents and teachers' associations, youth organisations, road safety councils, and so on, were associated with it. It is well known that to secure the support of the leaders of such local organisations is tantamount to having the huge bloc of votes under their control committed to oneself.

Of critical importance to the organisation and activities of a supporters' association of this type is the role of local politicians and the quasi-public agencies of local administration called the *chōnaikai* and the *burakukai*. As the nexus between a particular LDP member of the Diet and a multitude of

---

[11]Kuraishi Tadao, *Jimintōkindaika no ugoki to sono kōsō* (KSK Report, 40) (29 May 1961), pp. 19-21.

local voters, they play an indispensable, indeed predominant role. Numerically and otherwise the most important local politicians in this respect are the members of the forty-six prefectural assemblies, about 67 per cent of whom were officially affiliated with the LDP by October 1966. According to a recent detailed study of factional divisions in the Chiba Prefectural Assembly, virtually all of its conservative members were aligned with one of the members of the House of Representatives returned by their constituencies.[12] At the town, village, and hamlet levels, the nominally independent local politicians who control various quasi-administrative and functional organisations, notably the chōnaikai and the burakukai, are at the same time intimately involved in the leadership of particular supporters' associations. In a Diet election they not only themselves vote for the LDP candidates with whom they are aligned but often commit the large numbers of voters under their effective influence to the support of that particular candidate.

As suggested by Kuraishi's statement quoted above, these local supporters' associations function in some cases as fund-raising, as well as vote-gathering, machines. More frequently, however, they are financed by the politicians concerned, rather than financially supporting them, for, in Satō's words, 'Each member of a supporters' association may pay ¥100, but he receives in return ¥300 worth of food and drinks from the Diet member . . .'.[13] It is partly to finance this type of supporters' association, which has proved indispensable to their electoral victory, that most LDP members are compelled to seek funds from the official party treasury, a faction leader's purse, or one or more interest groups willing to make donations to individual rank and file Diet members. As pointed out in the preceding chapter, the resources of the party headquarters are usually far too limited to meet their demands, so that faction leaders and interest groups assume critical importance to many LDP back-benchers. The role of the factions in this respect has been fully discussed already, but the significance of relations between LDP Diet members and particular interest groups deserves a brief mention.

Previous studies have pointed out that the largest and most active interest groups (such as the Chūshōkigyō seiji renmei and the Nihon ishikai) officially endorse and support up to a few hundred candidates on a more or less non-partisan basis in each important election, providing them with fairly substantial funds. As a result of this practice there have emerged several distinctive clusters of Diet members who are tied up closely with particular interest

---

[12]In District 1 eleven prefectural assembly members were identified as Kawashima Shōjirō's supporters, four Shiseki Ihei's, and one Usui Sōichi's; in District 2 five supported Inō Shigejirō and seven Yamamura Shinjirō; and in District 3 six were aligned with Mizuta Mikio, five with Mori Kiyoshi, two with Nakamura Yōichirō, three with Chiba Suburō and two were uncertain. Ōhara Mitsunori and Yokoyama Keiji, *Sangyōshakai to seijikatei: Keiyōkōgyōchitai* (Nihonhyōronsha, 1965), pp. 108-45, esp. 126-7.

[13]Satō Eisaku, *Watakushi no jikyokukan* (KSK Report, 28) (18 February 1961), p. 8.

groups which support them and who engage in extensive and sustained lobbying activities within the party on behalf of these groups. Examples are the forty or so members of the *Shōkōgyō shinkō giindan* (Diet Members' Group for the Promotion of Commerce and Industry) established in July 1961, those identified with the *Ikeigiin renmei* (Diet Members' League Associated with the Medical Association), and those associated with the *Kankyō-eisei giin renmei* (Diet Members' League for Environmental Hygiene).[14] In addition to these two types of supporters' association, practically every LDP Diet member has been involved in one or more of these intra-party agencies of special interests in order to fill his needs for adequate material and moral support from external sources.

The linkages maintained by the LDP and its members with various external groups which have been so far considered are designed to provide them mainly with support in the form of funds or votes. As suggested earlier, it is obvious that support is given almost always on a reciprocal basis in return for specific services rendered or to be rendered by the party or its members. From the latter's point of view, to receive assistance from an external group, whether in the form of money or votes, is to surrender part of its freedom of action and to come under the donor's influence.

Big Business as an Interest Group

As the financial patrons of the LDP, the nation's larger industrial and business enterprises and their executives, especially those affiliated with the four representative business organisations, have naturally exerted a powerful, even predominant, influence on the fortunes and behaviour of the party leaders, the factions and the rank and file Diet members. The crucial role played behind the scenes by the leaders of these four organisations (particularly the Keidanren and the Dōyūkai), in the 1954 change of power from Yoshida to Hatoyama, in the merger of the two conservative parties in 1955, and in Hatoyama's resignation in 1956, has been described in detail in a previous study.[15]

Political and social stability under a conservative party government was the basic and minimum demand of big business at that time and it still remains so. If they achieve that, they are likely to find their vast contributions to the party, whether through the Kokumin kyōkai or otherwise, not entirely wasted. Beyond this generalisation, however, there are a host of much more specific

---

[14]The so-called 'environmental hygiene' trades include barbers, beauty parlours, entertainment industry, restaurants and tea houses, hotel and tourist industry, laundry business, food processing industry, etc., and their 15 million members are organised in the *Zenkoku kankyōeisei dōgyōkumiai chūōkai* (National Association of Environmental Hygiene Trades). They are regarded as one of the most reliable voting blocs for the LDP. Nakajima (interview, 20 January 1966); 'Ketsuzei bundori atsuryoku-dantai konkūru', *Shūkan Yomiuri* (28 January 1966), pp. 16-21.

[15]Shinobu Seizaburō, 'Dokusenshihon to seiji' in Oka Yoshitake (ed.), *Gendai nihon no seijikati.* (Iwanami shoten, 1958), pp. 224-36.

demands they want to have translated into public action by the government, at least partly with the help of the LDP.

As the history of Keidanren and Nikkeiren indicates, such demands are extremely diversified and complex. In the economic field they have concerned such matters as amendment of the laws related to economic deconcentration, taxation, stock exchange, price control, foreign trade and tariffs, the development of atomic power, defence industries, unemployment, management-labour relations, international economic co-operation, and so on. On each of these varied problems directly affecting their material interests, they have naturally conveyed their views to the LDP, whether officially or unofficially, publicly or privately.

As suggested by the 1954-6 situation discussed by Shinobu, the role of business has been especially important at times of party and government crisis, such as that caused by a particularly controversial political issue or change of top leaders. Its reaction to the Security Treaty revision crisis of 1960 took the form firstly of enormously increased contributions to the Keizai saiken kondankai and secondly of a campaign to replace Kishi by Ikeda. In the first half of that year only about ¥248 million passed into the hands of the Keizai saiken kondankai, but in the second half, that is after the riots and the peak of the crisis, as much as ¥1,143 million was poured into the coffers of the organisation by business groups. In the meantime, Ikeda received in the name of his Kōchikai ¥396 million for the year, as compared with ¥65 million of Kishi's Shinyūkai and ¥329 million of Satō's Shūzankai. When Ikeda resigned in late 1964, an overwhelming majority of top businessmen swiftly decided to swing their support behind Satō in his struggle against Kōno and Fujiyama. Not only the Dōyūkai leaders who had become by this time openly critical of Ikeda's economic policy, such as Kikawada, Iwasa, Nakayama, and Fujii, but also the 'strong men's group' represented by Kobayashi and so far intimately associated with Ikeda, gave almost undivided support to Satō. It was probably this particular factor, as much as the logic of intra-party factionalism, that ultimately determined the outcome of the contest. There is little doubt that under successive conservative party administrations of their own choice big business has earned handsome dividends for its material and moral support, in the form of generous consideration in the annual budget-making and a succession of favourable legislation. It is clear, for example, that the maintenance of an extraordinarily high level of investment and resulting high economic growth rate which was pursued by Ikeda in the name of an income-doubling policy was precisely what big business needed and wanted as it faced the prospect of imminent liberalisation of trade and investment. In fact, businessmen largely succeeded, thanks to that policy, in accomplishing large-scale technological innovation and rationalisation and thus increasing their competitive power in an open world market. Nor is there much room for doubt that the fiscal policy embodied in the annual budgets of successive governments has benefited them, often at the expense of other occupational groups, through the reduction of corporation taxes, increases in public works expenditures, and so on.

In assessing the role of big business in the party policy-making process, however, it is necessary to remember that its interests and opinions have never been completely uniform or united. It is probably correct to argue that big business has been in general agreement in the past few years on a few fairly specific demands, such as the stabilisation of commodity prices, improvement of the balance of international payments, the structural reform of individual enterprises to increase their international competitive power, economic co-operation with underdeveloped countries, and greater emphasis on national interests in the collaborative relationship with the U.S.A. On matters, however, relating to the fundamental character of the existing economic system and the balance of power obtaining between its component units, there have been sharp divisions of opinion between the senior leaders of Keidanren, represented by its president Ishizaka, and the relatively younger executives leading Dōyūkai. The bifurcation between the *laissez-faire* approach of the former and the 'modified capitalism' doctrine of the latter has been fairly evident throughout the postwar period, but it has been intensified more recently because of the trend towards business consolidation in the strategic sectors of the nation's industry such as iron and steel, automobiles, and petrochemicals. Despite the tendency to fuse the leadership of the two organisations, seen in the appointment in May 1964 of the four top leaders of Dōyūkai to Keidanren's board of standing directors, the differences in ideology and attitudes between them remain evident.

In addition to the fundamental conflicts of opinion between the leaders of these two large organisations differences also arise both between and within the business organisations over certain particular issues. The conflict which occurred in early 1963 over the abortive Emergency Measures Bill for the Promotion of Special Industries is a good example. This particular bill was originally proposed by the Ministry of International Trade and Industry and was subsequently supported by Keidanren, partially opposed by the National Bankers' Association, and completely opposed by the Kansai Regional Federation of Economic Organisations. Furthermore, Dōyūkai was divided against itself and was unable to express a clear-cut view one way or another. Under the system of free enterprise the relationships between individual enterprises or trade associations are generally competitive rather than collaborative and that often makes it difficult for them to unify their lobbying and pressure politics activities *vis-à-vis* the government or the ministerial party.

Because of these divisive tendencies within the business community, a single unified organisation such as the Keizai saiken kondankai or the Kokumin kyōkai cannot represent the whole of that community in consultations and negotiations with the LDP on specific matters of legislation or administration affecting the vital interests of its members. For this reason it is likely that the role of Kokumin kyōkai will remain limited to the co-ordination of fund-raising and the advocacy and propagation of points of view which are general and vague, rather than specific. On the other hand, the greater part of the dialogue between the LDP and the most influential members of that organisation is likely to be carried on through such separate channels as are offered by the informal societies of individual businessmen built around particular LDP politicians.[16]

The Intervention of the Bureaucracy

Whereas the demands of those who make fairly substantial monetary contributions to the party or its members usually concern matters of a more or less public nature and call for legislative or administrative action on the part of their recipients, those who help in gathering votes often seek more personal rewards for their contributions. Every LDP Diet member is constantly called upon to help a supporter's son in his hunt for a job on graduation, to help another to obtain a loan from a bank, to arrange a tour of Tokyo for a group of his constituents, and so on. This type of service, however, is of marginal significance for LDP policy-making. The rewards that require more or less official party decisions and therefore become by definition subjects of its formal decision-making process are to be considered here. Demands for subsidies and loans from the national government for all sorts of local public works projects as well as other forms of legislative and administrative action pertaining to particular localities or groups fall in this category. They are as a rule brought to the attention of the party or to particular party members through a variety of lobbying activities on the part of the external groups concerned.

By seeking and receiving support from external sources mainly in the form of funds and votes, the LDP inevitably gets caught in an endless input-output process of interaction with a wide variety of external groups. In order to terminate each round of this process the party must take concrete legislative or administrative action with a view to rewarding these groups for contributions already made and to encourage their continued support in the future. Such action, however, requires the participation not only of the LDP but also of the bureaucracy.

Administrative action naturally pertains to the bureaucracy. Hence both leaders and rank and file of the party turn to the public service for help in satisfying a large proportion of the demands which come to them from their

[16]In addition to those which were formed around Ikeda, Kōno, and Satō, Miki Takeo's *Kindai shihonshugi kenkyūkai* (Modern Capitalism Study Society) deserves attention in this respect. This group includes the top leaders of Dōyūkai, such as Kikawada, Iwasa, Nakayama, Mizukami, Imazato (Nihon Seikō Co.), Shōji (Nittō Chemicals Co.), and Fujii. Information concerning this group was supplied by Mr Iwano, Mr Miki's secretary, in an interview on 17 January 1966. See also Suzuki, *Seiji wo ugokasu keieisha*, p. 107.

M

financial and electoral supporters. In order to have a new licence issued to a local trucking company or to have a road or river system in one's constituency reclassified as 'state-administered' instead of 'prefecture-administered' and thus maintained at the expense of the national, instead of a prefectural, treasury, a member of the 'highest organ of state' does not hesitate to bow many times before a senior public servant. Even in the case of legislative action, the help of a relevant ministry has to be sought, though the power to take such action constitutionally belongs to the Diet and thus is shared by the parties. As pointed out in Chapter 4, neither the PARC nor the executive council of the LDP is adequately staffed or technically equipped to deal effectively with the needs of legislative action. Virtually all reference material vital to effective law-making is rigidly and jealously controlled by the individual ministries and other agencies of the national public service and is, as a rule, inaccessible to Diet members. As a result, nearly all of the few hundred bills introduced to the National Diet each year are actually prepared either entirely by bureaucrats or with very extensive help from them, and the organs of the LDP play merely a supporting role at the most.

It is important to note in this connection that, as is the case with the support given by private groups, the services of the bureaucracy are not offered free, but only on a reciprocal basis. In return for favours done by a ministry for a formal organ of the party, the latter undertakes to fight for increased powers or budgetary appropriations for that particular ministry. For services done personally and privately by a senior public servant, the politicians concerned often undertake to look after him after his retirement from the public service. This may involve either helping him enter politics or finding an attractive job with a public corporation or a private firm.[17]

It is evident that in their relations with the bureaucracy those politicians who have themselves been career bureaucrats before their entry into party politics enjoy many important advantages over those who come from other occupational backgrounds. Their relationships with their ministries of origin are frequently perpetuated by the existence of 'old boys' associations'. These may be confined to those ex-bureaucrats now active in party politics (as in the case of the Kōrakukai which consists of the LDP politicians connected with the Welfare Ministry), or it may include anybody who has been an official of the ministry, as in the case of the Kayōkai of former International Trade and Industry Ministry officials.

[17]This practice is often referred to as 'picking up the bones' of the public servant concerned, the implication being that, as far as his public service career and all the powers and prestige accruing from it are concerned, he is 'dead' and his remains must be collected and deposited at a proper place on his retirement. Thus, according to Okada, Suzuki Shun'ichi, long the Vice-Minister of Autonomy, was helped by Kawashima Shōjirō to get his nomination for the post of Tokyo's Vice-Governor, and one-time Construction Vice-Minister Ishiba Jirō was similarly seconded by Nanjō Tokuo for the post of Tottori's prefectural governorship. See Okada Tadao, *Seiji no uchimaku* (Yūki-shobō, 1963), pp. 226-8.

It has long been evident that the technical and administrative problems involved in public policy-making can be effectively disposed of only by or with the help of the bureaucracy and, for that reason, the latter's role and influence have been of critical importance in defining the nature of the LDP connections with external groups. However, more fundamental philosophical or ideological aspects of policy-making either at the party or the government level cannot always be adequately dealt with by the bureaucrats alone. Partly to fill this gap in the services rendered by public servants and partly to keep in touch with major trends in public opinion, many LDP Diet members have come to rely on a variety of other groups and individuals for advice and information on either general or specific policy matters.

Connections with Other Groups and Individuals

One of the commonest practices in this respect is to employ a number of private secretaries specialising in policy affairs in addition to the two clerical secretaries provided at public expense.[18] These secretaries, who are hired privately by the politicians concerned, not only read newspapers and magazines for them but frequently select books and journals for them to read. In some cases the work of such secretaries is reinforced and supplemented by more or less regular consultations with journalists, scholars, and businessmen. As of early 1966 about twenty LDP-affiliated Diet members were known regularly to meet and consult with their personal 'ideas men' at breakfast or luncheon sessions.

Ikeda's relationship with Shimomura Osamu, a director of the Development Bank, who built the theoretical and conceptual framework of his 'high-growth-rate' policy, is well known. Likewise, the views concerning the China issue of Matsumoto Shigeharu, director of the International House of Japan, have apparently been taken into consideration by Fujiyama Aiichirō in formulating his flexible approach to the Peking régime. The *Sōgō seisaku kenkyūjo* (Integrated Policy Research Institute), which is a well organised group of prominent economists and economic journalists, regularly advises both Satō and Miki. As of early 1966 this group involved Arisawa Hiromi (Emeritus Professor, Tokyo University), Inaba Hidezō (president of the Kokumin keizai kenkyūkai), Ōkita Saburō (director of the Nihon keizai sentā), Tsuchiya Kiyoshi (chief editor of the *Sankei Shimbun*), Kiuchi Nobutane (director of the Sekai keizai chōsakai), Enjōji Jirō (chief editor of the *Nihon Keizai Shimbun*), and others. Satō arranged regular monthly consultations with this group almost as soon as he was elected LDP President in 1964, while Miki has been also intimately associated with it as well as another set of his personal 'ideas men', the Chūō seisaku kenkyūjo.

[18]For this and the following discussion the writer owes information to many journalists associated with the *Hirakawa kurabu*, especially Mr Nakajima Kiyonari of *Asahi* (interview on 20 January 1966), and Mr Uchida Kenzō, assistant chief of the political affairs section of the Kyōdō News Agency (interview on 10 February 1966).

Probably more important has been the role played by Yatsugi Kazuo and his 'research' organisation, Kokusaku kenkyūkai, in the formation of LDP policy toward Taiwan and South Korea. According to his own accounts, Yatsugi was largely instrumental in bringing into existence the Committee for the Promotion of Sino-Japanese (Taiwan-Japanese) Co-operation and the Committee for South Korea-Japan Co-operation. Also in many ways he personally guided the LDP's efforts for the normalisation of diplomatic relations with Seoul which was accomplished in 1965. His Kokusaku kenkyūkai holds monthly discussions with the Prime Minister (LDP President), the LDP Secretary-General, and the Minister of Finance. The intimacy of the relationship between the party leadership and the organisation may be inferred from the presence of several prominent LDP leaders on the latter's board of directors, including in September 1964 Funada Naka, Ikeda Hayato, Ishii Mitsujirō, Kishi Nobusuke, and Satō Eisaku.

As the foregoing discussion has demonstrated, the LDP depends on external groups for the acquisition of the basic forms of support vital to its survival and progress. This dependence, which reflects the weakness of the party's formal organisation and the peculiarities of its membership composition, seriously limits its freedom of action and choice in policy-making situations. Considering that private interest groups and the bureaucracy support the party in order to obtain, if possible, policy decisions favourable to their own specific interests, it is hardly surprising that the latter should be concerned more with satisfying their demands than with its own independent policy-making. In other words, it is compelled to function as broker for its two major kinds of patron—a state of affairs that is likely to continue so long as it depends on them to the extent it does today.

Despite the importance of contacts between leading LDP politicians and persons or groups outside the party who are primarily interested in policy, the basic pattern of its external relationships may be seen as a triangular system of interactions linking the interest groups, the bureaucracy, and the party. The system operates on the basis of reciprocal give-and-take between any two of them, with influence flowing in either direction. In these circumstances the party's decisions (its only valuable output) are seen primarily as payment for support received from the bureaucracy and the interest groups. To that extent the LDP is subject to the considerations of their particular interests and wishes.

Even more important, however, is the fact that the formal party organisation and leadership is not directly involved in, or responsible for, more than a part of these relations. Nearly half of the corporations and business associations that provide funds, and important sections of the bureaucracy that supply administrative and technical assistance, do indeed have more or less direct connections with the LDP and its official leaders as such. On the other hand, nearly half the donors of funds, all the supporters' associations, which look after votes, and a large number of individual public servants, journalists, and businessmen, who can help with wide-ranging policy-making activities, are all tied directly to individual party members and only indirectly and incidentally to the party as such. This shows the singular organisational weakness of the LDP even more dramatically than does the fact of its overall dependence on external sources of support. It also indicates some important truths concerning the relations between the formal party organisation on one hand and informal intra-party groups and individual party members on the other.

The situation may be summarised roughly as follows. Each member depends entirely on his own vote-gathering machine for electoral victory, very considerably for funds on particular corporations and persons privately connected with him, and on personal help given by various policy advisers for ideas and plans. He benefits little from the financial assistance of the party treasury or the services of the bureaucracy rendered through the formal party organs. In brief, the presence of the party is incidental, rather than vital, to his electoral success and to much of his other political activity. It therefore seems reasonable to conclude that there is no sound reason for them to attribute a great deal of prestige, authority, or leadership to the formal party organs and officials. The centre of gravity has tended rather to remain with the individual members, and not with the party organisation as an integral entity.

The successive campaigns to 'modernise' the party have apparently been aimed at reversing this situation. Important progress has indeed been achieved in the efforts to centralise the flow of funds into the party, as is seen by the rather remarkable success of the Kokumin kyōkai. If the present efforts are continued, as they no doubt will be, members will become gradually more dependent for financial assistance on the official party treasury, and their relations with the formal party leadership will change accordingly. Moreover, the party as a whole, rather than individual members of it, will become increasingly dependent on the donors of funds and subject to their influence, especially the influence of the Kokumin kyōkai and its principal members. Since these are the big business groups, represented by the four national business organisations, this will mean that the LDP will become officially and even more intimately involved with big business interests. In other words, successful 'modernisation' of party finance will tend to make business influence less direct on individual members but more direct on the party as a whole.

As regards relations with the supporters' associations, the bureaucracy and personal policy advisers, however, there have been no signs of a drastic change. In view of the fact that voters at large tend to be interested only in the narrowly limited area of an electoral contest which they feel capable of influencing by their personal acts of voting, it seems inevitable that they will continue to identify themselves, not with the LDP as such but with a particular LDP Diet member returned by themselves. As a condition of their support, moreover, they bind the particular LDP candidate to work for their interests in a variety of ways, including the promotion of specific legislative action by the party. Thus a supporters' association can be formed only by and for a particular member returned by a particular constituency whose interests he feels obliged to represent and champion in the party and the Diet. Since this is the case, and since the supporters' associations have in the past almost completely dominated the electoral scene, it is hard to predict any significant change in their status or role in the foreseeable future.

Similar elements of inflexibility seem likely to prevent any appreciable change in the LDP's dependence on the bureaucracy. Despite the impressive increase since the war in the number of former senior public servants who on retirement have become LDP politicians, and the resulting 'bureaucratisation' of the party, the vital information and skills indispensable to law-making remain an exclusive preserve of the bureaucracy beyond the access of Diet members, including those affiliated with the LDP. As the LDP grows organisationally and in the range of its interest aggregation and articulation functions, its dependence on the bureaucracy is likely to increase rather than diminish at the levels both of its formal organisation and of the individual member. The role of personal policy advisers is unlikely to have a significant effect on this process, although their presence will no doubt help to prevent the complete control of the party policy-making process by the powerful interest groups, supporters' associations, and the bureaucracy.

**Part Three
Case Studies**

7 Compensating Former Landowners

Shortly before 11 p.m. on 28 May 1965 a controversial Cabinet-sponsored bill, popularly referred to as the Farmland Reward Bill, was passed by the House of Councillors and on 3 June promulgated as Law 121, 1965. It authorised the payment over ten years of some ¥145,600 million by the government to some 1,670,000 former landowners and their relatives dispossessed of their property as a result of the land reform in the wake of World War II. The opposition to this bill raised by the Socialists and the Democratic Socialists was such that it was voted through by the LDP majority in the House of Representatives Committee on the Cabinet on 13 May while a Socialist member was still speaking. Subsequently it was not until the Upper House plenary meeting on the 28th had sat continuously for forty-nine hours that the final vote was taken at which it passed by 121 votes to 69. Why the bill caused such controversy between the parties is in itself an interesting problem to explore, but why it was pushed through the Diet despite the controversy is even more important for an understanding of the pattern of policy-making in the LDP. In the present chapter an attempt will be made to analyse the interaction of the principal factors involved in the development of the issue, in order to explain the LDP's attitude towards it and the decisions made at different stages.

BACKGROUND

It is well known that land reform was one of the most important and effective of the many reform programs undertaken under the auspices of the Occupation in postwar Japan. In seventeen stages between March 1947 and December 1950 as much as 1,526,893 chō (1 chō equals 2·45 acres) of farmland and 232,910 chō of pasture were bought up by the government for redistribution among the actual cultivators, mainly former tenants. As a result, the number of pure owner-cultivators increased from 1,869,298 households in April 1946 (32·8 per cent of the total farming households) to 3,821,531 in February 1950 (61·8 per cent of the total) while that of pure tenant households dropped from 1,637,051 (28·7 per cent) to 312,364 (5 per cent) in the same period. This, however, left approximately one million

173

former landowners who were thus deprived of their estates deeply dissatisfied.

Their resentments have since been expressed both privately and publicly, with increasing force. In retrospect it seems that such sentiments on the part of the dispossessed former landowners (who have since made it a rule to refer to themselves as 'victims' of an 'unfair Occupation policy') were ultimately bound to move the government to take concrete legislative steps for at least some measure of redress, despite certain strong objections raised by the Opposition parties and others.

One of the most immediate and prevalent forms of reaction by the dispossessed landowners to the land reform program was the unilateral cancellation of tenancy contracts. They did this in order to cultivate the land themselves, sell it at black-market prices, or divide it up between their relations, rather than letting it be bought up by the government for redistribution at a fixed price. According to one estimate, by the summer of 1946 some 250,000 disputes were caused by such unilateral withdrawals of tenanted land by the legal owners. When, however, in March 1947 Iwata Chūzō (a former member of the House of Peers and Minister of Justice in the Higashikuni and the Shidehara Cabinets) publicly disputed the constitutionality of the reform program itself, many began to take the matter to the courts on the fundamental issue of constitutionality. Iwata questioned the validity of the program not emotionally but in terms of a basic constitutional principle, and thus provided one of the most powerful weapons for the dissatisfied former landowners to wield against the government in the subsequent years. His views were thus of crucial importance in the evolution of the issue.

In accordance with Article 6, Paragraph 3, of the *Jisakunō sōsetsu tokubetsusochi hō* (Law Relating to the Special Measures for the Creation of Owner-Cultivators, i.e. Law 43, 1946), which was the legal expression of the land reform program, the landowners were paid by the government forty times the legally fixed 'standard' rent for their rice land and forty-eight times the standard rent for their uplands. This meant that they received an average of ¥760 per *tan* (*tan* equals ·245 acres) for the former and ¥450 per *tan* for the latter. Although a modest amount of 'compensation' money was added to these prices, boosting them respectively to about ¥980 for rice land and ¥580 for uplands, most landowners were very unhappy with the arrangement, according to which only part of the money was paid in cash and the rest was given in government bonds unredeemable for two years. After two years from their issue the bonds could be redeemed in twenty-two even yearly payments at a 3·65 per cent interest. Except in the first of the twenty-four buying operations involved, when the government paid up to ¥4,000 per head in cash in addition to a fraction of less than ¥1,000, only the fraction was paid in cash and all the rest in bonds. As a result, only ¥2,944 million of the ¥12,006 million (24 per cent) paid up by the end of 1950 was given in cash.

In the face of the rapidly progressing inflation such an arrangement rendered the money actually received by the landowners almost worthless and added much to their resentment with the whole program.

Under such circumstances Iwata referred to Article 29 of the Constitution, according to which 'the right to own or hold property is inviolable' and 'private property may be taken for public use upon just compensation therefor'. He argued that the above-mentioned prices had been arbitrarily and unfairly fixed by the government and therefore could not be regarded as 'just compensation'. He also pointed out that the maintenance of the same low prices over a prolonged period of time in the face of drastic depreciation of the currency made the government buying operations even more unjust and unconstitutional. These views prompted many groups of the disgruntled former landowners to institute legal suits on this particular ground. By the end of June 1950 119 such cases had been brought before the courts, especially in the north-eastern prefectures. Although there was no case where a lower court gave a decision condemning the program as unconstitutional, it was not until 23 December 1953 that an end was put finally to this basic controversy by a decision of the Supreme Court which upheld the full constitutionality of the program.

The resentments of the dispossessed landowners were also reflected in the proceedings of the National Diet and opinions expressed publicly or privately in the parties. Although both the Liberals and the Democrats ultimately approved the legislation, many of their members were openly critical of both the underlying principles and purposes of the program. The policy plan of the Democrat Liberal Party, which on 22 May 1948 was presented to the Joint Assembly of its Diet Members, contained the following:

> We will resolutely oppose a third land reform program and see to it that the unreasonable aspects of the second reform are rectified. The prices at which land is bought by the government and sold to former tenants must be properly modified. The acreage limits imposed on the land cultivated by a landlord must be made more flexible and the practice of determining the limitations of such acreage on a family basis should be changed . . . Measures to rescue the landowners impoverished by the land reform must be devised and the cashing of the farmland bonds must be expedited.[1]

One year later a Democrat, Ōmori Tamaki, also bitterly condemned the program in the House of Representatives Committee on Agriculture and Forestry. There is little room for doubt that such sentiments were widely shared among the former landowners both in villages and in the conservative parties.

It was against this background that groups of the dispossessed landowners began to organise, first at the village and eventually at the prefectural and national levels.

[1]*Asahi*, 23 May 1948.

The small village level groups which were formed during 1946, typified for example by the *Bunka kyōkai* (Cultural Association) of Sumoto in Kumamoto Prefecture, the *Nōchimondai kenkyūkai* (Land Problem Research Association) of Hachiman in Ōita Prefecture, and so on, gradually grew into larger units after 1947, such as the *Ōitaken nōchi kyōgikai* (Ōita Prefectural Farmland Council) and the *Yamagataken jinushi yūshidan* (Yamagata Prefectural League of Landowners). They demanded from the authorities an increase in the acreage of land a former landowner was allowed to retain, the permission to withdraw his land from tenancy to avoid the application of the reform program, a substantial increase in the prices for the land taken by the government, and in extreme cases restoration of the title to land already redistributed to the original owner. Organised action of this kind did not prove very successful under the Occupation. The most extreme groups were openly suppressed, as was the case with the above-mentioned Ōitaken nōchi kyōgikai which was ordered to be disbanded a few months after it was formed in 1947. However, their activities set a pattern to be followed with increased vigour after the Occupation came to an end.

In August 1952 a national organisation, the *Zenkoku nōsei renmei* (National Agricultural Policy League) was formed and under its auspices was convened in November 1953 a conference of the National Council of Landowners' Organisations. A year later (in December 1954) their sustained efforts towards more effective unification at the national level resulted in the formation of the *Zenkoku kaihōnōchi kokkahoshō rengōkai* (National Union for Governmental Compensation for Liberated Farmland). Its first meeting was held in January 1955 with the participation of nearly 6,000 delegates from the prefectural groups, and its total membership at that time was estimated to be about 100,000.[2] However, conflicts developed between the majority of its formal leaders, who wanted only to exact from the government adequate monetary compensation for the material and spiritual damages caused by the land reform, and those who persisted in demanding restoration of their titles to the land already redistributed. These conflicts eventually led the organisation to split into three opposing groups—the National League for the Compensation by the State for Liberated Farmland, the Japanese League of Land Reform Victims, and the Federation for the Compensation by the State to Dispossessed Landholders.

It was through the mediation by the chairman of the LDP Special Investigation Committee on the Farmland Problem that the three groups joined hands for a second time in December 1957 and formed a new national organisation, initially called the National Farmland Liberators' League

[2]This and the following description of the organisational developments in the *Zenkoku kaihōnōchi kokkahoshō rengōkai* and its successor, the *Zenkoku nōchi dōmei* (the National Farmland League) is based largely upon the information supplied to the writer by Mr Hirota Yukinori, secretary-general of the latter organisation, in an interview on 21 February 1966.

(*Zenkoku nōchikaihōsha dōmei*) and subsequently renamed the National Farmland League (*Zenkoku nōchi dōmei*), hereafter referred to as the League. It was this organisation that spoke in the name of the 'three million victims of the land reform' in the subsequent prolonged negotiations with and pressure group actions against the LDP leadership and the government.

Prior to the formation of the League the government had consistently denied any intention to compensate former landowners, although it had at times vaguely hinted that those who found themselves in actual and serious economic difficulties as the result of the land reform might be helped by the special application of the social security program. For example, responding to a question asked by Narita Tomoni (JSP) on this issue in the House of Representatives Committee on the Budget in March 1957, Prime Minister Kishi had said:

> As you know well, former landowners have expressed many grievances. It is undeniable that there have been cases of injustice done to them in relation, for example, to the subsequent transfer of the title of the land which had been originally taken away from them. The land reform program was, however, originally executed by the government strictly in accordance with the relevant provisions of the laws and, therefore, I believe that this government has no obligation whatsoever to compensate these people. . . .[3]

Less than a week later, however, in his answer to another Socialist interpellator, Kobayashi Kōhei, in the House of Councillors Committee on the Budget, Kishi made a somewhat different statement. He thought this time that the land reform had been a truly revolutionary reform and, as a result of it, many people had suffered from a drastic change in the conditions of living. If the changes thus brought about had caused serious social disturbances and personal hardships to large numbers of people, then he would have to agree that it was within the limits of the obligations of a government to deal with the situation by, for example, providing for special applications of the social security administration.[4]

As far as the legal aspects of the land reform and its effects were concerned, the government had insisted that the matter was already closed and that, therefore, it was not obliged to make an additional payment to former landowners to make up for the allegedly unreasonably low prices for which their land had been bought up for redistribution. The only possibility at this stage of their ever being paid something by the government was that the government might act in their interests not on the basis of a legal argument but out of purely political considerations. Such an attitude on the part of the government made it necessary for the League firstly to renounce its intention to demand the recovery of the lost land, and secondly to confront the government (and public opinion) with concrete evidence that the dispossessed landowners

[3]See *26th Diet, H.R., Yosan, No. 16* (8 March 1957), pp. 2-3.
[4]*26th Diet, H.C., Yosan, No. 10* (14 March 1957), p. 15. See also Finance Minister Ikeda Hayato's views on p. 14.

were actually in economic difficulties and deserved special 'political' consideration. Consequently they were led to define their immediate objective as the establishment of an appropriate public body to collect evidence to justify their demand for compensation out of public funds.

Nine days after the League came into being the LDP Special Investigation Committee on the Farmland Problem decided to seek the establishment of a Cabinet investigating committee of about twenty-five members. This plan failed to be acted upon in its original form, but a 28-member Investigation Committee on the Farmland Problem was set up instead in the LDP PARC towards the end of February 1958 to replace the existing special committee. This body undertook in September of the same year a survey with a sample of about 8,000 dispossessed landowners throughout the country and submitted in December recommendations based on its findings to the PARC deliberation commission and the executive council. The recommendations proposed: (i) to establish in 1959 a Cabinet commission to study the treatment of former landowners and have it prepare a report within one year; (ii) to institute a tax on the transfer of the title or sale of land by the beneficiary of the land reform in order to discourage such action and also to provide funds for the amelioration of former landowners' living conditions; and (iii) to take without delay financial and other measures to help those former landowners who were currently in economic difficulties.

As a result of these recommendations, the Cabinet attempted to have a bill establishing a Commission on the Problem of Dispossessed Landowners passed by the Diet. After initial failures in the 31st and 32nd Diet sessions in 1959, this bill was finally passed in June 1960 during the 34th session.

The commission thus established (popularly referred to as the Kudō Commission after its chairman, Kudō Shōshirō) produced in May 1962 a detailed report on the conditions of former landowners' households. The report demonstrated, among other things, that the average living standard of these households was not lower but substantially higher than that of other households. For example, 5·9 per cent had an annual cash income of over ¥1 million as compared with 1·5 per cent of former tenant households and 2·6 per cent of other households; for taxation purposes 15·6 per cent were classified in the highest income group as compared with 4 per cent of former tenant and 4·6 per cent of other households; and only 0·4 per cent received special government allowances under the Livelihood Protection Law, as compared with 1·2 per cent of former tenant households and 2·5 per cent of other households. It also showed that a substantially higher percentage of members of former landowners' households held public offices of one kind or another and were thus influential within their local communities. For example, 6 per cent of them were currently city, town, or village mayors and 33.5 per cent held other public positions, as compared with 1 and 17·1 per cent respectively for former tenant households and 0·5 and 9·2 per cent for other households.

When it came to evaluating the land reform and its effects on their living conditions, the findings of the commission confirmed the allegations that former landowners and their families were subject to accumulated frustrations and dissatisfactions. While 27·7 per cent regarded their present living standards as better than the average (as compared with 8·4 per cent of former tenant households and 8·7 per cent of other households), 53·7 per cent believed that they had lived better before the war, as compared with 25·9 per cent of former tenant households and 31·2 per cent of other households. Only 6·3 per cent positively approved the land reform while 53·6 per cent positively disapproved of it. This contrasts with the corresponding figures of 69·6 per cent and 4 per cent for the former tenant households and 17·4 per cent and 7·2 per cent for other households. The objections to the reform were based mainly on the belief that the land had been bought by the government at an artificially and unfairly low price.

On the basis of these findings the commission recommended that the government extend special loans to those former landowners' households that were actually in financial difficulties and also consider preferential treatment for the school-age children from such households in the application of the scholarship program. A majority of its nineteen members, however, were sceptical about the wisdom of granting a large sum of money to former landowners as a whole and, consequently, the commission refrained from making a definite proposal in this respect.

Despite the scepticism expressed by the Kudō Commission, the government under the continuing pressure from the League proposed another investigation of the living conditions of former landowners and opinions about the compensation to be undertaken by a special section to be established in the office of the Prime Minister.

By March 1964 the Special Research Section thus established in the office of the Prime Minister had prepared four reports. As regards the relative living standards of former landowners' households, its findings agreed substantially with the conclusion of the Kudō Commission.[5] Among its findings was also the information that 999,123 landowners and 885,909 landowners' households had been immediately affected by the reform and that of these 748,006 landowners were still living in August 1963 (745,256 inside Japan).[6]

As far as the problem of compensation was concerned, 82·9 per cent of the former landowners themselves, 72·6 per cent of their relations, and 41·1 per cent of those who had neither been landowners nor had relations or close acquaintances who had been landowners, were in favour of compensation.

[5]It showed, for example, that their average annual income was about ¥540,000 as compared with ¥500,000 for the average household.

[6]It also found that the average landowners had been deprived as a result of the land reform of 14·8 *tan* of farmland, 24·5 *tan* of uncultivated land, or 46·4 *tan* of pasture and that the average landowner had received a total of ¥8,736·6 for his farmland, uncultivated land, pasture and facilities therein.

Altogether, 50·7 per cent were in favour, 26·1 per cent were opposed, and 23·3 per cent were uncertain. It should be noted, however, that of those who were found to be generally in favour of the government making some kind of monetary payment to the former landowners, only 23·2 per cent thought that all should receive such benefits, while 59·6 per cent believed that the money should be given only to those among them who were actually in financial difficulties.

Despite this important reservation and despite the continued opposition of the Socialists and the Democratic Socialists, the government decided that it was politically proper to go ahead with plans for legislation for the disbursement of public moneys to pay 'rewards' to all the former landowners. The payment was to be made, however, not as 'compensation' but as a reward for the former landowners' alleged contributions to the subsequent economic development of the country, partly because the successive LDP governments had so far consistently denied their legal obligations to pay them compensation. It was also felt that 'compensation' for landowners would lead various other groups—such as those which had repatriated at the end of the war from former Japanese overseas possessions leaving most of their property behind—to seek similar treatment by the government, thus imposing an unbearable financial burden on the state. In any event, the June 1959 Bill Relating to the Payment of Benefits to Dispossessed Landowners was finally passed on 28 May 1965.

As we shall see below the legislation of May 1965 represented the final outcome of the prolonged efforts on the part of the League (with its LDP collaborators) to force the party leadership against the contrary pressure of the Ministry of Finance and the Ministry of Agriculture and Forestry to change its negative attitude. It represented a partial victory or, depending on one's particular viewpoint, a partial defeat for either side. The alliance of the League and its sympathisers in the LDP managed to obtain the legislation it had been working for, but in the process the total payment had been cut down from the original target of about ¥1,000,000 million to ¥145,000 million. This was less than half even of the ¥300,000 million once suggested by the secretary-general of the party, Tanaka Kakuei. In fact, assuming that the total number of the recipients of the benefits would be about 1,670,000, each would get in ten years an average of ¥87,000, or ¥8,700 per year. This amount was so small that in January 1966 the League was officially proposing to pool all the money in a 'Farmland Fund' which would be established and made to earn a 5 per cent dividend through investment under government supervision. Under the arrangements envisaged each would get about ¥4,300 per year indefinitely instead of ¥87,000 in ten years. In brief, the result of the extensive campaigns carried out by the League was essentially a compromise not entirely satisfactory to either side but better than nothing.

Conflicts of Opinion and Attitude in the LDP

The LDP contained from the beginning a fairly large number of Diet members who were conditioned to respond favourably to pressures from the groups of former landowners (subsequently represented by the League).

Although it was not until January 1957 that a committee was formally established in the LDP PARC to deal specifically with the issue, a group of several Liberal Party members had looked into the matter as early as 1954. According to Tsunashima Seikō, who was a leading member of this group and subsequently was associated with the League and the LDP Investigation Committee on the Farmland Problem, it involved Matsuno Raizō, Sudō Hideo, Ide Ichitarō, Nemoto Ryūtarō, Tanaka Man'itsu, and himself. It was mainly Tanaka and Tsunashima who were responsible for the conduct of the substantive investigation on behalf of the group. Assisted by an official of the Ministry of Agriculture and Forestry, Saitō Makoto, they had recommended to the party's leaders that compensation should be made in one way or another. Of the members of this Liberal Party group Tanaka Man'itsu, who had ceased to be a Diet member before the LDP officially came into being in November 1955, subsequently became president of the League in March 1958, while his trusted collaborator Tsunashima, who remained in the Diet, led the LDP Committee first as an active member and after December 1960 as chairman, until he was nominated in March 1965 concurrently president of the League.[7] The LDP's membership contained from the outset at least a few like Tsunashima who had already come to be personally identified with the groups of former landowners and their interests.

It is important to note in this respect that the traditional relationship between a conservative political party and the landlord class, which had constituted the basis of the conservative hegemony in prewar local politics, had survived the war and the land reform. The landowners continued to be regarded as the symbol of conservative power in rural communities. In 1950, for example, about 85 per cent of the former landlords who had owned fifty *chō* or more were associated with the Liberal Party, 9·5 per cent with the Democratic Party, and only 4 per cent with the Socialist Party. The general pattern does not seem to have changed significantly in the subsequent years and this fact no doubt exerted an important influence on LDP members in general in their personal response to the pressure of the League. It is also probable that a fairly high percentage of LDP Diet members had come from

[7]Tsunashima was first appointed chairman of the LDP Special Investigation Committee on the Farmland Problem in December 1960 and subsequently reappointed in August 1961 and again in August 1963. See *Asahi*, 14 December 1960; 4 August 1961 (evening); 28 August 1963. He was elected president of the League in March 1965. See *Nōchi Shimpō*, 57 (1 April 1965).

the former landlord class and were therefore naturally inclined to be sympathetic to the movement represented by the League.[8]

The official attitude of the top LDP leadership, on the other hand, remained remarkably consistent in a generally negative response to the demands of the League until about the middle of 1962. Even after the executive council decided in April 1962 (under the pressure of the League and its sympathisers in the party) to make the government pay 'rewards', the party's top leaders refused for nearly a year to commit themselves explicitly to such a policy. It was not until March 1963 that the four leaders (i.e. the vice-president, the secretary-general, and the chairmen of the executive council and the PARC) finally admitted that rewards would be paid soon and that their commitment was endorsed by Party President Ikeda. Furthermore, during the period between January 1958 and June 1962 only three of the fourteen persons who were nominated to the rank of the 'Three Leaders'—namely the secretary-general, the chairman of the executive council and the chairman of the PARC —ever consented to being listed officially in the roll of the League's advisers (see Table 14). In view of the fact that the party officials of somewhat lesser importance, such as the remaining categories of the 'Seven Leaders', were apparently as ready to associate themselves with the League as the rank and file, this rigid attitude of the top leadership is even more impressive.

It is very probable, though never certain, that this negative attitude on the part of the LDP leadership was strongly influenced by the attitudes of the high-ranking officials in the Ministry of Finance and the Ministry of Agriculture and Forestry, particularly the former of which Ikeda and his closest advisers were trusted 'old boys'. Even as late as April and May 1964 the bureaucrats in these ministries were insisting on cutting the total payment to about ¥30,000 million, as compared with anything between ¥285,000 million and ¥1,000,000 million earlier proposed by the League and its supporters in the party.

The objections of the Ministry of Finance arose mainly from the fear that this would in itself add considerably to state expenditure (a prospect it would oppose under almost any circumstances) and set a precedent for multifarious demands for 'compensation' for damages caused or allegedly caused by World War II and the Occupation. The objections of the Ministry of Agriculture and Forestry, on the other hand, were less specific. Officials in this ministry had been largely responsible for the execution of the land reform, and to make a concession to the former landowners would be to admit that it had committed injustices against them. Moreover, its principal contemporary concern

[8]For example, Mr Sakata Michita, an LDP member of the House of Representatives, said: 'I was a landowner myself and suffered from all the difficulties caused by the land reform . . . It was thanks to that reform that Japan was saved from communism and I believe it is natural, even for that reason alone, that former landowners should be properly rewarded . . .' (interview, 1 March 1966).

TABLE 14

Distribution of the official LDP leaders associated with the National Farmland League, 1 January 1958 to 5 June 1962

	No. of leaders (A)	Appointed League's advisers (B)	(B)/(A)	Not appointed League's advisers
Secretaries-general	4	Fukuda Takeo	1/4 = 25·0%	Kawashima Shōjirō, Masutani Shūji, and Maeo Shigesaburō
Chairmen, executive council	6	Hori Shigeru	1/6 = 16·6%	Satō Eisaku, Kōno Ichirō (Masutani Shūji), Ishii Mitsujirō, and Akagi Munenori
Chairmen, PARC	6	(Fukuda Takeo) and Tanaka Kakuei	2/6 = 33·3%	Miki Takeo, Nakamura Umekichi, Shina Etsusaburō, and Funada Naka
3 Leaders	14		3/14 = 21·4%	
Chairmen, National Organisation Committee	6	Miura Kunio, Takeyama Yūtarō, and Kogane Yoshiteru	3/6 = 50·0%	Fukunaga Kenji, Imamatsu Jirō, and Ogawa Hanji
Chairmen, Diet Policy Committee	6	Murakami Isamu, Masuda Kaneshichi, Yamamura Shinjirō, and Ezaki Masumi	4/6 = 66·6%	(Fukunaga Kenji) and Ozawa Saeki
Chairmen, Party Discipline Committee	6	Kimura Tokutarō, Ishihara Kan'ichirō, Uetake Haruhiko, Kogure Butayū, and Kōri Yūichi	5/6 = 83·3%	Sakomizu Hisatsune
Chairmen, Public Relations Committee	4	Fukuda Tokuyasu, Hara Kenzaburō, and Shiga Kenjirō	3/4 = 75·0%	Shinoda Kōsaku
7 Leaders	35		18/35 = 51·4%	

Sources: *Nōchi Shimpō*, 24 (1 January 1958) to 53 (5 June 1962); *Asahi*, 10 and 13 July, 19 September and 31 December 1957 (all evening); 13 and 17 (evening) June, and 13 September 1958; 10 (morning and evening) and 26 (evening) January, and 17 and 19 June 1959; 19 and 21 (evening) July, and 14 December 1960; 6 April (evening), 18, 20, 22, and 25 (all evening) July, and 29 September 1961; and 17 (evening), 21 and 30 (evening) July 1962.

was to protect the interests of the beneficiaries, rather than the victims, of the reform.

The negative attitudes of the ministries concerned were reflected in the trends of opinion in the two PARC divisions directly tied to them—the Division on Finance and the Division on Agriculture and Forestry. It was for this reason that the sympathisers of the League in the party chose in January 1957 to set up in the PARC the Sub-Committee on the Farmland Problem as a new unit separate and independent from both divisions. The possible resistance from the ministries through their agents in the divisions would thus be circumvented.

It was in the light of this situation that the League had to map out its strategy towards the LDP and the government. It was obviously essential for it to change the attitude of the party leadership if it was ever to succeed in winning the desired legislation.

The Strategy of the League

The League (officially established on 12 December 1957) was a federation of forty-six prefectural leagues with branches set up in all cities and counties throughout the country. It was governed by a leadership group made up of a president, a few vice-presidents, several standing directors, secretaries, and advisers recruited from among Diet members affiliated with the LDP and, initially, with the Ryokufūkai of the House of Councillors. The membership of the organisation has remained 600,000 or more throughout its active existence. Its influence was believed by its own officials to be powerful enough to defeat at the polls any candidate in a Diet election whom it considered as *persona non grata*, if not to guarantee the victory of every candidate it might endorse. As regards its policy orientation, it explicitly renounced any intention to undo the land reform or its effects in order to restore to their original holders titles to land already redistributed. As was made clear in their appeal sent in the summer of 1961 to local administrators, politicians, and leaders of various organisations, those affiliated with this organisation were ready to uphold the fundamental spirit of the land reform and yet believed that many injustices had been done to former landowners and that they had the right to demand adequate compensation from the government for those injustices. Their complaints concerned basically the low prices at which their land had been bought by the government in the reform, but they also enumerated eighteen other specific 'injustices' for which they would insist on being compensated. Accordingly, the leaders of the League decided to concentrate their efforts on obtaining legislation that would compel the government to pay the dispossessed landowners 'fair and just' compensation. This policy in retrospect seems to have been well calculated to avoid unnecessarily offending public opinion and, possibly, giving rise to serious social disturbances in many rural communities. All subsequent efforts of the organisation were oriented generally towards the ultimate fulfilment of this objective.

In organising its pressure group activities directed at the LDP members of the Diet the League followed in the footsteps of its two predecessors. As early as November 1953 the Zenkoku jinushidantai kyōgikai had decided to engage in extensive lobbying and in the following month about thirty of its representatives had personally petitioned and exacted a promise of co-operation from nearly forty conservative members of the Diet. In the first half of 1956 the Zenkoku kaihō-nōchi kokkahoshō rengōkai had staged a series of deputations to individual LDP Diet members. The League engaged in similar activities but on a vastly extended scale, lobbying with zest and determination the whole body of the LDP parliamentary party.

The first and foremost point in the League's strategy was to force as many LDP Diet members as possible to commit themselves to its support by establishing formal relationships with them. At the very outset it appointed Yamazaki Takeshi, a former LDP MHR, as its first president, and four sitting LDP Diet members as its first standing advisers. It also decided to recruit *all* LDP and Ryokufūkai members of Diet as advisers. By early February 1958 it had succeeded in persuading about 120 LDP-affiliated MHRs and 50 MHCs to agree to the listing of their names on the roll of advisers. These numbers had increased by July of the same year to about 170 and 80 respectively, or about 60 per cent of the total LDP Diet strength at the time. The fact that only between 80 and 130 of them attended the 'advisers' conferences' more or less regularly suggests that a substantial proportion of them were thus affiliated with the League nominally rather than effectively, but there is no doubt that the organisation achieved a remarkable success within a relatively short period in its efforts to infiltrate the LDP. Even the number of standing advisers (presumably interested in the issue much more genuinely than most of the advisers) increased by January 1961 to 27, of whom 17 were sitting MHRs, 3 former MHRs, and 7 sitting MHCs.

Parallel with the efforts to induce as many of the LDP Diet members as possible to associate themselves formally with the League, an intensive program of pressure activities was undertaken. A big national rally was held in October 1958 with some 20,000 people participating, including 75 Diet members. Another was held in October 1962 with 25,000 people attending, including some 200 Diet members. Specifically to demand the immediate passage of a 'reward' bill, about 1,200 activists met in April 1964 at an indoor rally (attended by 175 Diet members), and again in March 1965, this time with an unprecedented number of 251 LDP Diet members attending. Even more effective, however, than mass rallies as a form of pressure group activity was a series of petitions systematically organised and directed at particular party and government officials.

The first wave of systematic petitioning organised by the League came immediately following the mass rally of October 1958, when seventeen 'peti-

tioners' units' were organised to visit and petition individual party and
government leaders. Each was led by two Diet members and consisted of
delegates from several prefectures. They visited and petitioned in person the
following government and party officials: Prime Minister (LDP president);
Ministers of Finance, Agriculture and Forestry, and State without portfolio
(Ikeda Hayato); Director-General of the Economic Planning Agency; Chief
Cabinet Secretary; Chairmen of the Standing Committees on Finance, Agriculture and Forestry, and Budget in the House of Representatives and the
House of Councillors; and LDP Six Leaders (Secretary-General, and Chair-
men of the Executive Council, the PARC, and the Committees on Finance,
National Organisation, and Diet Policy).

A second wave of petitions came in early 1959 when the bill establishing
an Investigating Commission on the Problem of Dispossessed Landowners
was being debated in the Diet. On that occasion nine selected officials were
called upon on 25 April by groups of League members, again nearly all led
by members of the Diet. Later on the same day a group of delegates from
nine prefectures led by the League's president, Tanaka Man'itsu, stormed
the meeting of the Seven Leaders inside the Diet Building. Early on the
morning of 2 December 1959 and again on 31 March 1960 the Prime Minister, Kishi, was subjected to a petition by a group of twenty or so League
members at his residence.

In May and June 1964, the private residences of the Prime Minister, Ikeda,
and the Finance Minister, Tanaka Kakuei, were scenes of mass petitions
practically every morning and in these two months an average of forty-five
prefectural delegates engaged daily in this type of activity. Following the rally
of 24 March 1965 in the last phase of the prolonged campaign, fourteen peti-
tioners' units in the 'third wave' of mass petition tactics confronted eighteen
key politicians with the demand that they co-operate with efforts to pass
the Reward Bill being debated by the House of Representatives Cabinet
Committee.

The Role of the LDP Diet Members Associated with the League

Crucial throughout the period of these intense pressure group activities
carried out by the League was the part played by those of its sympathisers
in the party who were personally associated with it, as mentioned earlier, as
its advisers or standing advisers.

In connection with the abortive attempt immediately after the formation
of the League in December 1957 to bring about the establishment of a
Cabinet investigating commission, the efforts of the standing advisers Hara
and Koyanagi, reinforced by several active advisers, secured a promise from
the secretary-general, Kawashima, that such a commission would be set up
with an initial budgetary appropriation of ¥30 million in the 1958 fiscal year.
This plan, as we know, failed to materialise, but their continued efforts did

result in the establishment of the 28-member investigation committee in the party. In October of the same year 106 of the advisers adopted a resolution calling for immediate aid to those former landowners' households that were in economic difficulties, prompt establishment of a Cabinet investigating commission, and the enactment of a bill relating to the financial aspect of the problem. There is little doubt that it was because of pressure exercised by the more radically committed Diet members, such as the standing advisers Hara and Asaka and the advisers Tsunashima and Katō, that in 1958 the chief of the Ministry of Agriculture and Forestry's Bureau of Agricultural Land, Itō, and the Minister of Agriculture and Forestry, Miura, had to retract their statements repudiating the League's demands.

After the Kudō Commission was finally set up in late 1960 and especially after its report was submitted to the Cabinet in May 1962, the role of the LDP Diet members as the agents of the League became even more conspicuous and decisive. It was directly as a result of their face-to-face pressure applied to the top party leaders that the latter in the spring of 1962 for the first time indicated willingness to raise the total amount of compensation from about ¥30,000 million as suggested by the Ministry of Finance to about ten times that figure. About two years later Tanaka Kakuei, who had then been the LDP PARC chairman, reminisced as follows:

There used to be rallies held in Hibiya Park [in central Tokyo] and I believe that successive secretaries-general of the Party attended them. This time[the rally of 23 March 1962?], however, it was decided that the PARC chairman should go on behalf of the Three Leaders and that is why I went there . . . About that time each of the Three Leaders was visited by the representatives [of the League] almost every day and one day I was asked to meet the deputation on behalf of all the rest of them. They were still insisting on obtaining ¥1,000,000 million from the government, but I told them that the sum was ridiculous and that they should know that in order to make it more or less feasible politically they would have to cut it down to something like ¥200,000 million or ¥300,000 million. It is the truth that I made that suggestion on that occasion . . . It seems that they went back to the organisation and told its officials that the Three Leaders were ready to take the necessary steps [for legislation], provided that they would accept the offer of ¥300,000 million . . . They [other party leaders] had wanted me to do something about it in order to get ourselves off the hook and therefore I could not have acted otherwise than I did. This is how I have got into the present predicament over this issue.[9]

Instead of getting themselves 'off the hook', Tanaka and other leaders of the party and the government were thus led to agree to do what they had so long denied any intentions of doing, namely to pay a substantial amount of money uniformly to all those who had been affected by the land reform. This was certainly a credit to the perseverance (or obstinacy) and loyalty to the League of its Diet member advisers.

[9]'Seichōkai jūnen no ayumi wo kataru', Seisaku Geppō, 100 (May 1964), pp. 141-2.

Domination of Party Organs

In addition to their role as the spearhead of pressure activities directed towards particular party and government officials, the standing advisers and advisers of the League appointed from among LDP Diet members had another important role to play on its behalf. This concerned the infiltration and domination of the party's decision-making organs, especially the Investigation Committee on the Farmland Problem set up in February 1958.

Of the seventeen LDP Diet members initially appointed to membership of this body, fourteen, including the chairman, Tago Ichimin, and the vice-chairman, Takeyama Yūtarō, were either standing advisers or advisers of the League. Together with five of the additional eleven members drawn from among 'men of learning and experience' outside the Diet, they easily controlled the committee and turned it into the League's mouthpiece. The numerical balance between those patently representing and speaking on behalf of the League and those who were at least officially in a position to criticise its demands in the committee was inherited basically unchanged by the temporary LDP Council on the Farmland Problem established in April 1962 and embracing all top-ranking officials of the party's policy-making and executive organs. Of the total of twenty-six members, five had been or were standing advisers and thirteen were advisers, making, in other words, a balance of 18 to 8 in favour of the former. The composition of its sub-committee was even more extreme; the balance was 11 to 2 and many of the eleven were the most active of the advisers and standing advisers.[10]

As mentioned earlier, the LDP Investigation Committee on the Farmland Problem thus dominated by the agents of the League was primarily responsible for the establishment of the Kudō Commission in 1960. Long before the latter's report was completed and presented to the Cabinet in May 1962, however, the LDP Committee decided to go ahead with its own plans to ensure that legislative action necessary for the payment of compensation to the former landowners be taken in due course. On 23 March of that year it decided at its plenary meeting to introduce in the current Diet session a members-sponsored bill authorising the payment of between ¥400,000 million and ¥600,000 million to them. Although this attempt was blocked by the opposition of the Cabinet and party leadership, it resulted in a resolution by the LDP Assembly of the Members of Both Houses of the Diet to the effect that appropriate action should be taken in the next Diet session in order to satisfy the demands of the League. The subsequent behaviour of the committee demonstrated even more conclusively that it was merely a mouthpiece

[10]The League's representatives in the sub-committee were Ikeda Masanosuke (sub-committee chairman), Kambayashiyama Eikichi, Ōishi Buichi, Honna Takeshi, Seto-yama Mitsuo, Tsunashima Seikō, Matsuzawa Yūzō, Arafune Seijūrō, Ikuta Kōichi, Masuda Kaneshichi, and Shigemasa Yōtoku. The two exceptions were Yamanaka Sadanori and Kobayashi Eizō. For the list of members see *Nōchi Shimpō*, 53. Regarding the function of the sub-committee see *Asahi*, 12 April 1962.

of the League and acted as an intra-party pressure group *vis-à-vis* the party leadership. For example, in February 1964 the committee nominated a 22-man team of its own members to conduct 'negotiations' with the party leadership and the Cabinet. At its meeting on 26 February this team resolved, among other things, to express regrets at the 'misconception that the LDP Investigation Committee on the Farmland Problem is a pressure group and not the official party organ that it actually is'.

The extraordinarily intimate identification of the LDP Investigation Committee and the League was dramatically symbolised by the fact that one of the League's most ardent supporters and future president, Tsunashima Seikō, was at the same time the chairman of the committee after December 1960. It also eloquently testified to the degree of success the League achieved in its efforts to infiltrate and dominate the crucial nerve-centre of the LDP. During the critical year 1964-5, when it forged ahead with dogged determination in its final attempt to secure victory, practically all of the party organs immediately concerned with official party decisions and attitudes regarding the issue succumbed to its influence and pressure. In the executive council, for example, those who were openly associated with it as advisers held a 16 to 14 majority over those who were not, while the former also prevailed by 7 to 6 in the PARC Deliberation Commission, by about 25 to 16 in the PARC Cabinet Division, and 39 to 35 in the Agriculture and Forestry Division.

It is more difficult to be specific about the overall degree of success achieved by the League in its bid to infiltrate and dominate the LDP as a whole. As already pointed out, by the middle of 1958 approximately 250 LDP Diet members (about 60 per cent of LDP parliamentary strength at the time) had consented to having their names officially listed as advisers or standing advisers of the organisation. Furthermore, 31 (7·2 per cent) of the 429 LDP MHRs and 10 (5·2 per cent) of the 191 MHCs who were returned during the four and half years between January 1958 and June 1962 were nominated as standing advisers to the League. Of the rest, 213 MHRs and 86 MHCs were listed as advisers at one time or another during the same period. In other words, 244 of the 429 LDP MHRs (56·8 per cent) and 96 of the 191 MHCs (50·2 per cent) were officially associated with the organisation.[11] Thus by mid-1962 not only the key policy-making organs but also a majority of the party-affiliated Diet members had come under the influence of the League, an achievement that is remarkable by any standards.

Characteristics of LDP Members Associated with the League

In terms of the LDP policy-making process two facts about the LDP members of the Diet who were thus formally associated with the League deserve

[11]Based on information compiled from *Nōchi Shimpō*, 24 (1 January 1958) to 53 (5 June 1962).

special attention. One relates to the role of former public servants. The other concerns the significance of intra-party factionalism in situations such as those under review.

Compared with other occupational categories of LDP membership, the percentage of former public servants officially associated with the League was generally higher than the average, being 63 per cent for MHRs and 50·6 per cent for MHCs (see Table 15). A closer examination reveals that the

TABLE 15

Distribution by occupational categories of LDP Diet members appointed advisers to the National Farmland League, 1 January 1958 to 5 June 1962

	Local politicians	Public servants	Business-men	Journalists	Lawyers	Misc.	Totals
MHRs							
Those appointed advisers	66	63	40	25	19	31	244
Those not appointed advisers	53	37	23	24	11	37	185
Totals	119	100	63	49	30	68	429
MHCs							
Those appointed advisers	22	37	10	2	6	19	96
Those not appointed advisers	12	36	19	0	3	25	95
Totals	34	73	29	2	9	44	191

Sources: Nōchi Shimpō, 24 (1 January 1958) to 53 (5 June 1962) ; *GSS: Shūgiingiin meikan* (1962) ; and *GSS Kizokuin sangiin giin meikan* (1960).

'old boys' from the Ministry of Finance in both Houses and those from the Ministry of Agriculture and Forestry in the Upper House tended to be some-what more cautious than others, but the percentage differences were insignificant (see Table 16). In any event, it is impossible to find positive evidence to prove that the attitudes of the two particular ministries seriously inhibited the behaviour of the former bureaucrats associated with them despite the efforts of the League and its sympathisers in the party. The statistical evidence available suggests, on the contrary, that they co-operated with the League as willingly as others and possibly even helped it to cope with the intransigence of the officials of the two ministries. At the minimum their presence was probably useful to the League just as much as to the ministries as links of communication and in the behind-the-scenes negotiations which were no doubt essential to the ultimate compromise.

It is significant in this context that the former Finance Ministry official, Ueki Kōshirō, and the former Agriculture and Forestry Ministry official, Shigemasa Yōtoku, were included in the initial membership of the 6-man

TABLE 16

Distribution by ministries of former public servants appointed advisers to the National Farmland League, 1 January 1958 to 5 June 1962

	Home Affairs*	Agri- culture and Forestry	Finance	Trans- porta- tion	Com- merce and Industry†	Foreign Affairs	Misc.‡	Totals
MHRs								
Those appointed advisers	23	5	9	7	4	5	10	63
Those not appointed advisers	14	2	7	2	5	5	2	37
Totals	37	7	16	9	9	10	12	100
MHCs								
Those appointed advisers	18	3	5	4	1	1	5	37
Those not appointed advisers	8	5	5	7	3	2	6	36
Totals	26	8	10	11	4	3	11	73

*'Home Affairs' here refers to the prewar Ministry of Home Affairs (the *Naimushō*).

†'Commerce and Industry' refers to the prewar Ministry of Commerce and Industry (the *Shōkōshō*) and the postwar Ministry of International Trade and Industry (the *Tsūsanshō*).

‡'Miscellaneous' includes the Ministries of Education, Welfare, Labour, Construction, Postal Service, and the Economic Planning Agency.

Sources: As for Table 15.

PARC sub-committee on the farmland problem in January 1957. Similarly, the membership of the Investigation Committee included in March 1964 three former bureaucrats, one each from the Ministry of Finance (Maeo Shigesaburō), the Ministry of Agriculture and Forestry (Sakata Eiichi), and the Ministry of Home Affairs (Koyanagi Makie). In the meantime, a majority of the 'old boys' from the two ministries immediately interested in the issue, 14 out of the 26 from the Ministry of Finance and 8 out of the 15 from the Ministry of Agriculture and Forestry, were persuaded by the middle of 1962 to become the League's advisers.

Regarding the role of the factions, it should be first noted that, except for the Kōno faction,[12] a majority in every faction were appointed advisers of the League and, except for the Miki faction, each contained at least a few who were willing to devote more time and energy than others to helping the League as standing advisers (see Table 17). On the other hand, the lobbying activities systematically undertaken by the League in collaboration with its

[12]According to Mr Fukushima Matsutarō of the Shunjūkai Secretariat, members of the Kōno faction 'tended to avoid taking sides' over the issue. (Interview, 20 January 1966.)

TABLE 17

Distribution of the League's advisers and standing advisers by factions,
1 January 1958 to 5 June 1962

	Total no. of faction members (A)	No. of those appointed League's advisers (B)	(B)/(A) %	No. of those appointed standing advisers (C)	(C)/(A) %
Fujiyama	28	20	71·4	3	10·7
Satō	55	37	67·2	6	10·9
Miki	44	27	61·3	–	—
Ōno	37	21	57·8	5	10·8
Ikeda	56	33	56·7	4	7·1
Ishibashi	9	5	55·5	1	11·1
Kishi	58	31	53·4	4	6·8
Ishii	30	16	53·3	4	13·3
Kōno	47	22	46·8	4	8·5
Uncertain	65	32	49·2	–	—
Totals	429	244	56·8	31	7·2

Sources: Nōchi Shimpō, 24 (1 January 1958) to 53 (5 June 1962); and *Kokkai binran*, 7th ed. (April 1957) to 20th ed. (February 1962).

agents in the party were never directed specifically at any of the faction leaders as such. None of the faction leaders ever became the League's adviser or standing adviser at any time. These facts suggest the irrelevance of the factions in the policy-making situation under review, largely no doubt because, as the fact that a majority in each became officially associated with the League suggests, they were uniformly vulnerable to the latter's pressure. Under the circumstances it was also impossible for the issue to develop into a truly controversial one within the party and thus to become an effective weapon for the dissident factions to utilise in their attempts to undermine the prestige and authority of the dominant factions. The consensus which emerged within the party as a result of the intense campaigns of the League and, especially, the conversion of the former Finance and Agriculture Ministry bureaucrats, removed the issue effectively beyond the influence of factionalism.

The League as a Provider of Votes

The relationship between the League as an interest group and the LDP cannot be fully explained in terms solely of the functions of the factors of LDP policy-making internal to the party. There is little doubt that the effectiveness of the pressure group technique adopted by the League depended considerably upon its actual or assumed ability to provide the party with specific and concrete support. In other words, whatever success the League achieved resulted, in the final analysis, largely from the widely shared belief that it controlled a sizeable bloc of votes and therefore was in a position to influence seriously the results of an election. In the light of such evidence as is available that belief was not completely justified but was sufficiently well founded to be accepted by most LDP Diet members or prospective candidates.

While there is no firm evidence to suggest that the League systematically involved itself in any House of Representatives election, it is known to have undertaken to ensure the victory of four LDP candidates standing for the national constituency at the June 1959 House of Councillors election. On that occasion it assigned several prefectural leagues (branches) and a team of campaigners to each candidate. For example, the prefectural leagues of Nīgata, Yamanashi, Kanagawa, Saitama, Gumma, Tochigi, Ibaraki, Nagano, and Miyagi, and a campaigning team consisting of the League's president, Tanaka, and the presidents of the prefectural leagues of Kanagawa, Nagano, and Tochigi, were assigned to the candidate Yamamoto Sugi. Three of the candidates thus supported by the League in this election, Okamura Bunshirō, Yamamoto Sugi, and Ōtani Yoshio, were successfully returned, while one, Konishi Hideo, failed. In the next House of Councillors election of July 1962 exactly the same kind of arrangements were made for four selected LDP-affiliated candidates running in the national constituency—Konishi Hideo, Shigemune Yūzō, Hitotsumatsu Sadayoshi, and Shimojō Yasumaro. In addition, each prefectural league undertook to work for one or two particular LDP candidates in each prefectural constituency who were believed to be especially helpful to the organisation and its objectives. Thus a total of forty-eight candidates in the prefectural constituencies as well as four in the national constituency section stood with the official support of the League and forty-one (85·5 per cent) of the former and two (50 per cent) of the latter were successfully returned. Considering that the average survival ratio for all LDP candidates standing in the prefectural constituencies was 78·6 per cent, those who were officially supported by the League did appreciably better than the average. The same does not seem to apply to the national constituency candidates, where the average LDP survival ratio was 53·8 per cent compared with 50 per cent for the four officially endorsed by the League. This was, however, because one of the two unsuccessful candidates was chosen by the LDP Election Policy Committee very much against the will of the League, and its support was therefore purely nominal.[13]

As far as the results of the 1962 House of Councillors elections are concerned, there is little doubt that the League's endorsement made an appreciable difference to the performance of the candidates concerned when com-

[13]Shimojō, who had been president of the National Union for Governmental Compensation for Liberated Farmland, and therefore been personally and deeply involved in its internecine factional conflicts in 1956 and 1957, was apparently *persona non grata* to the League's current leaders. He was accepted nominally as one of the candidates to be officially endorsed by it only because of the insistence on the part of the LDP Election Policy Committee and Ishii Mitsujirō. See *Nōchi Shimpō*, 53; Hirota (interview, 21 February 1966).

pared with those who did not receive such support. It is also evident that its influence in this respect was not lost on a majority of the sitting LDP Diet members or prospective candidates. However, before venturing a generalisation about this particular aspect of the League's activities it is important to consider the specific nature of its support. In sharp contrast to the kind of support the LDP receives from most external groups sympathetic to it (especially business firms and trade associations), the support given by the League in connection with the election campaigns was almost entirely in the form of votes and not funds. For example, of the fifty-two candidates who ran with its official backing in the House of Councillors election of 1962, only one—Nakano Bunmon of Hyōgo Prefecture—is known to have officially received any financial aid from the organisation, and the amount involved was a meagre ¥30,000. In fact, the League does not seem to have ever been in a position to give money away, since its annual budget was only about ¥6 million, out of which wages had to be paid to about six full-time members running the secretariat, and it also incurred substantial administrative costs. In any event, it is evident that the LDP's co-operation was won not in return for financial contributions but for the several million votes the League was believed to have under its control.

As mentioned previously, the number of the landowners directly affected by the land reform and alive in mid-1963 was 745,256, according to the report of the Special Research Section established in the Office of the Prime Minister. This was 1·2 per cent of the total population of qualified voters (58,281,641 in November 1963), which appears to be an insignificant proportion. However, one of the League's slogans at the 1958 Lower House election was 'Let each of us secure ten votes for the right man at the polls', which implied that most of these former landowners were capable of influencing a certain number of other voters.

Whether or not ten votes per head was a reasonable approximation to reality, it is clear that the number of voters they were in a position decisively to influence was far greater than their own number. In part this was because the former landowners had families who had presumably shared the same hardships and therefore had good reason to act with them. Another factor was the special position many of them occupied in local politics and the functions they performed as opinion leaders, especially in connection with the organisation and activities of the individual LDP Diet members' supporters' associations.

According to data collected by the Special Research Section of the Office of the Prime Minister, in October 1963 the former landowner's household had an average of at least 5·3 members and an average of 3·3 members of twenty years old or over, who were qualified voters. Each former landowner, therefore, was probably in a position to commit about three votes, including his own, from his household to the support of a particular candidate.

It is more difficult to assess with precision the extent of the influence that he could exert on voters outside of his own family. His relations, however, with the supporters' association of an LDP Diet member or prospective candidate no doubt played a very important part in that member's or candidate's calculations. As pointed out in Chapter 6, every LDP Diet member or prospective candidate depends for votes in an election on the work of his supporters' association operating at the constituency level. It is a variety of local notabilities, especially local politicians, administrators, leaders of trade, professional and civic associations that play a predominant role in the organisation and activities of a supporters' association and it is, in turn, the former landowners and the 'old middle class' represented by them that supply the greater proportion of such local notabilities.

According to the Kudō Commission's report, for example, the percentage of former landowners' households from which a member or members had been elected or appointed public officials in the postwar period was as high as 33·6 per cent; the percentage of those of which a member or members were currently (from 21 November to 7 December 1961) occupying such positions was 20·8 per cent. Since the total number of the former landowners directly affected by the land reform and living in 1963 was 745,256, presumably at least about 150,000 members of their households were available to participate in and lead the supporters' associations. Each of them within the special framework of activities associated with the supporters' associations must have influenced at least a few voters.

For these two reasons, it seems quite reasonable to suggest as a very conservative estimate that each former landowner was in a position to influence an average of four voters, that is five including himself. If this assumption is acceptable for purposes of our discussion, then we may base an estimate of the League's strength as a vote-gathering machine on the hypothesis that the 745,256 former landowners could, at least potentially, determine the attitude of about 3,726,280 voters, including themselves, or 6·3 per cent of the total number of qualified voters. This figure is probably not very far from the kind of approximation made by many LDP Diet members or prospective candidates in mapping out their strategies for a future election and deciding how to respond to the demands of the League. This was, then, the key to the relative success achieved by the organisation of former landowners in its attempt to make the LDP satisfy its demands by pushing the unpopular legislation through the Diet.

The grievances of the landowners who were deprived of their property as a result of the land reform undertaken during the Allied Occupation led to the emergence of organised pressure groups among them, which were eventually unified in the National Farmland League. The issue considered in this chapter developed largely in the context of the relationship between this particular external group and the LDP.

The top leaders of the party persisted until about 1962 in their negative response to the demand of the League for monetary compensation. The influence of the Ministry of Finance and the Ministry of Agriculture and Forestry, which were both firmly opposed to the proposed compensation, probably determined the attitudes of these party leaders.

With a view to forcing the party leadership to change its attitude and co-operate in the passage of an appropriate bill, the League attempted success-fully to build a sufficiently large group of its supporters in the party by appointing as advisers as many of the Diet members affiliated with the party as possible. These supporters in the party in turn succeeded in controlling the key party organs, particularly the PARC and the executive council.

Despite the opposition of the Ministry of Finance and the Ministry of Agriculture and Forestry, former high-ranking public servants in the party actively associated themselves with the League and its lobbying activities either as advisers to the League or as members of the appropriate party organs, especially the PARC Investigation Committee on the Farmland Problem. Those from the two particular ministries were no exceptions.

The role of the factions, on the other hand, was almost entirely negligible. There is no evidence to suggest that an LDP Diet member's response to the pressure of the League was influenced significantly by his factional affiliation. Moreover, like the top party leaders, all faction leaders uniformly avoided personal involvement in the campaigns conducted by the League. An impor-tant reason for this irrelevance of the factions in the development of the issue was probably the fact that the vulnerability to the League's influence and resulting support for its activity were cross-factional and, consequently, there was not much room for the issue to develop into a sufficiently controversial one within the party to make it attractive as a weapon for dissident factions to exploit in their opposition to the dominant factions.

The League and its collaborators within the party had very definite and clear-cut ideas as to who were the decision-makers who really mattered in the resolution of the issue. Almost invariably chosen for systematic lobbying were, as we have seen, for the Cabinet, the Prime Minister (party president), the Chief Cabinet Secretary, and the ministers with direct jurisdiction over the matter involved (Ministers of Finance and of Agriculture and Forestry) ; for the party, the six or seven leaders and the chairmen of the appropriate PARC committees; and for the Diet, the chairmen of the appropriate stand-ing committees of both Houses. This defines clearly the group of the principal decision-makers in policy-making situations of the kind under review. It should be noted that all of these decision-makers designated by the interest group were formal officials of the three entities involved, but that neither the members of the PARC deliberation commission nor those of the executive council were included as such. This was probably an indication of the some-what ambiguous character of the issue itself, which was evidently not a sub-ject of purely routine policy-making and yet never assumed a truly controversial character within the party to the extent of provoking factional strife.

Finally, the basis of the League's influence on the LDP concerning the disposition of the issue was the votes over which it was believed to have effective control. It was largely the significance of the nearly 4 million voters who were believed to be subject to its influence and who could make a significant difference to the performance of the individual LDP Diet members in elections that determined the attitude first of the rank and file and eventually of the top leaders of the LDP.

o

8 Constitutional Revision

Blaming the most flagrant of the social, economic, and political weaknesses found in Japan in the wake of the Allied Occupation largely on the 'mistakes' committed by the latter's initial policies, the LDP made an official and public pledge at its inaugural meeting on 15 November 1955 to amend the constitution of Japan. 'The Mission of the Party' adopted at the LDP inaugural meeting reads as follows:

> Turning one's attention to the domestic conditions, one cannot but be struck by the absence of patriotism and the spirit of self-reliance, the political stagnation, the inability to establish a viable national economy . . . Responsible for these conditions, at least partially, were the nation's defeat in the war and the errors committed by the policies of the Occupation in its initial phase. Although the democracy and freedom, which were greatly emphasised under the Occupation, must be respected and defended as the guiding principles of the new Japan, the weight given in the initial Occupation policies to the weakening of the nation led to the unwarranted suppression of the ideal of the state and patriotism and excessive fragmenation of the powers of the state. Such resulted from the reform of the constitution, the education system and other institutions. . . .[1]

On the strength of this argument, 'voluntary revision of the constitution' was defined as one of the six basic missions of the new party. It was also incorporated, together with a call for a general re-examination of all 'Occupation-sponsored' laws and practices, in the original platform of the LDP.

The course of action envisaged by the LDP leaders for the fulfilment of this pledge was outlined in the general policy program adopted on that occasion. While making an assurance, on one hand, that the basic principles of the existing constitution, such as democracy, devotion to world peace and popular sovereignty, would remain unchanged, it proposed to have a special commission officially established and investigations of the problems involved undertaken without delay. The Cabinet Commission on the Constitution, which began to function in August 1957 and subsequently provided the main

[1] See Jimintōshi hensaniinkai (ed.), *Jiyūminshutōshi* (1961), pp. 22-3.

arena of the controversy between revisionists and anti-revisionists, resulted directly from the LDP commitment made at its inaugural meeting.[2]

Japanese Responses to the Constitution of 1946

Both the content of the new constitution of Japan, promulgated on 3 November 1946, and the special circumstances under which it was drafted, were destined to make it a subject of an emotional and ideological controversy, so that the possibility of its revision became a great political issue in postwar Japan. When made public in its original form on 6 March 1946, its draft text was received by the press (which represented such articulate public opinion on the subject as existed at the time) not only with enthusiasm and praise but also with criticisms and scepticism.[3]

Commenting on what subsequently became the controversial Article 9, the *Yomiurihōchi Shimbun* had the following to say in its editorial of 8 March 1946:

> Nor are we without some misgivings concerning the other focus of this constitution, the eternal renunciation of war. We are convinced, to be sure, that an aggressive war should be banned for all time, but should we not be left with the right to fight a war of liberation, in case a foreign power should commit aggression against us and attempt to subject us to a state of slavery? If the right to wage a war should be totally given up, then the nation should have a status of permanent neutrality recognised, as is the case with Switzerland, and guaranteed by the United Nations, by force if necessary. While we would be the first to vote for the perpetuation of peace and abolition of war, we would also defend our nation's life and independence even at the cost of our blood . . .[4]

No particular objections were ever raised to the drastic change proposed in the GHQ draft in the status and powers of the Emperor, although almost exclusive attention had been paid to this problem in the preceding several months in relation to the prospective revision of the Imperial Constitution.[5]

[2]For a more extended discussion of the issue and its probable outcome in relation to the work of the Commission on the Constitution, see Robert E. Ward, 'The Commission on the Constitution and Prospects for Constitutional Change in Japan', *Journal of Asian Studies*, XXIV, 3 (May 1965), pp. 401-29.

[3]The 'GHQ draft' of the constitution, a summary of which was made public on 6 March 1946, had been preceded by and replaced two far more conservative drafts prepared by the Matsumoto Committee on behalf of the Shidehara Cabinet, as well as those for which the parties and private groups were responsible. For a detailed review of these drafts and the circumstances under which they were prepared, as well as the circumstances surrounding the making of the GHQ draft, see Kempōchōsakai, *Kempōseitei no keika ni kansuru shōiinkai hōkokusho* (July 1964). The text of the same report is available also in Kempōseitei no keika ni kansuru shōiinkai (ed.), *Nihonkokukempō seitei no yurai* (Jijitsūshinsha, 1961). For further references, see Ward, op. cit., p. 401.

[4]*Yomiurihōchi*, 8 March 1946. See also *Asahi*, 8 March 1946.

[5]Of the drafts of Japanese authorship, only those prepared by the JCP and Takano Iwasaburō had proposed to abolish the Emperor system and establish a republican form of government in its place. That of the Constitution Study Association had adopted the principle of people's, as opposed to imperial, sovereignty. Those of the JSP

In addition to the war-renouncing clause, however, a few other specific provisions received critical comments. The greatly increased power of the National Diet was, for example, considered by some to pose the danger of dictatorship by the majority and abuse of power by parties. The excessive emphasis on the rights and the lack of emphasis on the duties of the individual *vis-à-vis* the society and government was condemned by a Tokyo University professor as typical of the nineteenth-century model of democracy rather than that of the twentieth century. Takano, who had written the draft of a republican constitution, advocated proportional representation in the Upper House elections, administrative tribunals, a national referendum on the new constitution within ten years of its promulgation, and so forth.

Just as important as these criticisms relating to the substance of the GHQ draft were those which concerned its form and language and the manner in which it had been prepared. The comments made by two readers in the *Asahi* of 24 April 1946, for example, concerned the first of these aspects. Both deplored the lack of precision and elegance in the colloquial style Japanese language used in the translation of the GHQ draft, and one of them pointed out the repetitiveness and diffuseness that occurred especially in the Preamble and Chapter III. Criticisms of the manner in which it had been prepared were typified by the brief remark attributed to a member of the JSP's Central Executive Committee, Kōno Mitsu. While praising the progressive nature of the GHQ draft, which sharply contrasted with any of the drafts written by the Japanese (including his own party), he wished that it had been prepared 'democratically' and not 'behind closed doors'.[6] Although its reference was not to the procedures which had been already followed but to those which might be followed in future, the opening sentence of the *Yomiuri*'s editorial call for the convocation of a special constitutional assembly reflected the same kind of sentiment. It stated that 'a democratic constitution must be established by democratic means'.[7] So did the delicately circumlocutional editorial of the *Nihon Keizai Shimbun* titled 'Sorrow over the Gracious Constitution'.[8]

If the press comments which appeared after the publication in March 1946 of the provisional translation of the GHQ draft, followed in April by the colloquial style version, reflected articulate public opinion at the time, the attitudes of the parties also corresponded roughly to its various shades. Although they tended to be much more self-consciously couched in generalities

---

and the Round Table on the Constitution had placed the locus of sovereignty somewhere between the Emperor and the people. The two Cabinet drafts and those produced by the Liberal and the Progressive parties had all retained the principle of imperial sovereignty, at least implicitly. The controversy over the problem of constitutional revision up to the publication of the GHQ draft had centred largely on such differences concerning this particular issue. See Kempōchōsakai, op. cit., pp. 166-224.

[6]*Tokyo Shimbun*, 8 March 1946.
[7]*Yomiuri*, 14 March 1946.
[8]*Nihon Keizai*, 19 March 1946.

inoffensive to the Supreme Commander for the Allied Powers, the opinions expressed in the Diet during the deliberations over the drafts clearly demonstrated the presence in the parties of a significant amount of dissatisfaction as well as goodwill. As a foretaste of the pattern of party attitudes after independence, it was the Socialists who probably found the GHQ draft most agreeable and the Liberals and the Progressives who found it most distasteful.

The difference in the Socialist and conservative response to the GHQ draft when it was debated in the Diet was important. From our point of view, however, it is even more important to note that conservative criticisms were left almost entirely unheeded under the pressure of the Occupation administration. The critics were never completely convinced that their views were basically wrong or that those embodied in the GHQ draft were right. Their opposition was silenced first under subtle psychological pressure and later by the more direct method of removal from public office (including Diet membership and party posts) and a total ban on their political activities.

Once the contents of the GHQ draft were made known, leaders of the conservative parties made a sudden about-face in their public pronouncements concerning the problem of constitutional revision. This indicated the degree of psychological pressure which they felt under the circumstances rather than a genuine change of heart. When Hatoyama commented on behalf of the Liberal Party that he was greatly encouraged by the 'maintenance of the Emperor system, safeguards for fundamental human rights, the renunciation of war and the establishment of a democratic system of government' which characterised both the GHQ draft and 'the principles underlying our own draft',[9] he was surely expressing only part of what he must have thought was the truth. The forced duplicity was even more obvious, if anything, in the statement of Saitō Takao, chairman of the executive council of the Progressive Party. He was quoted as saying:

In connection with the revision of the constitution, our Party has always insisted on the preservation of the national polity and [therefore] we support it [the GHQ draft] wholeheartedly. Especially welcome, as far as we are concerned, is the fact that the oneness of the Emperor and the people, which has been characteristic of the nation since it was founded, is given in it an explicit form, thus providing the basis for its further growth and development with the imperial family as its centre. Also welcome is the fact that the renunciation of war is stipulated in the supreme law of the land and highest moral symbol of our people . . .[10]

Tokyo Shimbun reminded its readers on 7 April that Saitō had declared during the previous extraordinary Diet session in September 1945 that he would firmly oppose democracy if it meant people's sovereignty.

If the restrictions imposed on such prewar politicians as Hatoyama and Saitō had remained indirect and general (as was actually the case with the

[9]*Mainichi*, 3 April 1946. See also the party's Secretary-General Kōno Ichirō's comment in *Yomiuri*, 2 April 1946.
[10]Ibid.

latter), their grievances concerning the constitutional revision of 1946 might not have been so emotion-charged and explosive as they proved to be several years later. Their personal involvement in the Purge ensured that their reaction, when eventually expressed freely, would be anything but friendly towards many of the Occupation-sponsored reforms, particularly the new constitution. In retrospect, so far as the climate of opinion over the constitutional issue is concerned, the Purge program accomplished a forced silence in the short run only to prepare an eventual explosion of suppressed frustrations and resentments in the long run.[11]

The deliberations of the Imperial Diet over the draft of the new constitution lasted from 25 June to 7 October 1946. Apart from those initiated by the GHQ itself,[12] only a few significant alterations in the original text were made by the Diet, namely the addition of the vaguely qualifying phrases in the war-renouncing Article 9 and of several new articles in Chapter III providing for the rights and duties of the individual. In evaluating this apparently meagre achievement of a Diet under the almost complete sway of the conservative parties, it is necessary to take into account the fact that, thanks to the Purge program, its membership had been cleared of those prewar and wartime elements which could have been potentially the most vocal dissidents. Of the prewar MHRs elected in the first postwar election of April 1946 Hatoyama was disqualified in early May and two of his most trusted confidants, Miki Bukichi and Kōno Ichirō, were forced to resign in June.

What is significant is not so much that their presence would have made any important difference in the actual handling of the issue by the Imperial Diet—a possibility which was rather slight under the circumstances—as that those politicians who were thus excluded from the official debate on the new constitution were absolved of responsibility for its making. On the strength of this, they could later join with little inconsistency or guilty conscience such

---

[11]This is not to suggest, however, that a man like Hatoyama would have been willing to accept all or most of the measures sponsored by the Occupation, if only he had been saved the ordeal of the Purge. In the famous *Asahi* article of 15 September 1945 he was quoted as saying that the United States should be willing to admit that she had committed a contravention of international law and a war crime worse than an attack on a hospital ship or the use of poisonous gases by indiscriminately using the atomic bombs against the innocent civilians of Hiroshima and Nagasaki. This article caused a two-day suspension of the paper. The incident suggests that his criticisms of the Occupation administration and its ideological assumptions were deep-rooted. There seems no doubt, however, that the Purge added fuel to such dissension. This assessment of Hatoyama's views is based on the information supplied by Mr Wakamiya Shōtarō, Hatoyama's trusted secretary in his lifetime and actual author of the above-mentioned *Asahi* article, in an interview on 23 February 1966.

[12]The GHQ-inspired amendments include the following: a change in the phrasing of the parts relating to the people's sovereignty in the Preamble and Article 1, the addition of the words 'education, property or income' in Article 44, the insertion of the guarantee of universal adult suffrage in the election of public officials in Article 15, and of the requirement for Cabinet ministers to be civilians in Article 66. For the origins and circumstances of these and other amendments, see Kempōchōsakai, *Kempōseitei no keika ni kansuru shōiinkai hōkokusho*, pp. 471-552.

depurged public officials as Kishi Nobusuke, Kaya Okinori, Ino Hiroya, and Aoki Kazuo in a campaign for revision of the 1946 constitution.

Considering the background to the making of the GHQ draft and the general political conditions prevailing in the early phase of the Occupation, one is struck by the extent of the criticisms that were voiced or implied in the course of the Diet deliberations. Although the debate centred on the provisions relating to the national polity, the Emperor system, and the renunciation of war, it extended also to the other sections, especially those concerning the rights and duties of the individual. If one takes into account the points raised in the press and elsewhere, including the proposal, which appeared in an economic journal, for a presidential system in the election of the top national executives (the direct popular election of the Prime Minister and Deputy Prime Minister)[13] one may conclude that all the essential arguments which the post-independence revisionists were subsequently to employ to support their positions had already been heard by the end of 1946.

These criticisms all arose from three basic, interrelated propositions: (i) that the constitution of Japan must be established by the Japanese people themselves; (ii) that not only universal principles, such as democracy and freedom, but also the 'unique' history, traditions, individuality, and national character of the Japanese nation must be incorporated; and (iii) that the constitution must be both practical and effective.

Once the Cabinet-sponsored draft, which was a Japanese language translation of the original GHQ draft, was approved by the Diet with a few significant amendments and many minor ones and was duly promulgated on 3 November 1946, the constitutional issue became dormant almost overnight and remained so until about the middle of 1950. The reasons for the virtually complete absence of revisionist agitation during the three and a half years are not very far to seek. Firstly, the fact of continuing Occupation itself discouraged criticism of the constitution which was well known to have originated from the GHQ. Secondly, the Purge had driven from the public debate most of the nation's prominent opinion leaders and their place had been filled by those who benefited, in one way or another, by the new constitution and the 'Occupation régime'. And finally, people were generally much more concerned with immediate economic problems than with the theoretical question of the functions of the constitution, while those few who were interested were generally still confident in the adequacy of its provisions, regarding it as the symbol of a new Japan. They were busy trying to understand the mean-

---

[13]A leading article of the *Tōyō Keizai Shimpō* of 19 January 1946 proposed to institute the direct, popular election of Prime Minister and Deputy Prime Minister for a term of four years or so, to allow the Prime Minister so elected to choose members of his Cabinet freely from both inside and outside the membership of the National Diet, and forbid concurrent membership of the Diet and Cabinet. This was the prototype of what later came to be referred to as the doctrine of the popular election of Prime Minister.

ings of its novel provisions and did not feel sufficiently conversant with them to offer better alternatives at this stage.

The Birth and Growth of Revisionism

When the outbreak of the Korean War in June 1950 led General MacArthur on 8 July to instruct the Japanese government to create a Police Reserve Force of 75,000 men and an increase of 8,000 in the size of the Maritime Safety Agency, the constitutionality of the nation's rearmament in relation to Article 9 inevitably became a controversial issue. From this time onwards Article 9 has become the central focus of the controversy both in the National Diet and in the press. It was probably unavoidable that as the original Police Reserve Force (which officially came into being on 10 August 1950) was renamed the Safety Force two years later and in June 1954 became the Self-Defence Forces (made up of three fully-fledged services), the logic of this series of *faits accomplis* began to be felt with increasing force. Under such circumstances the government and the ministerial party naturally began to consider in earnest an amendment of Article 9, if not a complete revision of the whole constitution.

Political and military developments in the Far East, particularly the establishment of the People's Republic of China in 1949 and the Korean War, provided the objective basis for a reconsideration of Article 9. The return to public life after the outbreak of the Korean War of the politicians and public servants who had been purged, provided emotional backing for the revisionist movement. As pointed out in Chapter 2, in the October 1952 House of Representatives election the depurged politicians managed to win a total of 139 seats accounting for 33 per cent of Liberal MHRs and 37 per cent of Progressive MHRs. As it later turned out, the most dynamic and powerful impetus both for a conservative merger and for constitutional revision was supplied by a group of these prewar and wartime leaders.

As suggested earlier, many of those who had been forced into silence over public issues by the Purge were critical of the Occupation-sponsored reforms, particularly the new constitution. This was not only because of their basic disagreements with the reforms, but equally because they felt that they had been prevented under duress from expressing their views when the reforms were put into effect. It was characteristic of the sudden upsurge of revisionism in the first few years after independence that its emotional drive was generated directly by the personal experience and resentments of these people. Such was the basic tone of the views expressed, for example, by Hatoyama who subsequently said in his autobiography:

> I had always thought, during and after the war, that the Americans were capable of doing most outrageous things at the same time as they were professing belief in justice and freedom. For this reason I had a certain amount of contempt for them.

I was therefore not particularly surprised when they purged me. I just thought that they acted according to type. . . .[14]

A very similar sentiment had been earlier expressed by Ishibashi Tanzan when he had written:

However it may have been, it is clear that not all actions of the high-ranking officials of the Occupation Forces were fair and just. Examples of unfair treatment can be found in the manner in which the Purge program was actually executed. One such example was my own case. For reasons not known to myself, the Government Section of the GHQ began to manoeuvre for purging me in early 1947 . . . When the [screening] committee established by the Japanese government finally decided on 2 May 1947 against designating me for purposes of the Purge, the Chief of the Government Section, Whitney, sent a memorandum dated 7 May to the Japanese government in which he demanded that I be removed from office on the grounds that I had been editor and president of the Tōyō Keizai Shimpōsha, irrespective of the decision previously made by the Japanese committee. The government succumbed to this pressure and designated me at last on 17th of the same month . . . I do not think that the intentions of the United States to democratise Japan were wrong. I believe, however, that the United States herself was not entirely democratic. Nevertheless, those Americans who came over to Japan with the GHQ looked upon the Japanese as completely undemocratic and seem to have believed that they themselves were, in contrast, completely democratic . . . The dictatorial men of power of the Occupation . . . would not admit of a single criticism of their own actions, and yet they were as brazenly self-righteous as to insist that they had bestowed upon the Japanese the freedom of speech . . .[15]

While the fact of Japan's rearmament presented a practical and concrete case for an amendment of Article 9, the emotionalism introduced by the mass 'come-back' of the prewar men gave rise to controversies over the origin and authorship of the new constitution and put it in its entirety to a critical and questioning review.

In terms of inter-party relationships, the bifurcation between the prewar and postwar approaches to the 'Occupation régime' in general and the constitution of Japan in particular took the form of disagreements and conflicts between a majority in the Liberal Party on the one hand and, on the other, a minority in the same party and a majority in both the Progressive Party and the Ryokufūkai. In the one group the postwar elements held control and in the other the prewar elements ruled so far as the constitutional issue was concerned.

Yoshida's negative view of an early revision of the constitution remained consistent throughout the post-independence years up to the merger of 1955 and, indeed, long after that. In the middle of 1952, when the Progressive Party had already officially committed itself to 'a total reconsideration of the laws and institutions established under the Occupation, including the Con-

[14]See Hatoyama Ichirō, *Hatoyama Ichirō kaikoroku* (Bungeishunjūshinsha, 1957), pp. 49-50.
[15]Ishibashi Tanzan, 'Hambeikanjō hassei no riyū', *Chūōkōron*, 781 (November 1953), pp. 42-3.

stitution', constitutional revision could not be loudly talked about in the Liberal Party because of his well-known opposition. The anti-revisionist posture of the Liberal Party became more pronounced during the two periods when the minority and revisionist Hatoyama faction and Kishi's followers stayed out of the party to run a separate party of their own. The first of these periods lasted from the middle of March to the end of November 1953, when a majority of the 'Democratic League' members led by Hatoyama formed the separatist Liberal Party. The second lasted from late November 1954 to the conservative merger of November 1955. During this period the Hatoyama and the Kishi factions formed the Democratic Party together with those drawn from the Progressive Party and the small Japan Liberal Party. Although the opposition of the Liberal Party as a whole to the suggestions of constitutional revision was very much toned down and even reversed during the periods when these revisionist groups chose to stay with it, Yoshida himself remained remarkably consistent in this respect and continued to exert an enormous restraining influence on the party's executives. On the eve of the 1955 merger, for example, he made it publicly clear that he was still firmly opposed to an early revision of the constitution, and the same position was maintained in his four-volume autobiography and in his letter to the Cabinet Commission on the Constitution.

Despite Yoshida's negative attitude, steps inspired by and supporting the revisionist position were taken by the Liberal Party, particularly during the twelve months between November 1953 and November 1954 when the revisionist factions stayed with it. In accordance with the agreement made between Yoshida and Hatoyama on the latter's return to the Liberal Party, in December 1953 a Committee on the Constitution was established in the party and Kishi was appointed its chairman. Significantly, Yoshida absented himself from the committee's inaugural ceremony at which Hatoyama and Kishi emphasised the need for the earliest possible revision, referring to the abnormal circumstances under which the existing constitution had been drafted. By the middle of September 1954, this committee concluded (as many had anticipated), that revision had to be total, with special emphasis placed on Article 9, the definition of the Emperor's constitutional status, the balance between the rights and duties of the individual, and the relationship between the constitution and international treaties. Finally, the joint session of its five sub-committees approved a tentative draft of the revision on 18 October, which incorporated the above-mentioned points and was published as an 'Outline of a Draft of the Revised Constitution of Japan' on 5 November.

The movement for constitutional revision during this period was inseparably related to the movement for the unification of the conservative parties. Behind both were the same groups of prewar politicians and former high-ranking public servants. It is quite natural that they should have been so interrelated, since the primary objective of both movements was to change the *status quo* identified with the Occupation régime and Yoshida's rule. Furthermore, one was used as a means of achieving the other and vice versa. In the Liberal Party Kishi, who was the driving force for the 'New Party Movement' (the unification of the conservative parties), was known even before he was elected to the House of Representatives in April 1953 to be deeply interested in a drastic change in the political arrangements established under the Occupation. A Japan Reconstruction League had been formed under his leadership as soon as he was freed from the restrictions of the Purge towards the end of 1952 and one of its five principal objectives had been constitutional revision. When his close friends met at his invitation in November 1953, they were reported to be interested in uniting the three existing conservative parties specifically with a view to bringing about constitutional revision. Five months later he was one of the anonymous sponsors of a 'Volunteers' Meeting for the Creation of A New Conservative Party' at which forty-four MHRs affiliated with the Liberal Party adopted a five-point platform for the would-be new party which included revision of the 'Occupation-made Constitution' as well as the perfection of the nation's defence arrangements.[16] No other member of the Liberal Party personified as dramatically as Kishi the correlation between the interest in the conservative merger and in constitutional revision, but a majority of those who were positively identified with either movement shared that characteristic to a greater or lesser extent.

When the anti-Yoshida factions led by Hatoyama and Kishi walked out of the party for a second time in November 1954 to join the Democratic Party, the work of the Liberal Party Committee on the Constitution was abruptly interrupted. In the ten-point policy program prepared for the general election of February 1955 the top executives of the party (who had been hand-picked by Yoshida) declared that no early attempt at constitutional revision would be made by them. In the course of the election campaign Ogata, who had succeeded Yoshida as the new Liberal Party president, assured an audience at Morioka that he was definitely opposed to revision. He also charged the Prime Minister and President of the Democratic Party, Hatoyama, with contemplating not only an amendment to Article 9 but possibly also the reinstitution of conscription. It is admittedly hard to assess the attitude of the Liberal Party during this period solely by its public pronouncements, especially those made in the course of an election campaign. It is possible that the party's real position was much closer to that of the Democrats than it appears from the press reports. Its negative tendencies were, however, sufficiently evident to contrast the official position of the

[16]The other two anonymous sponsors were the party's vice-president, Ogata Taketora, and Ishibashi Tanzan. The meeting was arranged by their respective deputies, Takechi Yūki for Kishi, Tsugumo Kunitoshi for Ogata, and Ishida Hirohide for Ishibashi. *Asahi*, 15 April 1954.

Liberal Party with the attitude of the Progressives (subsequently Democratic Party).

The Progressive Party came into being in February 1952 through the merger of the National Democratic Party and several minor groups, including the *Shinsei kurabu* (New Government Club) of those associated with the prewar Minseitō led by Matsumura Kenzō. The party committed itself from the beginning to the earliest possible revision of the constitution. As already indicated, Point 5 of its platform called for a total reconsideration of the laws and institutions established under the Occupation, explicitly including constitutional revision. Although the creation of the Progressive Party Committee on the Constitution did not take place until the spring of 1954 (nearly five months after the establishment of its Liberal Party counterpart), concrete steps toward constitutional revision had actually been taken by the party in July 1953 when it had established a Special Committee on Defence. During the election campaign in the spring of 1953 the Progressive Party leaders, led by Ashida Hitoshi and Kiyose Ichirō, propounded the view that rearmament was compatible with Article 9. The introduction of this view exerted a considerable moderating influence and was responsible, at least indirectly, for the delay in the creation of the Party Constitution Committee. Nevertheless, it seems evident that, in sharp contrast to the situation in the Liberal Party, the revisionists were a majority in the Progressive Party and divisions of opinion over this particular issue were negligible at the time. In any event, the Sixth Progressive Party Conference of February 1954 decided to establish a committee on the constitution in the party and work towards the creation of a similar body at the government level in order to have the constitution re-examined in its entirety. In the meantime, the two largest factions identified in the party at the time expressed clear-cut revisionist views on several occasions. In November 1953, for example, about thirty members of the 'Radicals' faction led by Kitamura Tokutarō, Kawasaki Hideji, and Nakasone Yasuhiro resolved to press the party leadership to take a 'more positive' attitude towards the issue and in February 1954 decided to call on the other parties to join a Diet Members League for Constitutional Revision to be established. Similarly, the 'Neutrals' faction led by Furui Yoshimi, Igarashi Kichizō, and Machimura Kingo included a total revision of the constitution in the program of their intra-party group Dōyūkai formed in February 1954.

The Democratic Party resulted in November 1954 from the merger of the Progressive Party and the anti-Yoshida revisionist groups in the Liberal Party. It embodied the most pronounced of the revisionist tendencies among the parties and in the National Diet at the time. Point 2 of its Policy Program adopted at the inaugural meeting promised to amend the constitution, 'considering the circumstances of its establishment and experience of its practice', although without sacrificing 'the principles of pacifism and democracy'. It also proposed to set up in the Diet a deliberative committee on the constitution. In the 'Outline of the Basic Policies' subsequently ratified by the party's executive council and accepted by the Hatoyama Cabinet on 14 December 1954, the pledge to undertake constitutional revision was repeated, together with a parallel call to strengthen the nation's defence system.

Once, however, he had been elected Prime Minister as well as President of the Democratic Party, Hatoyama's references to the constitutional issue became at times so cautious and circumspect that he was charged with a change of heart by his Socialist and Liberal opponents in the Diet. In reply to these charges he insisted that his basic attitude had not changed at all but that the interpretation of Article 9 had changed in the minds of many people, including himself, to such an extent that it was now considered to be entirely in accord with the spirit of that article to rearm Japan without undertaking its formal amendment. It would nevertheless seem to be undeniable that Hatoyama had changed his mind about the issue of constitutional revision as such, probably largely as a result of the pressure applied by the Cabinet Legislative Bureau which refused to accept a radical departure from the negative position it had consistently taken under Yoshida's premiership.

In the meantime, an extreme revisionist view, according to which the constitution of 1947 was essentially null and void because of the peculiar circumstances under which it had been enacted, began to be voiced in the party with Hatoyama's restrained but obvious encouragement. In any event, his Cabinet proceeded in the summer of 1955 to introduce in the Diet a bill establishing a Cabinet Commission on the Constitution. After an initial failure in the Special Diet session of March-July 1955, this bill was finally passed in June 1956 under the Third Hatoyama Cabinet.

The merger of the two conservative parties in November 1955 represented the culmination of the revisionist upsurge which had started, as we have seen, in the last phase of the Occupation with the mass reinstatement of prewar and wartime leaders. As the most dynamic and influential proponent of the merger scheme, Miki Bukichi, declared in a public statement in the spring of 1955, the merger was conceived primarily as a means by which to achieve constitutional revision as well as amendment of the Election Law and expansion of defence facilities. The differences of attitude towards the merger did not strictly correlate with the divisions of opinion on the constitutional issue in either party. It is nevertheless significant that the groups most consistently revisionist—the Kishi, Ishibashi, and former 'Neutral' factions in the Democratic Party—provided the motive power for the merger movement as well. On the other hand, the merger movement was persistently opposed by the Liberal Party's Yoshida faction, which was also known to be least interested in constitutional revision.[17]

[17]About the attitudes of the different groups towards the merger, see ibid., 13 June 1955. It should be noted, however, that the reluctance of the Yoshida faction to see

It should also be noted that the strongest pressure for constitutional revision came during this period from the party out of power and within the party in power from the dissident groups. This fact reveals the partisan and factional causes and implications of the revisionist movement, which have continued to characterise it in the more recent years.

Extra-party Groups and Public Opinion

If the prewar-postwar dichotomy and the less clearcut yet relevant factional divisions typified the pattern of responses to the constitutional issue in the conservative parties, the conditions of opinion outside them were characterised equally by divisions and conflicts. On the one hand, the left-wing parties, especially the Socialists, were consistently and fiercely opposed to the suggested change, particularly (though by no means exclusively) of Article 9. On the other hand, representative business and industrial interests, especially those associated with Keidanren, were deeply interested in a *de facto*, if not *de jure*, revision of that particular article. They helped the creation of a united conservative party in the hope that it would prove powerful enough to push the matter through the Diet. As if sandwiched between these two extreme and articulate positions, public opinion remained indecisive and even indifferent.

The opposition of the JCP to constitutional revision may have been tactical rather than fundamental in view of its public commitment to 'abolish the Emperor system and establish a democratic republic'.[18] That of the Socialists was, however, much more genuine and consistent, though there were obvious differences in emphasis between the right and the left wings even after their unification in October 1955.[19] The latter's more inflexible position on the

---

the merger take place under the initiative of the Democratic Party was caused more by partisan considerations than by real differences of opinion on specific policy issues. The attitude of the former 'Radical' faction of the Progressive Party, now absorbed by the Democratic Party, was even more complex. It was basically revisionist and some of its members very aggressively so. Its opposition to the merger scheme was motivated partly (and paradoxically) by the fear that unification with the anti-revisionist groups in the Liberal Party would hamper, rather than facilitate, the attainment of the revisionist goal.

[18]See the 'New Platform' of 1952, in *Akahata*, 15 July 1952. According to this proposal, the Emperor would be replaced by a President elected for a term of four years, the National Diet would become uni-cameral, the minimum ages of electors and candidates in a Diet election would both be lowered to 18, the whole nation would constitute a single constituency, and the principle of proportional representation would be introduced. The JCP was willing, however, to play a leading role in the anti-revisionist movement, especially after the People's Confederation for the Defence of the Constitution was established in January 1954 under the leadership of a Right Socialist, Katayama Tetsu. See Nikkan rōdō tsūshinsha (ed.), *Sengo nihon kyōsanshugiundō shi* (1955), pp. 570–89.

[19]*Asahi*, 3 May 1952; 2 May 1953; *Mainichi*, 15 October 1954. The differences between the Right and the Left Socialists concerned mainly the evaluation of Article 9 and the attitude towards Japan's rearmament and neutralist foreign policy. For a detailed discussion, see J. A. A. Stockwin, *The Japanese Socialist Party and Neutralism: a Study of a Political Party and Its Foreign Policy* (Melbourne: Melbourne University Press, 1968).

issue was officially confirmed in the policy program of the unified Socialist Party and subsequently led to concrete actions both within and outside the Diet under the direction of the party's Special Committee on the Defence of the Constitution.

The aims and efforts of big businesses were the exact opposite of this. Their degree of interest in the earliest possible resumption of 'defence production' and their commitment to Japan's rearmament were embodied in the work of the Keidanren's Economic Co-operation Forum. Established originally in February 1951 as a US-Japan Economic Co-operation Forum and reorganised in August of the following year into a body with three working committees on general policy, defence production, and Asian reconstruction and development, this group led activities of the nation's businessmen broadly aimed at rearmament and constitutional revision. Particularly significant was the role played by the Defence Production Committee as a semi-official link between the government and business circles in the planning and execution of the series of defence build-up programs. In February 1953 it produced a 'Keidanren Plan' of rearmament, according to which Japan was to be equipped within the next six years with a land force of 15 divisions and 300,000 men, a maritime force of 290,000 tons and 70,000 men, and an air force of 3,750 aircraft and 130,000 men. In August 1954 it distributed copies of a pamphlet titled *The Need for the Maintenance of Self-Defence Forces and the Role of Defence Production*, which emphasised more vigorously than ever the group's revisionist views. It was under the pressure and with the advice of this group that organised research in guided missiles was initiated in 1954, the production of jet fighters (F-86-F and T-33-A) was officially started in 1955, and a joint Defence Production Liaison Council established in 1956 to co-ordinate the opinions and efforts of the government, the ministerial party, and industry. Against this background it is not surprising that those leaders of Keidanren who were personally involved in the activities of the forum should have also been keenly interested in encouraging the revisionist movement in the parties and, with a view to promoting it, in helping their merger and consolidation.

In sharp contrast to the differing positions of the Socialists and big business, public opinion remained ignorant, indifferent and, at the best, indecisive. The result of an opinion poll involving a sample of 3,000, which was conducted by the *Asahi* in February 1952, for the first time laid bare the harsh realities of what had come to be accepted as the basic and ultimate criterion of the soundness of public policy under the new 'democratic system'. To the embarrassment of both revisionists and anti-revisionists, 67 per cent of the respondents admitted that they had never read the text of the constitution, 19 per cent had read it in part, and only 14 per cent had read the whole of it. In the subsequent polls undertaken by the research section (*Shingishitsu* and, subsequently, *Chōsashitsu*) of the Cabinet Secretariat the percentages of 'don't know' responses in this extreme sense fluctuated between about 20 per cent and 45 per cent. The *Asahi* survey of November 1957, however, again reported a shocking 61 per cent.

The results of these and other opinion polls when classified according to the affirmative versus negative division, instead of the 'know' versus 'don't know' division, have demonstrated that a substantial proportion of the 'don't know' respondents were ready to take sides in the controversy. However, the general tenor of public opinion as revealed by these polls could hardly be considered as a positive factor from the point of view of either of the opposing positions.

Furthermore, so far as the more articulate and organised section of public opinion was concerned, the actual balance between the two positions was evidently more favourable to the anti-revisionists than to the revisionists. While the People's Confederation for the Defence of the Constitution embraced as many as 135 organisations and groups with an aggregate membership of at least several million, the revisionist position was supported by only one small group led by a few politicians, journalists, university professors, and writers. The attitude of the press was somewhat more encouraging to the revisionists on the eve of the conservative merger, but even here opinion was sharply divided and revisionism never became a majority view among the largest of the nation's daily newspapers except, probably, briefly in 1954.[20]

On the eve of the formation of the LDP there were thus factional and ideological divisions of opinion within the conservative parties themselves and a parallel lack of consensus between the articulate extra-party groups and among the media of mass communication. Public opinion in general was singularly ignorant and indifferent. It was under such political and psychological conditions that the inaugural pledge to bring about constitutional revision was made by the leadership of the newly formed LDP. By so doing, the party imposed upon itself an apparently difficult and politically dangerous task, as its leaders were soon to realise.

THE LIBERAL-DEMOCRATIC PARTY RESPONSE

Negative Factors

Article 96 of the Constitution of Japan specifies the requirements for amendments as follows:

Amendments to this Constitution shall be initiated by the Diet, through a con-

[20]The *Asahi* in particular was consistently anti-revisionist, while the *Mainichi* was fairly clearly revisionist. Compare, for example, the editorials of the *Asahi* on 30 April and 3 May 1952, 3 May 1953, 3 May 1954, and 4 January 1955, with those of the *Mainichi* on 3 May 1954, 9 January and 3 May 1955, etc. In 1954 twenty-five of the forty dailies which carried editorials specifically relating to the issue expressed more or less revisionist views, only eight anti-revisionist views, while seven were noncommittal. After the February 1955 election, however, a majority became much more cautious and began to emphasise the need to maintain the basic principles of the existing constitution (democracy and pacifism).

curring vote of two-thirds or more of all the members of each House and shall thereupon be submitted to the people for ratification, which shall require the affirmative vote of a majority of all votes cast thereon, at a special referendum or at such election as the Diet shall specify . . . .

Since the LDP came into being in November 1955 the party has never succeeded in satisfying the first of these requirements, for the percentages of its members returned in successive Diet elections have never quite reached two-thirds. In the 27th Diet session following the February 1955 House of Representatives election the LDP controlled 64 per cent of the members in that House and 64·4 per cent of those in the Upper House. The percentages of the party's members in the former following each subsequent election have been as follows:

May 1958—63·8%; November 1960—64·2%; November 1963—62·9%; January 1967—58·6%.

In the House of Councillors the corresponding percentages following each subsequent election have been as follows:

July 1956—61·2%; June 1959—58·4%; July 1962—57·2%; July 1965—58·4%.[21]

These figures indicate that the first of the hurdles to be cleared if constitutional revision was to be achieved has remained unsurmountable. The second hurdle might have been somewhat easier to clear until the late 1960s, if one may assume that the split of votes in a national referendum on constitutional revision would generally follow party lines as in an ordinary Diet election. In the four House of Representatives elections held between February 1955 and November 1963 the LDP invariably gained a majority of votes cast, as shown by the following percentage figures:

February 1955—63·1% (Liberal and Democratic votes combined); May 1958—57·8%; November 1960—57·5%; and November 1963—54·6%.[22]

Even here, however, the LDP's edge over the anti-revisionist parties steadily decreased and in the January 1967 election it failed for the first time to gain a majority of votes.[23] The prospects for a revisionist victory in a special referendum have thus become doubtful. According to the consolidated results of various public opinion polls on the issue, revisionists enjoyed greater grass-roots support than anti-revisionists before the merger of 1955, but they have since lost their superiority, the shift of their fortunes becoming increasingly clear after the middle of 1957 (see Table 18). Moreover, the change in the climate of public opinion has been accurately reflected in the attitude of the press which, as we have already seen, became extremely cautious in 1955 after

[21]The percentage figures are derived from Tsuji Kiyoaki (ed.), *Shiryō: Sengo nijūnen shi: 1 Seiji* (Nihonhyōronsha, 1966), pp. 221-4, and *Asahi*, 31 January 1967.
[22]See Shūgiin Jimukyoku, *Dai-30-kai shūgiingiin sōsenkyo ichiran (Shōwa 38-nen 11-gatsu 21-nichi shikkō)* (June 1964), p. 552.
[23]The percentage of the LDP votes in the January 1967 elections was 48·8 per cent. See *Asahi*, 31 January 1967.

P

TABLE 18

Public opinion on constitutional revision, 1952–63

Organisations responsible for poll	Dates	No. of respondents	Questions asked	Responses Revision-ist %	Anti-revision-ist %	Don't know, undecided %
Yomiuri Shimbun	February 1952	3,298	Revision after conclusion of the Peace Treaty?	47	18	35
Yomiuri Shimbun	April 1952	3,423	Revision, yes or no?	42	17	41
Cabinet Secretariat	October 1954	2,597	Revision, desirable or undesirable?	25	29	46
Yomiuri Shimbun	February 1955	1,365	Revision or no revision?	41	33	26
Mainichi Shimbun	February 1955	2,584	Revision, yes or no?	45	29	26
Cabinet Secretariat	June 1955	2,541	Revision, desirable or undesirable?	26	31	43
Cabinet Secretariat	August 1955	2,574	Revision, yes or no?	26	27	47
Asahi Shimbun	December 1955	2,930	Revision, necessary?	30	25	45
Cabinet Secretariat	February 1956	2,517	Would you vote for or against revision?	33	28	39
Shimbun yoron-chōsa renmei	March 1956	2,517	Revision, total, partial or neither?	43	19	38
Cabinet Secretariat	July 1956	2,516	Revision, yes or no?	20	43	37
Yomiuri Shimbun	August 1957	2,631	Revision, yes or no?	44	32	24
Asahi Shimbun	November 1957	2,433	Revision, necessary or unnecessary?	27	31	42
Cabinet Secretariat	May 1958	2,453	Revision, or no revision for the time being?	20	32	48
Cabinet Secretariat	August 1959	(20,000)*	What would you do about the constitution?	8	12	78
Cabinet Secretariat	August 1960	16,683	What would you do about the constitution?	8	8	83
Cabinet Secretariat	August 1961	16,437	What is your opinion of constitutional revision?	20	14	66
Cabinet Secretariat	August 1962	15,775	What is your opinion of constitutional revision?	19	19	62
Asahi Shimbun	August 1962	3,000	Revision, necessary or unnecessary?	27	38	35
Shimbun yoron-chōsa renmei	December 1962	2,500	Revision, yes or no?	27	31	42
Cabinet Secretariat	October 1963	(20,000)*	Revision relating to the Emperor's powers?	19	55	26
			Revision for rearmament?	30	30	40

*The size of the sample and not the number of actual respondents.

Sources: Naikakusōridaijin kambō shingishitsu, Kempō ni kansuru yoronchōsa: ōhōkoku, Furoku (June 1961); Naikakukambō naikaku chōsashitsu, Sengo nihon ni okeru kempōishiki to seron no dōkō (Shakaijūchō chōsa shiryō) 35 (September 1965); and Kobayashi Naoki, Nihonkokukempō no mondaijōkyō (Iwanamishoten, 1964), Appendix III, pp. 406-7.

a short-lived revisionist spree in 1954. In 1956 the ratios of revisionist, anti-revisionist, and uncommitted daily newspapers became something like 5-6-23 and it has since remained basically unchanged.

To make the situation even worse from the revisionist point of view, big business circles, best represented by Keidanren, ceased to show so much positive interest as previously in an early revision of the constitution. There is little doubt that, as pointed out in Chapter 6, business groups have been in a position to influence the policy-making process of the LDP more effectively than other extra-party groups. The general direction of their influence regarding this issue in recent years, however, hardly seems to have been towards an early achievement of the LDP's inaugural pledge. An important cause of this apparent change in the attitudes of many businessmen may be found in the increasingly wide acceptance of *de facto* rearmament (or at least acquiescence in this), which amounts to *de facto* revision of Article 9 on the part of public opinion and the press and, ultimately, by the Supreme Court.[24] In view of these developments business circles probably continued to regard revision as a desirable goal, if it could be achieved without much sacrifice. They ceased, however, to consider it essential. Businessmen had been concerned from the beginning not so much with the ideological arguments for the overthrow of the 'Occupation régime' as with the prospects for substantial defence contracts. So long as the latter were forthcoming without a formal amendment of the constitution, there was no compelling reason why they should identify themselves with the unpopular cause of revisionism.

Attitude of Top Party Leadership

Despite the evidently adverse conditions described above the LDP's official enthusiasm and optimism for an early constitutional revision were maintained for about half a year after the merger of November 1955. In December of that year Ogata, then a member of the initial 4-man Presidential Proxy Committee, defined it as a principal objective of the unified party, while the Prime Minister, Hatoyama, who was also a member of the Presidential Proxy Committee, confidently promised to attain the goal without delay. Half a year later, in June 1956, the secretary-general, Kishi, appealed to a meeting of the heads of the Party Prefectual Federations to ensure that the party won a two-thirds majority in the forthcoming House of Councillors election in order to make constitutional revision possible. In the meantime, the Commission on the Constitution Bill was introduced into the Diet in February and was passed against bitter Socialist Party opposition in June 1956.

[24]In its decision of 16 December 1959 in the controversial Sunagawa Case the Supreme Court avoided passing a clear-cut and articulate verdict on the constitutionality of Japan's rearmament in relation to Article 9. It held, however, that the controversial article did not require an entirely defenceless Japan but recognised her right to self-defence. The court thus legitimised by inference the existence and possible extension of the Self-Defence Forces.

Once the Cabinet Commission on the Constitution was established, however, the official attitude of the party's top leadership group became much more moderate and, at times, even negative concerning the issue. This change has been reflected, for example, in the treatment of the subject in the occasional public pronouncements made in the name of the party in connection with Diet elections and annual party conferences. Although references have been made to the issue in a number of such pronouncements, a comparison of the terms and expressions used in them reveals that, so far as the essential arguments are concerned, each was more or less a reiteration of the points previously made. Furthermore, the general tone of the arguments presented has become progressively more moderate and ambiguous.

In the meantime, the official organ of the PARC, *Seisaku Geppō*, has carried a fair number of solidly revisionist theses as if to make up for the inaction of the party's executives represented by the leaders' meeting. A careful examination of these theses shows, however, that a majority of them have been written by one theoretician on the staff of the PARC and a former purgee, Miyamoto Yoshio. Of the nineteen signed theses on this subject carried in the first (January 1956) to the 127th (August 1966) issues of the monthly organ, he contributed ten, including the unconcluded series titled 'Kempōkaisei hantai ron hihan' (Critique of the Opposition to Constitutional Revision) which was started in July 1965. Admittedly very persuasive though many of his revisionist arguments are, they impress the reader more with their increasing tendencies towards moderation and eclecticism than with the consistency of the revisionist emphasis. This is true especially of the most recent of his contributions.

Considering the rigid constitutional requirements, which the party's failure to control more than two-thirds of seats in both Houses of the Diet has made it impossible to satisfy, and the generally adverse situation of opinion outside the party, the deliberate evasion of the issue by the party's top leaders may have been tactically sound and even unavoidable. A greater emphasis on revisionism would probably have estranged a significant number of votes from the party and intensified the opposition of the other parties to the other parts of its policy program. This negative attitude of the party leaders, however, has not put an end to revisionism within the party but merely driven it into temporary abeyance. Its proponents have been associated first with the LDP Committee on the Constitution, then with the Cabinet Commission on the Constitution, and more recently with the informal intra-party group, Soshinkai.

The LDP Committee on the Constitution

As soon as the LDP was formed in November 1955, it officially set up a Special Investigation Committee on the Constitution in the PARC to continue the revisionist movement which had been an important reason for the merger. By the end of the same year this committee had decided to start in January 1956 a serious investigation of the problems involved and to prepare by May 1956 a provisional draft of the revision. As none of the permanent divisions or existing investigation committees of the PARC were competent to deal with this particular kind of issue, the establishment of the Committee on the Constitution was a step necessary in order to make any course of action, whether revisionist or anti-revisionist, official party policy. As indicated in Chapter 4, the party's official attitude towards the issue could be determined only when a decision recommended by this newly established PARC sub-division was approved first by the PARC deliberation commission and then by the executive council. The above-mentioned decisions of the committee were clearly predicated on the assumption that it was to play the role of policy-initiator and promoter in the organisational framework of party decision-making.

In reality, however, the LDP Committee on the Constitution has never produced a draft of the revision. Moreover, in July 1956 its chairman, Yamazaki Iwao, explicitly accepted the proposal of the top party leaders conveyed to him jointly by the secretary-general, Kishi, and the chairman of the executive council, Ishii Mitsujirō, to the effect that all concrete preparations for revision, including the drafting of a revised constitution, should be left entirely to the Cabinet Commission and that the work of the party committee should be confined to the education of public opinion and dissemination of information. The record of its subsequent behaviour proves that it has faithfully observed this agreement. Although it has not been formally dissolved, it ceased to function after the middle of 1956 until early 1961 and there is no evidence that it ever met officially during that period. It began to meet with some frequency in early 1961, but until the latter half of that year the meetings were devoted largely either to business of a procedural nature or to lectures given by invited guest speakers on subjects more academic than practical, such as the constitutions of foreign countries.

Originally, the main support for the committee no doubt came from groups of prewar politicians and bureaucrats such as Hatoyama and Kishi, who had brought to the early revisionist movement both leadership and emotional drive. It seems, however, that the initial enthusiasm and sense of dedication which had characterised their call to rectify the 'Occupation régime', of which the constitution was a basic part, dissipated rather quickly. Soon after the formation of the LDP the three most ardent revisionist leaders of the pre-merger period—Hatoyama, Ishibashi, and Kishi—all began to behave just as any prudent leaders of dominant factions would have behaved with a view to minimising causes of internal friction and estrangement of public opinion and to stabilising the *status quo*. The steady decrease of prewar elements in the overall conservative force in the Diet (Tables 19 and 20) also tended to reduce the importance of their role in the policy-making process.

Under these circumstances the committee was gradually divested of the emotional influence of the prewar men. At the same time, however, the domination of it by former high-ranking public servants became increasingly

TABLE 19

Prewar and wartime Diet members among conservative party members elected to the postwar House of Representatives, 1946–65

	Total no. of members	Prewar and wartime members	%
April 1946			
Nihon jiyūtō	152	40	26·3
Nihon shimpotō	112	21	18·7
Kyōdō minshutō	45	4	8·8
Kokumintō	33	—	—
Total	342	65	19·0
April 1947			
Nihon jiyūtō	133	25	18·7
Minshutō	135	18	13·3
Kokumin kyōdōtō	32	1	3·1
Total	300	44	14·6
January 1949			
Minshu jiyūtō	270	26	9·6
Minshutō	70	9	12·8
Kokumin kyōdōtō	14	1	7·1
Total	354	36	10·1
October 1952			
Jiyūtō	243	67	27·5
Kaishintō	89	29	32·5
Total	332	96	28·9
April 1953			
Jiyūtō	203	44	21·6
Jiyūtō (separatist)	35	15	42·8
Kaishintō	77	19	24·6
Total	315	78	24·7
February 1955			
Jiyūtō	116	19	16·3
Nihon minshutō	186	67	37·0
Total	302	86	28·4
May 1958			
Jiyūminshutō	302	59	19·5
November 1960			
Jiyūminshutō	296	52	17·5
November 1965			
Jiyūminshutō	294	38	12·9

Sources: GSS: Shūgiingiin meikan; GSS: Seitō kaiha hen; Kokkai binran, 21st ed. (October 1962) and 26th ed. (March 1964).

TABLE 20

*Prewar and wartime Diet members among conservative party
members elected to the House of Councillors, 1947–65*

	Total no. of members	Prewar and wartime members	%
April 1947			
Nihon jiyūtō	51	12	23·5
Minshutō	47	5	10·6
Ryokufūkai	92	13	14·1
Total	190	30	15·7
June 1950			
Jiyūtō	83	10	12·0
Kokumin minshutō	30	3	10·0
Ryokufūkai	58	7	12·0
Total	171	20	11·6
April 1953			
Jiyūtō	98	10	10·2
Kaishintō	18	5	27·7
Ryokufūkai	48	7	14·5
Total	164	22	13·4
July 1956			
Jiyūminshutō	130	20	15·3
Ryokufūkai	29	6	20·6
Total	159	26	16·3
June 1959			
Jiyūminshutō	138	19	13·7
Ryokufūkai	11	1	9·0
Total	149	20	13·4
July 1962			
Jiyūminshutō	142	14	9·8
July 1965			
Jiyūminshutō	139	11	7·9

Sources: GSS: Kizokuin sangiin giin meikan; GSS: Seitō kaiha hen; Kokkai binran,
21st ed. (October 1962) and 31st ed. (November 1965).

evident, until by the end of 1965 nearly half its members were drawn from that particular category of LDP member (see Table 21). The disproportionately high percentage of former public officials and the disproportionately low percentage of former local politicians has indicated significant differences in the degree of interest on the part of these two categories of LDP-affiliated Diet members in a primarily ideological issue such as the one under review.

In terms of the factional distribution of its members, on the other hand, no single faction had a conspicuously higher percentage of members affiliated with the committee than the others (see Table 22). Like most other formal party organs the faction led by the current President (Ikeda) contributed

TABLE 21

*Occupational backgrounds of members of the LDP Investigation Committee
on the Constitution, November 1965*

	MHRs	MHCs	Total
Local politicians	4	1	5
	10·5%	4·1%	8·0%
Public servants	17	13	30
	44·7%	54·1%	48·3%
Businessmen	2	2	4
	5·2%	8·5%	6·4%
Lawyers	5	–	5
	13·1%	–	8·0%
Journalists	2	–	2
	5·2%	–	3·2%
Miscellaneous	8	8	16
	21·0%	33·3%	25·8%
Total	38	24	62
	100·0%	100·0%	100·0%

Sources: Jiyūminshutō, *Seimuchōsakai meibo: Shōwa 40-nen 11-gatsu 10-ka genzai,*
pp. 27-8; *GSS: Shūgiingiin meikan; GSS: Kizokuin sangiin giin meikan; Kokkai
binran,* 31st ed. (November 1965), pp. 99-150.

a somewhat larger share than others, although the difference was not very
significant. So far as its membership composition is concerned, it is impossible
to identify the committee with any particular faction or factions. It was, in
fact, this very fact of impartiality or indifference in terms of intra-party
factionalism that has eventually led to a shift of the focus of revisionist
activity from the official Committee on the Constitution to the Soshinkai.

TABLE 22

*Factional distribution of members of the LDP Investigation Committee
on the Constitution, March 1964*

	Committee members (A) No.	Committee members (A) %	Total no. of faction members (B)	Percentages A/B
Ikeda	8	26·6	49	16.3
Kōno	5	16·6	48	10.4
Satō	4	13·3	48	8·3
Miki	4	13·3	37	10.8
Fukuda	3	10·0	21	14·5
Fujiyama	3	10·0	21	14·5
Ishii	2	6·6	14	14·5
Ōno	1	3·3	30	3·3
Kawashima	–	–	19	–
Total	30	100·0	287	10·4

Sources: Jiyūminshutō, *Seimuchōsakai meibo: Shōwa 39-nen 3-gatsu 1-nichi genzai,*
pp. 27-9; *Kokkai binran,* 26th ed. (March 1964), pp. 326-9.

Factional Implications of Revisionism

This distribution pattern of the members of the LDP Committee on the Constitution seems to imply that factionalism has been irrelevant to the development of this issue in the party. A closer examination reveals, however, that in rather subtle ways it has played a critical role in the process just as it has done in many other instances of party policy-making.

When the attitude of the top party leadership towards the issue conspicuously softened only half a year after the 1955 merger, most of those who would subsequently replace the prewar men as leaders of the revisionist movement in the party were associated with the anti-Hatoyama coalition of dissident factions, the Jikyoku kondankai. Since this coalition was led by the Yoshida faction, it was difficult for them to advocate immediate constitutional revision, which would have displeased the majority in that faction and consequently undermined the unity of the dissident factions built up over another controversial issue, namely opposition to the normalisation of diplomatic relations with the U.S.S.R.

When eight more or less stable factional units emerged out of the bitter presidential contest of December 1956, many of the potentially most aggressive revisionists were associated with two of them, the Kishi and the Ishii factions. Kishi replaced Ishibashi as Prime Minister only two months after the latter's nomination as LDP President and Prime Minister and, consequently, the Kishi faction acquired the status of a dominant faction. As a result the revisionists associated with it were put in a position where it was difficult to bring up this controversial issue at the risk of intensifying intraparty conflicts as well as provoking other parties and thus threatening their own factional hegemony. On the other hand, the revisionists in the relatively small Ishii faction could not launch an effective campaign by themselves.

Finding it difficult for these reasons to carry on revisionist agitation within the party, some of them turned to the Cabinet Commission on the Constitution when it was established in August 1957. With a hope of making it an official and respectable pressure group designed not only to 'educate public opinion' but beyond that also to prepare a workable blueprint of actual revision, they flocked to the Commission and tried hard to make it serve their purpose. However, because of the resistance of a small but determined group of anti-revisionist members led by Chairman Takayanagi Kenzō, they were made to realise before long that the Commission alone could not be relied upon as an effective pressure group of the kind that they had envisaged.[25] It was just when they were about ready to give up the attempt to turn the Cabinet Commission into an effective vehicle of revisionism that the Kishi Cabinet was replaced by the Ikeda Cabinet in the wake of the anti-Security Treaty riots of 1960. The consequent change of factional posi-

[25]Concerning the divisions of opinion within the Commission, see Ward, op. cit., pp. 407-15.

tions freed the revisionists associated with the Kishi faction from the restrictions which had bound them so long as theirs had been a dominant faction.

Now that they were driven to the position of dissident factions it became not only possible but tactically desirable (in terms of the game of inter-factional competition and manoeuvre) for the revisionists in the Kishi and Ishii factions to challenge openly the Ikeda and other dominant factions by raising whatever controversial issues were likely to embarrass and weaken them. Constitutional revision was well suited to this purpose and it was therefore most natural for the revisionists in the dissident factions to have seized upon it. Under these changed circumstances they attempted to revitalise the PARC Committee on the Constitution and also to build an entirely new dissident and revisionist group within the party, crossing factional lines and independent from the said committee.

The first sign of a systematic attempt to bring the LDP Committee on the Constitution back to life was given in December 1961 when the more militant of its members succeeded in having a decision made in its name to bring pressure to bear upon the party leaders so that they should take an unequivocally revisionist stand in the forthcoming House of Councillors election. Although this was firmly rejected by the leaders' meeting, which was, like most other formal organs of the party, under the effective control of the dominant factions, the committee became thereafter a much more articulate and active body than previously. For example, despite the restraint applied by the top party leadership, it managed to publish on 18 August 1962 a concrete revision proposal, enumerating nine specific parts of the existing constitution to be amended. These included Article 9 and the status of the Emperor. This resumption of an aggressive stance by the committee attracted wide attention, although only one week later it was virtually nullified by an official statement issued by the party promising to refrain from determining the actual content of revision until the Cabinet Commission reported its findings to the government.

The attempt by the revisionists associated with the dissident factions (especially the Kishi and the Ishii factions) to make the official party committee the principal base of their revisionist activities failed precisely because of their factional implications. Being under the control of the dominant factions, it proved impervious to the manipulation by the minority representing the dissident (revisionist) factions. In the spring of 1964, for example, the Fukuda (former Kishi) and the Ishii factions contributed between them only 16·6 per cent of its membership and the addition of the Satō faction's share would not bring the figure above 30 per cent (see Table 22). It was no doubt for this reason that they turned their attention to the possibilities of building a new intra-party group, Soshinkai, as a substitute for the Cabinet Commission and the party committee.

Soshinkai

Some time in 1959 about thirty revisionist LDP members of the Diet began to meet informally but regularly to exchange views on various controversial issues, including constitutional revision.[26] This group was named Soshinkai (Association of Pure Hearts) in June of the following year and by early 1966 had grown into a well established intra-party group of some one hundred members, a majority being incumbent members of the Diet.[27] Like any other significant political group in contemporary Japan, it professes above all firm commitment to a 'true democracy', but its more immediate concern is with the restoration of the traditions of the Japanese nation and control of international communism. Although it has interested itself in a wide range of ideological issues—the system and content of school education, national defence, the ratification of the ILO Convention 87, etc.—constitutional revision has been one of its basic and central objectives.

It is hard to imagine that the aggressively anti-communist line, compounded with traditional Japanese puritanism and moralism, which has been consistently advocated by the leaders of Soshinkai, will be accepted by a majority even within the party, let alone by public opinion at large.[28] As an intra-party pressure group, however, it no doubt has a very significant degree of influence on the policy-making process and has effectively used it in various ways. In addition to frequently 'advising' the Prime Minister as well as other members of the Cabinet on issues of its primary interest, the group presented its views, for example, on constitutional revision and the restoration of the prewar National Foundation Day to the party leaders before the 17th Party Conference of January 1966.

As in the case of the LDP Committee on the Constitution the percentage of former public servants has been very high in the membership composition of Soshinkai. In the middle of 1963, for example, fifty-six LDP-affiliated MHRs were officially associated with it, of whom forty could be positively identified. Of these forty presumably most active members twenty-two were former high-ranking public servants, as compared with four each of former local politicians and businessmen (see Table 23). In the case of the twenty-two MHCs associated with the group at the time fifteen could be positively identified. Of this latter number only four were former public servants, but it should be noted that even this percentage was twice as high as that of either the former local politicians or businessmen and that three of the six

[26]The following account of Soshinkai is based largely on the information provided by Mr Shimano Moribumi, secretary-general of Soshinkai, in an interview on 21 January 1966.
[27]According to Shimano, in January 1966 there were about 55 MHRs, 20 MHCs, and 25 former members of either House affiliated with the group.
[28]Soshinkai is firmly opposed, for example, to trade with the People's Republic of China and would prefer the restoration of the spirit of thrift and industry (traditionally characteristic, in the opinion of its members, of the Japanese nation) to the doubling of per capita income. Many of its members believe also that public opinion should not be followed but be led by the party and the government.

TABLE 23

Occupational backgrounds of LDP members associated with the Soshinkai, July 1963

	MHRs	MHCs	Total
Local politicians	4	2	6
Public servants	22	4	26
Businessmen	4	2	6
Lawyers	2	1	3
Journalists	3	0	3
Miscellaneous	5	6	11
Total	40*	15*	55*

*Only 40 of the 56 MHRs and 15 of the 22 MHCs could be positively identified.

Sources: *Soshinkai to wa*, leaflet (July 1963); *Kokumin seiji nenkan: 1962*, p. 602; *GSS: Shūgiingiin meikan; GSS: Kizokuin sangiin giin meikan; Kokkai binran*, 25th ed. (September 1963), pp. 97-150.

classified as 'miscellaneous' were former military leaders with backgrounds analogous to those of high-ranking civil servants. In any event, the numerical predominance of bureaucratic elements in the membership of Soshinkai is as evident as in the case of the LDP Committee.

Just as significant (though very natural) is the fact that the group has had a special relationship with the two particular factions respectively led by Fukuda (formerly Kishi) and Ishii. The percentages of the members of these two factions officially associated with the group in 1963 were respectively 37·5 and 35·7 per cent, both figures being more than twice as high as those of any other faction (see Table 24). Between them they constituted 35 per cent of the group's identifiable members with seats in the Lower House of the Diet, a ratio which is quite remarkable considering the fact that their com-

TABLE 24

Factional distribution of LDP MHRs associated with the Soshinkai, July 1963

	Members associated with Soshinkai (A)		Total no. of faction members (B)	Percentages (A)/(B)
Fukuda	9	22·5	24	37·5
Ishii	5	12·5	14	35·7
Ikeda	8	20·0	49	16·3
Satō	7	17·5	49	14·2
Miki	3	7·5	31	9·6
Fujiyama	2	5·0	23	8·6
Ōno	2	5·0	29	6·8
Kawashima	1	2·5	25	4·0
Kōno	1	2·5	31	3·2
Independents	2	5·0	3	66·6
Total	40	100·0	278	14·3

Sources: As for Table 23.

bined share of the party-affiliated MHRs at the time was a mere 13·6 per cent. If one adds the Satō faction's share of 17·5 per cent, the three dissident factions easily controlled a majority of members in Soshinkai.

The revisionist pressure which had grown largely out of the reinstatement of prewar and wartime leaders in the early 1950s constituted an important part of the ideological and political justification for the conservative merger of 1955. Considering the historical background of the merger movement, it was inevitable that the initial program of the LDP should have included an explicit commitment to the earliest possible attainment of constitutional revision. The establishment of both the LDP Committee on the Constitution and the Cabinet Commission on the Constitution under the Hatoyama Cabinet was a natural and logical consequence of the historical process.

Almost as soon as the latter came into being, however, the attitude of the party's top leaders became much more cautious, and even negative. This change resulted from the desire on the part of the dominant factions (represented by the successive presidents) to ensure the continuation of their own hegemony in the inter-party and intra-party power struggle. This they attempted to do by avoiding such controversial issues as might cause or intensify conflicts and destroy the minimal degree of consensus required for the maintenance of the *status quo*. Relevant in this respect were the rigid constitutional requirements for revision, the hostility of the opposition parties and groups, the generally negative state of public opinion and the decline of support for positive revisionist action from business circles. These factors combined to make it not only unrealistic but also politically dangerous for the party's leaders to emphasise the issue.

The negative attitude of the party leadership inhibited the activities of the PARC Committee on the Constitution, but it has not put an end to the revisionist pressure in the party. New groups of revisionists, who have largely replaced the prewar and wartime leaders, have been drawn mainly from the occupational category of former public servants. Just as significant is the fact that they have been associated with two particular factions—the Kishi (subsequently Fukuda) and the Ishii factions. Because of this factional implication of their activities, their attempt to use the LDP Committee on the Constitution as the principal base of their operations has failed. Since the centre of their activities shifted to the newly-formed unofficial intra-party group, Soshinkai, the elements of factionalism have become more pronounced than previously. In this respect a consistent and recurring pattern has appeared which deserves special attention.

Strong and overt revisionist pressure has emanated invariably from dissident factions and their leaders. Once they have succeeded in having one of their own faction leaders elected party president, thus putting themselves in the position of dominant factions, they have ceased to press aggressively for an immediate or early revision. Considerations about the continuation of their own rule in terms of the inter-factional balance of power have always proved more decisive than their ideological commitment to the cause of constitutional revision. Since the pre-merger days there has not been a single exception to this general rule. Now that Satō has been nominated party president and both the Fukuda and the Ishii factions have become automatically the hardcore of the new coalition of dominant factions, this familiar pattern seems likely to repeat itself. With the change in the fortunes of the factions involved, the emphasis in the activities of Soshinkai will also probably change. The LDP as a whole is no nearer today to fulfilling its inaugural pledge than it was a few months after it was formed.

9 Relations with the People's Republic of China

In the history of Japan's foreign relations no issue has received such attention from her leaders and people as relations with her vast continental neighbour, China. World War II merely increased the complexity of this centuries-old problem which is bedevilled not only by the differing attitudes of Peking, Washington, and Taipei, but also apparently irreconcilable divisions of opinion among the Japanese themselves. The issue has not only divided the parties from each other but has even divided the LDP itself. Indeed, conflicts seem to exist within the minds of many LDP members.

BACKGROUND

Phase I, 1949-52

Relations between Japan and the People's Republic of China may be divided into five fairly distinct phases. The first phase lasted from the establishment of the People's Republic in October 1949 to the middle of 1952 when the first private trade agreement was concluded.

In the first months after its establishment, the attitude of the People's Republic towards Japan was far from amicable. Its hostility was symbolised by the Sino-Soviet Treaty of Friendship, Alliance and Mutual Assistance (signed in February 1950) the first article of which was directed specifically against Japan. Both the contents of the Japanese Peace Treaty (concluded in September 1951) and the manner in which it was prepared were bitterly opposed by Peking. Neither the U.S.S.R. nor the People's Republic of China signed that treaty and the separate peace treaty which Japan concluded with Nationalist China in April 1952 naturally exacerbated her relations with Peking.

The exchange of persons and goods between mainland China and Japan during this period was negligible. Between 1949 and 1951 fifteen Japanese are known to have visited mainland China, but no mainland Chinese visited Japan until 1954. Japan was bound during this period by the trade embargo enforced by the United States and her Western allies through the Consultative Group (CG) based in Paris and COCOM and CHINCOM established under it. The embargo list which was applied to Japan was far more extensive than the 'international' or 'Paris' list prepared by and applied to the European members of CG, which she joined in September 1952; for she accepted a more restrictive list presented by the United States at the conference on Far Eastern trade held in Washington in July and August 1952.[1] Under the circumstances Japanese trade with mainland China fell from 6 per cent of her total exports and 3·6 per cent of her total imports in 1947-8 to 0·4 per cent and 0·73 per cent in 1952 (cf. the 1930-9 average of 21·6 and 16·6 per cent respectively) (see Table 25).

This decline of Japan's China trade involved a drastic change in her sources of basic raw materials and foodstuffs. Japan's purchases of soy beans, coal, and salt from the United States in 1951 increased by a factor of three, sixteen, and eighteen over the previous year. On the other hand, the values of her imports of the same items from mainland China in 1951 were 5·5, 8·8, and 3·7 per cent of those of the previous year.

Phase II, 1952-8

The second phase opened with the conclusion of the first private trade agreement in 1952 and lasted until early 1958, when the 'Nagasaki flag incident' temporarily interrupted the exchange of persons and goods between the two countries.

After 1952 it became customary for Peking to invite various Japanese groups to the mainland on the occasion of the annual National Day celebration, and the number of Japanese visitors to China steadily increased until it reached a peak of 1,243 in 1957. In the meantime, over one hundred Chinese visited Japan annually between 1955 and 1957.

Trade between the two countries was governed during this period by three non-governmental trade agreements, the first of which was signed, as already mentioned, in June 1952. The second was signed in October 1953 by a non-partisan delegation of the *Nitchūbōeki sokushin giin renmei* (Diet Members' League for the Promotion of Sino-Japanese Trade) and the China Council for the Promotion of International Trade. The third agreement (the first to be signed in Tokyo) was signed in May 1955. While the target envisaged in these three argreements was in each case £Stg 30m. each way, the rates of the fulfilment were 4 per cent for Japanese exports and 6 per cent for Japanese imports under the first, 27·7 per cent for exports and 41 per cent for imports under the second, and 36·7 per cent for exports and 91·3 per cent for imports in the first year of the third agreement.

[1]According to a journalist's account, the United States insisted at the conference, which was attended also by the United Kingdom, France, and Canada, that Japan should be governed by an embargo list more restrictive than the international list because the engagement of the United States troops in the war against China benefited her more directly than the European nations. See Shimazu Kuniomi, 'Chūkyōbōeki wa mada seijimondai' in Nihonshūhōsha (ed.), *Dokuritsu gaikō* (1954), p. 191.

TABLE 25

Japanese exports to and imports from mainland China, Taiwan, and the United States, 1946–66
(¥ million)

Years	Mainland China				Taiwan				U.S.A.			
	Exports to	%	Imports from	%	Exports to	%	Imports from	%	Exports to	%	Imports from	%
1946	221	(4·6)	273	(1·6)	1	(0·04)	30	(0·7)	1,472	(65·1)	3,516	(86·4)
1947	761	(5·9)	182	(1·0)	31	(0·3)	73	(0·3)	1,791	(17·6)	17,631	(86·9)
1948	287	(1·6)	1,275	(3·6)	5	(0·01)	610	(1·0)	16,894	(32·4)	37,583	(62·3)
1949	928	(0·6)	5,587	(2·4)	2,143	(1·6)	8,933	(3·1)	30,737	(18·0)	176,807	(62·1)
1950	7,068	(2·4)	14,158	(4·1)	13,684	(4·5)	12,894	(3·7)	64,547	(21·6)	150,565	(43·2)
1951	2,098	(0·4)	7,778	(1·1)	18,216	(3·7)	19,089	(2·5)	66,578	(13·6)	250,110	(33·9)
1952	216	(0·04)	5,365	(0·7)	21,840	(4·7)	22,955	(3·1)	84,355	(18·4)	276,588	(37·8)
1953	1,634	(0·3)	10,692	(1·2)	21,948	(4·7)	23,054	(2·6)	84,197	(18·3)	273,489	(37·5)
1954	6,875	(0·4)	14,677	(1·6)	23,737	(4·0)	20,552	(2·3)	101,731	(17·3)	305,537	(31·5)
1955	10,277	(1·2)	29,080	(3·3)	22,978	(3·1)	29,116	(3·2)	164,233	(22·6)	278,612	(35·3)
1956	24,242	(2·7)	30,113	(2·6)	28,029	(3·1)	16,383	(1·4)	198,142	(22·0)	384,202	(31·3)
1957	21,774	(2·1)	28,974	(1·9)	30,339	(2·9)	24,212	(1·5)	217,604	(21·1)	584,334	(33·0)
1958	18,216	(1·8)	19,594	(1·8)	32,414	(3·1)	27,231	(2·4)	248,638	(24·0)	380,194	(37·8)
1959	1,313	(0·1)	6,810	(0·5)	31,265	(2·5)	25,757	(1·9)	376,790	(30·2)	401,628	(34·8)
1960	981	(0·07)	7,462	(0·4)	36,805	(2·5)	22,868	(1·4)	396,593	(27·1)	559,272	(30·9)
1961	5,990	(0·4)	11,122	(0·5)	34,676	(2·2)	24,389	(1·1)	384,070	(25·1)	754,497	(34·5)
1962	13,846	(0·8)	16,567	(0·8)	42,687	(2·4)	22,095	(1·0)	504,083	(28·4)	651,228	(36·0)
1963	22,470	(1·1)	26,856	(1·1)	38,571	(1·9)	44,150	(1·8)	542,488	(22·3)	747,839	(32·0)
1964	54,986	(2·3)	56,790	(2·0)	49,641	(2·0)	50,726	(1·7)	662,969	(27·5)	840,975	(30·8)
1965	88,213	(2·8)	80,894	(2·7)	78,450	(2·5)	56,634	(1·9)	892,524	(29·3)	851,812	(29·4)
1966 Jan.-Sept.	87,615	(3·4)	83,572	(3·3)	61,454	(2·4)	43,430	(1·7)	786,888	(31·4)	701,167	(27·9)

Note: The figures in the parentheses are the percentages of the total Japanese exports and imports in the respective years.

Sources: Sōrifu tōkeikyoku, *Nihon tōkei nenkan*, Dai-9-kai (1958), p. 242; *Dai-16-kai* (1965), p. 294; *Nihon Tōkei Geppō*, 66 (December 1966), pp. 52-3.

Q

Despite the Korean ceasefire in July 1953 and the drastic relaxation of the embargo against the U.S.S.R. and the nations of East Europe in August 1954, rigid international control against trade with China was continued until the middle of 1957. Under the circumstances it was impossible for Japan to export many of the industrial materials, equipment, and machinery designated in the aforementioned unofficial agreements as Category A and this was largely responsible for the relatively low level of the Japanese exports. It was not until July 1957 that the Japanese government freed 170 of the 450 items listed in the CHINCOM list and not until one year later that the new embargo list (the current COCOM list) was further cut by about 70 items. In other words, it was impossible until the latter half of 1957 for Japan to increase significantly her exports to China since these by the nature of her economy and resources consisted mainly of manufactured goods and industrial equipment to which the international embargo applied.

Despite the barriers erected by the international trade embargo, various steps were taken in Japan during this period to encourage the growth of China trade. Following the conclusion of the third agreement a Special Committee for the Promotion of Trade was established in the House of Representatives on a non-partisan basis. Prime Minister Hatoyama promised 'support and co-operation' in the implementation of the agreement, and the first Chinese trade fair was held in Tokyo and Osaka in October and December 1955, which was reciprocated in the following year by a Japanese trade fair in Peking and Shanghai. Finally, a *Nitchū yushutsunyū kumiai* (Japan-China Export-Import Union) was set up with the official blessing of the government and the participation of about 240 private firms.

However, the situation changed in February 1957 when Kishi Nobusuke succeeded Ishibashi Tanzan as Prime Minister of Japan. After the new Prime Minister visited Taipei in June and reportedly encouraged Chiang Kai-shek to realise the reconquest of the mainland, the attitude of Peking began gradually to revert to the early hostility and distrust towards the Japanese government.

This sudden change in the climate of Sino-Japanese relations naturally interfered with the efforts to conclude a fourth trade agreement, negotiations for which were started in September 1957, interrupted in November, and resumed in February of the following year. Although the agreement was finally signed in Peking on 5 March 1958, the attitude of the Japanese government was far from enthusiastic, particularly because of the provisions it contained concerning the reciprocal stationing of permanent trade missions in the two capitals and the accompanying memorandum spelling out the legal privileges they would be entitled to receive from the respective governments. Particularly objectionable from the point of view of the Japanese government was Point 1 (4) of the memorandum, according to which each mission would be entitled to fly its own national flag at the building in which it was housed.

Also disagreeable was Point 2 which would exempt members of the Chinese mission and their dependants from finger-printing required by the current Japanese immigration regulations.

Chinese anger at the generally negative attitude of the Kishi government was ignited by a brief note the latter gave to the three Japanese signatories to the agreement on 9 April.[2] In this note Kishi promised to give support and co-operation 'within the limits of relevant Japanese laws, on the basis of the understanding that she [Japan] did not recognise it [the government in Peking], and considering existing international relations . . .' In his lengthy telegram of 14 April Nan Han-chen bluntly rejected the 'offer' of support couched in these qualifying phrases.

To make the break even more definite, two Japanese pulled down the Chinese national flag at the site of a Chinese postage stamps and colour prints exhibition in Nagasaki on the afternoon of 2 May 1958. The incident in effect brought the second phase of relations between the two countries to an end, and for about two years following it the Kishi government adopted a 'wait and see' attitude, while Peking promulgated 'three principles' of future Sino-Japanese relations. These 'principles' as outlined by Peking to a visiting JSP member of the House of Councillors, Sata Tadataka, in August 1958 were: (i) that the Japanese government should immediately give up words and actions hostile towards the People's Republic of China; (ii) that it should cease to participate in a 'plot to create two Chinas'; and (iii) that it should refrain from obstructing the normalisation of relations between the two countries.

Phase III, 1958-60

The sudden resumption of the 'cold war' between Peking and Tokyo was reflected in a decline both in the exchange of persons and in trade. Compared with 1957 when 1,243 Japanese visited China and 140 Chinese visited Japan, only 191 Japanese and not a single Chinese visited the other country in 1959. In the meantime, the values of Japanese exports to and imports from China in 1959 dropped respectively to one-twentieth and less than a quarter of what they had been in 1957 (see Table 25). In the process a total of 1,262 export and import contracts, involving about 110 Japanese manufacturers and trading firms and valued at £Stg 35m. were cancelled, not only causing enormous financial loss to the companies concerned but—probably more important in the long run—creating a deep psychological shock in Japanese business circles in general.

Despite its open and relentless attacks on the government of Japan, however, Peking continued to encourage the visits to China of Japanese indivi-

---

[2] The three signatories of the fourth agreement were: the Nitchūbōeki sokushin giin renmei, the Nihon kokusaibōeki sokushin kyōkai, and the Nitchū yushutsunyū kumiai. China was represented again by the China Council for the Promotion of International Trade.

duals and groups known to be opposed to Kishi either on ideological or partisan grounds. This dualism in Peking's policy became increasingly evident as the controversy in Japan over the proposed revision of the U.S.-Japanese Security Treaty intensified in 1959. In March 1959 a JSP delegation led by Secretary-General Asanuma visited Peking and caused both jubilation and dismay in Japan and elsewhere by publicly denouncing 'U.S. imperialism' as 'the common enemy of the Japanese and the Chinese peoples'. In June *Nitchūyūkō kyōkai* (the Japan-China Friendship Association, established on 1 October 1950) and the *Nihon chūgoku bunka kōryū kyōkai* (Japan-China Cultural Exchange Association, formed in March 1956) sent their representatives to China and issued a joint statement with the Chinese People's Association for Cultural Relations with Foreign Countries. More significant for their long-range political implications were the visits of two LDP politicians' groups a few months later. In September Ishibashi Tanzan went to Peking accompanied by two other LDP Diet members, and in the next month Matsumura Kenzō and his party followed. The personal involvement of these leaders of dissident LDP factions in people-to-people diplomacy during the crisis set an important precedent for the developments in the next phase.

Phase IV, 1960-4

The fourth phase, which began with the replacement in 1960 of the Kishi Cabinet by the 'low posture' and 'economic-minded' Ikeda Cabinet, saw a resumption of the trend towards increased trade and communication at the non-governmental level that had become evident in the second phase.

On the occasion of the National Day celebration of 1960 twelve Japanese groups were invited to Peking where they joined eight Chinese organisations in issuing an appeal for increased trade and an official governmental trade agreement. This was followed by Chou En-lai's three-point proposal (usually referred to as the 'three principles of Sino-Japanese trade') made during an interview with Suzuki Kazuo, the managing director of the Nitchūbōeki sokushinkai on 27 August 1960. These referred to the three different forms of trade which could develop between the two countries in the new period: (i) trade to be guaranteed by an official agreement between the two governments; (ii) trade supported by non-governmental agreements and contracts to be concluded between private Japanese firms and appropriate Chinese corporations; (iii) trade specially designed to suit the interests of small Japanese enterprises wholly dependent on Chinese supplies of raw materials and to be arranged by particular organisations, such as Sōhyō (Japan Council of Trade Unions) and the All-China Federation of Trade Unions. Hereafter a formula called 'friendly firms trade' began to be accepted as the principal type of Sino-Japanese trade. However, before this had been formalised by the signing of a protocol in December 1962, another formula was initiated by a memorandum signed on 9 December by a Japanese businessman and

LDP Diet member, Takasaki Tatsunosuke, and a deputy chief of the Chinese Staff Office of Foreign Affairs, Liao Cheng-chih. Sino-Japanese trade in the ensuing five years has developed largely in accordance with the terms of these two basic formulae.

The Liao-Takasaki memorandum on a long-term Sino-Japanese trade program envisaged import and export transactions amounting to an annual average of $US180m. for the next five years, China exporting mainly coal, iron ore, soy beans, maize, salt, tin, etc., and importing steel materials, chemical fertilisers, agricultural chemicals, agricultural machinery, and various kinds of industrial plant.

Under the arrangements based on the protocol (friendly firms trade formula) and the 1962 memorandum (referred to as the 'LT trade' formula), the volume of trade between mainland China and Japan increased quickly from the low level of 1960 and by 1965 recorded £Stg 88m. for Japanese exports and £Stg 81m. for Japanese imports, or 2·9 and 2·7 per cent respectively of total Japanese exports and imports in that year. In 1964, Japanese exports to and imports from the mainland each overtook those to and from Taiwan. By the middle of 1966 mainland China had become one of Japan's most important export markets and suppliers of her raw materials.

In the steady growth of Sino-Japanese trade under the Ikeda Cabinet particular significance attaches to the conclusion in July 1963 of an export contract between the Kurashiki Rayon Company and the China National Technical Import Corporation. This involved the sale by this well-known Japanese textile manufacturer of a vinylon plant worth about £Stg 7·4m. on a 5-year deferred payment basis at 5·5 per cent interest. By the middle of 1964, about a dozen similar contracts were either being negotiated or considered by Japanese manufacturers and appropriate Chinese corporations. These included another vinylon plant offered by the Dainihon Bōseki Company, a urea fertiliser plant offered by the Tōyō Engineering Company, and a 12,500 ton freighter to be built by the Hitachi Shipbuilding Company.

The 'forward-looking' view expressed in September 1963 by Japan's four most influential employers' organisations — Keidanren, Nikkeiren, Dōyūkai, and Nisshō — through their joint research machinery, *Nihon keizaichōsa kyōgikai* (Japan Economic Research Council) indicated the degree of enthusiasm shared by Japanese industrialists and businessmen for the growing China trade. An official report of this council recommended explicitly that Japan's trade with communist bloc nations, especially China, should be encouraged much more positively than heretofore. It is significant that the three managing directors of this group at the time were the vice-president of Keidanren, Uemura Kōgorō, vice-president of Nisshō, Nagano Shigeo, and an emeritus professor of Hitotsubashi University, Nakayama Ichirō. Even more dramatic and revealing was the attitude of Japanese political and economic leaders to Nan Han-chen's visit to Japan on the occasion of the Chinese trade fair held in Tokyo and Osaka in 1964. The chairman of the China Council for the Promotion of International Trade was met individually by such LDP leaders as Satō Eisaku, Kōno Ichirō, Fujiyama Aiichirō, Miki Takeo, and such prominent businessmen as Uemura Kōgorō and Suga Reinosuke of Keidanren, and Kikawada Kazutaka, Nakayama Sohei, Usami Makoto, Mizukami Tatsuzō, and Inayama Yoshihiro of Dōyūkai.

Furthermore, in accordance with the memorandum signed by Liao Chenchih, now president of the China-Japan Friendship Association (established in October 1963), and Matsumura Kenzō, a team of five Chinese trade representatives led by Sun Ping-hua arrived in Tokyo in August 1964. In return in January the following year a 3-man Japanese mission led by a minor official of the Ministry of International Trade and Industry went to Peking.[3] In accordance also with the same memorandum fourteen Japanese correspondents, nine of whom were to stay in Peking for a year and the remaining five only temporarily, arrived in Peking on 29 September, while on the same day seven Chinese correspondents arrived in Tokyo.

Despite, however, these promising developments up to the latter part of 1964, it gradually became evident in the following two and a half years that postwar Sino-Japanese relations were undergoing yet another important change and entering a fifth phase.

Phase V, 1964-7

The People's Republic of China with which the Satō government which came into office in November 1964 was to deal had now grown much more formidable a power for Japan to cope with, both ideologically and militarily.

The progress of the Sino-Soviet dispute, China's nuclear armament, and the Great Proletarian Cultural Revolution have combined to cause an unexpected basic realignment among the Japanese groups interested in the issue. On the one hand, the JCP and groups under its influence, which had always played a leading part in postwar Sino-Japanese relations until late 1965, have made a remarkable about-face and come to be regarded as Peking's 'enemy number one' in Japan. Less surprising but just as significant, Peking's relationship with the Satō government and the dominant groups in the conservative political hierarchy that it represents has also steadily deteriorated. On the other hand, the dominant groups in the JSP and, to a somewhat more limited extent, a minority in the LDP have virtually replaced the JCP and its front-groups as the main reservoir of goodwill and support for China in Japan.

[3]The chief Japanese representative, Sōma Tsunetoshi, was chief of the general affairs division of the ministry's Shikoku regional office. On appointment as the chief of the trade mission, he resigned the public service post and nominally became adviser to Nitchū yushutsunyū kumiai. This shows one of the more subtle ways in which the Japanese government had come by this time to take part in the direct dealings with Peking without openly abandoning the principle of non-recognition and political non-involvement. See *Asahi*, 31 October 1964, 25 January 1965.

In opposition to China's persistent attacks on Moscow and her refusal to co-operate with the Soviet 'revisionist' leaders (especially in supporting the South Vietnamese National Liberation Front and the North Vietnamese Workers' Party in their 'war of liberation' against 'American imperialism') the JCP began toward the end of 1965 to press openly for the creation of a broad 'anti-imperialist' international front linking the Communist and Workers' Parties of China, North Korea, North Vietnam, Japan, and the U.S.S.R. The exchange of opinion between the JCP delegation led by Secretary-General Miyamoto and the Chinese leaders in Peking in March 1966 failed to produce agreement and, following the return of the delegation to Japan, a series of articles openly critical of Chinese policy appeared in the official JCP organs.

Less unexpected or spectacular has been the deterioration of the relations between the two governments in the most recent period. Barely ten days after the new Satō Cabinet was formed in November 1964, it decided to turn down an application for Japanese visas made by a Chinese Communist Party delegation to be led by the then mayor of Peking, Peng Chen. When in August 1965 Nan Han-chen openly criticised the policy of the Satō government during his visit to Japan, the Vice-Minister of Foreign Affairs, Shimoda, responded with an extraordinarily strong denunciation of his action as a flagrant case of interference with Japan's internal affairs. Although his views were presented officially as those of the Ministry of Foreign Affairs alone, it seems evident that they had been cleared in advance by Satō and other senior members of the Cabinet. When a few months later opposition in Japan to the ratification of a treaty normalising her diplomatic relations with South Korea became intense, Peking demonstrated its objections to the treaty much more forcefully than other communist bloc governments. A New China News Agency despatch of 12 November branded it as 'criminal' and as a veritable step towards the creation of a 'North East Asia Treaty Organisation'. One week later fourteen Chinese organisations issued a joint statement condemning it and the Satō government, while a big protest rally was staged in Peking attended by government leaders, including Prime Minister Chou.

Nor have the attitudes of the two governments been very conciliatory with regard to trade. In contrast with the Ikeda Cabinet which had in 1963 allowed the Kurashiki Rayon Company to use the credit of the Export-Import Bank (a government corporation) to finance its export of vinylon plant to China, one of the first things the Satō government did in relation to Sino-Japanese trade was to deny on 21 January 1965 the same facilities to the Dainihon Bōseki Company. Less than a week later the Minister of International Trade and Industry, Sakurauchi, announced another Cabinet decision denying the bank's credit to Hitachi which was negotiating for the export of a freighter to China. These decisions were followed on 8 February 1965 by the Prime Minister's reference in the course of debate in the House of Representatives Budget Committee to the 'Yoshida letter' of May 1964 in which Yoshida, a former Prime Minister, had promised the Nationalist Chinese government that the credits of the Export-Import Bank would not be used to finance Japanese exports to mainland China, at least before the end of 1964. In protest against these decisions and the attitude of the Japanese government Liao Cheng-chih announced the nullification of the contract with Hitachi on 6 April, and on 30 April the contract with Dainihon Bōseki.

The increasing alienation between Peking on one hand, and the JCP (and groups under its influence) and the dominant groups in the LDP on the other, has led to the emergence of the left-wing groups in the JSP and the pro-Peking minority in the LDP as the main prop on the Japanese side of the relationship between the two countries. The traditionally pro-Peking JSP groups (represented by the *Shakaishugi kenkyūkai* of the Sasaki faction, the *Heiwa dōshikai* and the official Special Committee for the Restoration of Sino-Japanese Relations) have formed an *Ajiya afurika kenkyūkai* within that party. In the meantime, the pro-Peking elements in the LDP have organised themselves in the *Ajiya afurika mondai kenkyūkai* (Afro-Asian Affairs Study Group, hereafter referred to as the Afro-Asian Group). In competition with the anti-Peking group, the *Ajiya mondai kenkyūkai* (Asian Affairs Study Group, hereafter referred to as the Asian Group), this group has become a principal vehicle in the ministerial party of the movement for closer relations between Japan and the People's Republic of China.

THE LIBERAL-DEMOCRATIC PARTY RESPONSE

The Heritage of the Liberal and the Democratic Parties

Before the conclusion of the San Francisco Peace Treaty in early September 1951 the leaders of the government and the Liberal Party had taken generally positive views of Japan's relations with the newly established People's Republic of China.

Prime Minister Yoshida, in reply to questions in the Diet, explicitly rejected the extremist views of people like Kikuchi Yoshirō and advocated a closer relationship with Peking especially, but not exclusively, in the field of trade. That he and his government were not happy about the circumstances which compelled them to sign a separate peace treaty with the Nationalist Chinese government in Taiwan in 1952 seems to be beyond doubt. In 1963 Yoshida elaborated on this problem as follows:

> As far as the Japanese government was concerned, increased friendship and improved economic relations with Taiwan were naturally most welcome. On the other hand, it was our wish to avoid, if possible, going too far in that direction and manifestly renouncing the Peking government. Considering, however, that the Nationalist government had been the princpial belligetn in the conflict with us from the beginning, that it held an important place in the United Nations and

that we were obliged to it for the peaceful repatriation of our nationals at the end of the war, we found it impossible to ignore it. Then suspicions [about Japan's intentions concerning the choice between Peking and Taiwan] had been expressed by the United States Senate. While the relationship with mainland China was admittedly very important to us, it would have been intolerable to have the ratification of the Peace Treaty interfered with by it. We had to make up our minds in a hurry on the question with which government we should conclude a peace treaty, and under the circumstances we could not but choose the Nationalist government.[4]

Following the conclusion of the peace treaties, however, the official attitude of the Liberal Party became appreciably more negative and cautious. In fact, two days after the conclusion of the San Francisco Peace Treaty and more than half a year before the peace treaty with Taiwan the party's leaders publicly warned against optimistic expectations for a significant increase in Japan's trade with mainland China and gave assurances that Japan could hope to develop sufficiently large markets in Southeast Asian countries instead.[5] In the subsequent years the Liberal Party's attitude gradually moved to what has been defined as the doctrine of the separation of politics and economics in Sino-Japanese relations. The report of its Investigation Committee on Foreign Affairs published in September 1954 rejected an early recognition of the Peking government but called for efforts to increase trade and the exchange of persons concerned with trade between Japan and the mainland. This negative position was justified by the following reasons: (i) Japan had recognised the government of Nationalist China and it was impossible to recognise the communist government at the same time so long as both were firmly opposed to the 'two Chinas' idea; (ii) the Peking government was in military alliance with North Korea and to recognise it would jeopardise Japan's relationship with South Korea; (iii) the conditions presented by Peking as the prerequisites of normalising the relations between the two governments included termination of Japan's co-operation with the U.S.A. and the explicit renunciation of intentions for her rearmament; and (iv) Japan's recognition of Peking would considerably weaken the general anti-communist alliance system in Asia.

The policy of the Democratic Party (Progressive Party) before the conservative merger of 1955 had not been radically different from that of the Liberal Party. On the one hand, in 1951 the party's secretary-general, Miki Takeo, expressed his scepticism about the future of the Peking government and Japan's relationship with it. On the other hand, Kitamura Tokutarō, the chairman of the party's PARC, declared in 1952 that 'nobody who cared at all about Japan's economic independence would ever contemplate her separation from mainland China'. Although it was never forced to make a

---

[4]Yoshida Shigeru, *Sekai to nihon* (Banchō shobō, 1963), p. 146.
[5]The statement of the Liberal Party published on 20 September 1951, as quoted in Miyashita Tadao, *Chūnichibōeki no kenkyū* (Nihon gaiseigakkai shuppankyoku, 1955), p. 74n.

clear-cut and public decision regarding the legitimate government of China, there is no doubt that it faced the same kind of dilemma as the Liberal Party. When it came to power at last towards the end of 1954, Hatoyama and his advisers indeed had plans for the normalisation of diplomatic relations with the Soviet Union and hopes for improved relationship with the communist bloc nations generally. It was under the Hatoyama and Ishibashi Cabinets that the pre-1960 peak in both trade and exchange of persons with mainland China was reached, and at that time Peking-Tokyo relations were more cordial than ever. It seems equally evident, however, that they had no definite plans whatsoever for a drastic change in official Sino-Japanese relations as part of their 'independent foreign policy' program. According to Hatoyama's former secretary, Wakamiya Shōtarō, at that time the Democrat Prime Minister and his colleagues thought about the normalisation of Soviet-Japanese relations entirely independently and separately from the question of the Sino-Japanese relations. 'Time was not yet ripe' to take up the latter issue, as far as they were concerned. The recommendations of the party's PARC, *Jishu heiwa gaikō hōsaku*, published in January 1955, contained no specific proposals about the China issue, except for a call for increased trade. Theirs also was essentially a policy aimed at encouraging trade as much as possible but with no political involvement.

When the LDP was formed in November 1955, the only heritage in China policy that it received from its predecessors was therefore the doctrine of the separation of politics and economics (or rather trade). This had been developed mainly and more consciously by the Liberals, but it was now taken up by the LDP led by Hatoyama and his Democrat associates. In the actual practice of Japan's foreign policy, however, this simple principle alone was not sufficient as a guidepost. Both the international and domestic environment was too complex to allow the ministerial party and the government under its control to drift forever with the tide without making some painful decisions and choices. Internationally, the attitudes and policies of the United States and Nationalist Chinese governments in particular have compelled them to think and act in certain specific ways.

International Factors

Ever since General MacArthur's famous statement of 2 September 1949 on the prospects of Sino-Japanese trade[6] the successive United States governments have always opposed both Japan's prospective recognition of the Peking government and large-scale trade with mainland China. In recent years this view has been forcefully reiterated by such American leaders as

[6]In this statement MacArthur concluded that China was not likely to develop under communism into a promising market for Japanese products or an important source of raw materials, and that the great expectations found among Japanese business circles for the resumption of trade with her were entirely unfounded. See the summary of the statement in Arisawa Hiromi and Inaba Hidezō (eds.), *Shiryō: Sengo nijūnen shi: 2 Keizai* (Nihonhyōronsha, 1966), p. 169.

Assistant Secretary of State Harriman and Secretary of State Rusk.[7] In view of Japan's military dependence on and intimate economic relationship with the United States and the belief which is still widely shared among Japanese conservative politicians that one must above all be acceptable to Washington in order to make good in Japanese politics, there is little doubt that this attitude of the United States government has inhibited Japanese initiative in developing trade and other forms of contact with Peking.

Probably more direct and tangible has been the restrictive influence exerted by the Nationalist Chinese government. Politically and morally, Japan has been bound to Taipei not only by the peace treaty of 1952 but also, as many LDP Diet members have argued, by obligations personally owed to Chiang Kai-shek for his 'magnanimous' treatment of Japanese soldiers and civilians on the mainland at the end of World War II.[8] Economically, Taiwan has never been a major trading partner of Japan in the postwar period. However, it has been considered an important market for Japanese overseas investment and also a stepping stone to the vast though not yet fully developed market lying to its south. Between April 1951 and June 1964, for example, 39 of the 87 foreign capital investment projects set up in Taiwan have been Japanese (another 39 having been American) and 78 of the 117 technical joint ventures launched have been with Japanese firms. A number of large Japanese manufacturers have been involved in these investments and joint ventures, such as the Tōshiba Electric, Hitachi Manufacturing, Nissan Automotive Industry, and so on.

On the strength of such moral, political and economic ties, further reinforced by the connections centring around the United States and binding both Japan and Taiwan with the 'Free World' in an anti-communist alliance, the Nationalist government has actively interfered with Japan's efforts to increase trade and communication with Peking. As early as July 1952 the Nationalist government's Foreign Minister, Yeh Kung-chao, made it clear in the Legislative Yüan that it would regard Japan's formal resumption of trade with the mainland as a violation of the peace treaty, and in the following month an Osaka-based Japanese trading firm had its contract for the import of salt from Taiwan cancelled on the grounds that it had made inquiries with an import and export corporation in Peking for possible transactions.

[7]For Harriman's statement of June 1962, see *Yomiuri*, 24 June 1962. For Rusk's views expressed on the occasion of the fifth annual conference of the Joint United States-Japan Committee on Trade and Economic Affairs in July 1966, see the following: 'Seijishoku koi nichibei keizai iinkai', *Mainichi*, 7 July 1966; 'Satō Rasuku kaidan', ibid., 8 July 1966; 'Kuichigai nokosu chūgokumondai', *Asahi*, 8 July 1966; 'Keizaii wo shuzai shite: Nikkeikisha zadankai', *Nihon Keizai*, 8 July 1966.
[8]See the words of gratitude and appreciation expressed by senior LDP members, such as the then Prime Minister Kishi, Speaker of the House of Representatives, Masutani Shūji, President of the House of Councillors, Matsuno Tsuruhei, etc. at a mass rally held in September 1957 to welcome Chiang's envoy, Chang Chun, as quoted in Horikoshi Teizō, 'Taiwan to okinawa hōkoku', *Keidanren Geppō*, VII, 2 (February 1959), pp. 32-3.

More recently, Taiwan's active involvement in the efforts to prevent Japan's export of plant to China on a deferred payment basis has attracted much attention. In the summer of 1963, when the Ikeda Cabinet decided to approve finally the Kurashiki Rayon's proposed sale of vinylon plant to China, the Control Yüan in Taipei adopted a strongly-worded resolution in protest and the Nationalist government's ambassador to Tokyo, Chang Li-sheng, personally pressed Japan's Foreign Minister, Ōhira Masayoshi, to cancel the Cabinet decision.[9]

In order to assuage Taipei's anger over this issue, which was further complicated a few weeks later by the Chou Hung-ching incident,[10] former Prime Minister Yoshida visited Chiang Kai-shek in February and Foreign Minister Ōhira followed in July 1964. These Japanese visits were reciprocated in August by Chang Chun's visit to Tokyo to confer with the government and LDP leaders. In early 1965, it became known that one of the principal purposes of the Ōhira and the Chang visits had been to confirm and expand the Japanese government's pledge made in Yoshida's letter to Chang in May 1964 that it would not authorise further Export-Import Bank financing of plant exports to mainland China. It was this particular undertaking that has subsequently come to determine so effectively the Japanese government's attitude toward Peking.

Domestic Climate of Opinion

While the most obvious international influences affecting the behaviour of the LDP leadership have thus inhibited positive efforts on the part of Japan for increased trade and political communication with the People's Republic of China, the principal domestic factors seem to have had a much more complex and composite effect. Judging from the results of various public opinion polls, it is probably correct to assume that a majority of ordinary Japanese have been favourably disposed in recent years toward increased trade with mainland China and her early admission to the United Nations. Those opposed to this have remained a very small minority (a few per cent concerning trade and less than 10 per cent regarding China's admission to

[9]The resolution of 3 September 1963 of the Control Yüan called for: (i) reappraisal of the Nationalist government's trade and economic policy toward Japan, (ii) recall of Ambassador Chang, (iii) an effective boycott of imported Japanese products, and (iv) appeal to the other democracies to force Japan to suspend her 'aid' to mainland China. On the following day the Legislative Yüan Committee on Foreign Relations made similar recommendations. Two days after three Japanese Cabinet Ministers agreed to approve the transaction Ambassador Chang called upon Ōhira on 20 August to convey Taipei's strong objections to that decision.

[10]On the morning of 7 October 1963, Chou, a member of a group of Chinese technicians on an inspection tour of Japan, went to the embassy of the U.S.S.R. in Tokyo allegedly to seek political asylum in the Soviet Union. Subsequently he was reported to have expressed his preference for Taiwan and Japan. By the first week of November, however, he seemed to have changed his mind again and began to insist that he wanted to go back to mainland China after all. Despite repeated protests by the Nationalist government, he was repatriated to mainland China in early January 1964.

the U.N.). Regarding the choice between Peking and Taipei, significantly more respondents have preferred Peking, but a majority of those who have held articulate opinions one way or the other have opted for the 'two Chinas' formula, if such an alternative is offered. In other words, a majority of Japanese with opinions on the issue have wanted an increase in Japan's trade with the People's Republic of China, her speedy admission to the United Nations, and the general acceptance of the idea of 'two Chinas'.

The natural friendliness toward China and the Chinese (embracing, though not necessarily exclusively, the People's Republic) demonstrated by a majority of Japanese voters has on several occasions caused the National Diet and local assemblies to express their active interest in the issue. As early as May 1949 a non-partisan Diet Members' League for the Promotion of Sino-Japanese Trade was established with an initial membership of about ninety, recruited from both Houses of the Diet. Between then and 1958 this organisation sponsored a series of actions by Diet members aimed at promoting trade and exchange of persons between the two countries. For example, in July 1953 and December 1956 it led both Houses of the Diet officially to adopt resolutions calling for increased trade with China and in July 1955 had the non-partisan Special Committee on the Promotion of International Trade in the House of Representatives adopt a resolution on the relaxation of the COCOM restrictions. In October 1956 a representative director of the organisation, Ikeda Masanosuke, conferred with senior public servants concerned with Sino-Japanese trade with a view to easing the methods of payment between the two countries. In January 1957 Ikeda also called on Foreign Minister Kishi, International Trade and Industry Minister Mizuta, and Economic Planning Agency Director Uda to assist in the efforts to have the COCOM embargo relaxed. After the Nagasaki flag incident it ceased to be non-partisan because as a result of an informal instruction issued by the LDP Secretary-General, Kawashima Shōjirō, most LDP members withdrew their membership. Nevertheless, the organisation not only survived the crisis but by early 1964 had recovered its non-partisan character to a certain extent, since nearly fifty LDP Diet members had rejoined it.

At the local level, prefectural and city assembly members' leagues for the promotion of Sino-Japanese trade began to appear throughout the country in late 1952 and they were brought together in June 1953 into a national organisation called the Local Assembly Members' League for the Promotion of Sino-Japanese Trade. In July 1955 it was renamed Local Assembly Members' League for the Promotion of International Trade. It was obviously under the influence and guidance of its members that a series of resolutions have been adopted by various local assemblies on China trade and the restoration of diplomatic relations, until they finally provoked the LDP Executive Council to issue an official refutation in March 1964.

From the point of view of the LDP a rather disturbing aspect of these movements, which seem to have gained considerable public support, has been that the opposition parties, particularly the JCP and the JSP, have been closely involved. Until its open break with the Chinese Communist Party became public in late 1965, the JCP had been bound to the latter by 'fraternal' ties which looked unshakable to an outsider. Except for the familiar factional divisions of opinion, almost precisely the same would apply to the JSP, as the joint statements issued by its official delegations visiting China and the Chinese People's Institute of Foreign Affairs have unambiguously indicated.[11] Not only the organisations specifically aiming at cultural and political *rapprochement* with China but also those primarily interested in increased trade have been under the strong influence of these two parties.

The Bureaucracy and Business Groups

The decisions and behaviour of the LDP and its members have been influenced by the international and domestic environment as reflected in and defined by the attitudes of these and other interested groups. Frequently, however, these influences have not been directly applied but rather been filtered through the bureaucracy and business groups financing the party or its individual members. These are the two principal groups which are external and yet intimately related to the party and its policy-making process.

The official position of the Ministry of Foreign Affairs on the China issue in recent years has been quite simple. It has maintained that the formal diplomatic relations with the Nationalist government should be continued and developed but that unofficial, *de facto* relations with Peking, especially in the field of trade, should be encouraged on the basis of the separation of politics and economics. In the final analysis, this policy is obviously the formula popularly known as one of 'two Chinas'. It is probably the most logical response to the situation created by the presence of two opposing governments and is an expression of the desire to deal with both in a way as advantageous as possible to Japan, economically and otherwise. Applied to the practice of Japan's diplomacy on China's admission to the U.N., the principle led her up to the 15th General Assembly (1960) to back efforts to shelve the issue. Since the 16th General Assembly (1961) she has jointly sponsored resolutions to define the issue as 'important' (as that word is used in Article 18 of the U.N. Charter), so that a decision would require a two-thirds majority vote for adoption (16th and 20th General Assemblies), or has simply opposed resolutions to replace Taipei by Peking (17th-19th General Assemblies).

When applied to Japan's trade with mainland China, this policy has meant that short of the conclusion of a governmental agreement an increase in ordinary commodity transactions is encouraged as much as possible. When,

[11]See the texts of the joint statements signed by the first to the third JSP delegations visiting China in 1957, 1959, and 1962 in Tsuji Kiyoaki (ed.), *Shiryō: Sengo nijūnen shi: 1 Seiji* (Nihonhyōronsha, 1966), pp. 666-72, and that of the fourth delegation in *Mainichi*, 30 October 1964.

however, it comes to the question of plant export involving deferred payment arrangements and the use of Export-Import Bank credits, the Foreign Office has taken a much more negative attitude. By early 1963, under the direct or implied pressure of the Nationalist Chinese and the United States governments,[12] it had formulated three general principles to guide it in determining its attitude towards specific cases: (i) that the terms of treatment accorded to mainland China by the Japanese government in this matter should be equivalent to those granted to the latter by most nations of Western Europe; (ii) that the Export-Import Bank's credits should be used for aid to those underdeveloped nations which belong to the free world and withheld as much as possible from China trade; and (iii) that the expected reactions of the United States and the Nationalist Chinese governments to Japan's transactions with mainland China involving deferred payments should be fully taken into account.

These basic positions, which have emerged through a series of intensive deliberations both among the ministry officials themselves and by *ad hoc* councils specially set up to advise the ministry,[13] have become the basis of Japan's China policy.

The main guideposts thus established by the Ministry of Foreign Affairs concerning Japan's proper relationship with Peking have been generally respected by the successive Cabinets. However, the relative emphasis placed on political and ideological ties with Taipei and economic and personal ties with Peking have varied considerably from cabinet to cabinet. With such changes in the emphasis of Japanese policy the attitudes of Peking and Taipei have also fluctuated and it has been this continual interaction that has determined the character of Sino-Japanese relations at any particular time.

Furthermore, the preoccupations of the Ministry of Foreign Affairs with the reactions of Washington and Taipei have been sharply criticised from time to time by other sections of the bureaucracy, particularly the Ministry

---

[12]In August 1963, following the Cabinet decision to approve the Kurashiki Rayon's export of vinylon plant to China, the ministry instructed Japanese ambassadors to Washington, Taipei, etc., to seek understanding of the respective governments that the deferred payment arrangements did not make the export transaction an 'aid', for it had been approved merely as part of export-promotion method, and that the People's Republic of China had not been given preferential treatment compared with other developing nations. The same points were emphasised also by Foreign Minister Ōhira and Vice-Minister Shima in their talks with the Nationalist Chinese ambassador to Japan, Chang. See Ōhira Masayoshi, *Chokumen suru gaikōmondai* (KSK Report, 177) (3 February 1964), pp. 18-20; *Asahi*, 21 and 29 August 1963.

[13]Apart from the regular consultations of the heads of the Japanese diplomatic and consular establishments in the Asia-Pacific area which have devoted considerable attention to the China issue, the intra-ministerial discussions organised in early 1961 by its *kambukai* (ranking officials' conference involving all bureau chiefs) and the *Seisakukikaku iinkai* (Policy Planning Committee) no doubt contributed very significantly to these basic ideas. Probably not as decisive but certainly important have been the contributions of such *ad hoc* bodies as the *Chūgokumondai kenkyūkai* (China Problem Study Council) of 1955 and the *Gaikōmondai kondankai* (Foreign Policy Study Forum) of 1960-1, both consisting of journalists, academics, businessmen, etc.

of International Trade and Industry (hereafter referred to as MITI).[14] In September 1963, in the face of strong protests from the Ministry of Foreign Affairs, MITI let two officials participate in the Okazaki trade delegation to China. One was Murakami Kimitaka, a director of the government-subsidised Japanese Export Trade Organisation (JETRO) and former official of MITI, and the other was Ōwada Yūji, secretary-general of the Japan-China Export-Import Union. As we have already seen, in January 1965 a minor official of MITI was appointed head of the permanent Japanese trade mission in Peking with that ministry's obvious encouragement and support. There was also a division of opinion between the two ministries concerning the export of the Kurashiki Rayon's vinylon plant in 1963.

The division of opinion within the bureaucracy has had its parallel among those businessmen who were closely related to the LDP or its members. On the one hand, a dozen or so prominent entrepreneurs, especially from the Kansai district (which was heavily dependent upon China trade before the war),[15] have consistently advocated greater efforts to expand Japan's trade with mainland China. In addition to the thirty-six 'national bourgeois' businessmen who formed the Sino-Japanese Trade Association in June 1949, President Sugi Michisuke of the Osaka Chamber of Commerce and Industry, Kawai Yoshinari of the Komatsu Manufacturing Company, and Matsubara Yosomatsu of the Hitachi Shipbuilding Company have been typical of this group. On the other hand, there have been those typified by the presidents of the most influential employers' organisations, Keidanren and Nisshō, Ishizaka Taizō and Adachi Tadashi. In the wake of the Nagasaki flag incident in 1958 Ishizaka made it very clear that he was opposed to the attempts to expand China trade at the expense of Japan's existing political commitments. His sceptical attitude has been shared not only by Adachi but also by several other prominent business leaders, such as Ishikawa Ichirō (Nissan Chemical Industry), Nagano Shigeo (Fuji Iron Manufacturing), Satō Kiichirō (Mitsui Bank), and Shinojima Hideo (Mitsubishi Chemicals).

As pointed out already, such scepticism and negative forecasts about the future of China trade gradually gave way to a much more positive, even enthusiastic, attitude among the nation's business leaders during the first half of the 1960s, especially after the 'LT memorandum' was signed in November 1962. Nevertheless, there is no evidence to suggest that the division of opinion has disappeared. On the contrary, leaders like Ishizaka and Adachi seem to

---

[14]See, for example, the attitudes of the successive MITI ministers, such as Inagaki Heitarō and Okano Kiyohide in the early postwar years, Ishibashi Tanzan and Takasaki Tatsunosuke in the latter half of the 1950s, and Fukuda Hajime and Miki Takeo in the more recent years, in *7th Diet, H.R., Gaimu, No. 13* (13 February 1950), p. 13; *Asahi*, 27 May 1953, 16 December 1954 (evening), 3 June 1955, 20 August 1958, 7 August 1962, 28 March 1963, and 12 August 1965.

[15]In 1939, for example, about 80 per cent of the trading firms based in Osaka had been engaged in China trade and in 1955 nearly 80 per cent of the one hundred firms surveyed by the city were interested in at least sending inspection teams to mainland China to find out about the trade possibilities there.

have even strengthened their opposition to deliberate efforts to increase Japan's trade and other relations with mainland China at the risk of offending Washington and Taipei. This seems, for instance, to have been the case regarding the activities of the semi-official organisation working for Japan-Taiwan co-operation, the Committee for the Promotion of Sino-Japanese Co-operation (*Nikka kyōryoku iinkai*).

This organisation was formed in 1956 following the visit to Taiwan of a Sino-Japanese friendship mission led by a senior LDP member of the National Diet, Ishii Mitsujirō, and consisting of about two dozen politicians, business-men, and publicists.[16] In the course of its half-yearly meetings held alternately in Tokyo and Taipei the Nationalist government's tough attitude towards Peking and criticisms of Japan's 'friendly' relationship with it have come to be accepted by the Japanese members with increasing appreciation and confidence.

From the outset the Chinese (Taiwan) members of the committee sharply criticised the 'pro-Peking' and 'pro-communist' attitude of the Japanese government and people. Many of the Japanese members, however, initially refused to accept such criticisms and were in fact resentful of the Chinese high-handed, self-righteous accusations. Writing about his impressions of the first meeting of April 1957, a Japanese participant, the secretary-general of Keidanren, Horikoshi, said:

They insisted that Japan was pro-communist and wrong . . . They expressed dissatisfactions and misgivings specifically about the visits of many Japanese people to communist China and the efforts to allow Peking to establish a trade mission in Japan . . . Mr Ashida Hitoshi attended one of these sessions open to public and asked them a few questions about the conditions within communist China, saying that they should certainly know much better about the problem than the Japanese people. Their answers to these questions were, however, very disappointing indeed. Although we understand well how difficult it must be for them to obtain informa-tion concerning the situation inside the country with which it deals with firearms in its hands, we could not help wondering whether they were not a little too arro-gant in charging us with pro-communism, considering that they themselves were largely ignorant of the situation . . . When we asked them about the rumour that Mr Chang Chun had recently visited Peking . . . they again failed to give us con-crete information and just accused Communist China of doing things in cowardly ways. We were not fully satisfied on this point either. . . .[17]

Largely due to this kind of scepticism and irritation prevalent among the Japanese participants, the Chinese proposal to adopt a joint resolution against further increase in Japanese trade with mainland China was flatly rejected

[16]This and following accounts of the Committee for the Promotion of Sino-Japanese Co-operation are based largely on information supplied by Mr Yatsugi Kazuo, Standing Director of the *Kokusaku kenkyūkai* (National Policy Research Association), during an interview on 9 February 1966. Mr Yatsugi was instrumental in the formation of this organisation as well as its sister committee for Japan-South Korea co-operation.
[17]See Horikoshi Teizō, 'Dai-1-kai nikka kyōryoku iinkai', *Keidanren Geppō*, V, 5 (May 1957), p. 15.

R

in June 1958. By the same token, a resolution on political co-operation adopted at the fifth meeting in October 1959 admitted that the methods to be chosen by the two governments to cope with communist aggression might naturally be different.

More recently, however, the Japanese members have gradually moved closer to Taiwan's position concerning the relationship between Tokyo and Peking. The resolution adopted at the ninth meeting in December 1964, for example, contained the following sentences:

> (1) On the basis of our common beliefs in freedom, democracy and the cultural traditions of East Asia both [Japan and Taiwan] ought to undertake to adhere steadfastly to the uncompromising renunciation of the ideology of communism and oppression and to relieve and liberate those peoples who continue to live in misery behind the iron curtain;
>
> (2) Japan undertakes to reject government-supported trade in any form with the areas under Communist Chinese control and to deny financial and banking facilities to Japanese firms trading with such areas . . . .[18]

At the tenth meeting of December 1965 both sides agreed also to ensure by all the means at their disposal that China's seat in the United Nations should be retained by the Nationalist government.

In the development of the committee and its anti-communist program a central role has apparently been played by Yatsugi Kazuo, standing director of the Kokusaku kenkyūkai, while several LDP politicians have played a substantial part.[19] It should be noted, however, that Horikoshi Teizō, secretary-general of Keidanren and Ishizaka's right-hand man, has been one of its most active members from the beginning, and both Ishizaka and Adachi have been the official leaders of the Japanese delegations to the successive half-yearly consultations. Speaking in his capacity as the head of the Japanese delegation and chairman of the tenth meeting in December 1965, Adachi referred to mainland China as a 'madman in arms' and 'veritable destroyer of world peace'.

In view of these divisions of opinion and attitude especially within the bureaucracy and business circles, opinion has also inevitably been divided within the LDP on this complex issue. At one end of the spectrum stand, for instance, Ishibashi Tanzan, Matsumura Kenzō, and Utsunomiya Tokuma, while at the opposite end stand such men as Kishi Nobusuke, Ishii Mitsujirō, and Fukuda Takeo. Others like Satō Eisaku, Ōhira Masayoshi, the late Kōno Ichirō, and the late Ikeda Hayato, have stood somewhere in between. If one were to examine closely each individual's opinion, it would be possible to place the party's 420 or so Diet members across the whole range of the pro-Peking pro-Taipei continuum.

[18]Quoted from Tsuji, op. cit., p. 677.
[19]Yatsugi (interview, 9 February 1966).

The Pro-Peking Group

None of the LDP Diet members identified as pro-Peking has ever supported communism or Marxism as such, but most have argued that the basic force in contemporary China has been nationalism rather than communism. They also claim it is quite possible for a liberal democracy and a communist state to coexist in a mutually beneficial relationship and that the creation and maintenance of such a relationship between mainland China and Japan is vital to the peace of Asia and the world, regardless of one's ideological preferences. Following his visit to China in 1962, Matsumura said at a private meeting:

> To be sure, it will be necessary for us to be on the alert . . . But once we have pledged that we will not interfere with each other's political system, is it not very natural that we should promote economic and cultural exchanges? . . . Whether China will or will not eventually give up her communism is beyond me, but I suspect that her communism, if that is what it is called, will be very Asian and significantly different from the European model . . . We feel that it is after all the rise of national consciousness that we are witnessing in China today and, if so, it is going to be lasting, though mere communism as such would fail soon . . . .[20]

Utsunomiya's views have been based on similar assumptions, as his numerous published opinions have made very clear. Writing in early 1965 after his visit to China and North Vietnam, he said:

> It would be impossible to understand the north-south problem in Asia without understanding the new nationalism rising there, especially in China . . . In brief, what is happening in China and North Vietnam today has arisen from the very simple and basic national desire of the peoples to have a Shanghai or a Saigon of their own . . . The greater the resistance to national independence and the more the basic conditions for modernisation are lacking, the more radical the method of achieving independence and modernisation tends to be . . . .[21]

About five years earlier he declared that he had explicitly made it clear to the Chinese leaders he had met during his visit to Peking in 1959 that he was neither a communist nor a socialist but just a liberal interested in the possibilities of peaceful coexistence between the two countries.

It seems evident that the views which favour closer ties with Peking on the basis of assumptions similar to these have been shared fairly widely in the LDP. Furui Yoshimi, who has been led by Matsumura to interest himself deeply in the China problem, has expressed more than once his belief that Peking is sincere when it says that peaceful coexistence with Japan is just what it wants. He argues that Peking's attitude concerning this matter is governed essentially by security considerations. According to Matsumoto Shun'ichi,

[20]Matsumura Kenzō, *Chūgoku ni tsukai shite* (KSK Report, 109) (9 October 1962), pp. 10, 15, and 17.
[21]Utsunomiya Tokuma, 'Tōzainamboku no setten ajiya: Chūgoku indoshina hōmon kara kaette', *Asahi Jānaru*, VII, 7 (14 February 1965), pp. 89-90.

'most Japanese know by intuition and common sense that Japan and communist China must coexist in peace' and 'maintenance of friendly relations between the two countries will work as a safety valve for world peace'. Somewhat more vaguely the same ideas have been put forward also by two faction leaders other than Matsumura, namely Fujiyama Aiichirō and Miki Takeo. It would not be difficult to add a dozen or more examples of LDP members publicly taking similar positions.

When it comes to the concrete reasons for their commitments, however, the motivations behind their positive views are extremely diverse. In fact, they seem to share very little beyond their common interest in bringing mainland China and Japan closer together both economically and politically. The steps advocated by them concerning specific aspects and problems of the existing relations between the two countries, particularly regarding the future of Taiwan and the Nationalist government, are more often than not too vague to be spelled out.

It would be impossible to explain Utsunomiya's devotion to the cause of Sino-Japanese friendship without referring to the influence of Marxism (in which he was keenly interested while a university student) and his father (a general with a strong belief in Asianism). It is no secret that he self-consciously carries on what he believes to be the spirit of his father's will which envisaged solidarity of Asian and African peoples against Western domination. Matsumura's interest in China also dates back to his student days at Waseda University where he was a student of the Chinese language and came personally to know the well-known China specialist of the Minseitō, Nagai Ryūnosuke.[22] He visited China for the first time in 1904, and has since returned there about ten times, both as a member of the Minseitō and later as a senior LDP member. Considering the peculiar importance of personal experience and connections in his and other LDP politicians' roles in Sino-Japanese relations, it may be also relevant to point out that he has long been personally acquainted with many Peking leaders, including Prime Minister Chou and Foreign Minister Chen. The president of the China-Japan Friendship Association and Chinese signatory to the LT memorandum of 1962, Liao Cheng-chih, studied at Waseda University and is therefore Matsumura's alumnus. Fujiyama's cultural interest in China became very evident around 1937, when he sponsored a China Study Society and set out to collect some 60,000 books on modern China in the fields of local history, novels, poetry, etc.

These examples show that the motivations which have led these prominent LDP members to interest themselves in the China issue were above all particular, personal, and diverse. It would be idle to attempt to generalise about them in the familiar organisational or ideological terms. Similarly, much of

[22]Both for information and suggestions concerning Matsumura's relationship with Nagai, the writer owes much to Mr Matsumoto Shigeharu, director of the International House of Japan. An informal interview was held on 9 January 1966.

the pro-Peking feeling exhibited by LDP members has been general and emotional rather than specific and logical and, as a result, it is hard to pinpoint what they propose to do about making political arrangements with Peking or the future of Taiwan. Fujiyama, for example, argues:

> *Putting aside the problems of recognition, and so on,* I doubt whether it is desirable from the point of view of world peace to keep the 600 million Chinese people from the international community . . . *Without referring to recognition, admission to the United Nations, and so on* . . . would it not be a good idea to give her opportunities to speak on the official platforms of international politics . . . Frankly *I am not thinking in terms of recognition of the government or admission to the U.N.* . . . (My italics.)[23]

Fujiyama's ambiguities and evasiveness have been shared by many, in fact by most, of those who have been identified as pro-Peking in the LDP.[24] Even Matsumura has not gone much further in specifying his program than to reiterate his wish that Japan should play a mediating role between Peking and the governments of Western powers, especially the United States. Only Ishibashi and Utsunomiya have produced specific plans concerning the political aspects of Sino-Japanese relations. Regardless of whether these are realistic or utopian, they deserve attention because of their rarity.

Neither of the two interrelated plans advocated by Ishibashi is very original. On one hand, he calls for the conclusion of a treaty of alliance between four nations (or possibly five nations with Taiwan as an additional party), namely the U.S.A., the U.S.S.R., the People's Republic of China, and Japan—a plan which, he has claimed, was accepted in principle by Peking in 1963. On the other hand, he proposes to mediate between Peking and Taipei, so that Chiang may be accorded by Peking the status of generalissimo and the two governments may thus be unified. Provided that they were accepted by the governments concerned, these plans would be ideal from the Japanese point of view. There is no evidence, however, that there is much possibility of their being taken seriously by them in a foreseeable future.

Utsunomiya's plan for the solution of the Taiwan problem has emphasised much more boldly the need for its acceptability to Peking. It would involve making Taiwan a 'highly autonomous' province, 'somewhat resembling

[23]Fujiyama Aiichirō, *Jikyokushokan* (KSK 'Denā kurabu' kōen, 16) (5 September 1963), pp. 24-5.
[24]Yamaguchi Kikuichirō, who believes that it is important that an atmosphere of friendliness be fostered especially between nations ideologically opposed to each other, has had this to say about the Taiwan problem: 'If no war breaks out in East Asia within ten years or so, both Chiang Kai-shek and Mao Tse-tung will eventually be in their graves. All the troubles will be resolved by time. The passage of time is the key to peace.' Yamaguchi Kikuichirō, *Hoshutō kara mita shinchūgoku* (Yomiuri shimbunsha, 1955), pp. 114-18, and his talk at the 'Getsuyōkai' meeting of Kokumin seiji kenkyūkai on 18 January 1966. On his appointment as Minister of International Trade and Industry in 1965, Miki Takeo said: 'On the one hand, we want to develop trade with China, but, on the other, we have various other commitments . . . The Japanese people tend to wish that everything could be decided clearly one way or the other, but this issue of China could not be decided in such a fashion . . .' See 'Nanmon ni idomu shinkakuryō', Part 2, *Asahi*, 5 June 1965.

Byelorussia or the Ukraine in the U.S.S.R.', with powers over international trade, immigration and, possibly, even defence. It might also enjoy an independent seat in the United Nations General Assembly. Such an arrangement, however, would be of temporary duration and after the United States military establishments and troops were withdrawn the possibility of a different arrangement would naturally arise.

With a great deal of emotional enthusiasm and few concrete plans, these pro-Peking elements in the LDP proceeded in early 1960 to form informal intra-party groups called *Chūgokumondai kenkyūkai* (China Problem Study Group) and *Nitchū kaizen kenkyūkai* (Study Group for the Improvement of Japan-China Relations) led respectively by Matsumura faction members, and Utsunomiya and Ishibashi faction members. In December of the same year, these were unified into a single *Nitchūmondai kenkyūkai* (Japan-China Problem Study Group), but soon ceased to be active because of pressure from the party leaders who insisted that debate on the issue should take place within the official Investigation Committee on Foreign Affairs. However, four years later, in January 1965, this group was revived as the Afro-Asian Group, following by about a month the formation of the Asian Group by a rival 'pro-Taiwan' group in the party.

Sponsored by twenty-four of the most active pro-Peking members, including Matsumura, Utsunomiya, and Fujiyama, the Afro-Asian Group initially consisted of 104 members from both Houses of the Diet and set out to deal with such problems as Japan's attitude towards the forthcoming second Afro-Asian Conference, the Vietnam issue, and the Malaysian dispute as well as relations with the People's Republic of China. By the middle of 1966 seven sub-committees specialising in different areas had been set up under a loosely organised governing body made up of nine 'caretakers' and five standing directors.[25]

So far as the China issue is concerned, it proposes: (i) to have the People's Republic of China admitted to the United Nations; (ii) to refuse in the future to support any U.N. resolution to regard China's representation as 'important'; (iii) to encourage direct contact between the two governments through ambassadorial talks and other means; and (iv) to expand trade by the conclusion of an official agreement.

Apart from its weekly study sessions, attended by anything between ten and thirty of its members,[26] the Afro-Asian Group in May 1965 sent a 6-man delegation of its own members to Indonesia at President Sukarno's invitation, organised a widely publicised three-day 'teach-in' on the China issue in May 1966, informally sponsored the visit to China of an 8-member LDP delega-

[25]The sub-committees deal with the following areas: (i) Vietnam and Indo-China; (ii) China; (iii) Indonesia; (iv) Africa; (v) Korea; (vi) Middle East; and (vii) India and Pakistan.
[26]Much of the following description of the Afro-Asian Group's activities is based on information supplied by Mr Utsunomiya Tokuma in an interview on 11 February 1966.

tion in August and September 1966, and following its return organised a signature-collecting campaign against Japan's co-sponsorship of the U.N. draft resolution on the designation of China's representation as an 'important' question. However, by February 1966 the original membership of over one hundred had diminished to about eighty,[27] while the number of its members present at the above-mentioned 'teach-in' was said to have varied between one and thirteen. Therefore the group apparently failed to make much headway during the first two years of its existence.

The Pro-Taipei Group

In contrast to the above-mentioned group of pro-Peking LDP members represented by Matsumura and Utsunomiya, a numerically larger group, including such senior party members as Kishi, Fukuda, and Ishii, has taken a generally anti-Peking, pro-Taipei position.

Just as none of the pro-Peking members has ever advocated communism or Marxism, whether Chinese or otherwise, few of those associated with the anti-Peking group have in principle opposed trade relations with mainland China. Fukuda has said, for example, that he welcomes positive efforts to expand Japan's trade with China, provided that her independence and freedom of action is firmly upheld. The same idea was in fact expressed a few years before by another fervent advocate of the anti-Peking line, Kaya Okinori. He once declared:

> [Japan] ought to trade with any and every country. She cannot survive without importing raw materials. From such a point of view, it must be said as a matter of principle that she must have peaceful trade. In this respect a communist nation cannot be excluded . . . .[28]

In contrast to the pro-Peking group, however, they insist that such trade should not be expanded at the expense of the basic principles of Japanese foreign policy, which in their view include above all the maintenance and development of friendly relations with the United States and Nationalist China. Thus Fukuda followed up his above-mentioned statement in favour of encouraging mainland trade with a blunt endorsement of his questioner's suspicion that he would rather see such trade completely terminated than allow Japan to yield to 'unreasonable' Chinese pressure. Nor would Kaya ever agree to giving Peking terms in business transactions more favourable than those Japan grants to free world nations. He would not tolerate Japan's dependence on the communist bloc for basic and essential raw materials, nor the abandonment of the principle of the separation of politics and economics, nor violation of the COCOM restrictions.

[27]Utsunomiya (interview, 11 February 1966). According to other sources, there were 87 dues-paying members in March 1966 and 97 in May. It is possible that there was some increase during 1966 from the low point reached at the beginning of the year.
[28]Kaya Okinori, *Jimintō no shinseisaku* (KSK Report, 113) (5 November 1962), pp. 16-17.

While those associated with the pro-Peking group tend to emphasise the elements of nationalism in Chinese communism or Maoism, the anti-Peking group tends to view the relationship between Japan and mainland China under the present régime essentially as one of ideological struggle between a liberal democracy and a doctrinaire and destructive communist power. This leads them to the position that, in the interests of Japan's security, Nationalist China as well as South Korea should never be allowed to fall prey to communism and that, therefore, the Nationalist government should be helped to keep going by all means available. Many of them further feel that Japan's own economic prosperity has been achieved largely thanks to the enormous sacrifices made by these governments which have gallantly devoted a large part of their limited resources to the defence against Chinese communism not only for their own but also indirectly for Japan's sake.

These considerations about Japan's security interests are mixed with the emotional argument that, at the end of World War II, Chiang Kai-shek treated the Japanese in China, including prisoners of war, with unparalleled magnanimity, and that the Japanese are morally bound to repay his kindness. A typical example of this argument is found in the declaration of a mass rally organised to welcome Chang Chun on 19 September 1957, which was attended by many LDP members, including Prime Minister Kishi, Speaker of the House of Representatives Masutani, and President of the House of Councillors Matsuno. It enumerated Chiang's 'magnanimous' acts as follows: (i) at the Cairo Conference of 1943 he had firmly insisted on leaving the matter of deciding Japan's future political system up to the Japanese people themselves against the wishes of Roosevelt and Churchill; (ii) on hearing about the Japanese Emperor's acceptance of the Potsdam Proclamation on 15 August 1945, he immediately called on the Chinese people by radio to repay the Japanese wartime atrocities with forgiveness and generosity; (iii) unlike some 'other governments', he had seen to it that millions of the Japanese in China were repatriated and war criminals released promptly; and (iv) despite the enormous damages caused to China by Japan during the war, he had announced that he intended to give up China's reparation claims against Japan. As the Committee for the Promotion of Sino-Japanese Co-operation has become more and more openly and militantly anti-Peking, the most active of the LDP Diet members who fall in this category have associated themselves with it. Whereas until the middle of 1958 only Funada Naka had been officially associated with it while a senior member of the JSP, Matsuoka Komakichi, still retained his affiliation with it, by late 1959 there were half a dozen LDP men but no JSP member among its official affiliates, and by early 1961 the former number had increased to about a dozen. Through this organisation they have been directly connected not only with the official and business circles of Nationalist China but also with those Japanese business leaders who have constituted the hardcore of the anti-

Peking groups in the nation's business community, such as, for example, Ishizaka and Adachi.

At the same time, they have acted as intermediaries between the Nationalist and the Japanese governments, thus providing a semi-official line of communication between them. Following his attendance at the eighth meeting of the committee in May 1963, Funada Naka conveyed to the Japanese Ministers of Foreign Affairs and of International Trade and Industry Taipei's strong objections to Japan's prospective export of industrial plant to mainland China and to the Japanese leaders' personally meeting visiting Peking officials. The significance of the influences exerted by the committee's members in the making of Japan's China policy has also been implicitly acknowledged even by an official of the Ministry of Foreign Affairs.

Even more significant, however, was the formation in December 1964 of the Asian Group in the LDP. Organised under Kaya's leadership with an initial membership of ninety-eight LDP Diet members, it took from the beginning a fairly clear-cut position about Japan's future relationships with Peking and Taipei, which may be summarised roughly as follows:

(i) The People's Republic of China must not be admitted to the United Nations so long as it persists in its 'aggressive' intentions.

(ii) For reasons of Japan's own security, among other things, Taiwan must be kept from communist take-over.

(iii) The problem of China's representation in the United Nations must continue to be regarded as an 'important' question, requiring a two-thirds majority vote for adoption.

(iv) Trade with mainland China must be conducted on the basis of the separation of politics and economics without involving the use of Export-Import Bank credits or terms more favourable than those applicable to Japan's trade with South Korea, Taiwan or other 'Free World' nations.[29]

Apart from its *ad hoc* study sessions usually held every fortnight, the Asian Group sponsored the formation of an Asian Parliamentary Union in February and its first conference (in Tokyo) in December 1965 at which thirty-four delegates from nine non-communist nations in the region participated.[30] By the end of February 1966 six regional sections were established in the group and by May of the same year the number of members had increased to nearly 170. In September 1966, when the 8-man team of the Afro-Asian Group members was visiting the People's Republic of China and North Korea, Kishi led a delegation of nineteen recruited from the Asian Group to South Korea to attend the second conference of the Asian Parliamentary Union.

[29] The writer was supplied with the basic information concerning the Asian Group and its activities by Mr Tanigawa Kazuho, member of the House of Representatives, and the group's liaison officer, in an interview held on 11 February 1966.

[30] The nations represented at the conference were: the Republic of China, the Philippines, South Korea, India, Laos, Malaysia, Thailand, South Vietnam, and Japan. Tanigawa (interview, 11 February 1966).

As we have seen above, all the positions that the Asian Group has publicly advocated so far are basically defensive of the *status quo* on the China issue. There is little doubt that its minimal and most fundamental demand is the prevention of Taiwan's falling into the hands of Peking. Its active sponsorship of the Asian Parliamentary Union suggests, however, that its intentions are probably somewhat more vigorous. In many respects this organisation inherits the tradition of and works in close collaboration with the Asian People's Anti-Communist League, which was first formed in 1954 by Chiang Kai-shek and Syngman Rhee with a view to linking up the non-communist states in the region in a grand anti-communist, anti-China alliance. The Japanese delegation attending the league's Eighth Conference in Tokyo in 1962 was led by Kishi and included, among others, some of the most militant leaders of the Asian Group, such as Ishii Mitsujirō, Kitazawa Naokichi, Chiba Saburō, and Funada Naka. Needless to say, most of these LDP parliamentarians are at the same time leaders also of the Committee for the Promotion of Sino-Japanese Co-operation. Within the LDP itself the Asian Group is intimately associated, again not surprisingly, with the nationalist group, Soshinkai, as is suggested by the fact that thirty-six of its original ninety-eight members were formally affiliated with that group. These international and domestic linkages are then what define the basic character and functions of the LDP Asian Group.

LDP Policy-making

Between these two opposing groups nearly half of the LDP members have remained more or less uncommitted or floating in their attitudes toward the issue. The late Kōno Ichirō and the late Ikeda Hayato were typical examples. Kōno had apparently been favourably disposed toward an improvement in Japan's relations with mainland China before he travelled in the United States and Europe in late 1959. It was he who had in fact advised Prime Minister Kishi in February of that year to send an official LDP representative of a cabinet minister's rank to Peking. Following that trip, however, he became much more cautious and evasive over this issue. Similarly, Ikeda aired some positive views on the matter at one stage but subsequently considerably moderated his advocacy of a 'positive approach' in public statements. Satō Eisaku, Ōhira Masayoshi, Ishida Hirohide, and Shīna Etsusaburō have all been equally non-committal and deliberately vague in their public pronouncements on the subject.[31] Despite, however, the numerical importance of this

[31]For Satō's views see 'Nitchūmondai no haikei', Part 10, *Asahi*, 9 May 1961; and 'Nan Kanshin no yonjūnichi', *Ekonomisuto*, XLIII, 23 (2 June 1964), pp. 24-8. In his lecture of 28 January 1966 Ōhira advised that Japan's economic prosperity must be based upon co-operation with the 'Pacific' nations, that it would be impossible for her to rely on the 'continent' for future economic growth, and that the China issue must be considered above all in terms of Japan's security interests. According to Takahashi Takehiko of *Mainichi*, Ishida had made up his mind about May 1961 to keep silent on the subject for at least three years. See Fukuda Takeo, *Tōsanyaku ni kiku: Sono*

neutral group and the mediative influence which it is potentially capable of exerting on the antagonistic groups, opinion in the party concerning the issue has become increasingly polarised and the decision-making process has been complicated by the conflicts between the two groups.

As already pointed out, the motivations of individual LDP members for associating, or not associating, with either of the two opposing groups seem too diverse and personal to permit generalisation. It is nevertheless important to emphasise the significance of their occupational backgrounds as one of the factors involved. Most conspicuous in this regard is the behaviour of former public servants. Of those in the House of Representatives 46·5 per cent belong to the Asian and only about 11 per cent to the Afro-Asian Group (see Table 26). They are by far the largest component group (36·1 per cent) in the

TABLE 26

Occupational backgrounds of the Asian and Afro-Asian Group members, MHRs only, July 1966

	Members of Asian Group	Members of Afro-Asian Group	Members of both groups or neither group	Total
Local politicians	21	14	36	71
Public servants	34	8	31	73
Businessmen	13	12	21	46
Lawyers	3	1	9	13
Journalists	6	11	13	30
Miscellaneous	17	11	24	52
Total	94	57	134	285

Sources: Kokkai binran, 32nd ed. (March 1966), pp. 99-150; *GSS: Shūgiingiin meikan;* 'Saiten: Zen shūgiingiin no seijinōryoku', *Gendai no Me,* VII, 7 (July 1966), pp. 148-87.

former and nearly the least significant element (14 per cent) in the latter. Former journalists and businessmen, on the other hand, tend to prefer the Afro-Asian Group, an overwhelming majority of the former and nearly half of the latter being associated with it and together constituting 40 per cent of its total membership. Former local politicians prefer the Asian Group, by a ratio of about three to two, but due to their overall numerical size are the largest single category in the Afro-Asian Group, supplying about a quarter of its membership. It should also be noted that the former public servants and journalists are relatively the most articulate and committed.

(1): *Jikyoku wo kou miru* (KSK Report, 39) (22 May 1961), p. 31. Shīna's prescription has been: 'What is important is to keep in our minds that liberalism and communism are fundamentally opposed to each other. Without forgetting about that fact, we ought to trade, promote cultural exchanges, conclude treaties and co-operate economically with her [mainland China] . . .' Shīna Etsusaburō, *Dōwa to seiji* (Tōyō seiji keizai kenkyūjo, 1963), p. 147.

The contrast between the two groups in terms of the relative proportions of different occupational categories in their membership composition (symbolised and personified by Kaya in the one and Matsumura and Utsunomiya in the other) largely defines their respective relationships with the bureaucracy over the issue. From the foregoing description of their opposing positions it is clear that the Asian Group's views are basically the same as those publicly taken by the Ministry of Foreign Affairs, whereas those of the Afro-Asian Group are basically opposed to them. This means that one operates with the support and co-operation, direct or indirect, of the ministry, while the other has to act in the face of its actual or potential opposition and resistance. This contrast no doubt tends to strengthen the position of the Asian Group in relation to that of the Afro-Asian Group and a situation similar to that which exists between the LDP and the JSP at the level of national politics arises between them within the organisational framework of the single party.

What, however, makes the relationship between the two groups so complicated and charged with emotion as it has apparently become is not only the ideological and policy differences relating to the occupational experience and background of their members; it is also closely bound up with intra-party factionalism.

Certainly both groups are cross-factional in the sense that their members are drawn from all but two factional units identified in the party (see Table 27). Very significantly, however, over 60 per cent of the members of the Asian Group come from the Ishii, Fukuda, Miki, and Satō factions, only

TABLE 27

Distribution of Asian and Afro-Asian Group members by factions, MHRs only, July 1966

Factions	Members of Asian Group	Members of Afro-Asian Group	Members of both groups or neither group	Total
Ishii	12	0	2	14
Fukuda	11	1	8	20
Miki	16	2	12	30
Satō	19	3	22	44
Fujiyama	6	3	9	18
Kawashima	5	2	11	18
Maeo	12	6	29	47
Independents	3	4	9	16
Ōno	5	8	14	27
Kōno	5	22	18	45
Matsumura	0	6	0	6
Total	94	57	134	285

Sources: Kokkai binran, 32nd ed. (March 1966), pp. 332-5; 'Saiten: Zen shūgiingiin no seijinōryoku', *Gendai no Me*, VII, 7 (July 1966), pp. 148-87; 'Jimintō ni bunka genshō', *Sankei*, 4 May 1965.

about 5 per cent from the former Kōno, and none at all from the Matsumura factions. On the other hand, nearly a half of the Afro-Asian Group's members belong to the last two factions and only about 10 per cent to the other four factions combined. In the two extreme cases 85·6 per cent of the Ishii faction members and 100 per cent of Matsumura's followers belong respectively to the Asian and the Afro-Asian Groups. Between these two extremes all factions (with the single exception of the Fujiyama faction) conform to the basic pattern that the higher the percentage of members associated with one group, the relatively lower the percentage of members associated with the other group.

The relationship between the membership compositions of the two China groups and of the factions as indicated by the above-mentioned patterns assumes singular importance when it is realised that since Satō became Prime Minister towards the end of 1964 (which was when both China groups were formed), the four factions supplying the Asian Group with the bulk of its members have constituted the dominant inter-factional alliance (together with the Kawashima faction) while the two which provide the Afro-Asian Group with a half of its members have formed the hard core of the dissident factional alliance in opposition to it. Consequently, the competition and antagonisms between the two groups inevitably take on the character of familiar inter-factional rivalries between the dominant and dissident alliances. This is why the competition tends to become highly personalised and emotional as well as programmatic and ideological.[32]

Another important fact about the two groups concerns the role of the formal party organs in the making of the party's China policy. To be noted first of all in this respect is the fact that no formal party decision on the China issue has yet been made. In connection with the prospective conclusion of the fourth private trade agreement in early 1958 the executive council did take the step of officially advising the Cabinet to make sure that the text of the agreement should not include provisions which might be interpreted as a gesture of recognition by Japan of the Peking government. Also, it was the semi-official decision-making organ, the six leaders' meeting, which decided in June of that year to disband the Diet Members' League for the Promotion of Sino-Japanese Trade. Since then, however, the issue has been considered by the party almost exclusively at the level of the PARC Investigation Committee on Foreign Affairs, briefly supplemented in 1959 and 1960 by a PARC Special Committee on Sino-Japanese Trade.

The deliberations on the part of the Investigation Committee on Foreign Affairs have been decisively governed by the fact that members are divided

[32]'The war criminals and bureaucrats like Kaya dominate our party . . . They have a highly developed superiority complex and extensive connections with big business and interest groups, but they have no political scruples or morality . . . The Asian Group is run by the Taiwan and Korean lobby, but these countries subsist solely on the United States' anti-communist policy . . . How could you expect me to sit and talk with people like Kaya?' Utsunomiya (interview, 11 February 1966).

with Hitachi on 6 April, and on 30 April the contract with Dainihon composition the numerical balance of the two groups has been in favour of the Asian Group. This group (or before its formation those who would have favoured its position) has contributed over two-thirds of those committee members known to be committed to one position or the other. For example, counting only those MHRs whose affiliations with either group may be definitely ascertained as of November 1964, the ratios of the Asian and the Afro-Asian Group members in the committee were 2 to 1 for the vice-chairmen and 33 to 10 for other members, one vice-chairman and twenty-two other members being associated with both or neither. The comparable ratios in November 1965 were 5 to 3 for the vice-chairmen and 38 to 16 for other members, two vice-chairmen and twenty-one others being identified with both or neither. As a result of this division of opinion among its members the committee has found it impossible to produce clear-cut recommendations. By the same token, because of the imbalance in the numerical strength of the two groups pointed out above, when compelled by circumstances to outline its position, it has emphasised the views of the majority, which are generally opposed to closer political ties or communication with Peking.

An early example of its deliberate refusal to take a stand on the issue was when in May 1957 it included the China issue in a five-point investigation program but omitted it from the final report which emerged out of the investigation.[33] In August 1960, it prepared a 'Basic Policy on Foreign Affairs' which advised that the issue be properly dealt with, 'carefully taking into account both the attitude of Communist China and changes in international conditions . . .'.[34] The paper produced in May 1961 by the China sub-committee (established within the Committee on Foreign Affairs on 9 April 1960) has since been known as the 'Interim Report'. This would have become the first official party decision on China, for it was duly approved by the executive council and was reported to the Cabinet. It presented, however, no policy 'decisions' or specific proposals but merely enumerated and described the mutually conflicting and contradictory views heard in the course of its deliberations. The only conclusion it contained at the end of the report was exactly the same as the 'Basic Policy on Foreign Affairs' of the previous summer.

It is obvious that the ambiguities of the wording in the interim report of 1961 directly reflected the conflict between the majority and the minority groups in the committee. Against the former, members of the latter, such as Ide Ichitarō and Sakurauchi Yoshio, argued that an official trade agreement

---

[33]The study program included specifically the following five subjects: (i) Japan's position over the defence issue; (ii) the Security Treaty and the Administrative Agreement between Japan and the United States; (iii) Okinawa; (iv) Prime Minister Kishi's prospective Southeast Asian tour; and (v) the China issue. The 'Foreign Policy Report' which emerged out of the deliberations, however, included only the first four subjects.
[34]*Asahi*, 16 August 1960 (evening).

should be concluded between the two governments to encourage trade, while Utsunomiya Tokuma and Nohara Masakatsu went further to call for an immediate recognition of the Peking government. More recently, following the French recognition of that government in January 1964, the committee meeting on 22 January saw an open clash of views between Utsunomiya and Maeda Masao over the question of whether the Japanese government should follow the French example or persist in its refusal to deal officially with Peking.

The internal division of opinion, however, has not always prevented the majority point of view from being made known to outsiders, and the committee as a whole has exerted an influence suppressive of the growth of a pro-Peking climate of opinion in the party and official circles at large. At the time the negotiations on the fourth trade agreement were being conducted in early 1958 the party leaders were no doubt aware that a majority of the members of the committee were strongly opposed to some specific provisions of the draft agreement. When a delegate from the Tokyo Metropolitan Federation of the Party Branches, speaking to a meeting of branch officials in March 1961, referred to the need to put forward 'positive' views on China in order to win votes for the party at the polls, the committee's chairman, Nomura Kichisaburō, emphatically stated that most of its members neither regarded Taiwan as part of Communist China nor would they acquiesce in Japan's 'flirting' with Peking. Before he left for Peking in 1962 to sign the LT memorandum, Takasaki Tatsunosuke was 'invited' to meet the committee and was reminded that its members did not want him to arrange with the Chinese leaders a trade relationship which might benefit the communist bloc, especially such arrangements as might involve deferred payments.

In view of the tendencies typified by these examples it is hardly surprising that the Asian Group claims that it represents the official party line and insists that the only official party line is what a majority in the official Committee on Foreign Affairs defines to be such. On the other hand, the Afro-Asian Group just as understandably prefers to stay away from the committee.[35] In fact, it was precisely because of this anti-Peking inclination exhibited by the official party organ and the difficulty of changing it that the pro-Peking elements in early 1960 felt compelled to form the antecedents of the Afro-Asian Group.

In early 1965, following the formation of the two rival groups, the number of vice-chairmen of the LDP Committee on Foreign Affairs was increased from three to twelve in an attempt to force them to carry on the controversy within the framework of the official party organ. Two members representing each side were included in this enlarged group of vice-chairmen: Nadao Hirokichi and Ikeda Masanosuke representing the Asian Group and Furui

[35]Tanigawa and Utsunomiya (interviews, 11 February 1966). According to Utsunomiya, he had tried more than once to have the committee reorganised but had given up the attempt and now wanted to have nothing to do with it.

Yoshimi and Takeyama Yūtarō the Afro-Asian Group. At the same time, two advisers for each group—Ishii Mitsujirō and Kaya Okinori of the former and Fujiyama Aiichirō and Matsumura Kenzō of the latter—were nominated Advisers to the LDP Committee. These steps have, however, apparently failed to prevent the controversy from developing outside the official organ and, therefore, beyond the party leaders' direct control. As we have seen already, both groups have subsequently intensified, rather than reduced, their opinion-forming and policy-making activities and seem bound to continue to do so in the months to come. The Asian Group remains a numerically dominant group in power while the Afro-Asian Group continues as an ideologically radical and militant minority perpetually out of power and unable to secure a majority.

Given the conditions described above, characterised predominantly by divisions of opinion and attitude both among the bureaucracy and the financial patrons of the party and, more importantly, among its own members, the LDP has been unable to make its own decisions or put forward policy proposals concerning the China issue. The only notable exceptions have been the polemical statements attacking each of the successive joint communiqués issued since April 1957 by JSP delegations while visiting Peking, and the 'Unified Views' handed out to local assemblies to dissuade them from adopting or publishing resolutions calling for the early normalisation of diplomatic relations with Peking.

Apart from the extraordinarily aggressive and inflammatory language used in the attacks on the alleged role of the JSP as Peking's mouthpiece, the positions taken by the party leadership in the 'Unified Views' and other official pronouncements have all been mere reiterations of the Ministry of Foreign Affairs' basic propositions. They amount to the application of the principle of separating the official, governmental relations (which should be maintained with the Nationalist government and must not be established with Peking) from unofficial relations, especially trade (which may be, if necessary, maintained and developed with mainland China as well). In other words, the LDP has never made a policy of its own but merely followed the lead of the bureaucrats. The divisions of opinion arising from the peculiarities of the party's membership composition, magnified and complicated by the complex ties it maintains with extra-party groups and the influences of intra-party factionalism, have made it impossible for its formal decision-making organs to exercise a significant amount of initiative or leadership.

The policy towards the People's Republic of China, predicated on the assumption that official diplomatic relations and unofficial economic relations may be separated and that the latter should be promoted without involving the former, has been inherited by the LDP from the Liberal Party. The conflicting international and domestic influences have since prevented the party from developing its own policy beyond this general, somewhat ambiguous doctrine.

Internationally, the attitudes of the two governments most closely associated with Japan and most immediately interested in her treatment of the issue, those of Nationalist China and the United States, have both restrained active attempts by the Japanese government to increase trade and other forms of contact with Peking, not to speak of normalising official diplomatic relations. Domestically, however, both public opinion as reflected in various opinion polls and the national and local legislatures acting generally in accordance with the trends of such public opinion have worked as a pressure towards increased contact and exchanges with mainland China, at least at the unofficial level.

Much more decisive from the point of view of the LDP policy-making process has been the fact that opinion has remained sharply divided between the ministries, especially between the Ministry of Foreign Affairs and the Ministry of International Trade and Industry, and among leading business-men. In so far as the bureaucracy and the business world are related to the party as the sources of its material and technical support, the divisions in them have inevitably introduced similar conflicts of opinion within the LDP.

The pro-Peking group, represented after January 1965 by the Afro-Asian Group, has advocated a policy line much more positive than that so far pursued by the Ministry of Foreign Affairs. This group has, however, re-mained a minority in the parliamentary party and has not been able to go much further than opposing and obstructing the more negative majority line. The pro-Taipei group, represented by the Asian Group, on the other hand, has been insisting on maintaining the close political and economic ties with Nationalist China and preventing Peking from being admitted to the U.N. at the expense of Taipei. Outside the party this group has been associated both with the Committee for the Promotion of Sino-Japanese Co-operation and the Asian Parliamentary Union, and within the party with Soshinkai.

In terms of occupational categories, former high-ranking public servants have tended strongly to associate themselves with the Asian Group and former journalists and businessmen with the Afro-Asian Group. Former local politicians have shown a fairly neutral or non-committal attitude.

In terms of the intra-party factions, the one group has been supported by the dominant factions under Satō's presidency, the Ishii, Fukuda, Miki, and Satō factions. The other group, on the other hand, has been closely identified with the two most articulate dissident factions, the Matsumura and former Kōno factions. The factional implications of the conflict have naturally tended to make it much more bitter and emotional than it would have been otherwise.

It has been the Asian Group which has succeeded, thanks to its majority

S

position, in dominating the official party organs, particularly the PARC Investigation Committee on Foreign Affairs. The sharp division of opinion, however, has prevented the higher decision-making organs, the PARC deliberation commission and the executive council, from making clear-cut and explicit decisions in favour of one or the other position. As a result, the LDP as a whole has never been able to pronounce an independent policy of its own regarding the issue but has simply followed the lead of the Ministry of Foreign Affairs.

Conclusion

Policy-making in the Liberal-Democratic Party involves extremely complex processes of interaction between the four factors which have been chosen for intensive examination in this study. The patterns of interaction between these four factors and other less conspicuous variables are even more complex and difficult to formulate into neat generalisations. It will nevertheless be useful to summarise and integrate in a series of explicit propositions such findings and conclusions as have emerged from the present study which have so far been left largely implicit. These generalisations may not necessarily explain the party's behaviour in all actual situations of policy-making, but they will probably provide at least elementary clues to a fuller description and explication of the party's behavioural characteristics.

A fact of basic importance to be taken into consideration in a discussion of the LDP is that in terms of both its membership structure and organisational characteristics it is a typical parliamentary party. We have seen that its non-parliamentary membership is largely nominal and extremely unstable, that its local organisation is weak and ineffective, and that all positions at the headquarters are controlled exclusively by members of the Diet. Two important characteristics of the party's behaviour in policy-making situations derive from this fact.

For all practical purposes the formal policy-making process of the party may be regarded as a closed circuit originating and terminating within the confines of the parliamentary party organisation. It is hardly influenced to any significant extent by the wills or actions of the non-parliamentary party members or the local branches, neither of which are in a position to determine party decisions more effectively or directly than extra-party groups or ordinary voters. In none of the cases reviewed in this study have they ever played a role of any significance.

The other fact to be noted in this connection is that, because of the weakness of its non-parliamentary membership and local organisation, the LDP is compelled to depend very greatly upon various extra-party groups for the acquisition of funds and votes which are vital to its survival as an effective

263

party organisation operating under a competitive system. A corollary of this situation is that an important part of the party's policy-making activity is necessarily concerned with the task of rewarding such extra-party groups as are capable, whether actually or potentially, of supplying it with funds and votes. It was as much because of the votes believed to be under its control as of its intense lobbying activities that the National Farmland League finally moved the LDP to take steps necessary for the disbursement of public moneys for the sake of its members despite the opposition of the other parties and the ministries concerned. Conversely, the reason why it was dissuaded from taking positive measures in connection with the constitutional issue was partly the decline of enthusiasm on the part of business circles.

The technical needs of such policy-making activity on behalf of the providers of funds and votes require the assistance of the various ministries of the national public service. The acceptance of the latter's help in turn obliges the party to heed their wishes and *inter alia* to undertake legislative actions designed to enlarge their powers and budgetary appropriations. One of the reasons why the LDP leaders showed reluctance to deal speedily with the demands of the National Farmland League was the opposition of the Ministry of Finance and the Ministry of Agriculture and Forestry. The dominant view in the LDP on the relationship with the People's Republic of China has been strictly in agreement with the guideposts established by the Ministry of Foreign Affairs, embodied in the doctrine of the separation of politics and economics and implicit commitment to the 'two Chinas' formula. In both cases the party's hands have been bound to a considerable extent by the attitudes of the sections of the bureaucracy.

The policy-making organs of the party tend to be preoccupied with satisfying the demands from these two broad categories of extra-party groups. The interests and opinions of those who belong to neither are much less likely to become the subjects of the party's official policy-making activity.

Of the principal kinds of policy decisions made by the party in accordance with the wishes of interest groups or the bureaucracy, the bulk may be regarded as 'routine' and non-controversial. These are dealt with by a chain of formal policy-making organs consisting of the fifteen divisions and the deliberation commission of the PARC, and the executive council. When declared as 'party decisions' by the last, they are usually introduced as Cabinet-sponsored bills into the Diet by the LDP Diet Policy Committee, or referred to the appropriate ministry for administrative action. In this process former high-ranking public servants, who have unique educational and occupational experience, play a leading role, while former local politicians tend to play a subordinate and much less conspicuous role. The fact that each ministry has its parallel division in the PARC symbolises the relationship between the party policy-making process and the bureaucracy in routine policy-making situations.

If the issues involved are controversial, decisions cannot be made so easily and smoothly through this chain of formal policy-making organs. The PARC divisions are much too occupied with routine policy-making to deal adequately with such issues. It therefore becomes necessary for a controversial issue to be dealt with by an *ad hoc* investigation committee set up within the PARC separately from the divisions. The Investigation Committee on the Farmland Problem, the Committee on the Constitution, and the Committee on Foreign Affairs (especially its sub-committee on China) were all set up for the purpose of dealing with the special and more or less controversial issues which could not be disposed of by the existing divisions.

The role of former public servants is as prominent in relation to a controversial issue as in routine policy-making situations. It seems evident that a number of former bureaucrats were used by the National Farmland League as its official representatives in negotiations with (or blackmail against) the reluctant ministries. In connection with the constitutional issue one of the most prominent aspects of the official LDP Committee on the Constitution and the unofficial intra-party group, Soshinkai, has been the preponderance of former bureaucrats. They also provided the hard core of the pro-Taipei, anti-Peking group, represented by the Asian Group which works with the support and co-operation of the Ministry of Foreign Affairs. Apart from the tendency among them to associate with one of the two opposing intra-party groups over this issue, it should be pointed out that, together with former journalists they have been the most articulate group. In this respect they have contrasted sharply with former local politicians.

The factions have grown up as the basic units for distribution of government and party offices and tend to divide themselves into two opposing alliances—one dominant and one dissident. A controversial issue is apt to be used by the latter as an excuse to intensify its opposition to the former. Hatoyama and Kishi were most outspoken advocates of constitutional revision so long as they found themselves leading dissident factions challenging the hegemony of Yoshida. More recently, the Fukuda and the Ishii factions used the same issue at least partly to discredit the dominant factions led by Ikeda, until they succeeded in establishing themselves as part of the newly-formed alliance of dominant factions led by Satō. Similarly, the dissident Matsumura and former Kōno factions have called for a drastic change in Japan's policy towards the People's Republic of China and formed the Afro-Asian Group to compete with the alliance of the dominant factions represented by the Asian Group which has committed itself to the maintenance of the *status quo*. The pattern is well established that those associated with a dominant faction tend to avoid involvement in a controversial issue, while those of a dissident faction attempt to use one as a weapon in the inter-factional power struggle by emphasising the need for 'positive' action.

In order to be attractive to a dissident faction as such a weapon, however,

266 party in power

the issue must be sufficiently controversial within the party as well as in the society at large. An essentially ideological and political issue like constitutional revision and policy towards China is likely to develop into a controversial state much more easily than a basically economic or budgetary matter such as the compensation of former landowners. In the latter case a majority in all but the Kōno faction was officially associated with the National Farmland League, while no faction leaders as such were ever chosen for targets of intensive lobbyist activities of the League. Factions were irrelevant to the policy-making process involving this essentially budgetary problem.

The PARC deliberation commission and the executive council are both constituted on the principle of inter-factional balance, co-ordination, and compromise. For this reason they frequently find themselves unable to make decisions when opinion is divided between the factions, especially if the division is between the dominant and dissident coalitions. Concerning the China issue, the deliberation commission has never officially expressed its own views, while the executive council did so only on a few occasions around 1958 in connection with the negotiations for the conclusion of the fourth private trade agreement and the subsequent withdrawal of LDP members from the Diet Members' League for the Promotion of Sino-Japanese Trade.

Generally speaking, the role of the factions in a policy-making situation involving a controversial issue is disruptive of party unity, although it may be of decisive importance. Built neither on the basis of ideology nor policy, they are seldom capable of functioning as units of positive and united action in such a situation. For this reason an intra-party group primarily interested in effectively organised action concerning a controversial issue tends to be formed separately from the existing factions and on a more or less cross-factional basis. This was true in all three cases reviewed in this study.

Factionalism considerably weakens the authority and prestige of the party president, particularly because of the manner in which he is selected and his short term of office (two years). As a result, the president is usually unable to exercise strong leadership in the making of decisions in controversial situations. The office of the president played a decisive role in none of the three cases examined.

In order to cope with the adverse effects of factionalism and make up for the weakness of presidential power, a semi-official decision-making organ controlled by the dominant factions, the leaders' meeting, supplements or supersedes the executive council (and frequently the PARC deliberation commission as well) when the party faces a controversial issue. Thus an alternative chain comprising an *ad hoc* PARC investigation committee, the executive council, and the leaders' meeting (or simply a PARC committee and the leaders' meeting) has developed.

The intervention of the leaders' meeting, however, does not prevent a division of opinion from developing in the party over certain kinds of issues but merely minimises its vicious effects. There still remains the possibility of such a division being exploited not only by opponents outside the party (especially the opposition parties) but also by the dissident factions within the party itself. This prospect discourages the top party leadership, represented by the president and the leaders' meeting, from advocating or closely identifying itself with a controversial issue. Even in the least controversial of the three issues discussed in the present study, the compensation of former landowners, the three leaders were invariably noncommittal. In the case of constitutional revision the negative attitude of the top leaders seriously interfered with the work of the LDP Committee on the Constitution and drove the more militant revisionists to seek a new base of operations in the unofficial Soshinkai. On the issue of Japan's policy towards China the LDP top leaders have never gone beyond generally following the lead of the Ministry of Foreign Affairs. To get the party to deal officially with a controversial issue against the resistance of the top leadership takes enormous efforts on the part of the interested intra-party or extra-party group.

The above-mentioned functions of the four principal factors of policy-making in the LDP and the pattern of interaction between them show a degree of stability and even rigidity, if not immutability. They have emerged from a gradual process of historical evolution originating in the first years of the Meiji era when parties and party politics were first introduced into Japan. The remarkable staying power which they have proved before, during, and after World War II in spite of the great and drastic changes in both Japan's international environment and her domestic conditions points to their continued relevance to the basic characteristics of policy-making in the LDP and, possibly, in any other conservative parties that may emerge in future.

In the actual development of an issue and the LDP's response to it, factors other than those discussed in this study no doubt play an important, often decisive, role. The problem of the compensation of former landowners arose primarily from the effects of the land reform which was executed by those not related or only marginally related to the LDP, long before the party was formed. None of the four factors considered in relation to LDP policy-making was, up to a certain point, immediately responsible for the origin and development of this issue. The requirement that the constitution of Japan may be amended only with the support of two-thirds or more members in each House and in addition a majority in a popular referendum, exists independently of the LDP and its policy-making process. The attitudes of the press and public opinion on whether the constitution should be amended have been determined only very indirectly by the characteristic behaviour of the four factors we have examined. The same has been even more true as regards the attitudes of the governments of the United States or Nationalist China which have largely delimited the scope of action on the part of the Japanese government and other groups in their relationship with the People's Republic of China.

Furthermore, personal motivations responsible for the specific behaviour of individual LDP members in actual policy-making situations are much more complex, diverse, and particular than a few abstract categories may adequately represent and explain. The personal decision-making involved in the part of, say, Utsunomiya Tokuma, Matsumura Kenzō, and Fujiyama Aiichirō in relation to the China issue is not explicable primarily in terms of any of the four factors examined in this study or the general patterns of their interaction.

Provided, however, that one is aware of these obvious limitations, the series of interrelated generalisations presented above will be useful to an understanding and a more sophisticated analysis of the behaviour of the LDP. To the extent that the LDP has been continuously in power since it was formed in November 1955 and is likely to remain so for at least some time to come, these generalisations will also give some initial clues to a discussion of governmental decision-making in contemporary Japan.

Appendixes

APPENDIX I

Occupational backgrounds of conservative MHRs, 1890-1967
(in actual numbers and percentages)

	Local politicians		Public servants		Businessmen		Lawyers		Journalists		Miscellaneous		Total
	No.	%	No.	%	No.	%	No.	%	No.	%	No.	%	No.
July 1890													
Yayoi kurabu	96	71·6	33	24·6	34	25·3	13	9·7	6	4·4	10	7·4	134
Giinshūkaijo	31	73·8	8	19·0	14	33·3	2	4·7	8	19·0	2	4·7	42
March 1894													
Jiyūtō	90	75·6	17	14·2	16	13·4	14	11·7	7	5·8	8	6·7	119
Rikken kaishintō	36	75·0	11	22·9	9	18·7	3	6·2	6	12·5	3	6·2	48
March 1898													
Jiyūtō	74	75·5	12	12·2	21	21·4	6	6·1	4	4·0	10	10·2	98
Shimpotō	60	65·9	17	18·6	21	23·0	7	7·6	9	9·8	10	10·9	91
August 1902													
Rikken seiyūkai	146	76·4	17	8·9	47	24·6	29	15·1	11	5·7	16	8·3	191
Kenseihontō	60	64·5	17	18·2	22	23·6	19	20·4	10	10·7	12	12·9	93
March 1904													
Rikken seiyūkai	104	71·7	13	8·9	40	27·5	23	15·8	7	4·8	12	8·2	145
Kenseihontō	71	73·1	15	15·4	19	19·5	18	18·5	9	9·2	7	7·2	97
May 1912													
Rikken seiyūkai	126	56·2	20	8·9	84	37·5	42	18·7	18	8·0	19	8·4	224
Rikken kokumintō	50	52·6	5	5·2	26	27·3	15	15·7	20	21·0	16	16·8	95
April 1917													
Rikken seiyūkai	91	52·6	14	8·0	64	36·9	35	20·2	15	8·6	18	10·4	173
Kenseikai	77	58·7	10	7·4	46	35·1	14	10·6	25	19·0	19	14·5	131

APPENDIX I (*continued*)

	Local politicians No.	%	Public servants No.	%	Businessmen No.	%	Lawyers No.	%	Journalists No.	%	Miscellaneous No.	%	Total No.
May 1924													
Rikken seiyūkai and Seiyūhontō	110	47·0	18	7·6	85	36·3	40	17·0	28	11·9	29	12·3	234
Kenseikai	94	55·9	5	2·9	59	36·1	33	19·6	30	17·8	19	11·3	168
February 1930													
Rikken seiyūkai	66	38·1	17	9·8	48	27·7	29	16·7	25	14·4	32	18·4	173
Rikken minseitō	139	51·4	16	5·9	74	27·4	55	20·3	44	16·2	36	13·3	270
February 1936													
Rikken seiyūkai	82	47·3	9	5·2	42	24·2	36	20·8	23	13·2	34	19·5	173
Rikken minseitō	102	49·5	18	8·7	53	25·7	41	19·9	31	15·0	31	15·0	206
April 1942													
Yokusanseijikai	197	44·4	33	7·4	91	20·5	68	15·3	53	11·9	100	22·5	443
April 1946													
Nihon jiyūtō	78	52·3	3	2·0	38	25·5	18	12·0	9	6·0	37	24·8	149
Nihon shimpotō	62	55·3	5	4·4	37	33·0	10	8·9	10	8·9	21	18·7	112
April 1947													
Nihon jiyūtō	50	37·8	13	9·8	26	19·6	17	12·8	16	12·1	33	25·0	132
Minshutō	46	34·3	8	5·9	55	41·0	13	9·7	12	8·9	31	23·1	134
January 1949													
Minshujiyūtō	89	32·9	47	17·4	86	31·8	26	9·6	31	11·4	48	17·4	270
Minshutō	28	40·0	9	12·8	27	38·5	5	7·1	5	7·1	15	21·4	70
October 1952													
Jiyūtō	71	29·3	62	25·6	56	23·1	28	11·5	28	11·5	33	13·6	242
Kaishintō	24	26·9	15	16·8	21	23·5	11	12·3	5	5·6	27	30·3	89

273

APPENDIX I (*continued*)

| | Local politicians | | Public servants | | Businessmen | | Lawyers | | Journalists | | Miscellaneous | | Total |
	No.	%	No.	%	No.	%	No.	%	No.	%	No.	%	No.
April 1953													
Jiyūtō and Jiyūtō (separatist)	72	30·2	59	24·7	47	19·7	28	11·7	37	15·5	31	13·0	238
Kaishintō	20	25·9	15	19·4	21	27·2	4	5·2	5	6·4	25	32·4	77
February 1955													
Jiyūtō	30	26·3	32	28·0	25	21·9	9	7·8	12	10·5	17	14·9	114
Nihon minshutō	49	26·4	36	19·4	39	21·0	25	13·5	15	8·1	51	27·5	185
May 1958													
Jiyūminshutō	79	26·4	70	23·4	64	21·4	26	8·6	32	10·7	66	22·0	299
November 1960													
Jiyūminshutō	79	26·6	77	26·0	60	20·2	22	7·4	39	13·1	59	19·9	296
November 1965													
Jiyūminshutō	79	26·8	76	25·8	62	21·0	16	5·4	35	11·9	63	21·4	294
January 1967													
Jiyūminshutō	67	23·7	71	25·1	44	15·6	10	3·5	33	11·7	57	20·2	282

Note: Of the 2,900 MHRs examined (out of the total of some 4,800 elected in the House of Representatives elections Nos. 1–31) those with two or more occupational backgrounds were counted twice for the two principal categories. As a result, the totals of the numbers given for the five categories are larger than the actual numbers of members.

Sources: GSS: Shūgiingiin meikan (1962); *GSS: Seitō kaiha hen* (1961); Kikuoka Yaozō (ed.), *Kokkai binran* (Nihon seikei-shimbun shuppanbu), 1st ed. (April 1954) to 34th ed. (March 1967); *Shūgiin jimukyoku* (ed.), *Shūgiingiin yōran* ('Otsu' series), June 1955, October 1958, February 1961, February 1964, and February 1966; *Jinji kōshinjo* (ed.), *Daigishiroku* (1946); *Nihon minsei kenkyūkai* (ed.), *Shūsan giin binran: 1964-nen ban* (Hyōronshinsha, 1964); *Kōjunsha shuppankyoku* (ed.), *Nihon shinshiroku*, 52nd ed. (December 1960).

APPENDIX II A

'New face'—'old face' ratios of candidates in House of Representatives elections,
1946–67

	New candidates		Incumbent members		Former members	
	No.	%	No.	%	No.	%
10 April 1946						
Liberals	429	88·2	15	3·0	42	8·6
Progressives	339	89·2	18	4·7	23	6·0
Co-operatives	91	96·7	2	2·1	1	1·0
Socialists	305	92·1	7	2·1	18	5·4
Communists	143	100·0	—	—	—	—
Minor parties	565	99·1	1	0·1	4	0·7
Independents	752	98·0	4	0·5	11	1·4
Totals	2,624	94·7	47	1·6	99	3·5
25 April 1947						
Liberals	223	69·2	92	28·5	7	2·1
Democrats	239	72·2	83	25·0	9	2·7
National						
Co-operatives	67	60·9	41	37·2	2	1·8
Socialists	193	68·4	86	30·4	3	1·0
Communists	114	95·0	6	5·0	—	—
Minor parties	146	97·3	4	2·6	—	—
Independents	246	96·8	5	1·9	3	1·1
Totals	1,228	78·2	317	20·2	24	1·5
23 January 1949						
Democratic Liberals	207	53·4	152	39·2	28	7·2
Democrats	109	51·6	85	40·2	17	8·0
National						
Co-operatives	33	52·3	26	41·2	4	6·3
Socialists	65	35·3	107	58·1	12	6·5
Communists	107	93·0	4	3·4	4	3·4
Minor parties	109	68·1	47	29·3	4	2·5
Independents	232	94·6	7	2·8	6	2·4
Totals	862	63·1	428	31·3	75	5·4
1 October 1952						
Liberals	115	24·2	256	53·8	104	21·8
Progressives	59	28·2	60	28·7	90	43·0
Co-operatives	14	50·0	4	14·2	10	35·7
Right Socialists	38	35·1	30	27·5	41	37·6
Left Socialists	60	62·5	16	16·6	20	20·8
Communists	84	78·5	18	16·8	5	4·6
Minor parties	29	55·7	8	15·3	15	28·8
Independents	133	80·1	1	0·6	32	19·2
Totals	532	42·8	393	31·6	317	25·5
19 April 1953						
Liberals	56	13·4	234	56·1	127	30·4
Progressives	29	17·1	87	51·4	53	31·3
Right Socialists	39	32·8	58	49·4	20	17·0
Left Socialists	45	41·6	56	51·8	7	6·4
Communists	75	85·2	—	—	13	14·7
Minor parties	14	56·0	5	20·0	6	24·0
Independents	78	72·8	10	9·3	19	17·7
Totals	336	32·5	450	43·6	245	23·7

APPENDIX II A *(continued)*

	New candidates No.	%	Incumbent members No.	%	Former members No.	%
27 *February 1955*						
Liberals	25	10·0	171	68·9	52	20·9
Democrats	62	21·6	125	43·7	99	34·6
Right Socialists	43	35·2	60	49·1	19	15·5
Left Socialists	43	35·5	72	59·5	6	4·9
Communists	44	73·3	1	1·6	15	25·0
Minor parties	36	67·9	12	22·6	5	9·4
Independents	106	83·4	4	3·1	17	13·3
Totals	359	35·2	445	43·7	213	20·9
22 *May 1958*						
Liberal-Democrats	51	12·3	287	69·4	75	18·3
Socialists	73	29·6	156	63·4	17	6·9
Communists	97	85·0	2	1·7	15	13·1
Minor parties	26	78·7	—	—	7	21·2
Independents	106	73·1	3	2·0	36	24·8
Totals	353	37·1	448	47·1	150	15·7
20 *November 1960*						
Liberal-Democrats	58	14·5	278	69·6	63	15·9
Democratic Socialists	55	52·3	40	38·0	10	9·5
Socialists	49	26·3	119	63·9	18	9·6
Communists	102	86·4	1	0·8	15	12·7
Minor parties	31	91·1	—	—	3	8·8
Independents	81	82·6	1	1·0	16	16·3
Totals	376	40·0	439	46·7	125	13·2
21 *November 1963*						
Liberal-Democrats	48	13·3	270	75·2	42	11·4
Democratic Socialists	27	45·7	14	23·7	18	30·5
Socialists	46	23·2	134	67·6	18	9·0
Communists	104	88·1	3	2·5	11	9·3
Minor parties	63	98·4	—	—	1	1·5
Independents	102	85·7	6	5·0	11	9·2
Totals	390	40·2	427	46·5	100	10·9
29 *January 1967*						
Liberal-Democrats	48	13·9	270	78·7	25	7·2
Democratic Socialists	27	42·1	26	40·6	11	17·1
Socialists	56	27·0	129	62·3	22	10·6
Communists	111	90·2	4	3·2	8	6·5
Kōmeitō	32	100·0	—	—	—	—
Minor parties	12	75·0	1	6·2	3	18·7
Independents	117	87·3	1	0·7	16	11·9
Totals	403	43·8	431	46·8	85	9·2

Sources: GSS: Seitō kaiha hen; Asahi, 11 April 1946, 25 April 1947, 22 January 1949, 1 October 1952, 17 April 1953, 27 February 1955, 22 May 1958, 19 November 1960, 20 November 1963, 28 January 1967.

APPENDIX II B

*'New face'—'old face' ratios of elected members in House of Representatives
elections, 1946–67*

	Newly-elected		Incumbent members		Former members	
	No.	%	No.	%	No.	%
10 *April* 1946						
Liberals	103	73·0	13	9·2	25	17·7
Progressives	71	76·3	14	15·0	8	8·6
Co-operatives	12	85·7	1	7·1	1	7·1
Socialists	73	78·4	6	6·4	14	15·0
Communists	5	100·0	—	—	—	—
Minor parties	38	97·4	—	—	1	2·5
Independents	73	92·4	4	5·0	2	2·5
Totals	375	80·8	38	8·2	51	10·9
25 *April* 1947						
Liberals	59	45·0	71	54·1	1	0·7
Democrats	58	46·7	63	50·8	3	2·4
National Co-operatives	7	22·5	24	77·4	—	—
Socialists	69	48·2	71	49·6	3	2·0
Communists	2	50·0	2	50·0	—	—
Minor parties	17	85·0	3	15·0	—	—
Independents	9	69·2	4	30·7	—	—
Totals	221	47·4	238	51·0	7	1·5
23 *January* 1949						
Democratic Liberals	121	45·8	125	47·3	18	6·8
Democrats	23	33·8	39	57·3	6	8·8
National Co-operatives	—	—	14	100·0	—	—
Socialists	6	12·2	40	81·6	3	0·6
Communists	28	80·0	4	11·4	3	8·5
Minor parties	1	25·0	3	75·0	—	—
Independents	11	91·6	1	8·3	—	—
Totals	192	41·2	243	52·1	31	6·6
1 *October* 1952						
Liberals	52	21·6	132	55·0	56	23·3
Progressives	10	11·7	37	43·5	38	44·7
Co-operatives	—	—	1	50·0	1	50·0
Right Socialists	6	10·5	26	45·6	25	43·8
Left Socialists	25	46·2	16	29·6	13	24·0
Communists	—	—	—	—	—	—
Minor parties	2	50·0	1	25·0	1	25·0
Independents	14	73·6	1	5·2	4	21·0
Totals	109	23·3	217	46·5	140	30·0
19 *April* 1953						
Liberals	13	5·5	166	70·9	55	23·5
Progressives	6	7·8	52	68·4	18	23·6
Right Socialists	9	13·6	49	74·2	8	12·1
Left Socialists	14	19·4	53	73·6	5	6·9
Communists	—	—	—	—	1	100·0
Minor parties	1	16·6	4	66·6	1	16·6
Independents	4	36·3	5	45·4	2	18·1
Totals	47	10·0	329	70·6	90	19·3

APPENDIX II B *(continued)*

	Newly-elected		Incumbent members		Former members	
	No.	%	No.	%	No.	%
27 February 1955						
Liberals	6	5·4	81	72·3	25	22·3
Democrats	22	11·8	101	54·5	62	33·5
Right Socialists	8	11·9	50	74·6	9	13·4
Left Socialists	17	19·1	68	76·4	4	4·4
Communists	—	—	1	50·0	1	50·0
Minor parties	—	—	5	83·3	1	16·6
Independents	2	33·3	2	33·3	2	33·3
Totals	55	11·7	308	65·9	104	22·2
22 May 1958						
Liberal-Democrats	26	9·0	215	74·9	46	16·1
Socialists	34	20·4	121	72·8	11	6·6
Communists	—	—	1	100·0	—	—
Minor parties	1	100·0	—	—	—	—
Independents	5	41·6	—	—	7	58·3
Totals	66	14·1	337	72·1	64	13·7
20 November 1960						
Liberal-Democrats	29	9·8	226	76·3	41	13·9
Democratic Socialists	1	5·8	13	76·4	3	17·6
Socialists	26	17·9	103	71·0	16	11·0
Communists	—	—	1	33·3	2	66·6
Minor parties	1	100·0	—	—	—	—
Independents	3	60·0	1	20·0	1	20·0
Totals	60	12·8	344	73·6	63	13·4
21 November 1963						
Liberal-Democrats	33	11·6	224	79·1	26	9·1
Democratic Socialists	4	17·3	11	47·8	8	34·7
Socialists	22	15·2	108	75·0	14	9·7
Communists	1	20·0	3	60·0	1	20·0
Minor parties	—	—	—	—	—	—
Independents	8	66·6	2	16·6	2	16·6
Totals	68	14·5	348	74·5	51	10·9
29 January 1967						
Liberal-Democrats	26	9·3	235	84·8	16	5·7
Democratic Socialists	8	26·6	18	60·0	4	13·3
Socialists	33	23·5	90	64·2	17	12·1
Communists	1	20·0	3	60·0	1	20·0
Kōmeitō	25	100·0	—	—	—	—
Minor parties	—	—	—	—	—	—
Independents	9	100·0	—	—	—	—
Totals	102	20·9	346	71·1	38	7·8

Sources: Asahi, 15 April 1946, 27 April 1947, 25 January 1949, 3 October 1952, 20 April 1953 (evening), 1 March 1955, 24 May 1958, 22 November 1960, 23 November 1963, 31 January 1967.

T

APPENDIX III A

'New face'—'old face' ratios of candidates in House of Councillors elections,
1947–65

	New candidates		Incumbent members		Former members	
	No.	%	No.	%	No.	%
20 April 1947						
Liberals	74	100·0	—	—	—	—
Democrats	54	100·0	—	—	—	—
National Co-operatives	25	100·0	—	—	—	—
Socialists	102	100·0	—	—	—	—
Communists	42	100·0	—	—	—	—
Minor parties	35	100·0	—	—	—	—
Independents	251	100·0	—	—	—	—
Totals	583	100·0	—	—	—	—
4 June 1950						
Liberals	104	76·4	32	23·6	—	—
National Democrats	32	68·0	15	31·9	—	—
Ryokufūkai	37	63·7	21	36·2	—	—
Socialists	61	81·3	14	18·6	—	—
Communists	47	94·0	3	6·0	—	—
Minor parties	35	85·3	6	14·6	—	—
Independents	150	96·1	6	3·8	—	—
Totals	466	82·7	97	17·2	—	—
24 April 1953						
Liberals	64	70·3	25	27·4	2	2·1
Progressives	33	76·7	5	11·6	5	11·6
Ryokufūkai	9	26·4	23	67·6	2	5·8
Right Socialists	22	56·4	12	30·7	5	12·8
Left Socialists	39	78·0	9	18·0	2	4·0
Communists	9	75·0	2	16·6	1	8·3
Minor parties	15	88·2	1	5·8	1	5·8
Independents	152	94·4	7	4·3	2	1·2
Totals	343	76·7	84	18·7	20	4·4
8 July 1956						
Liberal-Democrats	63	53·3	50	42·3	5	4·2
Ryokufūkai	5	26·3	12	63·1	2	10·5
Socialists	44	53·6	34	41·1	4	4·8
Communists	29	85·2	1	2·9	4	11·7
Minor parties	17	85·0	2	10·0	1	5·0
Independents	63	92·6	3	4·4	2	2·9
Totals	221	64·8	102	29·9	18	5·2
2 June 1959						
Liberal-Democrats	48	47·5	49	38·5	4	3·9
Ryokufūkai	2	16·6	9	75·0	1	8·3
Socialists	47	60·2	27	34·6	4	5·1
Communists	35	97·2	—	—	1	2·7
Minor parties	22	95·6	1	4·3	—	—
Independents	73	91·2	3	3·7	4	5·0
Totals	227	68·7	89	26·9	14	4·2

APPENDIX III A (*continued*)

	New candidates		Incumbent members		Former members	
	No.	%	No.	%	No.	%
1 July 1962						
Liberal-Democrats	38	38·0	55	55·0	7	7·0
Democratic Socialists	16	66·6	8	33·3	—	—
Socialists	38	55·0	28	40·5	3	4·3
Communists	45	95·7	2	4·2	—	—
Minor parties	15	78·9	4	21·0	—	—
Independents	61	88·4	6	8·6	2	2·8
Totals	213	64·9	103	31·4	12	3·6
4 July 1965						
Liberal-Democrats	42	44·2	52	54·7	1	1·0
Democratic Socialists	17	80·9	2	9·5	2	9·5
Socialists	39	59·0	24	36·3	3	4·5
Communists	45	93·7	2	4·1	1	2·0
Kōmeitō	11	78·5	3	21·4	—	—
Minor parties	36	100·0	—	—	—	—
Independents	47	90·3	3	5·7	2	3·8
Totals	237	71·3	86	25·9	9	2·7

Sources: Asahi, 12 April 1947, 23 April 1953, 8 July 1956, 1 June 1959, 30 June 1962; *Nihon Keizai,* 2 June 1950, 14 June 1965.

APPENDIX III B

*'New face'—'old face' ratios of elected members in House of Councillors elections,
1947–65*

	Newly-elected		Incumbent members		Former members	
	No.	%	No.	%	No.	%
20 April 1947						
Liberals	39	100·0	—	—	—	—
Democrats	32	100·0	—	—	—	—
National Co-operatives	10	100·0	—	—	—	—
Socialists	47	100·0	—	—	—	—
Communists	4	100·0	—	—	—	—
Minor parties	10	100·0	—	—	—	—
Independents	108	100·0	—	—	—	—
Totals	250	100·0	—	—	—	—
4 June 1950						
Liberals	32	61·5	20	38·4	—	—
National Democrats	6	66·6	3	33·3	—	—
Ryokufūkai	6	66·6	3	33·3	—	—
Socialists	30	83·3	6	16·6	—	—
Communists	1	50·0	1	50·0	—	—
Minor parties	3	60·0	2	40·0	—	—
Independents	16	84·2	3	15·7	—	—
Totals	94	71·2	38	28·7	—	—
24 April 1953						
Liberals	29	63·0	17	36·9	—	—
Progressives	6	75·0	1	12·5	1	12·5
Ryokufūkai	2	12·5	14	87·5	—	—
Right Socialists	5	50·0	3	30·0	2	20·0
Left Socialists	13	72·2	4	22·2	1	5·5
Communists	—	—	—	—	—	—
Minor parties	—	—	—	—	—	—
Independents	30	100·0	—	—	—	—
Totals	85	66·4	39	30·4	4	3·1
8 July 1956						
Liberal-Democrats	26	42·6	33	54·0	2	3·2
Ryokufūkai	—	—	5	100·0	—	—
Socialists	20	40·8	26	53·0	3	6·1
Communists	1	50·0	—	—	1	50·0
Minor parties	1	100·0	—	—	—	—
Independents	7	77·7	2	22·2	—	—
Totals	55	43·3	66	51·9	6	4·7
2 June 1959						
Liberal-Democrats	29	40·8	39	54·9	3	4·2
Ryokufūkai	—	—	6	100·0	—	—
Socialists	14	36·8	22	57·8	2	5·2
Communists	—	—	—	—	1	100·0
Minor parties	—	—	1	100·0	—	—
Independents	9	90·0	1	10·0	—	—
Totals	52	40·9	69	54·3	6	4·7

APPENDIX III B *(continued)*

	Newly-elected		Incumbent members		Former members	
	No.	%	No.	%	No.	%
1 July 1962						
Liberal-Democrats	17	24·6	48	69·5	4	5·7
Democratic Socialists	1	25·0	3	75·0	—	—
Socialists	12	32·4	23	62·1	2	5·4
Communists	1	33·3	2	66·6	—	—
Minor parties	—	—	2	100·0	—	—
Independents	8	66·6	4	33·3	—	—
Totals	39	30·7	82	64·5	6	4·7
4 July 1965						
Liberal-Democrats	27	38·5	42	60·0	1	1·4
Democratic Socialists	3	100·0	—	—	—	—
Socialists	14	38·8	19	52·7	3	8·3
Communists	1	33·3	2	66·6	—	—
Kōmeitō	8	72·7	3	27·2	—	—
Minor parties	—	—	—	—	—	—
Independents	—	—	2	100·0	—	—
Totals	53	42·4	68	54·4	4	3·2

Sources: Asahi, 1 May 1947, 7 June 1950, 26 (morning and evening) April 1953, 11 July 1956, 4 June 1959 (evening), 3 (morning and evening) July 1962, 6 July 1965.

Notes on Sources

This bibliographical note includes only some of the most important sources used in preparing this book. For a more complete list, readers are referred to the bibliography in my Ph.D. thesis, 'The Japanese Liberal-Democratic Party and Policy-Making', a copy of which will be available for loan from the Australian National University Library.

Of the sources frequently used throughout the work the official gazette of the Japanese government, *Kampō*, was particularly valuable. Not only the regular issues of it but, more importantly, its special issues, or 'Gōgai', which contain the records of proceedings of the National Diet and various committees in it, were extensively used. These included the proceedings of the plenary meetings and of the Standing Committees on the Cabinet, Foreign Affairs, Agriculture and Forestry, and Budget, in both Houses. Of the non-official sources generally relied upon in addition to the large daily newspapers the most important were various kinds of yearbooks, such as *Asahi nenkan*, *Jiji nenkan*, *Kokkai nenkan*, *Kokumin jichi nenkan*, *Kokumin seiji nenkan*, and *Nihon tōkei nenkan*. The 12-volume compilation of materials on the Diet, Shūgiin and Sangiin (eds.), *Gikaiseido shichijūnen shi* (Ōkurashō insatsukyoku, 1960-2), and the 6-volume compilation on postwar Japanese history, *Shiryō: Sengo nijūnen shi* (Nihonhyōronsha, 1966-7), also proved indispensable. Kyoto daigaku bungakubu kokushikenkyūshitsu (ed.), *Nihon kindaishi jiten* (Tōyōkeizaishimpōsha, 1958) and Seijigakujiten hensanbu, *Seijigakujiten* (Heibonsha, 1954), were often consulted and usually proved helpful, despite the fact that much of the information contained in them was found to be dated.

Part One of the book was written on the basis of information obtained mostly from secondary sources. The books used for the description of the general political developments in prewar Japan included Ōtsu Jun'ichirō, *Dainihon kenseishi*, 10 vols. (Hōbunkaku, 1927-8); Osatake Takeshi, *Nihon kenseishi taikō*, 2 vols. (Nihonhyōronsha, 1938-9); Shinobu Seizaburō, *Taishō seijishi*, 4 vols. (Kawade shobō, 1951-2); Horie Hideichi and Tōyama Shigeki (eds.), *Jiyūminkenki no kenkyū*, 3 vols. (Yūhikaku, 1959); and Oka Yoshitake,

Kindai nihon seijishi, Vol. I (Sōbunsha, 1962). The works most useful to the discussion of the political parties were the descriptive histories of the two major parties of prewar Japan, such as Kobayashi Yūgo (ed.), *Rikken seiyū-kai shi,* 4 vols. (Rikken seiyūkai shuppankyoku, 1924-6) ; Kikuchi Gorō (ed.), *Rikken seiyūkai shi,* 3 vols. (Rikken seiyukai shi hensanbu, 1933) ; Kensei-kaishi hensanjo (ed.), *Kenseikaishi* (1926) ; and Rikken minseitō shi hensen-kyoku, *Rikken minseitō shi,* 2 vols., 1935. In addition, Shōji Kichinosuke, *Nihon seisha seitō hattatsushi: Fukushimaken jiyūminken undō shiryō wo chūshin to shite* (Ochanomizu shobō, 1959) and several articles supplied a substantial amount of factual information and insight. Examples of the latter are Hayashi Shigeru, 'Rikken Kaishintōin no chihō bumpu', *Shakaikagaku Kenkyū,* February 1958, pp. 78-135; Itō Takashi, 'Meiji jūshichi nijūsan nen no rikken kaishintō: Kokkaikaisetsu izen ni okeru seitō no ichikōsatsu', *Tokyo daigaku shakaikagaku kenkyūjo sōritsu jūgoshūnen kinen rombun,* 1963, pp. 255-94; and Masumi Junnosuke, 'Nihon seitōshi ni okeru chihōseiji no sho-mondai', *Kokkagakkai Zasshi,* November 1959–December 1962. Regarding the role of the *zaibatsu* in prewar party politics, *Nihon kontsuerun zensho,* 12 vols. (Shunjūsha, 1937-8) was extensively used, particularly the first three volumes, *Nihon zaibatsu ron, Mitsui kontsuerun tokuhon,* and *Mitsubishi kontsuerun tokuhon.*

Many biographies of prewar government officials and politicians were also consulted as an important source of information. These included, for example, Kōno Banshū den hensankai (ed.), *Kōno Banshū den,* 2 vols. (Kōno Banshū den kankōkai, 1923) ; Ōkumakō hachijūgonenshi hensankai (ed.), *Ōkumakō hachijūgonenshi,* 3 vols. (1926) ; Wakatsuki Reijirō, *Wakat-suki Reijirō jiden: Kofūan kaikoroku: Meiji taishō shōwa seikai hishi* (Yomiuri shimbunsha, 1950) ; Yabe Sadaji, *Konoe Fumimaro,* 2 vols. (Kōbundō, 1952) ; Matsumura Kenzō, *Machida Chūji ō den* (Machida Chūji ō denki kankōkai, 1958) ; and Aritake Shūji, *Maeda Yonezō den* (Maeda Yonezō denki kankōkai, 1961).

For the discussion of the postwar conditions and problems, Oka Yoshitake (ed.), *Gendai nihon no seijikatei* (Iwanami shoten, 1958) proved useful, although some of the materials and information on which contributors based their arguments and conclusions were found to be out of date. Matsushita Keiichi, *Gendai nihon no seijiteki kōsei* (Tokyo daigaku shuppankai, 1962) was also extensively consulted. Very helpful for the understanding of the role of business groups in postwar party politics were the histories of the large businessmen's federations, such as Keizai dōyūkai, *Keizai dōyūkai jūnenshi* (1956); Nikkeiren sōritsu jusshūnen kinenjigyōiinkai (ed.), *Jūnen no ayumi* (Nihon keieishadantai renmei, 1958); and Horikoshi Teizō (ed.), *Keizai-dantai rengōkai: Zenshi* and *Keizaidantai rengōkai junenshi,* 2 vols. (Keizai-dantai rengōkai, 1962-3). Some useful interpretative views based on the case studies of representative interest groups in contemporary Japan were found in Nihon seijigakkai (ed.), *Nihon no atsuryokudantai* (Iwanami shoten, 1960).

As was the case with the part dealing with the prewar developments, various biographical accounts of politicians and administrators directly involved in the process proved relevant to the understanding of postwar party politics in the period preceding the formation of the Liberal-Democratic Party. A few examples are: Hatoyama Ichirō, *Hatoyama Ichirō kaikoroku* (Bungeishunjūshinsha, 1957); Yoshida Shigeru, *Kaisō jūnen*, 4 vols. (Shinchōsha, 1957-8); and Mitarai Tatsuo, *Miki Bukichi: Minshūseijika no shōgai* (Shikisha, 1958).

In preparing Part Two of the book some census data compiled and published by the government were indispensable. Particularly widely used were Sōrifu tōkeikyoku, *Shōwa 35-nen kokuseichōsa: Zenkoku todōfuken shikuchōson jinkō sōran*, Part I, 1965 and *Shōwa 40-nen shūgyōkōzō kihonchōsa hōkoku: Zenkokuhen*, 1966. Just as important for general reference purposes were the 6-volume compilation of historical materials, *Shiryō: Sengo nijūnen shi*, cited already. Journalists' observations of contemporary Japanese politics represented, for example, by Okada Tadao, *Seiji no uchimaku* (Yūki shobō, 1963) and Kawada Jirō, *Desuku nikki: Masukomi to rekishi* (Mizuho shobō, 1964) were at least as interesting and useful as more academically motivated studies, such as Nihon seijigakkai (ed.), *Gendai nihon no seitō to kanryō* (Iwanami shoten, 1967). Of this latter publication Misawa Shigeo's 'Seisakuketteikatei no gaikan' and Masumi Junnosuke's 'Jiyūminshutō no soshiki to kinō' were especially relevant. For analytical insights into the nature and problems of local politics in contemporary Japan the joint book-length study by Ōhara Mitsunori and Yokoyama Keiji, *Sangyōshakai to seijikatei: Keiyōkōgyōchitai* (Nihonhyōronsha, 1965), and Akimoto Ritsurō's 'Chiikishakai ni okeru kenryokubaitai no rīda no kōsei' and Katsumura Shigeru's 'Chiikirīdā no kōsei to seisaku no kettei' in *Shakaikagaku Tōkyū*, June 1965, deserve special mention for their substantial contribution to my analysis.

The discussion of the Liberal-Democratic Party and problems directly related to it was based largely on information obtained from the various publications of the party itself and groups associated with it, as well as from personal interviews. These publications included such periodicals as *Jiyūminshu*, *Seisaku Geppō*, and *Soshiki Jōhō*. They also included the following non-periodical publications: *Wagatō no kihonhōshin*, July 1962, January 1964, January 1965, and January 1966; *Seimuchōsakai meibo*, March 1964, November 1964, and November 1965; *Soshikichōsakai tōshin*, January 1964; *Seisaku kaisetsu*, April 1959, October 1960, April 1962, October 1963, and May 1965; *Todōfuken shiburengōkai yakuin meibo*, 1959; and *Kakushudantai meibo*, 1966. Jimintōshi hensaniinkai (ed.), *Jiyūminshutōshi* (1961), also belongs to this category.

For the discussion of the intra-party factions and their functions, periodical and miscellaneous materials published by the factions themselves were extremely useful and extensively used in addition to the studies by Watanabe Tsuneo, *Habatsu: Nihon hoshutō no bunseki* (Kōbundō, 1964) and Yomiuri shimbun seijibu (ed.), *Seitō: Sono soshiki to habatsu no jittai* (Yomiuri shimbunsha, 1966). Examples of the faction publications so utilised are Shunjūkai's *Shunjū* and *Seisaku kenkyū shirizu*, both irregular; Kōchikai's *Shinro*, monthly; Kōyū kurabu's *Seisaku*, monthly; and Tōfūsasshin renmei's *Habatsu no honshitsu* (n.d.), *Sasshin renmei no kihonsenjutsu to sono hōkō*, etc.

Regarding the problem of political funds and contributions, Ichikawa Fusae's compilations of data relating to the election campaigns of 1960 and 1962 were very helpful; see her *Shōwa 35-nen 11-gatsu 20-ka shikkō shūgiin-giin sōsenkyo no senkyohiyō sōkessan* (1961) and *37.7.1 no sangiingin senkyo no hiyō to 37-nen no seitōtō no seijishikin to kaisha no seijikenkin* (1965), both published by Risōsenkyo fukyūkai. Kōmeisenkyo renmei, *Seijidantai to sono shikin* (1964), was used in conjunction, while Kokumin kyōkai's periodical, *Kokumin Kyōkai*, was consulted for information relevant to the activities of this particular organisation.

In addition to the above-mentioned sources a variety of reference materials was relied upon for basic data. For biographical information in particular the following sources were extensively exploited: Ōkurashō insatsukyoku, *Shokuinroku*, annual; Shūgiin jimukyoku, *Shūgiin yōran (otsu)*, irregular; Kikuoka Yaozō (ed.), *Kokkai binran*, irregular; and the *Shūgiingin meikan* and *Kizokuin sangiin giin meikan* volumes of *Gikaiseido shichijūnen shi* cited earlier. Extremely useful in innumerable ways as a primary source in the discussion of the Liberal-Democratic Party and its members were the two series of mimeographed records of talks given by various government, party, and interest group representatives for the private research association, Kokumin seiji kenkyūkai. One of these series was titled 'Getsuyōkai' (Monday Meeting) reports, as the talks were given regularly every Monday. More than thirty issues of this series were used, some very extensively. The other series, titled 'Denā kurabu kōen' (Dinner Club Lectures), was used but only to a limited extent.

Needless to say, three groups of sources were used in preparing Part Three of the book, each relevant to the particular case chosen for the intensive investigation. Most valuable to the discussion of the farmland issue were the reports of the special section established in the Prime Minister's Office. These included Naikakusōridaijin kambō shingishitsu, *Nōchihibaishūsha mondai chōsakai tōshin*, May 1962; Naikakusōridaijin kambō rinji nōchitō hibaishūsha mondai chōsashitsu, *Nōchihibaishūsha mondai ni kansuru seron-chōsa kekka*, March 1964; *Nōchihibaishūsha no seikatsujōkyō chōsakekka*, March 1964; and *Nōchihibaishūsha jittaichōsa kekkahyō*, March 1964. The practical implications of the compensation bill itself are explained by one of the officials directly involved in Masumitsu Jirō (ed.), *Nōchihōshō no kaisetsu* (Taisei shuppansha, 1965). In addition to these sources which concern the developments of the legislative issues as such, data published by the Ministry of Agriculture and Forestry at the time of the postwar land reform were also studied, including *Nōrinshō tōkeihyō* and *Nōchikaikaku shiryō*. A substantial amount of information was drawn also from Nōchikaikaku kiroku iinkai (ed.), *Nōchikaikaku tenmatsu gaiyō* (Nōchichōsakai, 1951). For the developments on the interest group side the organ of the National Farmland League, *Nōchi Shimpō*, and its occasional mimeographed publications, such as *Kokkaitaisaku hōkokusho: Shōwa 39-nen 1-gatsu 10-ka yori shōwa 39-nen 6-gatsu 26-nichi made* (n.d.), were invaluable.

For the issue of constitutional revision, the most important source was the publications of the Commission on the Constitution, particularly the main report, *Kempōchōsakai hōkokusho*, July 1964, and the series of appendant reports published simultaneously with it. The proceedings of the Commission, too, were frequently consulted. Of the numerous studies of the issue which had appeared in the form of books and magazine articles the following were found to be especially helpful: Arikura Ryōkichi *et al.*, *Kempōchōsakai sōhihan: Kempōkaisei mondai no honshitsu* (Nihonhyōronsha, 1964); Kobayashi Naoki, *Nihonkokukempō no mondaijōkyō* (Iwanami shoten, 1964); and Kempōmondai kenkyūkai (ed.), *Kempō tokuhon*, 2 vols. (Iwanami shoten, 1965). For the survey of public opinion on the issue the compilation of the postwar public opinion polls undertaken by the three major newspapers and their results available in Vol. 5 of *Shiryō: Sengo nijūnen shi* cited earlier and the mimeographed publication of the Cabinet Secretariat Research Section, *Shakaifūchō chōsa shiryō*, proved very useful.

The discussion of the China issue was based very substantially on information gathered from Chūgoku kenkyūjo (ed.), *Chūgoku nenkan* (Ishizaki shoten, annual, 1955-61); *Shinchūgoku nenkan* (Kyokutō shoten, annual, 1962-6); Nitchūbōeki sokushin giin renmei, *Nitchūbōeki giren shūhō*; and *Nitchūkankei shiryōshū*, April 1961. Almost as indispensable as these sources were the publications of the Ministry of Foreign Affairs, especially *Waga gaikō no kinkyō*, annual, and various publications of the Liberal-Democratic Party, mostly in mimeograph. The latter included, for example, the following: *Jimintō kettō irai no nitchūmondai ni kansuru shiryō*, n.d.; *Chihōgikai no nitchū kokkōseijōka nitchū yūkōshinzen sokushin ketsugian ni taisuru hanron*, March 1964; *Gaikōchōsakai hōkokusho*, July 1962; *Sankō shiryō*, August 1962; and Jiyūminshutō gaikōchōsakai chūgoku shōiinkai, *Chūgokumondai ni kansuru chūkanhōkoku*, May 1961.

There exists a voluminous literature on this subject and reference was made to wide-ranging books and articles. Examples of the books are Miyashita Tadao, *Chūnichibōeki no kenkyū* (Nihon gaiseigakkai shuppankyoku, 1955); Tokyo ginkō chōsabu, *Nitchūbōeki gaikan* (1958); Utsunomiya Tokuma,

Heiwakyōzon to nihongaikō (Kōbundō, 1960); and Nihon chūgoku yūkōk-yōkai, *Nitchūyūkōundō no rekishi* (1966). The periodicals consulted for relevant articles included the following (the locations of the particular articles are given in the bibliography of my Ph.D. thesis): *Ajiya Keizai Jumpō, Ekonomisuto, Gaikō Jihō, Gendai no Me, Jiyū, Keidanren Geppō, Kokusai Mondai, Minzoku to Seiji, Nippon, Saiken,* and *Shinkokusaku.*

Index

U

Japan Medical Association (Nihon ishikai), 95, 122, 151, 161
Japan Reconstruction League, 207
Japan Socialist Party, 28, 121, 140, 252, 256; members, 62, 63; farmland issue and, 173, 180, 181; constitutional issue and, 199n., 200, 201, 210, 211, 215; China issue and, 232, 234, 236, 242, 260
Japan-China Cultural Exchange Association (Nihon chūgoku bunka kōryū kyōkai), 232
Japan - China Export - Import Union (Nitchū yushutsunyū kumiai), 230, 231n., 234n.
Japan - China Friendship Association (Nitchūyūkō kyōkai), 232; cited, 287
Japan - China Problem Study Group (Nitchūmondai kenkyūkai), 250
Japan-South Korea Treaty, 101, 137, 150, 235
Japanese Export Trade Organisation, 244
Japanese Industrialists' Club (Nihon kōgyō kurabu), 44
Japanese League of Farmers' Organisations, 151
Japanese League of Land Reform Victims, 176
Jiji nenkan, cited, 282
Jikyoku kondankai, 221
Jimintōshi hensaniinkai, cited, 198n., 284
Jisakunō sōsetsu tokubetsusochi hō, 174
Jishu heiwa gaikō hōsaku, 238
jitsuryokuha, 157
Jiyū, cited, 287
Jiyū kokumin rengō, 148
Jiyūminshu, 78
Jiyūminshutō, cited, 67, 78n., 81n., 220, 284, 286; *see also* Liberal-Democratic Party
Jiyūtō, *see* Liberal Party
Joint United States-Japanese Committee on Trade and Economic Affairs, 239n.
journalists, 167, 169

Kaishintō, *see* Progressive Party
Kambayashiyama Eikichi, 69n., 188n.
Kamoda Sōichi, 110n.
Kampō, cited, 147, 149, 158n., 177n., 282
Kanda Hiroshi, 110n.
Kaneko Jun'ichirō, cited, 116n.
Kanemitsu Tsuneo, 24n., 36, 48
Kanke Kiroku, 117
Kankyōeisei giin renmei, 162
Kansai Regional Federation of Economic Organisations, 164
Kantō (Japan), 90

Karuizawa (Japan), 115, 117
Katakura concern, 25n.
Kataoka Kenkichi, 10
Katayama Tetsu, 210n.
Katō Hiroyuki, cited, 9n.
Katō Seizō, 187
Katō Takaaki, 29
Katsumura Shigeru, cited, 284
Kawai Yoshinari, 111n.; China issue and, 244
Kawakami Tamio, cited, 137n.
Kawamura Yoshikuni, cited, 113n.
Kawarada Kakichi, 46
Kawasaki Hideji, 47, 208
Kawashima Shōjirō, 91, 114, 123, 125, 127, 148, 161n., 166n.; quoted, 71, 131, 139n.; faction of, 91, 110, 111, 113, 115, 116, 155, 257; *see also* Kōyū kurabu; farmland issue and, 186; China issue and, 241
Kaya Okinori, 203, 257n.; cited, 251n.; China issue and, 251, 253, 256, 260
Kayōkai (of Ikeda Hayato), 153
Kayōkai (of Ministry of International Trade and Industry officials), 166
Kazami Plan, 32
Keidanren, 44, 164, 245, 246; relationship to Liberal-Democratic Party, 50–1, 152, 153, 162, 163; constitutional issue and, 210, 215; Economic Co-operation Forum, 211; China issue and, 233, 234, 244
Keidanren Geppō, cited, 287
Keidanren Plan, 211
Keizai dōyūkai, *see* Dōyūkai
Keizai saiken kondankai, *see* Economic Reconstruction Forum
Kempōchōsakai, cited, 199n., 200n., 202n., 286; *see also* Commission on the Constitution
Kempōmondai kenkyūkai, cited, 286
Kenseihontō, 15, 26, 72
Kenseikai, 22, 26–9, 30
Kenseikaishi hensanjo, cited, 283
Kenseitō, 15
Kikawada Kazutaka, 163, 165n.; China issue and, 234
Kikuchi Gorō, cited, 19n., 22n., 27n., 283
Kimura Tokutarō, 183
Kindai shihonshugi kenkyūkai, 165n.
Kinki (Japan), 90
Kinko (Japan), 124
Kishi Nobusuke, 48, 71, 90, 97, 108n., 115, 116, 124, 128, 129, 136, 138, 148, 163, 168, 221; cited, 98n., 115n.; quoted, 177; faction of, 46, 49, 108, 109, 110–11, 115n., 116n., 120n., 122,

Seisaku kondankai, 155
seisha, 9, 10, 12
Seishin kurabu, 122, 123
Seiyūkai, 30; members, 16–17, 22, 27, 29, 35, 72; organisation, 17–21, 24, 90; factions of, 22–4, 26; Mitsui and, 24–5, 32, 121
Sekai keizai chōsakai, 167
Sekiyōsha, 10
Self-Defence Forces, 204, 215n.
Self-Defence Forces Law, 51, 92
Sengoku Mitsugu, 29
Senkenkai, 138
Senshū University, 125
Setoyama Mitsuo, 112, 188n.
Shibusawa Eiichi, 16
Shidehara Kijūrō, 29, 42; Cabinet of, 174, 199n.
Shiga Kenjirō, 183
Shigemasa Seishi, 71, 111, 119, 120
Shigemasa Yōtoku, 188n., 190
Shigemitsu Mamoru, 114
Shigemune Yūzō, 193
Shikoku (Japan), 90
Shima Shigenobu, 243n.
Shimada Saburō, 12
Shimada Toshio, 24
Shimano Moribumi, cited, 223n.
Shimazu Kuniomi, cited, 228n.
Shimoda Takezō, 235
Shimojō Yasumaro, 193
Shimomura Osamu, 167
Shin seiji keizai kenkyūjo, 132
Shin seiji keizai kenkyūkai, 154
Shin zaisei kenkyūkai, 118, 154
Shina Etsusaburō, 116, 183; quoted, 255n.; China issue and, 254
Shinkokusaku, cited, 287
Shinobu Seizaburō, 163; cited, 25n., 162n., 282
Shinoda Kōsaku, 183
Shinojima Hideo, 244
Shinro, 117, 118n.
Shinsei kurabu, 60, 208
Shinshinkai, 41
Shinyūkai, 132, 163
Shiseki Ihei, 161n.
Shōda family, 125
Shōji Kichinosuke, cited, 283
Shōji Takeo, 165n.
Shōkōgyō shinkō giindan, 162
Shokuinroku, cited, 65, 285
Shōriki Matsutarō, 50, 108
Shōwa Electric Industry, 125
Shūgiin Jimukyoku, cited, 213n., 285
Shunjūkai, 119, 137n., 138, cited, 285
Shūzankai, 112, 132, 138, 163

Sino-Japanese Trade Association, 244
Sino-Soviet dispute, 234, 235
Sino-Soviet Treaty of Friendship, Alliance, and Mutual Assistance, 227
Small and Medium Enterprises Basic Bill, 151
Small and Medium Enterprise Political League (Chūshōkigyō seiji renmei), 151, 161
Small Industry Finance Fund, 160
Socialists, *see* Japan Socialist Party
Sōgō seisaku kenkyūjo, 167
Sōhyō, 232
Sōma Tsunetoshi, 234n.
Sōrifu tōkeikyoku, cited, 229, 284
Soshiki Jōhō, 78, 101
Soshinkai, 107, 140, 150, 223, 254, 261, 265; cited, 224; constitutional issue and, 216, 220, 222–5, 226, 267
South Korea, 253; relations with Japan, 168, 252
South Vietnam, 235
Stockwin, J.A.A., cited, 210n.
Study Group for the Improvement of Japan-China Relations (Nitchū kaizen kenkyūkai), 250
Sudō Hideo, 152, 181
Suehirokai, 153
Suga Reinosuke, 234
Sugi Michisuke, 148; China issue and, 244
Suhara Shōichi, 110n.
Suiyōkai, 117, 122
Suiyō kurabu, 116, 138
Sumitomo zaibatsu, 25n.
Sun Ping-hua, 234
Sunada Shigemasa, 138
Sunagawa Case, 215n.
supporters' associations, 159–61, 169, 170, 195; as source of Liberal-Democratic Party members, 74, 77, 79; as means of securing votes, 100, 135, 145
Supreme Commander for Allied Powers, Government Section, cited, 38n.
Suzuki Kazuo, 232
Suzuki Kisaburō, 23, 24
Suzuki Shun'ichi, 166n.
Suzuki Yoshio, cited, 107n.
Suzuki Yukio, cited, 152n., 165n.
Suzuki Zenkō, 118
Syngman Rhee, 254

Tago Ichimin, 188
Taiseiyokusankai, 16, 33–4
Taiyōkai, 41
Takada Sanae, 12
Takahashi Kamekichi, cited, 25n.

ABOUT THE AUTHOR

Haruhiro Fukui obtained his master's degree at Tokyo University and his doctorate at the Australian National University. He also spent some time at the University of Michigan as a Fulbright exchange student and as a research assistant, specialising in political science.

Since January 1968 he has been Assistant Professor of Political Science at the University of California at Santa Barbara.

Designed by Arthur Stokes

Text set in 10 pt Intertype Baskerville, 2 pt leaded, by J. C. Stephens & Company, Melbourne, and printed on 85 gsm Burnie English Finish paper by Halstead Press Pty Ltd, Sydney.